PSYCHIATRY AND THE WAR

*A Survey of the Significance of Psychiatry
and its Relation to Disturbances in Human
Behavior to help provide for the Present War
Effort and for Post-War Needs*

A RECORD OF THE CONFERENCE ON PSYCHIATRY
HELD AT ANN ARBOR, MICHIGAN,
OCTOBER 22, 23, AND 24, 1942,
AT THE INVITATION OF
THE UNIVERSITY OF MICHIGAN
AND
McGREGOR FUND

Published under the Auspices of
McGREGOR FUND

DETROIT

PSYCHIATRY AND THE WAR

A Survey of
the Significance of Psychiatry
and its Relation to Disturbances
in Human Behavior to help provide
for the Present War Effort and
for Post War Needs

EDITED BY

FRANK J. SLADEN, M.D.

PHYSICIAN IN CHIEF
HENRY FORD HOSPITAL, DETROIT
TRUSTEE, McGREGOR FUND

CHARLES C THOMAS, PUBLISHER
Springfield, Illinois & Baltimore, Maryland

COPYRIGHT, 1943, BY McGREGOR FUND, DETROIT, MICHIGAN

Published by CHARLES C THOMAS
220 EAST MONROE STREET, SPRINGFIELD, ILLINOIS

First Edition

Printed in the United States of America

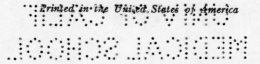

To
TRACY W. McGREGOR
AND
KATHERINE McGREGOR

The Values of This Conference

By FRANK J. SLADEN, M.D.

Physician in Chief, Henry Ford Hospital. Chairman of the Conference on Psychiatry

THIS VOLUME has taken on the form and dress that will most persuasively tempt its useful and interested reading by those into whose hands it will fall. All available skills have been called into service to attain this end. As with the speaker who knows he has a real message and strives to capture the attention of his audience, an absolute faith in the contents of this volume prompts these efforts to make its study immediate not postponed, tempting not difficult, and in all a happy experience.

In truth the thirty papers and the two symposiums reported in this volume represent the contributions of some forty leaders in the special field of psychiatry and its closely allied interests.

To gain the advantages of the earliest possible publication and availability has proven no easy task in these days of more difficult transportation and transaction. To aid this, authors have been generous in delegating much of their editorial prerogatives; and, in some instances, cutting and trimming has been done to convert a somewhat informal, almost conversational style into appropriate part and parcel of this book. It is true the papers were presented as part of a planned conference and are now made to fit harmoniously into a volume which aims at more than the status of proceedings. A synopsis of each paper's essential points has been introduced by the editor at the beginning of each paper, for the convenience of the reader.

The Committee on the Conference on Psychiatry was chosen long ago as representative of the various applications of the psychiatric specialty in medicine. Its members, experienced, resourceful, untiring, developed after countless hours together the vision of an opportunity for psychiatry to look itself over, to examine its past experiences and its present techniques, to consider its relationships, satisfactory or not, and to reshape, if needed, its aims and goals.

This committee was composed of:

DR. JOHN M. DORSEY

President, Michigan Society of Neurology and Psychiatry, Detroit.

DR. THOS. J. HELDT

Physician in charge Division of Neuropsychiatry, Henry Ford Hospital, Detroit.

DR. RAYMOND W. WAGGONER

Chairman and Professor of The Department of Psychiatry, University of Michigan, Ann Arbor.

DR. ORUS R. YODER

Medical Superintendent, Ypsilanti State Hospital, Ypsilanti.

and

THE EDITOR.

The expert and untiring labors of this Committee resulted in the building and execution of the plan of this Conference on Psychiatry, for which McGregor Fund again acknowledges its indebtedness. That the exacting obligations of the profession were fulfilled is evidenced by quotations from the letters of those who attended.

"And the planning of the program to bring together the full sweep of psychiatric thought in the country and to focus it on the urgent problems we are facing today is calculated, I am convinced, to leave a permanent impress for good on American psychiatry."

"It was most stimulating from many angles. I am sure that a great deal of good will come from it, and that the influence of psychiatry, not only in the prosecution of the war, but in the readjustment which must ultimately follow, will be distinctly felt."

". . . expressed his pleasure in the fact that so wide a diversity of approach was possible without stirring up acrimonious debate."

"For this excellent broad presentation of many divergent trends I think you and your Committee deserve not only our thanks but our congratulations."

"I have just returned from attending the Ann Arbor Conference on Psychiatry and am glad to find upon looking back that there is no abatement of the enthusiasm which I experienced while the meeting was in progress.

"I have attended many meetings but never have attended a psychiatric meeting after which I felt so stimulated and enriched. So far as I know this is the first time a selected group of psychiatrists wrote on an assigned topic.

"The program was splendidly conceived, superbly executed."

"The Conference was peculiarly fruitful in that it developed a rather complete perspective on psychiatry coming out of the experience of a great many leaders. In that respect it differed from most of our conferences that are expressions of individual interests.

"I think the McGregor Fund is to be congratulated on having developed this unique sort of program."

Frances Bradley Chickering, A.B., Bryn Mawr, has worked unceasingly, first on the Conference project, then on the meetings themselves, and now on the preparation of this volume. As correspondent and secretary, in administration and management, editing and correction of copy, and finally proof reading, her work was done with enthusiasm, efficiency and expedition. We acknowledge here the great value of her contribution.

The Philosophy of Psychiatry was chosen as the title for the first general session of the Conference; *Research in Psychi-*

atry and *Psychiatry in the Training, Experience and Education of the Individual* for the second and third. These were planned in great detail to explore significant relationships and applications, to consider the future of the specialty and its sources of advance, and to deal very really with lives and life's most pertinent areas of activity and occupation. First the subjects were chosen. Then the best man to present each was sought. Invariably the assignment was accepted, and these papers are offered as evidence of the wisdom of this Committee and its judgement in making the choices. Not every author is a psychiatrist. Dr. Heinz Hartmann, Dr. Norman Cameron, Dr. Percival Bailey, Dr. Carl Camp, Dr. Cyrus C. Sturgis, are among the psychologists, neurologists, surgeons and internists who made noteworthy contributions. Several after-dinner and introductory remarks are not included, since the form of a volume of proceedings is not being followed.

The cross currents of religion and psychiatry received masterly handling from a man who not only was thoroughly at home with the subject and had addressed such gatherings of professional men before, but who expressed the psychiatric as well as the religious principles and practise in a most understanding and scientifically acceptable manner.

The natural, acknowledged leadership of Dr. Adolf Meyer was felt from beginning to end. Many requests for this and that paper have been received.

Psychiatry is considered in Parts I, II, III as a foundation, a background, for the papers of Part IV, entitled *Psychiatry and the War*. With the approval of the Surgeons General of the Army and Navy and their participation through appointed representatives, the relation to the present unusual service and civil problems and situations colored all discussions. The Army, Navy, Aviation and other papers brought into the open the most critical psychiatric topics of the day. Part V of this book is a record of the discussions of all preceding papers, under capable leadership.

The purpose of the Conference of which this book is the record is expressed by the following reprint from the program.

The Conference on Psychiatry will offer an opportunity during this national emergency to emphasize the importance of phychiatry in the solution of the problems of human relationships.

The scope and aims of psychiatry, and its principles and advancements, will be reviewed with the object of creating new values in its disciplines and techniques.

For psychiatrists, the Conference is dedicated to the orientation and crystallization of unified thinking; for others, to their understanding of the place of psychiatry and its usefulness.

A survey of the significance of psychiatry and its relation to disturbances in human behaviour will be made at this time in order to help provide for the present war effort and for post-war needs.

Again the evidence which the papers of this volume give shows the accomplishment of this purpose.

The University of Michigan and McGregor Fund joined hands in sponsoring the Conference. The University of Michigan through President Alexander G. Ruthven, was host to the attendance and provided an environment conducive to both comfort and undivided attention, in the Horace H. Rackham School of Graduate Studies. McGregor Fund of Detroit made the Conference possible and undertook the publication of this book.

Attention is called to two significant facts. First, a group of laymen living in an industrial center reached out to join hands with a willing University to institute a project of this sort. This is a significant contribution to united effort, not entirely new, perhaps, but well worth recording. Second, a group of laymen in their capacities as trustees of a fund took the initiative in their desire to do something to help psychiatry help itself; and in that way, to enhance its usefulness to mankind. This, too, is noteworthy and should be on record.

These Trustees all had the good fortune to know well the founder of the Fund. They are Henry S. Hulbert, Kenneth L.

Moore, William J. Norton, Frank J. Sladen, M.D., Cleveland
Thurber, and Renville Wheat, all of Detroit. The founder of
the Fund was Tracy W. McGregor of Detroit. Judge Hulbert
speaks intimately of Mr. McGregor in the Foreword. You are
advised to read it.

These Trustees, a bank executive, a realtor, an executive in
social work, a physician and two lawyers, have held fast to the
interests of the founder and have thus tried to express his desires as they could be imagined in this day.

Mr. McGregor died in 1936, after forty-five years of unselfish service to the unfortunate of mankind. From his father
came the responsibility at twenty-one, of the McGregor Mission for homeless men. Here were countless opportunities to
study the homeless man in all his types and aspects.

Nothing interested him more than the health of these men
and the handicaps and subtractions which beset their health.
Here came the beginnings of a deep interest in personality
problems and mental disturbances, their cause, their relief,
their prevention. Here, too, came the evaluation of best health,
its loss, its recovery, convalescence, and the needs for one of
his creations, the present McGregor Health Foundation.

In January, 1910, he published *The Story of a Man Without a Home*. Later, in 1916, came *An Introduction to Twenty
Thousand Men*, which was an analytical survey of 23,508 of
these men in one year of the institute's work. At the session
of the National Conference of Social Work in June, 1933, Mr.
McGregor read a paper afterward printed in book form, entitled *Toward a Philosophy of the Inner Life*. It should be
read by everyone caught by an interest in this remarkable man.
For it expresses well his philosophy of life.

In April, 1939, The Tracy W. McGregor Room was dedicated in the Alderman Library of the University of Virginia
at Charlottesville. The year before, his carefully chosen library
of early American history and contemporary English literature had been presented to the University in keeping with the
terms of his will.

Mr. McGregor's [1] "name has become a tradition in that Detroit in which he lived and worked; a quiet, unassuming Christian gentleman, with high spiritual attributes, a tower of civic strength, and one who felt deeply his responsibilities to the community in which he lived. He gave little thought to self, and his modesty was one of his most lovable qualities." "A scholar who had searched for knowledge in the writings of men and tempered it with a deep understanding of life, a philosopher who had found for himself happiness and understanding amidst all of the perplexities of modern life and who knew how to help others to find it, a friend who deeply loved his fellowmen and did not hesitate to make any personal sacrifice to help them, however lowly their station in life might be, it has been given to few men to attain a place so close to the hearts of the people of a great industrial community as had Tracy McGregor."

[1] Hulbert, H. S. Tracy W. McGregor. Address, at the University of Virginia, Charlottesville, Virginia, 1939.

Foreword

By HENRY S. HULBERT

President, Board of Trustees, McGregor Fund

In opening this Conference on Psychiatry in behalf of the Trustees of McGregor Fund, it seems fitting that I should say something concerning the devoted couple whose benevolent forethought made this, as well as many other important philanthropies, possible—Tracy W. McGregor and his wife, Katherine McGregor.

Tracy McGregor was a quiet, unassuming gentleman whose interest in life covered many widely different fields. His keen, kindly, but altogether merry eye found a constant interest in his fellow man, in his ambitions, his weaknesses, and his strength, together with those attributes of character that go to make up this thing we call the "human being."

When at the age of twenty-two, his father's death caused Mr. McGregor to take over the work that his father had begun in Detroit for destitute and homeless men, his intense interest in his fellow man and an overwhelming desire to be of service and to help solve some of his many problems, enabled him to make a complete success of the task his father had just commenced before his death. This little Mission later became McGregor Institute and had the well-earned reputation of being the most intelligently managed institution for transient and homeless men in this country.

During the hours he spent with these men, Mr. McGregor found both time and opportunity to study the causes of human failure and the effects of the impact of circumstance on human lives. He was apt to put his thoughts into brief essays and in one written many years before his death, which he entitled *Twenty Thousand Men,* he made the observation which somewhat reflects his creed:

"One should remember that the mystery of human failure will be more clearly disclosed by first-hand knowledge of one individual than by a casual acquaintance with many. By sympathetic searching into the history of the man who does odd jobs for you, or whose instability as a worker in your office frets you, such original and independent insight may be had. Truth, thus directly conveyed by living personality, will impressively influence one's whole attitude toward mankind. It will enrich the soul; it will relieve class isolation, and beget patience, kindliness, humility, and breadth."

His deep and sympathetic understanding of all kinds of problems is well evidenced by the statement of the barber who for many years served him at the Detroit Club:

"I feel that I have lost the one genuine friend I had in the world. I never had a problem that I couldn't have taken to Mr. McGregor with assurance that he would both understand and help me."

It was that broad interest in mankind which caused him to form the fund that now bears his name; and it is this same broad interest in mankind which we Trustees are trying in his absence to carry on. Throughout his whole life he realized fully the effect of the nervous and mental diseases of man and sought continually to find some kind of an answer to some of the problems. I think it was that which caused him to seek and follow the advice of Thomas Salmon, for instance, and of others of that generation whom Mr. McGregor regarded very highly and spent as much time with as he could.

His Trustees have participated in this Conference with the idea that whatever is new, whatever has occurred in psychiatry or in neurology that is helpful to the world, might perhaps through your efforts be put in writing and made clear, to the end that it would be of use to humanity in the days to come.

Psychiatry and the War

CONTENTS

PART II

RESEARCH IN PSYCHIATRY

PART III

PSYCHIATRY IN THE TRAINING, EXPERIENCE AND EDUCATION OF THE INDIVIDUAL

PART IV

PSYCHIATRY AND THE WAR

PART V

REVIEW OF THE SUBJECTS OF THE PAPERS OF PARTS I, II AND III, AND THOSE OF PART IV IN TWO SYMPOSIA WITH SELECTED LEADERSHIP AND ASSIGNED AND OPEN DISCUSSION

FIRST SYMPOSIUM: The Philosophy of Psychiatry

Discussions from the Assembly

Closing Discussion

SECOND SYMPOSIUM: Psychiatry and the War

Introduction

Presentation of the Subject

Scheduled Discussions

PSYCHIATRY AND THE WAR

*A Survey of the Significance of Psychiatry
and its Relation to Disturbances in Human
Behavior to help provide for the Present War
Effort and for Post-War Needs*

PART I

THE PHILOSOPHY OF PSYCHIATRY

Introduction to Part I

By RAYMOND W. WAGGONER, M.D.

Professor of Psychiatry, University of Michigan Medical School; Director, The Neuropsychiatric Institute, University of Michigan. Member of the Committee on the Conference on Psychiatry

RARELY DOES one have the opportunity to listen to such a notable group of psychiatrists as we shall have at this Conference on Psychiatry. The need of such a conference is emphasized in an article by Dr. Allen Gregg of the Rockefeller Foundation, published in the September issue of the *Bulletin of the Menninger Clinic,* who writes: "I could not be satisfied with the definition of psychiatry as that specialty of medicine which deals with *mental* disorders. Like a bad newspaper headline such a definition confines while condensing and misrepresents by oversimplifying. Psychiatry deals also with the disturbed emotional and social life of man, not merely his reasoning mental operations. Insofar as experience has shown you that emotional thinking is different from logical reasoning, you see why mental is an inadequate word. Indeed the province of psychiatry is the disturbances in the conduct of man, his experiences and his way of experiencing, his reactions, his behavior as an indivisible sentient being with other such beings. Until recently medical attention has been given only to grossly disordered conduct—to persons locked up in asylums—but now the field is far more inclusive because it spreads into the anxieties, the fatigues, the instabilities, the maladjustments, the disturbances of normal everyday living and also because it includes the effects of mental and emotional functions upon the component organs of the body, as well as the effects of the disordered organs upon the function of the human being as a whole. The psychiatrist, then, studies emotions as well as mental processes, and over the whole vast range from optimum health to incurable disease."

Consider for a moment the tremendous emotional stimuli being generated in the world at the present time, particularly in relation to the war and its multiple ramifications. Consider the social and economic adjustments necessary now and the readjustments which will be necessary when the war has been won. Consider the care with which the problems of adjustments in the education of the individual should be studied. Consider the emotional factors associated with the tremendous speed-up in industry and the need of the armed services. Consider the need for research, the result of which should help us in handling problems which are developing or which will develop in the future. And consider, finally, the need for correlating the various disciplines of psychiatry and the need for marshaling every psychiatric resource which can be utilized in the solution of these problems,—and the value of this Conference becomes obvious.

Psychiatry: Its Meaning and Scope

By ADOLF MEYER, M.D.

Psychiatrist-in-Chief, Emeritus, Henry Phipps Psychiatric Clinic, The Johns Hopkins Hospital; Henry Phipps Professor of Psychiatry and Director, Department of Psychiatry, The Johns Hopkins University

PHILOSOPHY INVOLVED IN PSYCHIATRY • MEANING OF PHILOSOPHY • DEVELOPING RELATIONSHIPS • THE BRAIN THE ORGAN OF MENTAL FUNCTIONS • A VACATIONAL PEREGRINATION IN 1894 • HOSPITALS OF NEW YORK, OHIO AND MICHIGAN • SPHERE OF PHILOSOPHY • CHALLENGE OF THE WORLD SITUATION • NEUROPSYCHIATRISTS AS PHYSICIANS FIRST • DANGER OF LEADERSHIP THROUGH DOMINATION • POWER FOR CREATION, NOT DESTRUCTION • THE PRESENT ON THE MARCH • ERGASIOLOGY, A CONCEPT FOR ACTION • MEANING AND SCOPE OF PSYCHIATRY

ONE MAY wonder about the meaning and scope of psychiatry, particularly in its relation to the philosophy of psychiatry. I must confess that I could indeed not think of the topic without being confronted immediately with the extent to which philosophy is involved in the question of the general concept and direction of that which we call psychiatry. I have often felt with regret that there is a great confusion in terminology and ideology when we come to the word "philosophy." Most people seem to think that it must be largely "metaphysics" in a sense of dealing with imponderables. That is not, I take it, what the invitation meant to imply. Philosophy, indeed, calls for something very specific and concrete, including the "physics" and not only the "meta." There has been a great deal of "meta" this and "meta" that, lately. The philosophy I should like to speak about is the intrinsic sense and general orientation and the extent of liberty the individual has in applying all that is in him in a reasonably orderly form to what he has to make his unit of concern.

5

To discuss this here at the University of Michigan is particularly stimulating to me, because it takes me back to the early important contacts I had with psychiatry and its wider span and relations with philosophy as they actually developed in this country. It was in 1894 that I used my first vacation for a trip to visit some of the institutions and colleagues in the field of work which I found myself thrown into—because psychiatry was not my primary intention; it was the need of access to brains that led me to blend certain philosophical interests and actual medical training and work in the direction of psychiatry. At the time of my Zurich and wider medical preparation, psychiatry figured as any physician's business when the mental condition or psyche was involved. "Insanity" was the summary legal term in America, which then, as to the present day, has very largely dominated a great deal of the concern with psychiatry. Another term was "mental disease," and there may be misapprehensions with regard to the word "mental." Evidently Dr. Gregg thought of it especially in terms of, I suppose, intelligence—and what does that mean? To me intelligence always means literally the capacity to be "selective among the many things." It is *inter-lection*. Certainly in the *choice* of things it is not only so-called mentality in the sense that so many people will attribute to "mind" that should perhaps figure as a derivative for the specific concept and word roots of *memory* and of *meaning,* etc. Meaning immediately includes very much more than mind in its narrow and static sense. It certainly also includes our real attitude to *what things mean to us,* and if there is not an element of dynamics and of emotion in that, I should like to know what live selection and choice could be. After all, most of us have our main impulses not merely in the refined sense of purely intellectual differentiation. Evidently that "selective capacity" includes all there is to us, in asserting ourselves and finding our way, our orienting ourselves and our proving ourselves and our make-up, as the whole of man—with one or another degree of efficiency.

At any rate, it was a special necessity that introduced psychiatry as a positive practical emphasis and a leading concern at the time. My human interest no doubt was comprehensive, demanding the inclusion of the whole of man, in which the specific "research" interest happened to be one in connection with the comparative anatomy and the comparative physiology of the brain, so that in 1893 I accepted a position as pathologist, which offered the brains of those who were committed, who were the inmates as we called them, of one of those remarkable asylums beginning to be called hospitals. That seemed to me to be the place where one might get systematic access to brains, to the organ of the *"mental functions* of the individual,"* and what I would also call the *social organ* of man.

I must not lose time by giving you the whole record of that vacational peregrination, which was an exceedingly interesting and concrete experience. As I said, in '94 I visited hospitals of New York State and Ohio and Michigan for the first time, after a year's experience in the Illinois Eastern Hospital at Kankakee. At that time there were two places in this state which I visited. The first was the Battle Creek Sanitarium, which was not supposed to be a place for "inmates," but a place of broad general medical activity, which also included some special topics, like hydrotherapy and laboratory work and general hygiene. I considered these essential for the type of patient which, in the meantime, I had become responsible for, although still too exclusively when dead and only to some extent when alive. The second hospital visited was that in Kalamazoo, which proved to be a good match of that new institution with twenty-two hundred patients, to which I belonged, in addition to my connection with the University of Chicago. At Kalamazoo there was a contact with an active clinical staff, and somehow, with a spontaneity which at present looks to me almost like well-meaning arrogation on my part, there arose the determination to bring together those who had to do the work, the assistant physicians of those neighboring hospitals, in an association which would bring in the working psychiatrists, and not particularly the organizers and administrators constituting the association of the superintendents. We had our first meeting at Kankakee. At any rate, it was the neighborliness with Michigan physicians and Michigan hospitals which gave rise to the temptation to bring together those who, as I say, were the specifically medical workers in these hospitals. This association of assistant physicians of Illinois, Michigan and Iowa hospitals remained active a number of years.

But there was also another point. In my status as docent in neurology at the University of Chicago, I had some neighborly contacts with some new arrivals, and they were arrivals from Michigan. The University of Michigan gave the young University of Chicago John Dewey and Mrs. Dewey—I have to mention them both. Actually a pragmatic "definition of philosophy" arises from the practical occurrence there of the influence of four personalities: first, a philosopher with psychological interest and background, a man brought up in a Hegelian system of absolutism and asserting himself in the direction of what John Dewey probably already was fundamentally at the time, and certainly became, and made himself so remarkably effective in, in connection with the educational element that created the school which formed, as it were, the foundations of philosophical thinking in a pragmatic sense; second, George Herbert Mead, a supplement to John Dewey, who was professor of philosophy and psychology, when philosophy and psychology still held together, the philosopher of social tendencies as much as of the individual, and who undoubtedly was influenced by the third personality, a man whom perhaps relatively few know of, but who seems to have been, in the University of Michigan, one of the relatively silent but intensely studious and thinking influences, Charles Horton Cooley, sociologist and social philosopher you might call him; and fourth, James Hayden Tufts, who was the strength of the ethical development, which must not be lost sight of as one of the fundamentals of the philosopher and of philosophy.

We have to recognize that philosophy is the broad sphere of arousal of human spontaneity, a study of the interests and mutual workings of the nature and driving influences and the goals of man; and that philosophy is meant to be the working-sphere of that large function which we might call the essential function of man, that of organization of life, of life intent and life performance. It may seem trifling, perhaps, to refer to a summer vacation experience and some events which might be passed by casually. I would say, however, that as soon as the University of Michigan and the agencies in Michigan which work with the funds in behalf of support of the human interests are mentioned, I cannot but look back upon the contribution of the University of Michigan to the University of Chicago at that time—a general but substantial rounding off of truly vital and effective concern. And philosophy then began to take form as that which is capable of going from that supreme typically German systematization—tendency of absolutism, to where it puts the head close to the feet, and the feet on the actualities, in the characteristic creation of pragmatism and the willingness to take the facts as one actually meets them and as one *uses* them.

Certainly the stirring and appalling situation in which we stand, not only in this country but in the world, makes a special challenge to this conference of psychiatrists, viz., to make sure that we get a clear idea of where we are going to put our feet and raise our head and turn the combination into action. This has got to be a meeting on the philosophy of psychiatry, on medical thought for use. There may be few things which one can attribute to war and be appreciative about, but one is that it makes us sure that we have to think of the *use* of things. That certainly is important. That we have got to learn it sometimes by war, is a tragedy.

I cannot help but follow freely my trend of thought of the moment, rather than one or another of those trends which developed themselves in the preparation of this communication. Here we are, brought together as psychiatrists—or, I have already heard it said, as "neuro-psychiatrists." I like to say, first of all, as physicians—and, I hope, physicians because of their drive and their training and their internal necessity of finding ways, not only of patching up, but of heeding the internal working of events, looking for ways of reducing the facts to terms of something workable. We know in connection with the pragmatism and with the operationalism which came out of it all, that we are on typically American ground, on ground which today has to prove itself in all sorts of directions. The supreme absolutists would like to have it at the place where John Dewey began in the spirit of his teachers. We want to have it where John Dewey showed his real nature and his development, and where the American spirit has given us the opportunity and the obligation, and also the ethical necessity of making life, the disturbances of life and the means of regulating life-function as remedy and prevention and something which allows us to forget the mere misery part and to think of construction. That is what I see in this preamble, and what I think may well pervade the sense of our being together for these three days.

Let us say that in the first place we are to be human beings worthy of the name. Let us realize that we are part of a world which is absolutely in flux, and which has so missed connections that at present it is doing its best to destroy. You may say, "No, it is not to destroy; it is to gain supremacy." Well, you know, supremacy is a rather dangerous thing. When I use the word "dangerous," I touch the very essence that combines in the word. "Danger," our expression for something which makes us alert and on the lookout, derives from "dominiarium," from "domination." And it is interesting that we have to admit that humanity has managed to bring it to pass that leadership, and that position of being the master, the *dominus*, the head of the household, came to include such abuses that the only word we finally have for danger in English and French is the degradation of "dominiarium," leadership, dropped out of its essential role and become sheer domination, and thereby a danger. And that is what one would like to bring to the fore again as one of the elements which might dominate *our* thought. We have to see that we get our working together in the development of *"power,"* so that it will so allocate itself and so divide itself and organize itself that it becomes creation and not the destruction that it smells of today. Thus goes our broadly human urge.

That we have become adepts of various forms of training in

that which makes us physicians, immediately brings up a *second emphasis*. It is the emphasis on *action* in the very substance of our field; it is a practice in life; it is also a question of philosophy which we then might call in, if we have a sense in calling things names. *Physician* is a name for a group of people who, in the course of time, through common experience, wrested a specific domain from the primitive priesthood in its status of healers. Through experience and training, and attention to what they might learn from their activity, physicians have been allowed to form a particular group, what we call a profession. And that profession had a somewhat delicate task, because it could not help arrogating an important function from those who long were the sole or supreme representatives, as they would consider themselves, of God, of the highest powers, of that which was the outgrowth of the particularly human bent of man in the way of religion. Religion, to me, is the "boundenness" of the individual to the things one has to be bound for. It is a "tie-up," and unfortunately the tie-up for the most part was made rather one-sidedly, not particularly for life, but for the life as seen by a particular power group, but really a very thoughtful and important center of construction of that type of imagination which has to lead humanity. Personal and groupwise religion—yes, that is what it is in its most valuable part; but unfortunately its larger part clings to dogmatic theology, to that which has taken so many deplorably conflicting forms, and largely along the urge of building up powers avowedly outside of nature, the supernatural, but particularly also from the oldest sources of medical culture and organization of thought. Hippocrates, in the fifth century before Christ, was clear enough in telling the world of his time that, when he spoke of epilepsy, then commonly called the Sacred Disease, he dealt with something that is just as much of nature, of that which has to be born, has to develop, and with which all of us start, as anything else. The Sacred Disease was, of course, one of those forms of mental changes of a momentary character which showed in the convulsions peculiar to people who had that affliction, the awe-inspiring features interpreted in keeping with what philosophy one would take for the interpretation of its nature and its treatment. Hippocrates showed so clearly that the physical and general measures which we have and use with it, after all, have just as much right to have divine affiliation as that which has been too exclusively attributed to revelation, and embodied in the form of soul, and in the affiliation to the highest forces and thoughts which people have felt themselves drawn to, and receptive for, in a sense of "revelation," and more and more in the philosophy and function of observation, of experience, that had to become the main standby of hope for the future, especially in the Occidental world.

At that point man and his language had been so long confronted with the extreme development of "animism," which attributed something like the concept developed from human life-experience, life-breath and sleep and dream, as "back of" the wind (anemos) or "back of" anything that moves, and in the further development of the theory of the world and of the mind, and in the theory of investigation that too one-sidedly took to the description of sensations, and not to the meaning. *Meaning* points to having intermediate "middles," connective links between stimulus and performance in the delayed reflex, out of which the most important considerations of human life arise as mentation. Instead of allowing the word "mental" to be interpreted in line largely with "intelligence," I would say that the same word-root serves for mind and meaning, memory and man, and the "meaning" is the tying together of those things in ourselves which form the intermediaries, or links and steps between stimulus and reaction, between past and future, and, as mentation, mind and spirit, the essential driving force and goal in the concept for differential and fitted *action*. It gives therefore a picture of what happened, in this sense, that one side of our organization, the sensation fact, and the sensation result, goes into an orientation or direction in a form of thought-symbols, and particularly in the human being, of course, with words, and then the building up of the word-symbols into concepts, and into perspectives and action-tendencies and action. That is the sense and nature of meaning-function and mentality. Therefore our idea of "mental" is that of the cultivation of meanings which are the intermediaries and progressions in our type of life-process.

This is the next point I want to emphasize, the relation between philosophy and psychology in the narrower sense. *Meaning-function* is that which the individual develops for and in the contact with the outside world in the actual construction of a person, an entity which gets an organization of "mind" or better, mentation, characteristically of the nature of symbols and symbol-function, in which the direct experience and the memories of the past and the vision of the future are all brought on one denominator, into that which gives us the concept of mental *process,* which is always something that happens and operates in *statu nascendi.* It was Dr. Mead who worked a great deal with this as the "function of the present and the now," in his teaching. Unfortunately he shared with some of us the tendency of not being particularly the writer to be read, but the one who was ever willing and able to discuss, and to convey and to demonstrate in action. He showed the importance of the moment, the importance of the time during which action is actually budding and at work. He developed the philosophy of the *present on the march.* And if you then bring in the brother or cousin in this family of Michigan-born philosophy, Professor Tufts' sphere, you realize that it naturally includes in complex man the *sense of responsibility,* the sense of duty, the sense of the way to achievement of a philosophy of the now and here when one is up against things. It is the now and here of process in the broad individual and social setting, which we have to prepare ourselves with and for. It is this "now and here" when thoughts come and where one or the other gets on the top and becomes the leader and, with it, the actual performance.

Well, that is my conception of philosophy, of mental process, and in a way gives you a picture of what I consider the conception of the average life, and the conception of the one who wants to make himself helpful in distress, who becomes a physician, not just a "physicalist"; one who has a conception of realities, of actualities, and who wants a psychology and a man-science of action and not largely of sensation and hedonism and pleasure-principle. Of course, we actually use terms the naive and natural meaning of which we forget and often abuse. *Psyche* is the breath, and if there is anything in what any average human being can most readily recognize as evidence of living and life, it is the fact that the individual breathes, and the breathing is used as that essence, as the *intrinsic part,* to which one turns when one wants an expression and understanding of the human being and life, and which has actually developed into the prime human sign-function and basis of culture, as voice and language. We are in a world of tremendous complexity, and the fact that we have learned to use signs—the productive sensitiveness in attitudes, language, and concept and the capacity to answer to stimulation with the working together of symbols in a setting of a breathing and living entity in a plastic world—that had to be both philosophy and psychology, the human sense, the leading person-function. That in academic circles the psychologist defends himself against including philosophy in his own choice and privilege, but he should not be unable to cultivate their union when needed.

Psychiatry is that which is handed over to licensed physicians, physicians who have to prove that they have a familiarity and a training which entitles them to take the leadership for people who are in distress, and especially for people who cannot use their own judgment effectively. Every physician has to be "psychiatrically intelligent" to be a good physician, and there must be those who then have to push the opportunity, the duty, and the privilege, to a degree of orientation and organization which makes them worthy of a particular title to a specialty.

It is unfortunate that psychology has become wedded so strongly to what seems to be so largely sensation-derived symbol-production. It is essential to have a concept for *action* in that whole field, which we call, therefore, *ergasiology.* It is not, as some rather ungracious critics will have it, that one Greek word, psychology, is just being transferred into a supposedly stranger Greek word. It is in the sense of that self-referring, responsibility-making type of action—not merely happening, but action—that the middle form of the Greek verb is required. *Erg* is exactly the same root as *work,* and we all know it in allergy and in energy, and as the unit of energy in physics. In the *ergazomai* form it is not only happening, not only chance doings, but that doing which points back to the subject, the person, to the self, and to the part one plays within the group of selves. That is what ergasiology wants to imply, and does imply. It is behavior, but free of a split of the person into mind and body, as if the two could exist by themselves. We accept many, many words in a rather irresponsible way. I rather think that this is the best word, born of and for responsibility and a goal. But let us forget the words now. Let us go to meaning and scope of our psychiatry.

Psychiatry has got to be that work of the physician, or somebody of the physician's caliber, which deals with those items that either are directly of the nature of person-function, or play a role in the shaping of person-function. And there finally, instead of "psyche" as the heading of things, I wish I had a word which would more adequately render that other rather queer word *person.* It is odd that we should use the word "mask" for that which *we* ought to *be* most fundamentally, most characteristically, most actively, most faithfully. I do not want any psychology which is just a mask. It has got to be the mark of what we are, from the moment of conception, in our function of life, a consistent entity as far as possible, to go through the privilege of life, which in the human goes through a longer period in which one is not completely made responsible, to a period where full responsibility is expected, and ought to be enjoyed and to be made effective, but which toward the end, in the course of nature, will again lead to a reduction and to death. This has to be the conception of the individual life, and of the social life—because no individual could exist by itself or will continue as such forever. It is always part of a highly inter-penetrating sort of an entity of life at large. That is what we have to bear in mind. It is a product of *nature,* and by nature I mean growth, and growth in which it also becomes most expressive and firm: it is the soft *G* of growth replaced by the strong *C* sound which makes "growth" a "creation" in doing and shaping. It is a problem of *creation,* including responsiveness and responsibility, including religion, the sense of belonging and reciprocity, a natural, deeply felt, and deeply active union, with a concept of the whole worthy of the relative immortality carried according to the contribution that may linger connected with the person.

And that is more or less the picture which presents itself to me in the midst of this group. We are here together to get in as concrete a form as possible the various expressions of what actual workers are doing with themselves in behalf of a large cause, the cause of having this moment's happening, the happening of the now and here, become pointed toward a goal which will be enduring.

Psychiatry: Its Relationship to Psychological Schools of Thought

By HEINZ HARTMANN, M.D.

Editor, International Journal of Psychoanalysis and Imago, New York City

PRACTICAL APPLICATION OF PSYCHIATRY • ORIGIN OF PSYCHOLOGICAL SCHOOLS OF THOUGHT • PSYCHODYNAMICS • OBSERVATION OF MULTIPLE DIMENSIONS • FORMULATION OF THEORIES • ACTUAL LIFE SITUATIONS • CORRELATION • MECHANISM OF REGRESSION • DEFENSE MECHANISMS • SOCIAL FACTORS • DYNAMIC PSYCHOLOGY • DOCTRINE OF SYMBOLS • THE EXPERIMENTAL METHOD • COLLABORATION AMONG THE BRANCHES OF PSYCHOLOGY • THE GIFT OF PSYCHOLOGICAL INSIGHT

WHEN WE think of the manifold tasks which face the psychiatrist in the present emergency, and of those which, in our opinion, will face him after the war; when we compare the present state of affairs with that forty years ago, we see clearly how much we in our field have profited from the development of psychopathology. For the great majority of these tasks can only be solved—and often only be approached —as a result of the revolutionary change which psychiatry has undergone under the influence of the various psychological schools. The psychiatrist as assistant, adviser, collaborator in internal medicine, in surgery, in pediatrics; his role in the mental hygiene movement, in education, in criminology; his part in individual as well as collective prophylaxis; his right and his duty to define his position with regard to social, and even certain political questions,—all these are phenomena which can be understood only as a result of the constantly growing psychological knowledge within the field of psychiatry. And I have merely mentioned a number of the most important practical

17

aspects of psychiatry; its application in the purely scientific sense is still more far-reaching. Yet a systematic enumeration seems unnecessary. All of you have lived through this development and many of you have contributed to it.

I will not deal much with the influence the modern psychological schools had and have on the practical aspects of psychiatry, as my paper is supposed to treat the theoretical side only. Nor can I give you a systematic account to-day. I have to make a selection and am aware of the fact that every such selection contains a personal element.

Some psychological schools which have influenced psychiatry have grown out of observation of the sick; others out of experiences related to the healthy person. Some are clinic-born, others laboratory-born, from experiments on man or on animals. This factor explains many differences. The importance of clinical observation, not merely as starting point, but also in the development of theory, is clear in psychoanalysis, as it is in its French forerunners. In psychobiology, too, we find an intimate relationship to clinical thought. Here we may as well speak of schools of psychiatry which had an influence upon general psychology, as of psychological schools which became important in psychiatry. Some schools have enriched psychiatry through a new approach to research, others have also tried to connect the diversity of psychopathological phenomena by developing different theories. In so doing they followed the example of biology for the most part, but, to a certain extent, also of physics.

Behaviorism, for example, has introduced a new point of view into psychiatric research, and advocated distrust of another, introspection. The formulation of a specifically psychological theory however is here not explicit. Psychoanalysis combines introspection with the objective viewpoint; in the formation of theories it went farther than most of the psychological schools of our time. Quite different was the development of Gestalt-psychology, which, originating in a theory of perception, gradually spread to other fields of psychology. Brain pathology and branches of biology have also profited from this school. Emphasizing the importance of total situations has rendered it of great significance to modern psychopathology where even other schools—less radical perhaps—have pointed out the totality of the personality. Its most interesting results however, from the point of view of psychopathology, seem to me to lie elsewhere, namely where Gestalt-psychology, going beyond its original objective, begins to investigate the relationship of the configurations to the concrete experience, under the influence of psychoanalysis.

This trend is clearly perceptible in the works of Kurt Lewin and his group, as well as, for instance, in a work such as the visual motor gestalt test by Bender. Collaboration between clinic-born and laboratory-born psychological trends has thus been shown possible. The same applies to the behavorists' contributions to psychiatry. All these different points of view can be co-ordinated to some extent; the contradictions are found between basic theoretical positions which may be opposed to each other or mutually exclusive.

Many schools which have exercised a particularly strong influence on modern psychiatry show a common trend which frequently goes under the expression psychodynamics. The concepts of psychological mechanisms, energetic notions, are characteristic of these schools; one speaks of a psychic equilibrium, its disturbances and its restitution (here, by the way, Spencer was a forerunner); or of psychic tension—a notion that occurs also in Gestalt-psychology. Many of these notions share some characteristics with physiological ones, as we find in the work of Meynert (Freud's teacher) and Jackson, later in Head or Sherrington, and others. This similarity is in some cases the result of a direct influence, the best example here being Freud's concept of a psychic regression. I believe we all agree that it was Freud who was most responsible for the acceptance of this type of psychology. In this country, Adolf Meyer recognized the importance of psychopathological dynamics very early; he thus helped to shorten the phase of a purely classificational psychiatry. McDougall's teachings had an equally strong influence on the development of psychodynamics. All schools emphasizing the dynamic point of view supplement descriptive terms through explanatory ones. Most of them take unconscious factors into account. In many of these schools this train of thought has led to basing dynamics on the genesis. The choice of mechanisms, their fixation, etc., can be derived from life history.

To characterize all these schools as psychodynamic is correct, though insufficient for some. The dynamic method can in principle be applied to peripheral as well as to central psychic layers. A number of experiments, often most interesting from a purely scientific point of view, belonging to the first group, has therefore remained without influence in the field of psychiatry. In psychoanalysis, however, and other related schools, dynamics has been supplemented through a theory dealing both with the structure and the driving forces of the human personality. The basis for the analytical and related theories as mentioned before goes beyond the psychical cross section and back to the genesis. I do not believe it to be an accident that the knowledge of mechanisms has borne fruit in the field of psychiatry mostly within the framework of a biological and genetic theory. The genetic approach is still the most fruitful one and I think it would be precocious to constitute psychology as an ahistorical science to-day—though in future it may become possible. At present the psychic dynamisms, which we can recognize in the various conflict situations, have to be understood not only in their interrelationship but also through the part they have played in the development. We thus arrive at a psychopathological form of observation of multiple dimensions; this method has helped much to bridge to a certain extent the gap that previously existed between subjective and objective, between descriptive and constructive psychiatry.

Theories of that kind Freud considered to be the coping of psychology rather than its foundation stone; they may be replaced if necessary. In any case we will not make such a change arbitrarily, and only if we are able to replace the coping with a more suitable one. The majority of psychopathologists is in agreement on some of these points, even though no agreement exists as to what extent it would be necessary and fruitful to correlate theoretically the multitude of new observations, or as to which degree of generality in the theoretical field would be most apt to further our psychological work. On the whole, however, we might say that we are here faced with a process which has taken place earlier in related fields. The importance of the formulation of theories is to-day more clearly recognized in the field of psychopathology; its scientific and practical role is clearly seen, and the distrust of the formulation of theories is disappearing in the entire field of psychology. J. F. Brown has recently expressed this by saying that even if we possessed none but false theories it would still be better than having no theories at all.

The dynamic and genetic approaches have made it possible to understand the *meaning* of psychic symptoms, in that they show their dynamic function and their place in the life history. What this has meant in the understanding of neuroses, of schizophrenia, and eventually in the field of psychiatry in general has often been pointed out. To-day I must be satisfied with merely mentioning it.

I should like to deal briefly with another related problem. Traditional psychology neglected the interrelationship between thought or feeling and concrete life situations. We understand that such a purely formal psychology could contribute little to psychiatry. Psychoanalysis, on the other hand, from the beginning, owing to its origin in the clinic, studied the content of experiences, i.e., their relation to the concrete objects of desire, love, hate, fear. So did other psychodynamic schools. Thus we have learnt to discover a human being in his actual situation instead of in his laboratory situation. This emphasis on the actual life situation further led to recognition that human being in a definite social environment is the object of psychology. The problem of adaptation, all important in psychopathology, thus could be treated on a scientific, empirical basis and a true psychology of action becomes possible. Former psychological schools paid too much attention to the phantom of an *isolated* individual, a human being without a correlated world. You realize that the above mentioned development signified an important step, in particular as applied to social science and social practice. The influence of John Dewey has proved particularly fruitful as far as this progress is concerned.

This step would have remained incomplete had one not attempted to correlate the behavior of a person toward certain objects or situations in terms of rules and laws. Occasional observations of an individual in his environment may here and there suggest a clinical connection. It may lead to a philosophical aperçu or to artistic elaboration but not to science. On the other hand, the laws of dynamics, independent of their interrelationship with certain classes of objectives, remain more or less empty shells. Such had been the case in psychiatry,—individual, brilliant, clinical-psychological observations, aphoristically formulated, without scientific background on the one hand and purely formal psychology, a science of rules, on the other. The combination of both, a psychology of concrete, situational problems, but tending toward certain definite rules, (as already discernible in the "Studien ueber Hysterie") signifies the breakthrough of a new trend. We find a similar design in the early works of Janet but his tendency toward the psychological law lags behind in comparison with his feeling for good clinical observation. To-day many psychologists and psychopathologists realize that progress in the direction of the psychological law cannot confine itself to purely phenomenological findings but must necessarily include elements of the unconscious. What I wish to say is that such psychology, ceteris paribus, will be most useful to psychiatry as is best capable of retaining this polar tension between the consideration of the multiplicity of life situations on the one hand and the tendency toward formulation of laws on the other hand. If psychology loses contact either with that multiplicity or with the scientific conception of its observations, its usefulness for psychiatry decreases. I wish to make it clear that I do not want to present here a methodological criticism. The meaning intended is rather a pragmatic one which is, in my view, valid in the present stage of our science.

It is obvious that all these psychological trends, as far as they could contribute to a psychiatric formulation of disease, had also to come into conflict with the old and fixed nosological schemes. Adolf Meyer in his doctrine of reaction types has gone further than anyone by way of criticism. Yet many adhere to the disease entities in psychiatry and many still regard schizophrenia as an organic disease even though it may be influenced by the psychical. Freud, at the same time, tried to develop a classification in the field of neurosis which, apart from its symptomatology, rested primarily upon the different *defense mechanisms* and the *degree of regression*. There can be no doubt that there is a definite correlation between stage of regression and type of neurotic reaction. In this connection of disease and regression lies also the origin of a research trend which investigates the relation of the neurotic and psychotic with primitive thought and feeling. The basis of a new concept of health is contained in this genetic criterion. This concept of regression, originating in the field of neurology, has, owing to Freud, become an essential part of our psychiatric thinking. It offers a good example for the problem of content and form in psychiatry at which I have hinted before; for regression means to go back on the one hand to earlier experiences, and on the other hand to primitive forms of thinking and expression.

The second question which is of importance is whether the defense mechanisms, sublimation, isolation, projection, etc., constitute a determinate specificity. It seems to be the case that these psychic mechanisms, or rather some of them, are, as a rule, found more frequently in certain forms of neuroses than in others, as the phenomenon of isolation, for example, or of undoing in obsessional neurosis. This justifies the attempt at coordination. Apart from the mechanism itself it is necessary to consider its topical value and its dynamic effect. That means not only its existence or non-existence but also its place in the psychical structure and the energy which it represents.

We will not, however, speak of specificity in the strict sense of the term. But we may say that in this respect, and perhaps only in this respect, psychiatry has developed its own concept of disease.

It remains an open question how far it is possible to classify psychoses according to mechanism and degree of regression. A number of melancholias offer the clearest picture in this respect. And yet, without thorough and detailed empirical investigation, we may certainly not assume that the psychopathological point of view is necessarily applicable to all other fields of psychiatry as the most suitable basis for determining diseases. Opinions regarding this question of the psychoses are sharply divided, just as they are still divided with regard to the etiological importance of present and childhood experiences.

This applies, to an even larger extent, to the evaluation of social factors and their importance for the origin and form of psychic disturbances. Psychopathology, like psychology, to be really useful must be social psychology; it must see a human being in his relationship to other human beings. The early social contacts of a human being are at the same time biologically decisive, for the child is infinitely more dependent upon the love and the protection of the adult than the young animal is upon that of his mother. This very helplessness and dependence of the child, which further the differentiation and the development of the Ego, are, according to Freud, also one of the most general factors responsible for the origin of neuroses, because this situation gives a particular biological emphasis to the need of being loved. The peculiarities of early relationships are of the greatest importance for the later life of a person in disease as well as in health. Biological and social factors can not be separated on this level, while it is perfectly possible to study these very factors from either a biological or a sociological point of view. It was relationships of this kind which became the central object of psychoanalysis and the basis for its applications to sociological phenomena. But there is no reason why we should limit the effect of biological factors on the psyche to those which are at the same time social factors. This seems as wrong as to neglect the significance of social factors, as earlier psychologists used to do. Apart from these differences of opinion the fact remains that the consistent widening of the doctrine of human relationships and their interrelation to human needs has enabled the psychiatrist to have access to social science and social practice. There are important contributions of psychiatrists to the problems of group psychology, of morale, of propaganda, etc. To-day his attitude towards these questions is no longer that of a dilettante; he is no longer someone whose hobby it is to concern himself with sociological problems. He can take a definite attitude, because his own science, in its present stage, has found useful access to that field. In modern psychopathology the social element is a basic one; it is not confined to a chapter of psychology called social psychology, as it was at the time when Spencer, Tarde, LeBon, Wundt lived. It is possible that the relations with sociology will in turn influence the development of psychological theories. The process of enrichment may well be mutual.

All this sounds rather schematic. I am afraid, however, it must be so, as I want to show you just a few points in present psychology, in which the actually fruitful trends of thought intersect each other. Thus the many concrete psychiatric questions, branching off at these points, which I can not discuss to-day, become most easily traceable.

The trends of dynamic psychology also have lent new stimulus to other psychological schools and have brought some of them into closer contact with psychiatry. Psychological experiments played a role in psychiatry in and even before the era of Kraepelin. But those experiments, despite their scientific interest, never gained full significance in psychiatry because they necessarily confined themselves to the peripheral psychic layers. To-day the situation has changed. We are faced with a large number of findings and hypotheses regarding personality due to the investigations of psychoanalysis, psychobiology and other schools. Experiments may be oriented in accordance with these findings. Actually an ever growing number of experiments is to-day concerned with this more ambitious task. Let me give you a few examples. The analytical doctrine of symbols, first based upon dream analysis, and later found invaluable in the doctrine of neuroses and psychoses, has often been experimentally verified and essentially corroborated. Other theories have been verified through investigations of identical twins, investigations which, under certain conditions, have experimental value. Even within the field of analysis we find situations which approach the experimental level, as, for example, when we give a patient an interpretation based on a well worked-out psychic situation, and then observe his reaction to such an interpretation. Incidentally, here we have a case where the analytical method makes it possible to predict psychic happenings with a fair degree of accuracy.

To corroborate analytical hypotheses, experiments with animals have been conducted, such as Miller's experiments as to displacement of affection, Mowrer's experiments and others. Murray's book constitutes a valuable contribution, as do investigations by Cameron and others; also those conducted by Brown. I am thinking of Sear's work of amnesia, and a number of works about Korsakoff; I am thinking of the Yale studies by Dollard, Miller and others which are based on the analytical hypothesis of the connection between frustration and aggression. This connection is used as a preliminary hypothesis which should lead to more precise and more detailed research findings, findings which in turn may be used for the more precise formulation or even revision of the original hypothesis.

Psychological schools have the natural desire to express in their own language whatever has been recognized as correct. Some of it is, in a sense, translation work. A large part of analytical results, for example, have been translated into the language of reflexology. But even such translations can be useful in as far as they help to establish a connection with different fields and methods of research.

Those verifications of which I have spoken represent, if positive, not merely a corroboration of those findings but also of the methods by which they have been found. The value of such experiments is obvious. The results can more easily be formulated, they are more distinct, easier to check, they demonstrate the generally known logical advantages of the experimental method.

A greater unification of psychopathological terminology may be possible and would be of great advantage to psychiatry. To-day we are still far from it. Confused by the mass of psychological doctrines, the psychiatrist often turns to methodology, only to find, if possible, even greater contrasts here. For him it is decisive to select a method which is close to his object, suited to this object and actually fruitful. In the field of methodological criticism, however, it happens only too often that two totally different questions are not sufficiently distinguished: the first question is that of the greater or lesser logical perfection of a method; the second, that of its purely empirical suitability in finding new facts and new connections. Methodological criticism must not deteriorate into a collection of prohibitions, but must teach us constructively to contribute to the development of our science and to avoid erroneous ways of approach.

To compare the different psychological schools within the field of psychiatry according to their logical and theoretical bases and to assign them their respective function would be a legitimate and urgent task for methodology. Several times such a comparison has been attempted without having ever been satisfactorily completed. Important in this connection is the comparison between topological psychology and psychoanalysis, as attempted by Brown and Lewin. Years ago Lewin's psychology was brought into contact with psychoanalysis, as in the field of obsessional neurosis psychology. To-day we witness the development of a methodologically serious, objective and sympathetic collaboration between the two schools, which may well serve as an example for the possible collaboration among other branches of psychology. It may help psychoanalysis to come to a clarification of the relationships existing between three main parts of its theory: dynamic,

instinct theory, and structural concepts. New ways of verifi-
cation may be discovered and the formulation in terms of
laws may be promoted. All methods which have contributed
something original and positive to the development of psychology contain problems which can best be solved through
collaboration. Even behaviorism and psychoanalysis, which
for some time were regarded as irreconcilably opposed to each
other, have found some common ground.

I do not forget that, in mentioning the usefulness of different
psychological schools in the field of psychiatry, we also refer
to the extent to which results may be of help in our medical
and extra-medical action, how far they help us, as psychiatrists,
to solve our tasks toward the individual or society. To-day I
can not investigate the effects of all these trends on education
or upon the means and goals of psychotherapy. In ending, I
wish to touch upon one point only, the human side, if I may
say so, of our problem. I am referring to our own attitude
to psychic diseases, and more particularly our attitude to the
patient. I believe that the attitude of many psychiatrists has
changed basically, and that on the whole this change has been
to the good. We have learned to eliminate sources of error,
blind spots in ourselves that had hampered the progress of
our psychological insight. We better understand our own role
as psychiatrists in relation to the individual as well as to
society. The problems of transference and of counter-transference, in its most general meaning, became definitely less
mystic and easier to control. This enables us to attain a greater
objectivity and maturity in our relation to the sick person and
to master the therapeutic situation. This change in the attitude
of the psychiatrist constitutes one of the greatest gifts which
psychological insight has presented to psychiatry.

Psychiatry: Its Significance in Internal Medicine

By OSKAR DIETHELM, M.D.

Psychiatrist in Chief, The New York Hospital, Payne Whitney Psychiatric Clinic; Professor of Psychiatry, Cornell University Medical School

PSYCHIATRY AND THE TOTAL PHYSIOLOGICAL FUNCTIONING • THE PSYCHIATRIST A PHYSICIAN TRAINED IN PHYSIOLOGY • MUTUAL INTERESTS WITH INTERNISTS • CONTRIBUTIONS OF THE PSYCHIATRIST • MEDICAL ASPECTS OF PSYCHIATRIC PATIENTS • SOUND PSYCHOPATHOLOGY • CLINICAL PSYCHIATRY • MEDICAL TREATMENT AND PERSONALITY FACTORS • INVESTIGATION • TEAM WORK • MUTUAL COOPERATION

INTERNAL MEDICINE and psychiatry are both based on physiology and psychobiology. In considering the physical functions of a person, one must evaluate the individual personality setting. For instance, it is impossible to study physiological functions without considering the emotions present at the time of the investigation. This principle has become accepted to a certain extent in human physiology, but it is largely discounted in animal experimentation. The difference between physiological studies of human beings and of animals can be explained by the fact that animal psychology does not consider the individual animal, whereas human psychology has begun to appreciate the role of the personality of the individual and to be guided by a psychobiological concept.

Psychiatry realized the value of physiology and of internal medicine after it had freed itself from the influence of a neurology which had limited the interests of the psychiatrist to the organic factors of the brain and neglected the total physiological functioning. This phase was followed by an interest in toxic and endocrinologic factors. Gradually a need to consider the total integrated organism developed. In this present phase of psychiatry, the psychiatrist must always feel obligated to consider physiologic as well as personality factors, physical illnesses as well as personality disorders. A dynamic conception which took into consideration the personality (i.e., psychodynamic factors) as well as physical and environmental factors became the basis for study and treatment.

The result was an extension of psychiatry from the limitation of the study and treatment of hospitalized cases to that of all kinds of major and minor personality disorders whether transient or lasting in nature. The part played by emotions in physical functions, a topic which had been buried for 150 years after a promising start at the end of the 18th century, became of increasing interest. The problems which are peculiar to the developing personality in childhood and adolescence, and most recently those of the aging period, became topics of inquiry. The psychiatrist began to request medical advice readily whereas the internist asked for aid only when his cases became unmanageable. However, it should be kept in mind that medicine in general has changed from the consideration of isolated functions and diseases to the study and treatment of the patient as a whole with his individual personality. The psychiatrist, being a physician trained in physiology, was ahead in this development. The physical illnesses of his patients forced him to keep abreast of medical progress. The failure of the development of a psychology which might be of equal value as physiology to a physician and the lack of adequate teaching of psychiatry prevented the internist from obtaining a sound basis for appreciation of personality factors and personality disorders.

Internal medicine should have the same relationship to psychiatry as psychiatry has to internal medicine. Until very recently there remained a one-sided separation of internal medicine from psychiatry which was not overcome by the expansion of psychiatry into the general hospital. The psychiatrist became the consultant who knew special techniques useful on the medical pavilions; he formed the liaison between to two separated disciplines. This liaison did not lead to an integrated working-together of internist and psychiatrist.

At present, it is accepted that all the various aspects of the patient should be investigated and treated. Both psychiatrist and internist should know the fundamentals of physical and personality functions, but each should know more than the other in his own field. The working-together of internist and psychiatrist in teaching and in medical practice should lead to mutual counsel, teaching and learning. There is no need to fear that the psychiatrist will take over an increasing part of internal medicine. Instead, the psychiatrist should teach the internist appropriate techniques for the evaluation of personality factors in diagnosis and treatment.

The requirements for a sound development of psychiatry and internal medicine include a basic training in psychiatry all through medical school, internship and graduate training. Psychobiology, i.e., the study of the functions of the personality, should be parallel and integrated with physiology. In using the term "psychobiology" in this discussion, I am not referring to any special school of thought but to the psychobiological concept as it is now recognized and used everywhere in medicine, under whatever name it may be called. Psychopathology should be taught and considered parallel with pathology with the same clarity of definition, observation and description, and critical investigation of all the factors which play a role. Clinical instruction should include the teaching of personality factors in medical patients and the internal medical aspects in psychiatric patients. All these principles should be applied to in- and out-patients and to fostering the health of family and community. In our own group at Cornell University Medical College, these principles of teaching have been used for several years. The medical students receive in psychobiology special instruction in the relationship of emotions and physiological functioning. In physiology, special lectures are devoted to presenting psychological factors. In the clinical years, somatic factors are stressed in the psychiatric teaching at the Payne Whitney Psychiatric Clinic and in the pavilions of the general hospital, and the clinical clerks in medicine are requested to pay special attention to psychological factors. The teaching is done by the psychiatrist as well as the internist. The same policy exists in the general out-patient department. The resident staff in medicine is urged to discuss personality aspects with the psychiatrist who attends the pavilions daily and to practice the study and treatment of personality aspects under his supervision. The integrated teaching of psychiatry and internal medicine has resulted in increased demands on the time of students and members of the resident staff. Considering such a development a necessity, ways can be found to save time in requirements which have become less important with the progress of medicine; for instance, the time spent in teaching and carrying out laboratory methods.

One of the essential ways in which psychiatry contributes to internal medicine is by offering the internist additional tools for the study and treatment of his patients. It is important that he learn to take a history in such a way as to give the patient an opportunity to tell his own story under the guidance of the physician and to present his complaints thoroughly. A well-organized history, which includes the genetic and dynamic aspects of the illness and the personality, results. Another point to be considered is the correlation of the facts obtained. This is best achieved by organizing material along the lines of physical development and illnesses, general life development, and environmental factors, obtaining as correct dates as possible. By the correlation of these various facts, dynamic factors become obvious and may be explained by the individual's personality reactions. Furthermore, the psychiatrist should teach the need to investigate all possible leads whether they be physical, psychological, or socio-economic. In order to be able to carry on the investigation, one has to know how questions should be asked and how the patient should be observed. The use of all available resources should be stressed, including the direct means of studying the patient as well as the indirect; for instance, obtaining information from relatives and social agencies. It is the obligation of psychiatry to make physicians aware of the intricate patient-physician relationship. A diagnosis of psychopathology should be based on positive facts and not on the absence of physical findings which could explain the complaints of the patient. The fundamentals of treatment of personality must be understood. The physician, by formulating the factors involved, should be able to offer an explanation which will satisfy the patient. The technique of offering reassurance based on facts rather than mere words has to be mastered. The knowledge of the use of suggestion and a critical awareness of the influence of suggestion in a therapeutic situation are important. The analysis of complex situations leading to a practical synthesis is frequently essential. Every internist should be aware of the significance of dreams and their relationship to personality or toxic factors. The more complex psychotherapeutic methods belong to the special equipment of the psychiatrist.

From this brief review, it becomes obvious that psychiatrists should bring to internal medicine a broader understanding of the personality and its role in health and illness. In addition, a broader concept of pathology than has heretofore existed should evolve. The pathology of the functions of the personality, i.e., psychopathology, should be recognized as being of fundamental importance to internal medicine. The essential characteristics of pathology remain the same whether one deals with somatic or psychopathologic disorders; findings which are unusual in degree, or occurring within the wrong age period, are pathological. In addition, psychiatry stresses the feature of unusual and disturbing behavior in interpersonal relations. Consideration of this feature should prove stimulating to medicine in general, especially when practiced outside the confines of the hospital. It might be pointed out here that in recent years psychiatrists have unfortunately been vague in their formulations of psychopathology. The philosophy of general pathology and internal medicine is gradually bringing greater clarity and definition into psychopathology. So-called borderline cases are investigated with a critical curiosity and can frequently be formulated in a more concrete form. In physiology and internal medicine, many borderline findings have been explained by the influence of emotions.

A knowledge of the fundamentals of sound psychopathology and clinical psychiatry is necessary in the field of internal medicine. Only with such basic knowledge can the physician proceed to a study of the less marked but frequently more involved personality problems. In this connection, it might be mentioned that the old dichotomy of psychoses and neuroses, which is the hangover of an outmoded type of psychiatric thinking, should be given up entirely. This demand does not imply an elimination of well-defined psychopathologic pictures and illnesses but a guarding against generalizations. The most recent fallacy along these lines is the claim that psychosomatic disorders are psychoneuroses. Such a statement disregards the advances of psychobiology and dynamic psychopathology. Investigative work has demonstrated that in the majority of psychosomatic cases one does not find psychopathologic conditions which can be considered psychoneurotic. It may well be that the dynamic factor of suppression of emotion is present in psychosomatic conditions, whereas repression (with dissociation, displacement and substitution) characterizes psychoneurotic reactions. There are no doubt other factors which have not yet become clear.

A knowledge of psychopathology permits the internist to recognize and understand the many types of personality disorders with which he is confronted. In the medical pavilions and in the practitioner's office may be found depressive reactions of physically ill and physically well patients, schizophrenic illnesses among chronic invalids, indistinct paranoic reactions, delirious and toxic psychopathologic reactions of varying degree, early signs of brain damage caused by arteriosclerosis or by brain injury, with surprisingly marked psychopathologic findings.

Treatment in internal medicine cannot be carried out without consideration of personality factors. An internist should be able to study, understand and treat depressive reactions in his patients, whether these reactions belong to the group of psychiatric disorders called depressions or are a mild depressive mood reactive to personal problems or to physical illness with its many possible implications. Among these may be included the meaning of the illness, its economic complications, and its interference with carrying one's responsibility. The period of convalescence as well as changes caused by aging give rise to disturbing emotional reactions. Personal difficulties of adaptation may be expressed in queer or suspicious behavior, in paranoic delusions, in antagonism to or overdependence on the physician, in jealousy reactions, or in schizophrenic withdrawal. The sexual life of most patients presents either some aspects which are unclear to them or definite difficulties which might be discussed to the patient's advantage. There is no patient who will not benefit greatly by a review of his mode of living and an investigation of whether, according to his individual needs, he balances work and recreation and pays adequate attention to his physical needs, especially food intake, activity, rest, sleep and sexual satisfaction.

Considering special problems of investigation which psychiatry has brought into the field of internal medicine, one should point out first that interest in the influence of personality factors on physical illnesses has led to uncritical overemphasis and bias. Emotions are always present in a human being and their significance depends on the type of emotion, its strength, its duration, as well as the general psychobiological constellation. The need for simplification and classification resulted in formulating special personality types which predispose to specific physical illnesses. The mere description of dynamic factors was considered of far-reaching investigative value which, it was claimed, answered the problems of the internist. Far from doing this, it disturbed the internist who could not believe that his philosophy of research and his criteria had been so wrong. Fortunately, this phase of psychiatric investigative attitude has passed and the contribution of psychiatric thinking and procedures has become clarified. The main features are the need to consider the individual at the time of the investigation with his life-determined attitude to any given situation, the need to elicit emotions present, and the need to evaluate psychobiologically all the factors found. Psychiatry has emphasized the point that investigation along any line should be considered fundamental if carried out critically and pushed far enough. Besides studies of a well-defined laboratory nature, broad clinical investigations have become more worth while than previously. Personality reactions to convalescence and to chronic and crippling disorders became promising fields of investigation. In disfiguring illnesses, social implications as well as the patient's conception of body image are important. An exceedingly important contribution is the change of attitude of the investigator to the patient. Realizing that any inconsiderate action will provoke corresponding complicating emotions in the subject studied, the investigator will try to avoid them. In other words, the critical clinical investigator must be a conscientious physician.

Although the development of joint study and treatment of a patient's disorders by various specialists cannot be attributed to psychiatry, psychiatric thinking certainly has contributed considerably to the attitude of integration in medical practice.

The psychiatrist's need to be concerned with the socio-economic situation, good or poor, has made itself felt in the field of medical social service. It seems a fact that wherever a strong psychiatric influence exists, internists are interested in the social needs of their patients and therefore request the aid of psychologically trained social workers.

A recent outcome of psychiatric thinking in internal medicine is the study of the relationship of the physician to the patient and his family. This interest presents an important step in the direction of assuming responsibility for helping the patient in illness and in maintaining his health.

In conclusion, it can be stated that the significance of psychiatry in internal medicine can be evaluated only by considering at the same time the significance of internal medicine in psychiatry. Through psychiatry, medicine has recognized the psychobiologic unit and has obtained the necessary psychological basis. A change in medical thinking has affected the physician's attitude to the patient and influenced undergraduate and graduate teaching and research. On the basis of mutual cooperation, it has become recognized that there is a difference of emphasis along various lines between internal medicine and psychiatry, but not a separation between the two fields. The physicians in these two fields will hold each other in mutual esteem and the result will be physicians with a broad outlook and self-reliance guided by their recognized limitations.

Psychiatry: Its Significance in General Surgery

By PERCIVAL BAILEY, M.D.

Professor of Neurology and Neurological Surgery, University of Illinois

CONCERN OF SURGEON WITH PSYCHIATRY • SURGICAL DIAGNOSIS AND PSYCHIATRIC PROBLEMS • ANXIETY STATES AND OPERATIONS • POLYSURGICAL ADDICTIONS • MOTIVATION TO OPERATION • SURGERY AND PSYCHOTHERAPY • HEADACHE • THE CHALLENGE OF LOW BACK PAIN • SIGNS OF NEUROTIC MECHANISMS • NEED OF PSYCHOLOGICAL INVESTIGATION • PAINFUL COCCYX • PLASTIC SURGERY • ESSENTIAL HYPERTENSION • GRAVES' DISEASE • EFFECT OF FEAR • THE SPIRIT OF THE PATIENT • PRE-OPERATIVE AND POST-OPERATIVE CARE • THE SURGEON HIS OWN PSYCHIATRIST

THE CONCERN of the surgeon with psychiatry is an eminently practical one and in reflecting on the matter it has seemed to me that there are three particular times when the surgeon needs psychiatric orientation, namely, before the operation, during the operation and after the operation.

During the Middle Ages, when the surgeon acted merely as the tool of the physician, except in the treatment of such obvious things as war wounds, he needed little equipment except manual dexterity and intestinal fortitude. But when he ventured out on his own, and cast off his leading strings, he began immediately to need also the knowledge and diagnostic skill of the physician. This meant that he had to take into account not only the organic causes of the troubles he tried to relieve but the psychic causes also; in other words, he tried to solve the physician's problem and determine for himself in what cases the therapeusis he had to offer was appropriate. For this task his preparation and temperament were not always adequate. Who does not remember the waves of ovariotomy, appendectomy, uterine suspension, nephropexy and other ill-advised operations for disorders now known to have been largely of psychic origin? At the present time I believe that much fewer unnecessary operations are done on patients of this type but they still occur. Any doctor with a large consultation practice knows well the patient who has been around to all the clinics, and recounts endlessly his experiences, interspersed with caustic remarks about the shortcomings of doctors in general and in particular. If his complaints are concerned principally with his abdominal viscera, his abdomen is apt to look like a European battlefield.

As I look back on my own experience as a neurologist, I can recall several thyroidectomies on confirmed neurotic patients and two in the early stages of organic neurological disorders, one multiple sclerosis and one Parkinsonian syndrome. A little tremor and a slightly elevated basal metabolic rate were sufficient for them to lose their thyroid glands, at least in part. Perhaps you will think that such errors could only occur in some isolated place. These two patients were operated on at one of the largest surgical clinics in the country (not in Chicago). I saw both patients in consultation before operation and believe that neither of them had Graves' disease. Several patients have been under my care with severe anxiety neuroses who have been partial thyroidectomies; some I have seen before operation, and some only afterward, but I am convinced that this error is made not infrequently. If the surgeon had a better understanding of the anxiety neuroses such mistakes would be oftener avoided.

I suppose there are unscrupulous surgeons who, for gain or for prestige, will persuade naive and credulous patients into needless operations but certainly such instances must be rare in comparison with those neurotic patients who persuade the young and unsuspecting surgeon into inadvisable operations for reasons quite apart from the correction of any organic defect. The relief of depressions and neuroses by intercurrent disease or injury is well known to psychiatrists, in fact, is the basis of treatment by fixation abscess, malaria, insulin shock and others of their ilk. A surgical operation may act similarly and many neurotic patients seem to have some subconscious impulsion to seek relief in this way. You are all familiar with such patients. I do not need to recount histories.

We have all seen these patients with their abdomens looking like well-plowed fields. They go from surgeon to surgeon until they find someone to make another operation. If rebuffed they may become paranoid and be a great nuisance to the doctor. These patients have anxiety neuroses. They have found that it is a relief to substitute an actual danger for the constant apprehension and, after operation, for a time at least, are better. Also the operation reduces the patient for a time to an infantile situation of helplessness, dependence and need for special care. There is a certain heroic excitement to the situation; the whole family rises to the emergency and the patient is the center of attention.

Alvarez has described the great difficulty the physician has in convincing such patients that an operation is unnecessary. Many will turn away from the able clinician or old family doctor who tries to convince them that an operation will, in all probability, only aggravate their symptoms. They have, unfortunately, learned from experience that the doctor, if they turn for a moment from their complaints to discuss their social difficulties, soon loses interest, begins to look at the clock, then to scold, then gives a sedative and pushes them out of the consultation room. So they keep to their leading complaints with such insistence that the surgeon, reflecting on the latest case in which he overlooked a serious lesion which was discovered by his principal competitor, or genuinely impressed by the apparent suffering, salves his conscience by reflecting that, if he does not operate, the patient will go perhaps to a less able or maybe unscrupulous operator, and so adds another scar to the already overdecorated abdominal wall. If young and inexperienced, he is apt to be chagrined later, on telling the patient that he found nothing wrong, to find that the patient concludes that he is lying or that he does not know his business.

Even if the doctor persuades the patient that his troubles

rest on something other than an organic ailment and the patient agrees to consult a psychiatrist, often the engagement is not kept. This usually means that the patient, once out of range of the persuasive influence of the doctor, feels unable to acknowledge to himself that he could be so weak as to suffer from an "imaginary" ailment and is even more unable to face the chorus of "I told you so" from his relatives, and the reproaches over the wasted money and time. So he will go again on the search for the surgeon who will adopt a more heroic therapeusis and drown the reproaches of his relatives in their sympathy with his intolerable and interminable suffering.

And, after the operation, in such cases the patient is often better for a time and apt to return to gloat over the conservative surgeon or, more often, to spread abroad the news of his incompetency. Such a patient may do an incalculable amount of harm to a careful and conservative surgeon's reputation. The young surgeon fears this possibility and, conscious of his inexperience, may be led into exploring. If he is going into the abdomen he should be taught to explore thoroughly and not content himself with removing the appendix through a two-finger incision. The young surgeon may console himself with the thought that, if he finds nothing serious in the abdomen, he can at least remove the appendix and do the patient no harm. He should beware of that thought; his simple laparotomy may be the beginning of an intractable and irreparable polysurgical addiction. The belly never feels the same again, as anyone knows who has had his abdomen opened. New discomforts appear, another surgeon is consulted who finds adhesions, another laparotomy is made, and so it goes on until the patient is a confirmed invalid and financially ruined.

There is no need to detail, for the benefit of a group of psychiatrists, the various subconscious needs which push neurotic patients into seeking relief in a surgical operation. Often the motivation is fairly simple and easy to discover. One of the most common has seemed to me to be the need of an inadequate person to secure the solicitude or care of relatives and friends who always gather around the sufferer facing a serious crisis such as a surgical intervention. Others resort to this means of avoiding facing something to them more fearful; thus a fiancee who puts off her wedding date again and again and finds a serious illness the only means of holding her lover a little longer. Perhaps some gain from a father-transference to the surgeon who is often a strong, domineering, cocksure type. Perhaps there is a trace of exhibitionism at times in the gynecological field, but the deeper motives such as those described by Menninger may be left to the analyst to uncover. It suffices for the surgeon to detect their existence.

If the conditions which gave rise to the neurosis have in the meantime changed, the operation may really solve the patient's problem and he remain well, but the surgeon can never count on such an outcome and should never perform an operation as a psychotherapeutic measure; nine times out of ten it will recoil on him. Operations done to "satisfy the patient" are equally risky. Surgery and psychotherapy should not be confused.

Nothing is more disastrous than to tell the patient that nothing is wrong. This leaves the patient frustrated because he knows "something" is wrong. The patient has unconsciously translated his troubles from the psyche to the soma and the surgeon must recognize the frequency of this mechanism and be trained to recognize it even though he does not wish to deal with the situation personally.

A very frequent neurotic complaint is pain about the head and, in my capacity as neurologist and neurological surgeon, I have seen a large number of such sufferers. One has always to be on his guard against these patients. The older surgeon learns usually to detect these people after bitter experience, but there is no reason why the younger surgeon should not be taught to detect this sort of case. Of course, what arouses the suspicion of the experienced surgeon is the fact that the story is not according to Hoyle. He proceeds to rule out organic disease as thoroughly as he can and, when he has assembled the data, he finds that there is a discrepancy between the complaints and the findings, that the symptoms spread more widely than can be accounted for by any hypothetical cause, also, if he is alert and pushes his investigation further, that this is only one of a long series of varied complaints which have, nevertheless, left the patient in quite passable condition. All of this does not ring true. The patient complains overmuch, has his symptoms too much in his consciousness, exhibits excessive fear, and perhaps obviously uses his symptoms to gain some advantage.

The young surgeon is seldom taught these simple rules, and some surgeons never learn them. So patients with pain around the head, if they complain long enough and consult surgeons enough, come finally with teeth removed, tonsils removed, and sinuses drained, thus reducing materially the things the last consultant can think of to do to them.

I have reason to suppose that the situation is not much different in other fields of surgery. One of the most frequent neurotic complaints, apart from headache, is low back pain. I have seen a great many such patients. After all possible or probable organic causes have been ruled out, so far as possible, there is a numerous residue which can be greatly helped by psychotherapy. Again I have found it necessary to warn the young surgeon that he cannot make a diagnosis of neurotic backache from his inability to find an organic cause. He must be able to demonstrate positive signs of neurotic mechanisms, as I have indicated briefly in discussing headache. It is important that these patients be detected early, before a brace has been given them and they have found how useful to them this crutch may be in obtaining various social, economic or emotional advantages. Such patients abound in the practice of chiropractors and osteopaths and too often in that of orthopedic surgeons. I have had them come to me after spinal or sacroiliac fusions, and I have a vivid recollection of one on whom I operated for a supposed herniated intervertebral disc. The differentiation of back pains of neurotic origin from those of organic origin should be thoroughly taught to every student. Fetterman notes that "The recognition of neuroses in the differential diagnosis of back symptoms is an everyday challenge to the industrial surgeon; nor is it infrequent as a problem of general practice," and adds, "An able orthopedic surgeon with whom I have seen several patients in consultation, and who had been skeptical about vertebral neuroses, now lists this condition as one of the commonest afflictions in the patients whom he sees."

One of the systems of organs most adversely affected by emotional stress is the female genital tract. The menses may be arrested or increased in amount. Pain at the menstrual period may become intolerable. Ovariotomies are no longer performed with the frequency of earlier days but, doubtless with the best intentions in the world, surgeons are pushed into attempting to relieve such patients by operations which could be avoided by adequate psychological investigation and treatment. Any psychiatrist can cite a long list of such cases. It seems to be particularly common at the menopause, when women are emotionally upset, and fear cancer, that such unnecessary operations are prevalent. I should perhaps mention here the pain in the coccyx which so often afflicts the unmarried spinster and which the unwary surgeon may attempt to relieve by operation.

The field of plastic surgery is also infested with neurotic patients. Blair and Brown advise caution in the correction of slight defects to which the individual seems to attach an exaggerated importance. They mention many cases in which the operation was clinically successful but the patient remained as dissatisfied as ever and they also mention cases in which the clinical result was not successful but it appeared to satisfy the patient surprisingly well. They deplore the "morbid neurotic craving on the part of these patients to have something done to correct a supposed defect which they rarely evaluate objectively."

It is unnecessary to go through the whole field of surgery. In the case of every organ in the body the repercussions of the psyche must be remembered. In short, the surgeon must take into account all those diseases in which the physician also has learned to reckon with psychic causes. Diseases which come frequently into this category are essential hypertension, Graves' disease, gastric and duodenal ulcer, cardiospasm, spastic colon and mucous colitis. Many of these are apt to fall into the surgeon's hands and he should never forget that a large proportion of such patients can be relieved by psychotherapy.

Patients with essential hypertension are found by Moschovitz to be tense, serious and irritable, unable to relax. Palmer estimates that with rest, conscious relaxation, psychotherapy and sedation, symptomatic relief can be obtained in ninety percent of mild cases, seventy-five percent of moderate cases and fifty percent of late cases. Patients with Graves' disease are hypersensitive, emotionally unstable people whose troubles often date from a sudden emotional crisis. With rest and iodine much can be accomplished with them. Certainly no one should be rushed into an operation on the basis of such a fallible datum as a moderately elevated basal rate, yet I have seen just this happen. Patients with duodenal ulcer are irritable, sensitive and introspective. With medical management and psychotherapy many can be cured. Dragstedt has maintained that the neurogenic origin of this disease seems to be soundly established, with hyperchlorhydria as the immediate mechanism.

The psychiatric needs of the surgeon do not cease, however, when an operation has been decided necessary. An operation is, for many patients, a serious psychic trauma. Crile, who has so elaborately investigated the effects of surgical trauma upon the human organism, has also eloquently described how disastrous may be the effect of terror and anxiety, natural to the patient who contemplates a surgical operation on himself, even if all effects of actual trauma are discounted.

If this is true of the adult, how much more true it must be of the child. Few surgeons realize what a barbarous procedure it is to take a child into a strange room containing impressively terrifying instruments, surrounded by solemn persons, garbed and masked like a Ku Klux Klan, who suddenly seize him, close his eyes, and put something over his face from which comes a foul choking odor. The terror of this experience survives as attacks of anxiety for a long time or may never be effaced.

We have all read the numerous stories recounted by ethnologists of savages who have been told by their medicine man that they are going to die. Under these circumstances, to the astonishment of the civilized observer, healthy men have actually lain down and died. We are not so far removed from primitive man as we sometimes think. Every surgeon knows that his results are better on a stolid unimaginative patient than on a high-strung sensitive one. If he can inspire quiet confidence in the patient the chances of a good result are greatly increased. On the contrary, fear and anxiety prejudice the outcome. It is a commonplace for patients to enter the hospital with a fever and rapid pulse; this even occurs on a visit to the doctor in his office. Even more often may be seen before an operation increased blood pressure, rapid heart beat, sweating, dry mouth, tremors, and other signs of terror. I have no doubt that, even in civilized communities, a settled conviction that he will die leads occasionally to a fatal outcome after an operation not lethal in itself.

The patient may be convinced that he has an incurable disease and will not believe the surgeon who informs him that no serious derangement was found. Surgeons are always faced with the problem of how much to tell the patient. I remember a former football hero who had been at Yale with Dr. Cushing and wanted to know exactly the situation, adding that he could take it. Dr. Cushing told him frankly, but not brutally, the actual condition, whereupon the tough guy wilted in the most complete funk I have ever seen. The last I saw of him he was still in a state of complete emotional demoralization. On the contrary I know that a well-known society woman, from whom her true condition was concealed but of which she learned from relatives to whom it had been revealed, went about town vilifying the surgeon for months before she finally died. If patients hear about such cases, or if as doctors and nurses they may have been parties to such evasions and present a real problem in psychotherapeusis to the harassed surgeon, he sees his patient failing in spite of a deft and faultless operation and in spite of an apparently satisfactory physiological healing. If the patient does not try to get well he may really die unnecessarily.

The responsibility of the surgeon does not begin or cease in the operating room. He should see to it that the patient meets with nothing but courtesy and kindness and consideration from admitting officer, orderly, nurse and interne, that no tactless conversations occur in the neighborhood, that there is no unnecessary roughness or noise, and that he himself is patient and solicitous. The surgeon may go home afterwards and take it out on his wife, but to the patient he must be graciousness personified. In short, the patient must be treated as a person, not as a case, and as a person in a trying, even terrifying situation. This solicitude over the patient's legitimate anxiety begins as soon as he enters the surgeon's care, and increases as the hour of operation approaches. It is often wise to give a sedative on the night before an operation and repeat it in the morning. When apprehension is obviously excessive, especially in thyroid cases, the anesthetic is often begun in the patient's room, even without the patient being aware of what is happening.

When it is necessary to operate under local anesthesia some surgeons have had soothing music played to distract and quiet the patient. After observing the antics of some surgeons, I have often wondered whether it would not be advisable to resort to this method or some other to quiet the surgeon. The behavior of certain surgeons in the operating room reminds one of the temper tantrums of children, nowadays generally considered to be in the field of the child guidance expert. I have known a good surgeon in this way to completely disrupt his operating team and cause the death of a patient.

After the operation every surgeon knows that his responsibility does not cease. He studies long and arduously methods of combatting shock, maintaining blood pressure, replacing fluids, etc., but he should not forget the patient's morale. He should know how to inspire hope and confidence which are necessary to prompt recovery, how to promote comfort and allay irritation. More than that, he should recognize that the psychogenic factors which played a role in the causation of the trouble for which he has just operated will probably continue to influence the patient after discharge. They should be actively combatted. To take duodenal ulcer as an example, if a gastroenterostomy is made and the patient left in the old tense situation the hyperacidity will continue and the patient will probably develop soon a jejunal ulcer. An inquiry should always be made into the personal and social problems of the patient and an attempt made to remove the sources of irritation and tension.

I shall not discuss the actual psychoses which patients may develop after operation. We are all familiar with the low muttering delirium of the exhaustive illness or the more acute deliria of fevers, but with these matters we are not now concerned. They are sufficiently obvious to everyone. But the more subtle situations giving rise to the neuroses must also be familiar to the surgeon. He cannot thrust all the problems off on the psychiatrists and then taunt them by remarking, as one surgeon did to me, that their business is to take care of those patients who have nothing wrong with them or for whom nothing can be done.

The surgeon must learn to be his own psychiatrist to a large extent, especially in smaller communities and under unusual circumstances such as war.

Soldiers are often no less terrified of an operation than laymen. It is one more trying situation to meet at a time when the soldier's resistance is lowered by pain and loss of blood, and after the operation the instinct of self-preservation will drive many to seek refuge in continued illness. If in peace times a woman will prolong her illness in order not to take up her relations again with a brutal husband, one may imagine the feelings of a sensitive man to whom war is a horror which a successful operation makes it necessary to face again. In war time, as in peace time, the surgeon must have always in mind those fundamental mental mechanisms which modern psychiatry has so brilliantly elucidated.

Psychiatry: Its Significance in Pediatrics

By LEO KANNER, M.D.

Associate Professor of Psychiatry, The Johns Hopkins University School of Medicine; Director, Children's Psychiatric Service, Henry Phipps Psychiatric Clinic and Harriet Lane Home for Invalid Children, The Johns Hopkins Hospital

PEDIATRIC SPECIALIZATION NOT LIMITED TO SPECIAL ORGANS • HEALER OF CHILDREN • ALL PROBLEMS AND PUZZLEMENTS • 70% PROBLEMS OF BEHAVIOR • 30% SOMATIC DISORDERS • PARENT-CHILD UNIT • DEVELOPMENTAL CONTINUITY • PEDIATRIC-PSYCHIATRIC ALLIANCE • MENTAL HYGIENE OF INFANCY AND CHILDHOOD • RESISTANCE OR REMONSTRANCE • PUNITIVE ORIENTATION • CHILD REARING • ANOREXIA NERVOSA • DEMOCRATIZATION OF THE AMERICAN HOME • HUMANIZATION OF MEDICINE • IATROGENIC CONDITIONS OF PERSONAL MALADJUSTMENT • WARD ROUNDS AND CASE PRESENTATIONS • CHILD PSYCHIATRY

THE SPECIALTY of pediatrics differs from many of the other branches of medicine in a number of features which, at least theoretically, should make it seem like a next door neighbor to modern psychiatry:

1. Specialization in medicine has proceeded on the basis of preoccupation with specific organs or organ systems (e.g., ophthalmology, cardiology, neurology), or in consideration of special maladies (e.g., syphilology, tropical diseases, allergic phenomena), or according to certain technical procedures of examination and treatment (e.g., roentgenology, surgery, orthopedics). Pediatrics, built around the factor of age as the principal nucleus of its concern, goes beyond the limitations of interest in special organs, diseases and techniques; it professes the assumption of full medical responsibility for human beings starting out on their life's journey. In this our era of emphasis on "the person as a whole," the pediatrician can point with pride to the original and still valid meaning of his voca-

tional designation as the healer of *children,* while even the psychiatrist must feel somewhat embarrassed at being tied etymologically to a psyche rather than to man in his functioning totality.

2. Pediatrics is a specialty only insofar as it does not minister to adults. The laity looks upon the pediatrician as a child specialist, a person to whom one turns with *all* problems and puzzlements about children's health in the broadest sense of this word. The laity makes no essential distinctions between the sources and implications of the problems and puzzlements. Measles and repeated failure of grade promotion, rickets and capricious eating habits, rheumatic fever and nightmares, chorea and tics are all considered as being legitimate items in the roster of pediatric concerns. It has been variously estimated that between 50 and 70 percent of children brought to the pediatrician's attention present problems of training and behavior rather than exclusive problems of somatic disorders.

3. The pediatrician, unlike most other specialists, hardly ever deals only or even primarily with the one individual who is the patient. He is always prepared to be confronted with a group of at least two people: the child and his mother. He usually directs his prescriptions and other therapeutic arrangements not so much to the child himself as to the family on behalf of the child. He is the child's physician by being the parents' adviser. He is thus inevitably introduced to the realities of parent-child relationship. He cannot help but notice that the manner of domestic training expresses in the main the way in which parents relate themselves to a child, and that a child's behavior reflects the way in which he attempts to relate himself to his family and to his world in general.

4. The pediatrician, who is in a sense a general practitioner for people in the first decade and a half of life, is consulted for various reasons and at different times in the course of the same child's period of growth and maturation. He is, therefore, more than most other specialists, in a position to maintain a record of biographic and developmental continuity. He

is even better off than the psychiatrist, who must satisfy his curiosity by going *backward* with his patients in terms of retrospective retracing of earlier and earliest happenings. The pediatrician can go *forward* with his patients and has, over and above, an opportunity to modify and reshuffle situations as he goes along.

5. The pediatrician, when confronted with what Douglas A. Thom has aptly called the everyday problems of the everyday child, has a very significant advantage over physicians to whom adults with personality difficulties appeal for medical help. He is not weighted down with the traditional ballast of bagsful of terminological strait-jackets and pseudo-diagnostic swear words. He cannot, with an erroneous sense of convenience, dismiss with a placebo and with the label of neurosis, neuropathy, psychopathy, hysteria and the like those patients whose troubles require more than the ordinary pharmaceutical or manipulative management. The contemporary parent will not allow him to sequester so-called problem children from his office as if they were foreign bodies. He simply cannot afford to divide his patients into children with somatic ailments to be treated earnestly and neurotic children to be kidded along or got rid of as painlessly as possible.

All these features make it easy to assume that the very nature of the pediatrician's occupation should create in him a far greater readiness for psychiatric orientation than might be the case with many other specialists. As a matter of fact, the very first full time psychiatric liaison arrangement anywhere was established at the invitation and with the wholehearted collaboration of a pediatric clinic, with the eventual inclusion of psychiatry as an integral part of ward, outpatient and private consultation routine, undergraduate and interne instruction, and participation in staff conferences. This particular exercise in intimate pediatric-psychiatric alliance, which is now going into its thirteenth year, has offered a practical background for the study not only of the type of problems for which psychiatric intelligence is wanted, but also of the significance of psychiatry in the attitudes and functions of the pediatricians themselves.

The first thing which stands out conspicuously is the pediatrician's unique and unrivaled opportunity to serve in the front trenches of the mental hygiene of infancy and early childhood. Psychiatrists, even in those communities which have them, are rarely brought into play before something has gone noticeably wrong with a child's emotional reactions and performances or with the parents' evaluation of a child's behavior. For this reason, many students of children's personal difficulties are compelled by circumstances to exclude from their scope the first two or three years. Stevenson and Smith made it clear that most child guidance clinics are hardly ever given a chance to become acquainted with infants and with parental perplexities about infants. And yet it is at this age that the groundwork is laid significantly for attitudes and patterns of living together of a child and the members of his family. And it is also at this age that unwholesome reaction tendencies can be pried loose with relatively greater ease before they have begun to attach themselves adhesively enough to form the core of future character and outlook on life.

Before the pediatrician rather than the psychiatrist come the earliest multiform outcroppings of what has been termed the infantile period of resistance or remonstrance. They come as complaints of disobedience, stubbornness, dramatic breath-holding spells, temper tantrums, exasperating refusal to eat with or without gagging and vomiting, bedtime pranks, chamber pot antics and other transgressions against expected conformity. German psychologists have spoken of this so-called period of resistance as being anchored in the anlage—a concept somewhat akin to that of the original sin. A less fatalistic orientation shows that infantile remonstrance is nothing more or less than the expression of a child's struggle to establish a way of living amidst a confusing and upsetting welter of educational inconsistencies. These inconsistencies are based partly on the parents' personal emotional needs for smothering overprotectiveness or nagging perfectionism and partly on culturally determined parental bewilderment when it comes to the issues of authority and discipline.

Autocratic systems make things ominously easy for parents and pediatricians alike. The idea of child rearing as a preparation for blind submission is an invitation to a punitive attitude which makes the educator feel justified in terrorizing a child into obedience. A book on childhood neuroses published in Naziland in 1939 by Franz Hamburger, Professor of Pediatrics at the University of Vienna, has in its subject index not less than fourteen references to corporal punishment as a desirable educational method in the name of the Führer. The infliction of pain, restraint and humiliation, miniature concentration camp methods in the form of uncomfortable isolation, stupefyingly large doses of sedatives, and application of the faradic current are favored in what is euphemistically called the "treatment" of spite, anger, enuresis, vomiting and tics. This, offered with characteristic distortion of logic as helpful and benevolent training, is the representative attitude of pediatricians in an autocracy.

Punitive orientation is still much more prevalent among many parents in our own midst than one should like to believe. But since its enactments lack public approval, there is considerable surreptitiousness about them. At the same time, the picture is peculiarly complicated by the existence of another extreme which, instead of the assertion of parental sovereignty, tends to turn complete domination of the domestic scene over to the child. There is, to be sure, nothing new in the custom of obsequious pampering of children; it was known and criticized in Biblical days. But over and above its function of satisfying more or less deepseated parental needs, it has of late received strange reinforcements growing out of contemporary cultural phenomena and affecting principally the intellectual and pseudointellectual sections of our population.

The oversimplifying and ill-digested popularization of recent psychological theories has created the impression that children should be granted free range of undisciplined conduct, should be allowed to express their personalities unhampered by adult interference and to give vent to their emotions as they well up, lest frustrations play havoc with satisfactory development. This notion is based on the two major fallacies that an infant is a priori possessed of a ready-made personality and that undisciplined behavior precludes frustration. In reality the child's *enfant terrible* shenanigans are often enough the very manifestations of existing frustration resulting from the absence of needed guidance in his fumbling efforts to fit himself to group living.

Matters are still further complicated by the manner in which medical and hygienic advances have transmitted themselves to the laity. The formula of spoiling and giving in would be as simple as that of adult despotism if it were not for the frantic concern about standard weights, calories, vitamins, the required number of stools, sources of contagion, and the supposedly dire potentialities looked for in any slightest behavior deviation from postulated perfection. The idea of prevention, intended as a set of guides to calm and wholesome living in the present, becomes a nightmarish bugaboo full of anxieties and visions of anticipated disaster. Radio and magazine ads which have products to sell, and popular books and articles which have theories to peddle help to spread the panic among parents. Child rearing becomes a mass of polypragmatic agitation with the view of averting calamity.

Few children, and by no means the sturdiest, submit without resistance to all this overabundance of frenzied activity. The biological acquisition of the ability to choose between compliance and non-compliance presents infants with effective weapons of insurrection. The home is apt to become a battlefield. The parents open the offensive by throwing around the infant a smothering blanket of solicitous demands and regulations. The infant has at his disposal an assortment of refusals, chief among them the refusal to take nourishment, which, as "anorexia nervosa," is known and dreaded as "the crux of the pediatricians." The parents fight back with more agitations, with various means of counter-resistance, with perpetuation of this undeclared warfare. In such a setting, an infant, whose limited experience keeps him unaware of the existence of other patterns of interpersonal relationship, cannot help but conceive of the process of group living as an unending tug of war between himself and his elders. To the parents, under these circumstances, child rearing becomes a chore; maternal genuineness and naturalness and spontaneous enjoyment of motherhood give way to uncertainty, uneasiness and fear of wrongdoing.

It is quite possible that this is a somewhat exaggerated picture of domestic confusion as seen by a clinician whose material is made up in a large proportion of the consequences of such early contests between parents and children. But the number of such instances is very considerable, and the variety of symtomatic complaints is legion. When they come to the psychiatrist, patterns have already been established, annoyances have reached a high point, the war has been on for quite some time. The pediatrician, and nobody but the pediatrician, observes these entanglements at their very onset and, instead of trying to do away with full-fledged agitations, apprehensions and hostilities, has a chance to nip them in the bud. The pediatrician is the only person in our civilization who can, whenever this is necessary, guide parents and infants from the beginning to a healthy mode of living together. He can spot and allay anxieties, clarify confusions, correct erroneous notions, try to understand and influence attitudes, and raise or reduce the parents' sense of obligation to its proper proportions. He can do much to mollify parental sternness and relieve the basic situations which lead to infantile rebellion. And, most significant of all, he can thus contribute a lion's share to the democratization of the American home. Hamburger's book indicates with repulsive clearness how Nazified pediatrics is trying to turn the German home into a miniature totalitarian state. This book should serve as a challenge to American pediatricians. It should stimulate them to foster a spirit of reciprocity, mutuality and reasonable compromise in the family as the best and most efficient introduction to, and preparation for, democratic living in the community. There is hardly a better, and certainly no earlier, object lesson for this than the situations arising from the so-called period of resistance in infancy and early childhood.

The second major contribution of psychiatry to pediatrics, of pediatrics to psychiatry, and of both to the mental hygiene of infancy and childhood is intimately connected with the pediatrician's primary task of treating sick children. Medicine, largely under the influence of modern psychiatry, is moving away a little shamefacedly from the attitude that a patient, as far as the physician is concerned, is a pair of lungs or kidneys lying between two bed sheets. Patients are being advanced from the status of "cases" to the status of persons who are ill. A "case" of this or that disease is an abstraction, a reference to a certain chapter in a textbook, a handy, useful and necessary focusing on the selective direction of investigation and appropriate therapy. Twenty cases of pertussis are similar, though not quite identical, abstractions. But the pertussis is an episode in the lives of twenty different children. There is a common etiology and symptomatology, yet the children differ even with regard to the illness itself. Some vomit profusely and others very little. Some are frightened by the paroxysm and others wait patiently until it is over. There are those of preschool age whose illness bears no relation to marks and promotion, and the older ones whose classroom work is interrupted by the enforced absence. Some develop a habit of coughing and vomiting after the cessation of the pertussis, while others resume their normal prepertussis behavior. Some parents smother their whooping children with morbid solicitude, while others maintain their usual emotional equilibrium. Pertussis is incidental to a child, and not a child to pertussis.

Such observations are prone to make the pediatrician especially well suited for participation and even leadership in the progressive humanization of medicine. Much more than in dealing with adults does the patient's and the family's behavior play a part in ordinary pediatric examination and treatment. The pediatrician must always be prepared to find a complying or resistive, well-trained or pampered, friendly or sulking child and a calm or agitated, helpful or interfering parent. He must be prepared to supplement his technical abilities with the equally important skill which makes it possible to quiet a fretful child or a fluttering mother or grandmother. He knows from experience how difficult it is at times to take a good look at the throat or to succeed with an injection. He knows how his indispensable quarantine order not infrequently influences the domestic, scholastic and vocational routine of the whole family group. When the telephone rings at night, he has sufficient experience to distinguish between the ranting of a frantically oversolicitous mother and objectively justified distress which causes him to jump instantly into action. The little boy whom he is just treating because of scarlet fever is not just another "case," but little Johnny whose early nutrition he has supervised, whom he has vaccinated, whose mother he has reassured about his weight. There is hardly a better basis on which to build psychiatric insights.

These needed psychiatric insights are still overgrown to some extent by a number of traditional views and practices which modern teaching is trying to weed out in enlightened pediatric clinics. The consequences of their infringement on the mental hygiene of childhood are sometimes spoken of as *iatrogenic,* or physician-determined, conditions of personal maladjustment. The medical alarmist and polypragmatist are now fortunately on their way out. The pseudodiagnostician who endows children with "touches" of pneumonia and rheumatism or with "verges" of breakdowns and St. Vitus' dance is also becoming extinct. But there is still room for improvement in the pediatric handling of a child's and his family's attitudes toward sickness and health.

When an acutely sick child gets well, his sickness usually becomes a thing of the past. But sometimes the sickness, even though no longer present, keeps exerting its influence on the family and the patient. A child who has had pneumonia is normally one who no longer has pneumonia, is again healthy, may return to school and play outdoors, and resume all the functions, obligations and privileges which have been his before. Yet there are children whose pneumonia or other cured disease is allowed by overanxious adults to linger for months and years as the starting point of agitated solicitude. For a long time to come, a sickroom atmosphere continues to pervade the home and the attitudes of the parents. The child is loath to part with the special attention which he has received when he was sick in bed. He takes advantage of the ensuing parental anxiety. He remains a child who "has had" pneumonia. Under such circumstances, a pediatrician's guidance can do much to lead a child definitely out of his sickness into real health, not only in body but also in attitude and in the eyes of the family. The pediatrician is in a strategic position to prevent the formation of invalidism in children and to treat that peculiar type of maternal invalidism which chooses the child as its preferential organ of hypochondriacal complaining.

In instances of chronic illness, the pediatrician can give valuable advice. He can find ways to occupy and cheer up the rheumatic child, to steer the neurologically or orthopedically handicapped child toward vocational usefulness, to bring some variety to the diet of the diabetic child, to make the epileptic child acceptable to his environment and liberate him from the ostracism which so often is his lot. He can find ways of precluding self-pity, boredom, brooding, excessive daydreaming in chronically ill children whose formative years are often wasted in the hapless monotony of uninterrupted idleness.

Most of these principles have nowadays become an integral part of pediatric thinking and teaching. But the tyranny of tradition has not as yet allowed the teachers to apply the ax to a long-established custom which still disregards the sensitivities of sick children. This custom goes under the time-honored name of "ward rounds." On ward rounds, a small congregation of white-robed people assembles near a patient's bed. One of the group recites a story about the recumbent white or colored male or female, who hears something about his early feeding and development, his present illness, and diagnostic terms. Some of the words he understands and some he does not understand. He learns things about diseases in his family. Then follow repeated palpations, percussions and auscultations; someone does not forget to voice his prognostic opinion, and then the procession moves on to the next bed. And there lies a living, thinking and feeling human being, who is left to ponder about the things that were said about him, to brood over his condition and his prospects of getting well. This is equally true of case presentations in lectures to students. It seems that the patient's presence is considered indispensable during the declamation of his case history. He hears all about the mortality rate of his illness and the complications which may arise from it. It is difficult to see what the students could possibly gain from the opportunity to gaze at a child during the teacher's talk. But it is easy to see how seriously a child may be harmed by the practice of having him witness unnecessarily the physician's discussions of his illness on ward rounds and during presentations to medical students. The abolition of this custom will doubtless signify the ultimate triumph of the humanization of pediatrics.

The last decade has witnessed a great deal of this humanization and a great deal of pacific penetration of psychiatric principles into the realm of pediatrics. Only in the past 20 to 30 years have psychiatrists themselves become acquainted with children and their problems. By the same token, it has been only in recent years that pediatricians could turn to psychiatry with the reasonable expectation of practical help. When, in the teens of this century, child psychiatry was still in its infancy, pediatrics and psychiatry were complete strangers to each other. The pediatricians, confronted with unfamiliar concepts and unfamiliar terminology, sat back with an attitude of watchful waiting, if not derisive suspicion. They were kept out and allowed themselves to be kept out of the hopes and activities of the National Committee for Mental Hygiene and of the work of the child guidance clinics in their own communities. But eventually child psychiatry got over its children's diseases and was able to demonstrate its usefulness to all comers. At that point the pediatricians did not hesitate to invite the psychiatrists to give them of their experience and, in the past few years, a number of pediatric clinics have opened their doors wide to psychiatry. Psychiatric service was established as a liaison arrangement in the pediatric departments of an increasing number of medical schools. The American Academy of Pediatrics now has a standing Committee on Mental Health. The country's pediatric journals regularly publish informative articles and reviews on topics pertaining to child psychiatry.

This is indeed an encouraging development. After all is said and done, psychiatry has succeeded in making one great fundamental contribution to pediatrics: the pediatrician, under its influence, is definitely adopting the attitude that, to paraphrase Gertrude Stein, a child is a child is a child is a child.

Psychiatry: Its Significance in Geriatrics

By CARL CAMP, M.D.

Professor of Neurology, University of Michigan

THE AGING PROCESS • PROGRESSIVE RETROGRESSION • FIRST, DEGENERATIVE STATES • PHYSIOLOGICAL MENTAL CHANGES • LOSS OF MEMORY • FEELING OF INFERIORITY • INELASTICITY OF THOUGHT • EXAGGERATION OF EARLIER TRAITS • AVAILABILITY AS MAN POWER • SECOND, DEGENERATIVE DISEASES • ARTERIOSCLEROSIS • THIRD, OTHER DISEASES IN OLD AGE • BRAIN TUMOR • NEUROSYPHILIS • USE AND ABUSE OF DRUGS • MALNUTRITION • PERNICIOUS ANEMIA • PSYCHONEUROSES

To DISCUSS the changes in old age in twenty minutes would, I think, be something of a triumph in condensation and I am further embarrassed by the fact that I am talking to an audience of expert psychiatrists and I am not one myself. But I have been interested in the study of the neurological and medical disturbances associated with old age for a number of years.

As a matter of fact, the aging process begins with life itself and only ends with death. Some organs show these aging changes early in life. The brain apparently is one of the later organs to undergo these retrogressive changes. According to Miles of Yale, who has collected statistics on the subject, the average age is around sixty-five. At that time the mental faculties seem to be undergoing a slight retrogression which is progressive. However, that is only the average. It is extremely interesting to me to see that as he draws the curve, there are many individuals who do not retrogress at even seventy. They are way above this normal line. So it seems that if at that age you are not peculiarly bad, you are peculiarly good.

The mental changes that occur in this aging process, which

we must regard as in a way physiological, are often disturbing to the community and to the individual's adjustment in that community. We can consider these, in a group, as physiological changes, consistent with age of the patient, but varying in their onset anywhere from fifty to perhaps seventy-five.

We must also consider as a cause of mental disturbances another group of cases, those that are associated with definite pathologies. For instance, arteriosclerosis and subsequent cerebral softening, Alzheimer's disease, Parkinson's disease, and the like are not physiological conditions. They are definitely pathological but they are usually considered to be due, at least in part, to the age of the patient and coincident with the physiological changes.

A third group of conditions in old age which must always be borne in mind is the possibility of lesions which might occur at any age, and are just as likely to occur in old age. I refer to such conditions as brain tumor and syphilis of the nervous system, nutritional disorders of one kind or another, pernicious anemia, the use or abuse of drugs, the endogenous psychoses and the psychoneuroses.

To return to the first group, the physiologic disturbances: here we find listed a number of symptoms or conditions, such as, for instance, disturbances in memory, disturbances in attention, tendency to repetition, inelastic thinking, a tendency to get set in their ways, irritability and along with that a certain amount of increased suggestibility, and a lack of control of emotional expression. These seem to be the major mental disturbances which could be considered as the ordinary concomitants of old age.

To take these up in more detail; there is, first, the question of loss of memory. This is usually described as a loss of memory for recent events, so that the older man remembers what occurred when he was twenty-five, but he forgets what occurred yesterday. Of course, in part, this is due to lack of attention, to lack of interest in what occurred yesterday.

Some years ago I had the opportunity of comparing two acquaintances, one about thirty-five and one seventy-two. They were both professional men with about the same cultural background, occupation and also about the same economic situation. I carried out a series of tests. One of them, for instance, was a situation in which we all three saw a slight accident, and on purpose I discussed this with both of them so as to make the details sure in their minds—the number of people in the car, the make of the car and so on. Then I wrote down the facts, and casually about three weeks later I discussed with each one individually this incident, bringing it up and asking whether or not they remembered this and that. Now I found somewhat to my surprise, that the older man remembered the incident and the details just as well as the younger one. Of course, in this case their attention had been carefully directed to these points.

Another experiment along the same line but with their consent and consciousness was to request them to learn a certain page of prose. The younger man learned the thing and recited it, making ten errors. He took about thirty-five minutes to learn it. The older man took sixty-two minutes, and then recited it with six errors. He explained afterwards, spontaneously, that he thought that he had learned it in a much shorter time, but that he read it over a number of times to be sure. It betrayed a characteristic mental attitude of old age, and that is the feeling of inferiority or unsureness that is so likely to crop up at that age. They do not want to have anybody think that possibly they are losing their memory or their ability to learn, etc. This question of loss of memory, while it is perfectly valid in the later years, is often in the earlier years largely a question of attention and a question of a feeling of uncertainty and insecurity which makes people try, as it were, to remember rather than remember without trying, so to speak.

The feeling of inferiority which is common and often concealed, I think explains some of the peculiar activities of older men. They do not want to be considered as growing old and consequently they often defend themselves against that by perhaps wearing youthful clothes and cultivating an exaggeratedly youthful manner which is liable to attract attention and to make others regard them as peculiar. One should understand what underlies this situation. We find many examples of an older man swindled by people who flatter him on his youthfulness. Now we think of that as being a mental abnormality but if his relatives or friends who try to rescue him would understand the underlying situation, they might do a better job. Instead of increasing his inferiority by pointing out his age, if they would use the same tactics as the swindler in the case, a little flattery, they might possibly do a much better job.

The inelasticity of thought is often remarkable in these patients. They get very set in their ways. Nevertheless, it is not necessarily a great handicap if this is understood, because the preservation of certain skills to an old age is not uncommon. I know a cabinet maker, for instance, who does beautiful work, although his mental condition outside of his particular skill is very poor. The General Electric Company in the last few years has had occasion to recall certain men whom they had retired years before, and they have found that their particular skills were still adequate to the job even though they had some mental peculiarities which would unfit them for general work.

The irritability and suggestibility of these patients go hand in hand, and along with these one often sees a lack of control of emotional expression which is often distressing to those around these older people. They cry easily or they show anger easily, and yet they probably do not feel such emotions any more than they ever did. We find also that in many older people a control of their desires, so to speak, their emotions or feelings is decidedly lessened. We find, for instance, that often when an old man becomes a miser, a careful study of his previous life history will show that he has been a very thrifty individual but has been prevented from being miserly by the opinions of other people and his own judgment. But as he grows older and this judgment becomes impaired and he loses this control, he exaggerates those previous traits. We find the same thing often when we study the case of an old man who becomes an exhibitionist or develops some lack of sex control. In all probability if one studies his previous history, one finds that he has had similar desires but in his younger days he has been able to control them, and it is only when he loses this control by a degenerative change in his brain that these desires become obvious and, perhaps in many cases, so disagreeable.

Many of these conditions can be managed. We have no cure for old age, of course; the changes are physiological and are bound to occur sooner or later, but if they are understood, I think the availability of the older person for work or for his own amusement can be well taken care of. In these days, when manpower is at a premium, this is an important point.

In reference to the second group of cases—the arteriosclerotic and the other pathologic changes, I have only a few observations. One of them is that it is difficult to determine in some cases whether an old man is suffering from arteriosclerosis or some organic change of that kind, or whether it is simply the physiologic changes of old age. One may say, however, that there are certain fairly definite clinical differences. In the first place, arteriosclerosis is likely to show its signs rather earlier than the degenerative changes, between sixty and sixty-five; whereas the truly degenerative cases could not develop until perhaps seventy or seventy-five. As Waggoner pointed out, sometimes these early arteriosclerotic changes may be overlooked and regarded as psychoneurotic. The arteriosclerotic changes are more likely to cause symptoms coming on rather suddenly; that is, the patient will suddenly develop an aphasia or some other disability rather than pursue the gradual course of the degenerative type. Furthermore the arteriosclerotic case is likely to suffer more from headaches, dizzy spells and somatic symptoms, so that, while the two are frequently concomitant, they can be differentiated.

The third group of cases are the diseases and conditions which exist in old age but which could occur at any age. Brain tumor, for instance, is not uncommon in old people. Moersch of the Mayo Clinic reported one hundred cases of brain tumors in patients over sixty years of age. The possibility of a brain tumor must always be kept in mind. It may be difficult to make a diagnosis on some of these aging patients. But the presence of a choked disk and especially such tests as the electroencephalogram and pneumoencephalogram should rule out this condition. It is desirable in many of these cases where there is any suspicion of it to carry out such tests.

An old man can have neurosyphilis. I have seen a case of paresis developing in a man aged eighty, and his initial infection in fact had occurred not many years before that. Here again we have signs of a degenerative disease of the brain, a condition which is treatable and which is, of course, difficult to differentiate from senility unless one has serological tests.

Another common cause of mental disturbances in old age is the use of drugs, especially the barbiturates. Personally I am very much opposed to use of barbiturates in elderly people. I think it often aggravates the other signs of senility which they are likely to show. I have, for instance, seen a woman about seventy who when she came to us could not walk without assistance. Her mental confusion was intense and she was drooling. She was the picture of what you might call a senile dementia. A couple of weeks in a hospital with no drugs of any kind and you would hardly have known her. She brightened up, she was able to walk quite well, there was no longer any drooling, and she did not have to be fed, etc. The history was that she had had insomnia for some time and had been given increasingly large doses of barbiturates until she had reached the condition in which I first saw her. The same thing can occur from the use of bromides and some of the other sedative medicines which are likely to be given to these patients to allay their irritability but which I think is a bad practice and is likely to lead to a mistake in diagnosis.

Another important part of this same situation is the nutritional disturbance in old age. We find that these patients gradually lose their appetite. They develop fads in eating or perhaps the gastric mucosa is not as good as it was when they were younger. As a combination of these circumstances, they will develop a starvation psychosis. We now, of course, recognize that this is probably due to a lack of certain vitamins. These patients will show a mental confusion also, with memory disturbances, irritability, often some of the paranoid delusions and suspicions that go with old age, and they are very likely to be put down as beginning senile dementias or pre-senile anxiety psychoses. Yet a proper management of their dietetic needs, possibly in some of those cases the injection of vitamins in large doses, brings back such a decided recovery that one can hardly think of the likelihood of a senile dementia. Pernicious anemia may occur in elderly patients, and pernicious anemia occasionally causes brain changes just as it does in the spinal cord. The late Dr. Albert Barrett published descriptions of these changes in the brain as occurring in pernicious anemia as far back as 1911. Now again we have a picture similar to that of a senile dementia with suspicions, irritability, set ways, certain mental attitudes. It is characteristic to find patients of that kind disregarding the doctor's orders; they know better. That sort of mental characteristic is so common in old age. Yet the treatment of pernicious anemia in these cases relieves, or may relieve, the mental symptoms as well as the spinal cord changes.

There is the possibility that an endogenous psychosis, a manic-depressive psychosis can occur in an old person. And again the psychosis may be attributed to the age of the patient. I have seen several patients of this kind. A patient, for instance, an elderly woman, showed signs of deterioration with extreme mental depression. It would have been easy to call her a case of senile mental depression, but the history was that she had had three previous attacks of typical manic-depressive psychosis and this happened to be the fourth one. Without any special treatment, after a period of six months or so, she recovered from the mental depression and her apparent deterioration was much lessened. She took an interest in things and became quite a normal woman for her age.

As a final point, I would call attention to the fact that the psychoneuroses are not uncommon in advanced years. We are usually prone to think of hysterical paralysis and hysterical disturbances in general as being the prerogative of youth, and, of course, they are much more common between the ages of, let us say, twenty and forty, or possibly even younger. But they often persist into old age and sometimes I am quite sure that they have their initial development in these people in advanced years.

PART II

RESEARCH IN PSYCHIATRY

Introduction to Part II

By JOHN M. DORSEY, M.D.

Training Psychiatrist, Children's Center; President, Michigan Society of Neurology and Psychiatry. Member of the Committee on the Conference on Psychiatry

ATTENTION IS directed to the purpose of the meetings of this Conference on Psychiatry. We have gathered in order to experience one another's best, particularly with regard to psychiatry's significance in terms of our country's most urgent needs.

Medicine has been able to learn much of the operations of normal health through the study of man fighting off his illness. Similarly, the past has taught us, medicine can learn much of value for post-war life from the experience of war. Seen this way war need not mean entirely a collapse of civilization, or a refusal to acknowledge human imperfections and their consequences.

We live in a psychological world and our understanding of the working of the human mind is indispensable to operating the causes that make for human efficiency and happiness. Bringing psychiatrists, civil and military, together at this time indicates an awareness both of war as the consuming reality of our day and of our dependence upon our understanding of the mind for coping with that painful reality.

Psychiatry and its basic sciences, psychology and psychopathology, have made some advances which already await application. Operating as a laboratory the Conference can remedy this situation: psychiatrists can investigate the needs of the armed forces; the armed forces can be supplied with what data psychiatry has already accumulated. From these contacts it is possible that all may be stimulated to further relevant endeavor in the field of research.

War intensifies the struggles of the human mind. In war time, planning assumes the more acute significance of strategy; instruments develop the more urgent values of weapons; disregard for facts has more immediate life and death meaning; and discoveries are more telling conquests. Now more than ever the needs for psychiatric research must be felt.

To know is to be strong. To know is to be free. It is by means of our senses, our powers of observation, that we bridge the fateful gap between the known and the unknown. Research is the truth-inspirited interest or discipline that recognizes fully the value of our senses and ability to accept the evidence of our senses.

Not only the study of the psychological level of the body but also every critical examination of facts contributes to understanding and, by the same token, to mental health and growth. Every science is relevant to finding the way in psychiatry and the Conference can survey psychiatric research only in a general and incomplete way. Perhaps there is no better introduction to the examples of productive inquiry that follow than our observation that until research wrests more power from mankind's common enemy, the unknown, we must make the best of our present strengths.

The Future of Medical Research

By CYRUS C. STURGIS, M.D.

Chairman, Department of Internal Medicine, University of Michigan; Director, Simpson Memorial Institute for Medical Research

A PROGRAM OF SUCCESSFUL RESEARCH • INTELLECT AND PERSONALITY OF INVESTI-GATOR • FOUR GROUPS • GENIUS AND THE SPIRIT OF INQUIRY • UNPARALLELED PROGRESS IN MEDICINE • CHANGES IN MEDICAL EDUCATION • CONTINUED PRO-DUCTIVE EFFORT • THE NEAR GENIUS • THE AVERAGE OR SUBSTANTIAL INVESTI-GATOR • FECUNDITY OF AGGREGATION • THE NON-PRODUCER • PRIVATE ENDOW-MENT • FEDERAL AND STATE AID • WAR A TRAUMATIC EPIDEMIC • DISEASE FATALITIES EXCEED WAR CASUALTIES • FUTURE TRENDS • SENESCENCE • SULFON-AMIDE THERAPY OF INFECTIONS • GRAMICIDIN AND PENICILLIN • CONTROL OF RHEUMATIC FEVER • ARTERIAL HYPERTENSION • THE COMMON COLD • FUNC-TIONAL NERVOUS DISORDERS

To ATTEMPT a prediction concerning the future of experi-mental medicine and research during a world-wide con-flict, when so many features of our mode of life are imperiled, is, to say the least, venturesome. And to be so reckless as to record one's thoughts in writing where they will remain a per-manent record of perhaps miscalculation, causes one to pause and ponder seriously. After almost thirty happy years of asso-ciation with investigators and investigations, however, it gives me genuine pleasure to contemplate what has transpired in the past, in the hope that a faint gleam of light might be perceived which will give some information concerning the future course of events in the development of medicine.

It has been said that "The best prophets are children and fools." The implications are, first, that it is poor judgment to prophesy, and, second, that a true forecast is the result solely of fortuitous circumstances. On the other hand, the world has existed long enough for the past to be utilized to foretell, with considerable accuracy, the course of some of the trends which are at least under partial control of the human mind. It is with this consoling thought that I approach my subject timidly, in the spirit more of an alluring adventure than a dogmatic recital of what I consider to be assured events.

The following are a few of the obvious questions which pertain to the conduct of medical research both in the immediate and distant future. They are mentioned now as my remarks will center about these in a very general way.

1. Will research continue at the same tempo and with the same degree of productiveness in the future as it has in the past one hundred years?

2. Who will do research in the years to come and how will such projects be supported?

3. What may be the defects of our present methods of fostering, promoting and guiding research?

4. And, finally, what will be the trends of future medical investigations, or, in other words, what are the most promising fields for exploration and what are our most demanding needs?

There are multiple factors which contribute toward a program of successful research, among which may be mentioned adequate financial support, equipment, availability of clinical subjects and laboratory material, stimulating associations, freedom from the cares of making a living, and the urgency or necessity of securing the answer to certain questions, a condition such as is provided by the present war. But none of these is the prime essential determinant which has the most important bearing on the success of any given investigation. This has not yet been mentioned. It is the intellect and personality of the man who is given the opportunity to do the work. The scarcity of such persons, with their peculiar and highly desirable mental endowments, is the only restraining influence which prevents an almost endless expansion of beneficial inquiries in experimental medicine. It may be surprising to some of you to learn that of 176,000 physicians in the United States, only 930 are devoting their time exclusively to medical research at present.

If the individual is the most essential factor, then what manner of man is he who is best fitted for this scientific work? For our present purposes, all men may be classified into four groups, in relation to their ability to accomplish research. These may be stated as follows:

The Genius. There are only a few such persons in each century. A real investigator is born, not made; he has inherent in him the rarest, and in some respects the most precious and productive of all intellectual qualities, that inborn and undefeatable spirit of inquiry which cannot be submerged permanently. Such a man creates his own opportunities and never encounters a situation which delays him indefinitely, or seriously interferes with his ultimate aims. Year after year he adds significantly to our sum total of medical knowledge. Fortunate indeed is the university or institute or organization which more often than not falls heir by mere chance to such a personality. Not all administrative authorities appreciate such persons. Far from it. They are usually non-conformists and often dissenters who do not follow rules very well. Their best work is not done when the time spent on the job is recorded by means of the clock. When interested, however, they will labor for many more hours than most persons in the department, and usually, when a long period is considered, work harder and much more productively than their critics.

President Hadley of Yale once told Graham Lusk that the great work of the world was done by men who were a little lazy and had good consciences. Such men, when they saw a chance to do worthwhile things, were driven to complete them by their keen sense of obligation and duty. It has also been said, with regard to work in the laboratories of experimental medicine, that it is far better to do too little than to try to do too much. This, I believe, is a proper concept but one which is not in entire accord with the trend of modern life in this country.

The world often considers that a genius is erratic and one who is likely to bestir himself in a regretfully sluggish manner. To some university authorities they are a nuisance, but others are more enlightened and, as one said, it is of first importance that "the life of the scholar and the man of science be made inviting, comfortable and secure." Their welfare should be a matter of great public interest and concern. Such a man may become the most important one in any organization, but this should not be recognized by making him the head of the department. This is for several reasons. In the first place, by so doing an excellent investigator will soon become lost in the maze of administrative details, many of which are relatively unimportant; second, a genius of this kind is usually a very poor administrator because his mind is not of the type which adapts itself to ordinary routine procedures; and, finally, good administrators are relatively easy to find as compared to the great rarity of the able investigators. But how are we to find such exceedingly desirable and rare men and women? This is the question which cannot be answered with finality at present. The solution of that problem, I hold, is the most important one concerned with the future of research.

With the intelligent development of education facilities, it is possible that geniuses will be recognized more frequently in the present and future than they have been in the past. It does not seem logical or reasonable to assume that any particular era has had a monopoly on men of ability. Does it not appear more likely that in each generation there is probably an equal number of such persons seeded throughout the countries of the world? Yet, all will admit that in the past hundred years there has been unparalleled progress in medicine which probably equals in importance all of the advances made previously in the entire history of the world. Can not this best be explained by acknowledging that men of ability have been recognized, their work encouraged and supported, and their bent directed into the proper channels? Is not a continuation and amplification of this attitude an intelligent attempt to recruit genius? This has been accomplished in the United States and other countries by the spirit of research which pervades some medical schools. The entering student on the day of admission perceives this, and it is continually impressed on him throughout his undergraduate education. In some hospitals this stimulating influence is felt throughout his period of intern and resident training.

It is clearly the duty of every teacher in a medical school, and even those in colleges and secondary educational institutions, to subject his pupils to a discerning appraisement in the attempt to select and encourage those who may be future genuine contributors to medical science. Furthermore, medical schools should make a radical change in their curricula which would permit certain qualified students considerable liberty and choice in the selection of their work. The difficulty at present is that too often a false value is placed on memorized information, and all students, bright and dull, are compelled to conform to the same course of studies. Such intellectual deterrence is stifling and almost repugnant to men of genius. Such a student would be reprimanded, or at least frowned upon, if the routine work were slighted and an attempt were made at anything which smacks even remotely of originality. One of the first and most important steps in the development of future medical investigators is a radical reorganization of the method of teaching in some medical schools. The most needed change is one which would make available a certain amount of unassigned time for a student to think, instead of memorize. Not all men of genius require much directed education. Some, as the great ones of the past, such as William Harvey, Lavoisier, Pasteur, Robert Koch, Ehrlich and many others with similar qualifications, will develop by themselves, even under the greatest of difficulties, and despite all handicaps and obstacles. There is not a great deal that can be done for them, nor, fortunately, does neglect submerge them. Adequate help at the proper time, however, might well augment their output and possibly direct it into more productive channels. But usually they thrive with very little assistance. For example, perhaps one of the most fundamental investigations with far-reaching possibilities which has ever been completed at the University of Michigan was the observation that pigeons could be immunized to huge amounts of rattlesnake venom, by the injection of gradually increasing doses. This was done by Dr. Henry Sewell, Professor of Physiology, in 1887, and it preceded and perhaps laid the foundation for the development of diphtheria antitoxin by Roux and Yersin and von Behring. This was the original work which demonstrated the principle of antitoxin production. It was a monumental and original contribution, accomplished by a genius working with a small amount of venom which had been collected for him by another member of the University staff in this vicinity, by a few bits of simple nondescript apparatus and some pigeons, and, greatest of all, a precious idea which arose spontaneously in the mind of a remarkable man, who in addition had the enthusiasm to carry to completion his plans and publish them to the world.

Let me reiterate for purposes of emphasis, that rare genius is characterized by at least two outstanding qualities; namely, (1) his remarkable ability to overcome all obstacles great or small, in order to achieve his ends and aims in research, and (2) the continued productive effort which causes him to complete new and worthwhile investigative projects, and outstanding knowledge year after year; indeed, this highly desirable quality may continue to operate until ripe old age.

The Near Genius. But all of us cannot be born as geniuses. Can investigators be developed? Are they ever overlooked and lost to the world? Are there different degrees of geniuses? Can any sensible person be stimulated to accomplish a certain amount of worthwhile research? Fortunately, there are a considerable number of near geniuses to be found in the population of every country. They have some of the outstanding qualifications of those with extraordinary powers of origination but require stimulation, encouragement and often direction for their development, especially in their younger years. Whether they succeed or fail may depend on extraneous influences. It is to be regretted that they may be of the type who accomplish a brilliant research early in life and then, for one reason or another, completely forego investigative work thereafter and fall to the level of mediocracy in some other branch of medicine. These men are priceless, and deserve all of the encouragement that can be given to them because, due to the paucity of real geniuses, they must serve for them. And well they might, for with the proper assistance, they have produced research of the most important and highest quality and will continue to do so. It is this type who should receive abundant help and encouragement from institutions and foundations.

The Average or Substantial Investigator. These make up the men and women who are doing the bulk of the research work in medicine today, and for that reason their future merits serious attention. Furthermore, the practical results of their labors, and the influence of their conduct and effort, must be considered to be well worthwhile contributions to the profession of medicine. Many such men are to be found on the staffs of the medical schools of this and other countries. It is proper that they should be, because it is highly desirable that at least some medical teachers in the clinical branches should be on a university basis, which implies that they should advance knowledge as well as impart it. It is the former obligation which distinguishes them from teachers in secondary schools.

It is my opinion that almost any person of average intelligence who has received a satisfactory basic education in science and in medicine, can be molded into a useful investigator of this type, provided the proper influences are brought to bear early enough in life. Often their work is not highly original, but it serves a useful purpose for several reasons. Frequently it is confirmatory in nature; it may provide an opportunity to summarize critically the literature bearing on certain subjects, and emphasize the importance of various phases of disease; but, perhaps most of all, it assists in developing in them the spirit of investigation, and fosters and diffuses this scholarly attitude of mind into their associates and students. They sometimes turn up a new idea which remains dormant and then, years later, it comes to the surface again as the stimulus for an epoch-making contribution by a real genius. Such men will always comprise the great bulk of investigators. They should by all means be encouraged for their influence is salutary. Under the proper direction they assist in keeping a department alive in thought, in freshness of teaching, and in the development of men to greater heights. Their attitude, moreover, insures that the patients under their care receive the most intelligent attention.

When a group of such men are gathered together for the common purpose of investigating a medical problem, regardless of its complexity, the result almost always justifies the classic remark of Josiah Royce, the great philosopher and teacher. It was he who said that you can always depend upon the "fecundity of aggregation." Or, in other words, if a group of substantial investigators concentrate their efforts on a given problem of disease, something new and useful will always be brought to light. It may have to do with the cause, the diagnosis, the management, or, possibly, the prevention or cure of the condition. Or, a fact may emerge which seems remote or disconnected from the disease under consideration, but one which will lead ultimately to real progress. The mere formation and recognition of such a group is thought-provoking with reference to the problem at hand.

There are some aspects of teaching which actually submerge any research ideas. Almost all persons are born with an innate sense of curiosity and an inherent desire to devise or invent something. This is apparent in a great majority of children. Sometimes our educational system operates to dull or discourage this highly desirable asset by the obstinate insistence on conformity to established and accepted thought. The great Galen made himself so emphatic that for a period of fourteen hundred years no one dared question his authority on medical or human anatomical questions, although his knowledge of the latter was based largely on dissections of apes and swine. As a result, progress in medicine practically ceased for this long period. We see it even now in some teachers of the best institutions who have an almost baneful Galenic influence, in a more restricted sphere. Many of them are regarded as outstanding in their ability to instruct, largely because they are dogmatic and emphatic in their statements. This always makes it easier for the novice to acquire information, even if it is incorrect and antiquated. They are usually regarded by the contemporary student body as the best teachers. But this method of instruction is a rigid and stifling one. Does it ever occur to such a professor that even if he may be expressing the best contemporary knowledge, it may be obsolete within a few months? Would it not be better to encourage an intelligent skepticism and a spirit of the quest for knowledge in the hope of stimulating, or at least preserving, his native curiosity and inventiveness? Some of my ideas in regard to the relation of the research attitude to medicine have been expressed clearly by the late William W. Holmes, formerly Professor of Medicine at Northwestern University. Among other things he says, "The mere accumulation of facts, however valuable they may be in actual practice, cannot be regarded as an ideal form of education. The student who is interested in acquiring only immediately useful facts becomes a sort of tradesman or artisan actuated by the viewpoint that his sole obligation is to treat disease, the particular disease which a patient may happen to present." "This," he goes on to say, "inevitably leads to an atrophy of the critical faculties."

It has been said that a physician, and I do not see why it should be confined to our profession, is either forgetting or learning, and that any department which does not foster and accomplish research has ceased to think. With these sentiments I fully agree but I should like to emphasize that it is usually the average investigator, as previously defined, who is of the greatest assistance, when stimulated, in dispelling this fact.

The Non-Producer. Finally, I come to the last group, who have many admirable qualifications, but the ability to investigate is not among them. They are non-producers and I do not mean to say this in a derogatory way, for without them the care of patients would undoubtedly suffer. They are not, however, endowed with what it takes for even the simplest concep-

tion of a problem, and its successful culmination. It would not
be wise to spoil a good practitioner to make a poor investigator. These men are often highly successful in the care and management of patients and hence they should restrict their activities to such a field. They acquire their knowledge almost exclusively from what is told them or what they read. Often they
have an excellent grasp of a large fund of information but they
are lacking in even the faintest spark of originality. It is pa-
thetic to behold such a man when, as the result of some unfortunate accident or chance, he is precipitated into a position in
which research activities are expected of him. Usually he is
the first to appreciate that investigation is not for him but his
pride prevents an early admission of this and he stumbles awk-
wardly on, until the situation is exceedingly painful to all concerned. It should be impressed upon him that he has other
talents, which should be developed and that, furthermore, the
inability to do research is certainly not a stigma or a serious
reflection on his actual intellect.

As previously emphasized, one of the most important reasons for the phenomenal growth of medicine in recent years
has been the increase in knowledge in the basic sciences of biology, bacteriology, pathology, physiology, chemistry, and their
sub-divisions. Undoubtedly this fundamental influence will
continue to act in the future. There has been in the past, and
will continue to be in the future, however, a regrettable lag between the time new and often badly needed information is
made available in the basic sciences and its recognition and
utilization by those engaged in clinical research. Let me relate
one impressive illustration as a characteristic example. With
the introduction of potent anti-pneumococcus serum in 1913,
it was emphasized that the early typing of the pneumococcus
and prompt administration of the proper serum was absolutely
essential for the optimum, and often life-saving, therapeutic effect. For a period of many years, however, pneumococcus typing was a procedure which required eighteen to thirty-six hours
or longer because the only method then available was the time-
consuming one of mouse inoculation. Finally, in 1933, the im-

mediate and amazingly simple Neufeld technique of typing directly from the sputum was introduced into clinical medicine. This provided something earnestly sought for by physicians for twenty years, as the result could be determined in a few minutes. The tragedy is that Neufeld described the phenomenon upon which this test was based, in 1902, thirty-one years before it was utilized clinically. How many deaths could have been averted, had the Neufeld method been introduced into clinical use at once, can only be a matter for gloomy speculation.

Other illustrative examples of similar delays could be cited. Many have occurred in the past, and they will continue in the future, although their incidence will diminish. A number of remedies could be employed which might assist in the solution of this difficulty. They are: (1) the training of more internists for two or three years in some basic medical science, after graduation from Medical School and following at least two years of clinical training in the hospital; (2) the attendance and participation of those interested in clinical medicine, in meetings of the physiologists, biochemists, bacteriologists and pathologists; (3) fostering small discussion groups composed of clinicians and those trained in the basic sciences, for frequent informal meetings to consider problems having an interdependence; (4) arranging joint teaching exercises for undergraduates and the hospital staff in which the clinical and basic science groups participate; and finally, (5) an appreciation by university teachers that a free exchange of information between all departments is highly desirable, and that this should be promoted with the utmost cooperation from all members of the faculty. This appears to be a mutually beneficial idea, but now, although the departments are usually separated by only short distances, the barrier is as great as if the Atlantic Ocean intervened. If predictions can be based on needs, it is safe to say that in the future, research will be expedited vastly by an improvement in this situation.

One of the most gratifying and productive ventures in this country has been the large financial gifts in support of science and medicine. One hundred years from now our descendants will consider these altruistic donations and their judicious management as one of our country's greatest contributions to modern civilization. They have pioneered the rough and unchartered way. All credit should be accorded those whose thoughts gave rise to their origin. Their inspiration has resulted in a notable impetus to the expansion of modern medical research in the United States and elsewhere. Furthermore, they have played an important role in improving the standards of medical teaching. No doubt these endowments will continue to foster deserving projects and exert a tremendous influence on medical research in the years to come. But it is unlikely that they will be the sole, or even the major, source of financial aid to research henceforth. This is because they are dependent mainly upon the beneficence and wealth of individuals. Matters so important as scientific discoveries cannot be left to any method which involves the slightest element of chance but must receive assured, adequate and sustained support, not for brief intervals, but for long periods. Worthwhile research is usually not accomplished rapidly but results from a long, well-organized program centering about an individual or a group of individuals. Support should be in the form of an annual appropriation, just as funds are allotted for fire, police protection, education, the practical aspects of Public Health, and other matters of general welfare. Already the cities, counties, states and the federal government have made substantial and efficient steps in this direction through health departments and the granting of subsidies for special research. As a federal agency, the Public Health Service has made an excellent record in the investigation of certain diseases, of which one of the most outstanding examples is the study of the cause and the prevention of Rocky Mountain spotted fever in their institute at Hamilton, Montana. The fact that this, and other major research projects have been completed under government auspices, is ample proof that important inquiries can be supported and accomplished efficiently with federal aid. By making such funds available, it should assure more permanence and stability of support, which is much to be desired. Furthermore, such funds are derived directly from the proper source, namely, from the persons who will receive the ultimate benefit of their expenditure.

It is not my intention to make more than a passing reference to the present world-wide conflict, but two matters of interest relative to war and medicine will be mentioned briefly. In the first place, as many writers have previously emphasized, medicine always advances during war time because so many opportunities are then offered for the observation and control of pathologic conditions which are rarely presented in civil life. Someone said, very properly, that war is "a traumatic epidemic" which presents the best experimental laboratory for surgery. But medicine, too, is offered unparalleled opportunities for experiment under the most powerful influence of necessity. The recent wholesale inoculation against yellow fever, for example, bids fair, once and for all, to offer the definitive solution to one of the most devastating of all diseases. In a way, this situation is analogous to the brilliant solution of the typhoid fever menace of many wars which yielded so successfully to the measures instituted by the army physicians.

A second point which causes one to ponder is that war is comparatively feeble, at least up to the present time, as far as this country is concerned, in its killing power when compared with the deadly effect of ever-present disease. For example, Livingston and Pack, in a comprehensive analytic study recently of a survey of the surgical treatment of cancer of the stomach, have made the following comparisons. In the fifteen years, which was the total time covering the six major wars in which this country has been engaged since 1776, about 250,-000 soldiers died of wounds received in action. Compare this with the fifteen years of peace from 1923 to 1937 inclusive, when almost 450,000 persons died from injuries received on the highways of the United States. But even more revealing are the figures in relation to carcinoma of the stomach. According to the data furnished by the American Society for the Control of Cancer, approximately 40,000 individuals die annually from cancer of the stomach. In fifteen years, therefore,

600,000 persons have succumbed to this condition, which is nearly two and one-half times as many as were killed in all the major wars in which the United States have been involved. Fortunately in war, the slaughter is only periodic; that is, war happily is interrupted by long intervals of peace. This is not so with disease, which moves relentlessly on, silently but constantly on the march, without respect to age, person or nationality, grimly reaping its quota day after day, year after year and century after century, until it brings on the inevitable end of all mankind, which can only be delayed, not averted, by human efforts.

It is stimulating to contemplate the future trends of research because the outlook is so promising. Although remarkable progress has been made in the past hundred years, all indications are that even greater advances are to be anticipated in the next generation. This is because an increased number of well qualified workers will be engaged in this aspect of medicine, and because of the continued progress in the various branches of the basic sciences, chemistry, physics, biology, genetics, and the sciences more closely related to medicine, as physiology, pathology, bacteriology and others.

Obviously with such an enormous number of potentialities, some of which are now wholly unrecognized, it is not possible to do more than to make a few random, incomplete and disconnected remarks relating to specific research projects that may be accomplished in the not too far distant future.

Most certainly, greater efforts will be directed toward the solution of the problems incident to senescence, for there is a greater need for such research as the span of life lengthens. According to the authoritative remarks of Dr. Louis I. Dublin, the average American can now expect to live for a period of approximately sixty-four years, as compared with an average of under thirty years for India, forty-eight years in Japan and fifty-five in Italy. In America the life span was a little more than forty years in 1850, about fifty years in 1900 and now it is sixty-four years. In the past decade, from 1930 to 1940, four years have been added to our span of life. From these facts it is apparent that ever more demanding in the next generation will be research directed toward the two most important conditions which are rife in old age, namely, cancer, and arteriosclerotic changes with their secondary manifestations throughout the body but especially in the brain, the heart and the kidneys.

Now let me turn to one of the most promising discoveries in the history of medicine, namely, the improved means of controlling certain infections. For many years physicians have hopefully awaited the discovery of an agent which would kill infectious organisms in vivo and yet spare the host from significant injury. Arsenic in syphilis and quinine in malaria have for a long time provided ample evidence that such an action could be attained. With the introduction of the sulfonamide type of therapy by Gerhard Domagk in 1935, this miraculous-like form of treatment for various bacterial infections has arrived. Consider what these preparations have accomplished even if not a single additional thing is done to perfect and improve their actions. They have reduced the death rate in pneumococcus pneumonia from a long time average of approximately twenty-five to thirty percent, to eight or ten percent. They have brought the cure of gonorrhea to a certainty in most cases, within a few days. They have introduced new hope in the treatment of puerperal fever and cerebrospinal meningitis.

But consider their future possibilities. With the aid of synthetic chemistry to develop new preparations, and by observing their effects on animals in which an experimental infection has been induced, a phenomenal advance in this direction cannot fail within the next few years. It is possible that variants of these drugs will be developed which will be highly effective against the typhoid and colon bacilli and other micro-organisms which are now refractory to such action. Furthermore, there is evidence which suggests that the highly resistant tubercle bacillus will in some not too far distant day succumb to the influence of this type of medication.

One of the most amazing aspects of this modern specific drug therapy is that now, after many years of waiting, the medical profession is presented not only with the sulfonamides but also with two other wholly different preparations which have considerable promise for the control of various infections. I refer to gramicidin, derived from soil bacilli, which was introduced into medicine by René J. Dubos in 1940, and penicillin, a product obtained from molds, discovered by Alexander Fleming in 1929, and in more recent years made available in a more refined state as the result of the work of several investigators. Time only will decide the definitive value of these promising substances. It seems safe to state, however, that revolutionary results have been obtained already by their use in medicine and future developments in this direction will undoubtedly be epoch-making.

Another fascinating possibility to contemplate is the great good which would follow the successful control of rheumatic fever, the major etiologic factor in the causation of valvular heart disease. Consider the debt which countless generations to come would owe the fortunate investigator who devised some means whereby this disease might be prevented from inflicting cardiac damage. Thus by one colossal stroke, such a person would eliminate from this and other countries approximately one-third of all the crippling cardiac disorders with their attendant suffering, and at the same time conquer the disease which is the leading cause of death between the ages of ten and fourteen years. That such might be accomplished is a reasonable hope to those familiar with the problem.

All indications are that research activities dealing with the subject of nutrition in health and disease will expand rapidly and result in a notable improvement in the welfare of mankind throughout the world. It is amazing to consider the progress, for example, which has been made in the field of the vitamins since the initial fundamental contributions of Casimir Funk in 1911, and of F. G. Hopkins between the years 1906 and 1912.

Our knowledge of normal and abnormal functions of the endocrine glands, which now seems to consist of about twenty percent fact and eighty percent speculation, will undoubtedly expand rapidly within the next few years. It has been less than one hundred years since Claude Bernard laid the experimental foundation for this important aspect of medicine. George Murray, who died only a few years ago in England, was the first to produce a beneficial effect from the administration of an endocrine product when he injected a glycerin preparation of thyroid material into a patient with myxedema, about fifty years ago. This subject which has had such a rapid, and, let us say, at times, an uncontrolled growth, holds great promise for the future.

All indications are that we are approaching the solution of the hypertension problem, in which progress has not been made for a good many years. It was only about a century ago when that restless genius, the Reverend Stephen Hales, inserted a tube into the carotid artery of a horse and discovered that there was such a thing as blood pressure. Consider also that it was as short a time ago as sixty-one years that Ritter von Basch, at one time personal physician to the ill-fated Emperor Maximillian of Mexico, actually measured for the first time the blood pressure in a human being. Now with a renewed interest in this subject, which has resulted largely from the observations of Goldblatt, a new light which might well lead to a method of controlling this common abnormality, has been shed on this condition.

Let me hasten to add that I am in perfect accord with the idea that it is one thing to live for a long period of years and quite another to be happy and content. The fact that an appreciable number of persons terminate their lives by their own hands, indicates that mere existence is not the sole criterion as to the desirability of continuing it. It was Herodotus who, four hundred and forty years before the birth of Christ, said with unwarranted pessimism that "the trials of living and the pangs of disease make even the short span of life too long." The aim of medical research should not be solely to prolong life but also to make it a happy, gratifying and efficient state while living. To some individuals, there are much worse things than death. Further research will, therefore, endeavor to combat the innumerable, annoying and often exasperating conditions which contribute to much discomfort and, as one writer has aptly said, "take the keen edge off of living." For example, the common cold is not important as a cause of death but the man who discovers the means of preventing or curing it undoubtedly will receive the gratitude of countless millions who have been distressed by this minor ailment, since the beginning of the world.

I come now to an aspect of medicine about which I speak more with a sense of sincere appreciation and hope, rather than with any idea of predicting its future. I refer to one phase of your own field of psychiatry. A better method of dealing with the commonly encountered functional nervous disorders is a necessity of paramount importance to all clinicians in every branch of medicine and surgery. We observe such conditions in a majority of our patients, and they frequently are either a primary or secondary cause of many of their complaints. Any advance in the management of such disorders should ideally be available not only to the trained psychiatrist, but in the form of therapeutic assistance which can and will be utilized by the practitioner. The skilled psychiatrist must necessarily delegate the care of some such patients to others. It is unnecessary to emphasize to you that the treatment of functional nervous conditions by the average physician leaves much to be desired.

In my own experience, and I am sure most internists will agree, the so-called "nervous" patients contribute more to the sum total of discomfort and anguish in this world than any other non-fatal condition. If urgent need is any criterion as to the likelihood of the development of helpful research in any given field, then we should have every hope that assistance in this direction will be forthcoming in the very near future.

In conclusion, permit me to summarize briefly what I believe will be the future development in medical research:

1. Although remarkable progress has been made in the past one hundred years, even greater advances are to be anticipated in the next few immediate generations. This will be due largely to the expanding knowledge in the basic sciences and because more accomplished investigators will be recruited by attractive offers. Enlightened medical schools will continue, even among

undergraduate students, to foster research and encourage an increased number of qualified workers to enter the field.

2. The situation in experimental medicine will be greatly improved because there will be a closer correlation with the basic sciences.

3. Private endowments for medical research must be credited with a most gratifying development of the field in this country, and they will continue to sponsor medical investigations of great importance. It appears likely, however, that ultimately the State and Federal Governments will very properly assume an increasing responsibility in this respect.

4. With the amazing increment to the span of life, it is certain that cancer and arteriosclerotic changes will demand an added amount of investigation with a resultant increase in our knowledge of these conditions. It seems likely also that the next few years will see the acquisition of new and important information concerning many phases of medicine. Special mention, however, has been made of only a few which include specific therapeutic agents for the control of infections, advances in the fields of nutrition, the endocrine glands, functional nervous diseases, hypertension, the prevention of rheumatic heart disease, and many non-fatal conditions which detract so much from the normal enjoyment of life.

The Controversial in Psychiatry

By C. MACFIE CAMPBELL, M.D.*

*Professor of Psychiatry, Harvard University Medical School;
Director, Boston Psychopathic Hospital*

THE FIELD OF PSYCHIATRY AND DIFFERENCES OF OPINION • CONTROVERSIAL PROBLEMS • THE FIELD OF PSYCHIATRY AND THE PSYCHIATRIST • RESPONSIBILITY VERSUS FREE WILL • MISGUIDANCE OF CHILD GUIDANCE • DISCIPLINARY PROBLEMS AND THE ARMY PSYCHIATRIST • THE WORKING MAN IN THE FACTORY • TRAINING OF THE PSYCHIATRIST • "ASYLUM PSYCHIATRY" • THE ALIENIST • THE PSYCHOLOGICAL AND THE PHYSIOLOGICAL • FREUD'S FORMULATIONS AND CLAIMS • PSYCHOANALYSIS • FOCAL INFECTIONS • TREATMENTS • NEED OF RESEARCH

YOU ALL know the famous remark of the bystander, "Is this a private fight or can anyone join in?" It is supposed to be said by an Irishman, but it represents the general human trait of getting a certain amount of pleasure out of controversy for one reason or another. I was not sure whether I should deal with the controversial in psychiatry or the controversial in psychiatrists. I found it difficult to make my topic precise and I apologize for my discursive, unsystematic and quite general remarks which do not particularly fit into the subject of the general discussion, "Research in Psychiatry."

It is difficult to know what will arouse controversy. When I was in Paris, I remember there was most violent controversy in the Society of Neurology whenever the question of the histopathology of tabes dorsalis came up. One only needed to introduce the topic of aphasia to have a real fight. The discussions there were always quite interesting. When I went to the quiet atmosphere of Nissl's laboratory in Heidelberg, I felt that there one would have peace; in order to induce peace and

[* This article and the discussion on page 402 are among the last contributions of this much beloved and respected leader of his profession. Dr. Campbell died August 7, 1943.   Editor.]

sleep I read the Doctrine of the Neuron. I did not realize that so much emotion could be put into a discussion of the intimate structure of the central nervous system. So the topics that may arouse controversy are numerous. In the field of psychiatry I suppose there is an indefinite number of formulations and views with regard to which there is a difference of opinion.

I want first of all to make some remarks upon the field of psychiatry in general. There may be some difference of opinion even with regard to what the field of psychiatry is. There is considerable difference of opinion as to the most important topics to be investigated. Sometimes controversies arise where the antagonists do not come to grips with each other but where each person presents a variety of data and formulations for which there is a certain justification, while those who have a somewhat different point of view bring up completely different data. If one takes, for instance, the comparative roles of heredity and environment, one finds a great deal of very vigorous controversy, although it looks frequently as if the protagonists were discussing two sides of the same shield. Both groups are discussing the concrete life of an individual with his own special endowment and with his own special development in an environment which has helped to mold him. The final situation with which the psychiatrist has to deal is the actual trouble of that individual, with his original make-up modified by the past and exposed to the actual strains of his present life. Some, interested in the family history, find in that an adequate cause for the fact that this person broke down at a certain time, whereas others would emphasize the privation and the stress and strain of his life.

Before we can come to any agreement with regard to problems like that, we may have to scrutinize the terms which we use. We may have to review a term like "cause." What we are dealing with is the segment of an individual life which we hypostatize as the "psychosis"; and in this phase of the individual life we see the importance both of the original endowment and of the environmental factors. Obviously it is extremely important for us to make as precise as possible those genetic factors which enter into the endowment of the individual and which make him vulnerable. But it is of equal importance to consider the contribution made to the disaster by unfortunate domestic or social factors. The individual who considers heredity exclusively is apt to be rather fatalistic with regard to the problem presented by the individual case. The person who overstresses the influence of environment may spend an enormous amount of energy, perhaps unproductively, with undue optimism and be quite disillusioned when he gets very poor results from all the effort he has put into his attempt to manage the environment of the individual case. So it is rather important in psychiatric controversies to consider how far we are dealing with a question of emphasis, and to make sure that we pay due allowance to those aspects which we are ourselves perhaps not primarily interested in or not specially working at.

As to the field of psychiatry, there may be some difference of opinion as to what the field essentially consists of. Ernest Jones, for instance, would look upon the field of knowledge which deals with the study of human behavior as psychoanalysis, which, starting with psychoneuroses, has broadened out until it covers the whole fabric of our civilization. According to this view, psychoanalysis deals with the adaptation of the individual to the problems of his life; those who get along fairly well give you the field of normal psychology. Those who break down in a way not psychoneurotic give the material for the psychiatrist; the psychiatrist is looked on as dealing with those serious types of breakdown which cannot be investigated in very great detail because they are not cooperative. Thus psychiatry only deals with patients from the outside, in a way that is rather unfruitful. This is the so-called "asylum psychiatry." Jones admits that the psychiatrist, although willing to confine his contacts to his asylum friends, is forced by public opinion to take an interest in the psychoneuroses in addition to his basic preoccupation with the practical aspects of mental hygiene. Now this presentation may well be a topic of controversy.

The psychiatrist in general, I think, takes a somewhat different attitude toward the problem. He feels that psychiatry is a specialized medical discipline, dealing with human ailments wherein the very center of the problem is a disturbance of the equilibrium of the personality, whether called a neurosis or a psychosis. There is no strict barrier, no strict separation between the one group of disorders and the other. The psychiatrist does not necessarily think in terms of "neuroses" and "psychoses"; he may even be faintly amused when he reads scholastic discussions as to whether a neurosis can turn into a psychosis, or vice versa.

As to other views of the field of psychiatry, we have some rather extensive claims. Colonel Rees (of the Tavistock Clinic of London) claims that every delinquent act is a mental disorder, a medical problem. It is a psychiatristic challenge. In his own words: "I venture to regard practically all delinquency as a symptom of illness, though I do not mean that every delinquent is necessarily sick in the ordinary sense of the word." Well, it may be quite wise to have every delinquent examined to see whether there may or may not be some basic ailment, which is the special field of the physician, but as to considering every delinquent a case of mental disorder, a case of sickness, although in a rather Pickwickian sense, that perhaps is a little more than the ordinary psychiatrist would claim. The psychiatrist dealing with the delinquent may try to trace the actual delinquency, the concrete problem back to earlier factors, to constitution and conditioning factors, but he may be willing to allow the concept of responsibility and not feel that merely because he is a physician he thereby discards the concept of free will. But I do not suppose this session has time for a discussion of the problem of responsibility versus free will.

If one is going to deal with environmental problems in psychiatry and to take up problems like those of child guidance, there has been a certain amount of difference of opinion, I believe, as to the actual results attained by child guidance, as to how far delinquency can be prevented, as to how far the psychiatrist is a beneficial influence. Dr. Brenneman (I do not know what his views are now, but I think he presented a paper on *The Danger of the Psychiatrist*) felt that in standardizing wayward youth you may be doing it a disservice and that much child guidance is rather misguided solicitude. Is child guidance a problem of psychiatry or does child guidance rely essentially on the pediatrician or on the psychologist, or is the teacher the person strategically situated to be the child's guide? Quite apart from any official designation, what special training, what personal equipment, should the guide have? There has been some controversy over these topics, but some of the friction may have been of the nature of jurisdictional disputes over trade union rights.

There are other human difficulties where there may not be agreement as to the role of the psychiatrist. Can disciplinary problems and failures in school and college be adequately dealt with by the dean or the teachers or the psychologist, or are they primarily a problem for the psychiatrist? And in the Army, what is the role of the psychiatrist with regard to disciplinary problems? Are his claims sometimes contested by line officers or psychologists?

In the factory or store or office, what is the role of the psychiatrist? Has he a role there? I judge that Elton Mayo is a little sensitive as to the role of the psychiatrist in a plant. He suggests that the important human problems there are not of the kind that the psychiatrist deals with. They are not "mental disorders"; they are maladaptations and difficulties and frustrations and compensations, but they can be dealt with adequately by the foreman or the personnel manager or perhaps the non-psychiatric interviewer. Elton Mayo almost suggests that the psychiatrist may be something of a danger there, although he leans very heavily on psychiatric formulations as he attacks the problems of industrial hygiene. I think that no more important problems face our present society than the problems presented by the working man in his factory, the environmental conditions of the average worker, the conditions in his home, the conditions in the factory and the conditions with regard to recreation and with regard to his personal development. These are problems deserving a great deal of research, with regard to which the body of psychiatrists is insufficiently instructed and in which the average psychiatrist takes little interest. I do not know whether you are all familiar with Elton Mayo's *Human Factors in an Industrial Civilization* or his colleague, Roethlisberger's book on *Worker and Management* dealing with the same material, or Whitehead's book on *Leadership in a Free Society*. These books based upon work done at the Hawthorne Works of the Western Electric Company are profoundly important, not only with regard to the mental hygiene of the individual worker but with regard to the reorganization of our social and economic life, to which psychiatrists can perhaps make their special contribution.

If the psychiatrist is going to deal with some of these wider problems and if he is not going merely to look after committed patients in mental hospitals, then the question is what sort of training should the psychiatrist have? With regard to that I believe there is room for a great deal of discussion. There is, as a matter of fact, a great deal of difference in the actual arrangements made in medical schools; our colleagues may not be willing to accept our formulations, and psychiatrists themselves do not agree as to what is the ideal training of the psychiatrist in the medical school, the internship and post-graduate study. In medical education at present there is a trend toward attributing increasing value to work in what I call the more elegant branch of psychiatry, the psycho-neuroses and so-called psychosomatic disorders, that is, with patients who come spontaneously to you, are grateful to you and refer freely to your ministrations. There is a tendency to depreciate work with the more serious mental disorders, which is apt to be referred to as "asylum psychiatry."

The difference of opinion with regard to these matters may not be very controversial here. In Great Britain it has been something of a controversial issue. There has been a tendency, as one can judge from various brief communications in the *British Medical Journal,* to suggest that the treatment of the

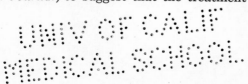

milder and incipient cases of mental disorders could hardly be entrusted to those familiar with "asylum psychiatry." "Asylum psychiatry" is supposed to dull the fine cutting edge of the intelligence, which has to be sharpened if you are going to deal with the milder and incipient cases. In an announcement of a vacant post of psychopathologist for a general hospital it was specified that no "alienist," i.e., no psychiatrist with sound experience in a mental hospital, need apply. That may be a little outside of the question of research, but seems to be inside the sphere of the controversial.

If one turns from the broader controversies with regard to the field of psychiatry and the training of the psychiatrist, etc., and takes the material itself, I suppose that the most familiar topic of controversy again is a question of emphasis. It is the artificial antagonism between the psychological and the physiological, the organic and the functional, the psychogenic and the symptomatic. In individual cases and in group discussions one worker points out emotional factors and past experiences and the other worker emphasizes the focal infection or the endocrinopathy. Well, both series of facts may be true, but a great deal of heat may develop in the presentation of this material. When I brought up to a French psychiatrist the fact that emotions might upset people seriously, he swept aside the suggestion that a person could develop a mental disorder merely on the basis of the difficulties of life, frustrations and bereavements and the attitude of other people, absence of affection, etc. For him all that was "the psychology of the janitor"; it was just interpretation of a lay kind. For him there was only one thing to do—*"Cherchez l'organicité"*—find out something wrong at the physiological level. That, he maintained, was where you find the explanation. That is one of the most frequent controversies that crop up. Some cannot accept an explanation which consists merely in an extremely thorough reconstruction of the evolution of the individual from the time when he was mixing with his neighbors in an apparently normal way until the time when the surface

adaptation was disturbed, and he was recognized as mentally sick.

Some people feel it is not possible that there can be such continuity, that if there is such a thing as a mental disorder and a respectable sickness, there must be some discontinuity; something must have happened at a basic level, you must look for something at that basic level; and if you find something there, then that is the peg upon which you hang the weight of the whole disorder. It is excellent to look for whatever you are curious about, and we cannot make our observations too precise, but the question is whether, in the presence of certain major difficulties in life and complicated factors which seem to explain the behavior of our patient (just as much as we can understand the behavior of any individual), we must necessarily lay the whole onus of the disorder on the fact that there is something wrong with a molar tooth, or the basal metabolism deviates from an accepted norm. The issue raised is of practical importance; if we ignore the concrete circumstances of the individual life, if we fail to recognize the specific needs of the individual in view of his constitution or his specific sensitiveness and if we merely pay attention to the impersonal factors, then we sometimes bar the possibility of helping that person. A person may be helped by kindliness or by the reconstruction of a social situation, just as a baby may put on weight when a kindly nurse is allowed to pick it up and fondle it a little, whereas if it is brought up according to Hoyle and with very little human affection, it may not thrive. I speak with all deference in the presence of Dr. Kanner.

In our whole psychiatric work these contrasting points of view give rise to much controversy.

In no field of psychiatry has there been such vigorous and open controversy as with regard to the formulations and claims presented by Freud and his pupils. These have been lumped together under the term "psychoanalysis" and not infrequently one is challenged with regard to one's attitude on the subject. One is asked, "What do you think of psychoanalysis?" If you ask exactly what the inquirer means, what is the formulation that he has in mind, he might say that he has none particularly; he is just thinking of psychoanalysis as a whole. Psychoanalysis has had its own history—first of all, a method of treatment and then a method of study and then a body of doctrines. With regard to each of these topics there may be a good deal of discussion as to the precise nature of the procedure, as to the dynamics involved in this procedure, as to the results of treatment. Perhaps we may gradually attain some sort of consensus of opinion. I do not know that there is so very much controversy about these matters now. There used to be very violent controversy. If you felt that a meeting was getting dull, you had merely to drag in some psychoanalytical formulation or perhaps just mention the name of Freud, and at once everybody was up declaiming pro or con. Now people are more or less working along each in his own line, so far as this controversy is concerned; the psychoanalytic groups are going on gathering their own data, discussing their own formulations and realizing that there are other points of view of some importance. Psychiatrists in general appreciate the contribution made to psychiatry by the psychoanalytic school. Head-on collisions are fewer than they used to be. This is perhaps to be regretted, because violent controversy has the great advantage of developing a temperature, making people very eager, and apt to work harder.

Among detailed topics for further research one may mention the following: what does infantile sexuality amount to, what sound data do we have, how far are we entitled to use the term "sex" with regard to certain manifestations, how far in every child or in the great majority of children are there incestuous wishes toward the parents, what is the best formulation of the personality, is there any special value in the formulation of super-ego, ego, and id, and how far is the psychoanalytic presentation of the forces at the basis of the personality the best formulation? And then, if you wish to get into trade union questions or jurisdictional disputes, we can bring in the problem as to whether an analyst must be a medical person or can be a lay person. There has been some difference of opinion on that in the past between Vienna and New York. I suppose that instead of psychiatrists looking upon psychiatry as a branch of a wide field of general psychoanalysis, the psychiatrist looks upon psychoanalysis as one method of examination which any psychiatrist can apply if he goes through the necessary preliminary procedure, and the doctrines which are brought forth are general psychiatric doctrines and the results of treatment have to be estimated according to the general canons by which we determine the results of any treatment.

I do not wish to stay too long on this one topic with regard to which you are familiar. I might mention the controversy about focal infection with regard to which the temperature was very much elevated about fifteen years ago, when we had the doctrine that most mental disorders of the so-called functional type were essentially due to non-recognized focal infections and primitive psycho-surgery of those days was invoked in order to improve our patients. The acute controversy has subsided, temperatures are normal, the psychiatrist tries to identify focal infections of his patients without losing his sense of perspective.

I might refer to schizophrenia and suggest that that is a somewhat controversial field; the controversy, however, has some of the aimless quality of a battle royal or meleé. Many general statements are made. There is active discussion and criticism; but at the same time "schizophrenia" remains merely a name, and one does not know to what the statements refer. I have the 1940 annual report from Burghölzli dealing with admissions and readmissions. Of the admissions there were, for 1940, 871. Of these, 578 were first admissions; 289, readmissions. Of the 578 first admissions, there were 196 "schizophrenic forms," and 2 "manic-depressive forms." For readmissions, there were 147 "schizophrenic forms" and 5 "manic-depressive forms." Well, in Burghölzli it seems they have only 7 manic-depressives in one year and between three or four hundred schizophrenics. Reports of the results of various treatments may seem interesting and may be accepted; but you are very anxious to know just what it is they have been treating. You have no idea.

Thus in relation to the treatments of the last five to ten years, the shock treatments with insulin, metrazol, alternating current, etc., it is extremely difficult to know what has actually been under treatment. We are in a situation where controversy in regard to these treatments is perhaps inappropriate, where further data are required with clear thinking and precise formulation. It will be quite some time before the situation is clarified.

In this field as in regard to many other psychiatric topics there is still great need of research of rather prosaic type, which aims at solving some of our problems by the accumulation and analysis of very detailed life histories, paying due attention to the inner evolution as well as to the external reactions of the person.

Psychological Research in Psychiatry

By NORMAN CAMERON, M.D.

Professor of Psychology, University of Wisconsin

RELATIONSHIP OF PSYCHOLOGICAL RESEARCH AND PSYCHIATRY • OLD ALLIANCE RE-ESTABLISHED • TECHNIQUES IN STUDY OF PSYCHIATRIC PATIENTS • NORMAL BE-HAVIOR • TESTING DEVICES AND TRAINED PERSONNEL • INDEPENDENCE FROM THE CLINICIAN • SOUND MODERN BASIS • BIOLOGIZING THE PSYCHE • PSYCHOSO-MATIC MEDICINE • LOCALIZATION OF PSYCHE • LANGUAGE BEHAVIOR • MODERN SCIENTIFIC PSYCHOLOGY AND CLINICAL PSYCHIATRY • SOLVING OF MUTUAL PROB-LEMS • RECIPROCAL NEEDS

T HE PSYCHOLOGICAL research that has definite implications for psychiatry is scattered over a wide area, and there is a great deal of it. If I were to try to arrange, classify and detail this to you, it would require as many hours for the presentation as I have been allotted minutes; and most likely no one here would be willing to sit through it. What you want in a conference like this is some notion of how things look to the worker from the inside, what the obstacles are that stand in his way, and what the future seems to promise. I shall try, in what follows, to touch upon each of these aspects of the situation.

It is becoming more and more evident to those of us who are concerning ourselves seriously with the scientific study of human conduct that we are entering upon a new and critical phase in the relationship between psychiatry and psychological research. As one who has divided his time during the past fifteen years almost equally between the duties of experimental psychologist and clinical psychiatrist, I welcome the opportunities for reorientation that this state of affairs is bringing to both disciplines. In days past it was not so unusual for contributors in one of these fields to be men of recognized eminence in the other. Psychology has, for instance, received benefits from the hands of such medical men as Wundt, James, Kraepelin, Meyer, McDougall, Freud, Binet, Prince, Janet and Jung. I am convinced that psychology and psychiatry should never have parted company; they need each other badly. To-day it begins to look as though there were definite hope that we shall live to see this old alliance reestablished.

There are two rather distinct ways in which psychological research has recently been playing a role in psychiatric advances. One of these involves a very direct relationship in which psychologically trained men have been working with psychiatric patients, investigating the character, developments and effects of altered function which are present, by the techniques of psychological experimentation and controlled observation. The other way is much more indirect and not so generally recognized; but it is fully as significant and in the long run may turn out to be more so. Research within the fields of *normal* behavior has gradually swung the study of human psychology over, from the older highly individualistic and introspective techniques toward a more objective and verifiable approach. Call it more social if you like; it certainly places the effects of the whole human environment on a par with the personal and biological factors.

Psychologists have found that isolationism does not work in the science of human behavior any better than it does in politics; so they have come out with their problems into the world of social behavior. This has especially important implications for psychopathology. Modern psychological research has also been developing more adequate and objective criteria of what constitutes valid experimentation and valid interpretation in work with human beings. This advance has reduced the prestige formerly enjoyed by methods of anecdote, and by elaborate deductive systems of interpretation which could be applied in such a way as to explain everything as it came up; but it has brought the methods and results of human psychology in line with those of other natural and social sciences, and made it possible to express them in an intelligible common language.

Competent psychological research of importance in psychiatry has been carried out over many decades. Among its early fruits are the various testing devices now adopted as routine, in one form or another, in most of the leading clinics and hospitals. Of course, such tests of performance samples were originally no more a matter of haphazard guesswork or uncontrolled speculation than were the clinical laboratory tests now routine technical procedures in medicine. They serve a purpose quite similar to that served by medical laboratory data by furnishing aids to the clinician in his problems of diagnosis and prognosis; they are sometimes useful also in the clinical planning of therapeutic and social rehabilitation programs for the patient. There is also the same danger here as there is in clinical laboratory data, that attempts will be made by the impatient or poorly qualified to misuse tests and measurements as substitutes for trained clinical judgment, instead of as auxiliaries. To a very large extent the business of developing and adapting tests of performance at a research level is still actively in progress as, for example, in the significant work of the psychologist, Ward Halstead, and the medical man, Kurt Goldstein.

I have singled out the testing field as an example only because it is the best known and by now the most firmly established in American psychiatry. It is impossible for me to do justice to the other direct attacks that have been made and are being made upon problems of psychopathology, through formal experimentation and controlled observation, within the scope of this report. Even the good ones number in the hundreds. They have opened up many fields for investigation and raised many genuine questions which are susceptible of controlled and verifiable inquiry. The most serious obstacle in the way of more rapid and dependable progress lies in the fact that in little more than half a dozen spots in the United States are sustained programs of psychological research in relation to psychiatry being encouraged and supported. This is at once, in my opinion, the most serious and the most remediable gap in American psychopathology. I should like, therefore, to turn next to a brief statement of some of the measures which we as psychiatrists must take if this defect is to be filled in.

1. Perhaps the most fundamental consideration is that of rendering the study of psychopathology dispassionate. Investigation in this field must be *detached* from the direct demands of therapy, and it should never be carried out in the service of any sectarian theory. If scrupulous attention is not paid to this aspect, research is very apt to become the handmaiden of personal or of in-group self-justification. It is then likely to be used to provide evidence either of one's own skill and success in the management of patients, or in support of some interlocking system of hypotheses. Conversely, the cause of experimentation is not apt to be well served if its outcome tends to reflect public discredit upon the therapeutic skill of the experimenter or the collaborator. The same is true if the outcome of experimentation and controlled observation tends to disrupt or repudiate a fixed system of professional beliefs with which the experimenter or collaborator has identified his own integrity.

On the other hand, the detachment which is demanded for valid observation and experimentation means, of course, the loss of a sizable portion of the clinical services of a would-be experimenter, or the engagement of non-clinical personnel to carry it on. Sustained research always costs money. If it is important enough to be worth the time and devotion of skilled personnel it is also worth supporting financially.

2. Psychological research programs in psychiatry should not be arranged in such a way that a responsible experimenter is merely the psychiatrist's *assistant,* or is directly dependent upon his approval of the data and the conclusions for his livelihood or his advance, or even for permission to publish reports. Neither should the common policy be continued of attaching the name of a prominent clinician to every research

paper, as a sort of rider without which the report cannot be passed for publication. I believe that the relationship toward which we should work is something like that now existing between the internist or the surgeon and the pathologist. The research psychopathologist who is well grounded in the study of normal behavior may safely be left to form his own opinions concerning the dysfunction he studies. If he is competent, he should be able to contribute independently something in addition to and beyond the conclusions of the clinician, whose attention is focussed upon the diagnosis and treatment of individual cases. These two persons should be colleagues whose functions are regarded as of equal status. They should be able to differ sharply, as pathologists and surgeons differ; they should be prepared sometimes to clash and perhaps throw off a few bright sparks for others to profit by or enjoy.

3. The question of *competence* deserves special attention. Not everyone who would like to carry on psychopathological research is prepared to do so. Wanting to experiment does not confer the ability upon the wisher any more than just wanting to be a doctor makes one able to practice medicine. There are numerous pitfalls, as we all know, in the mere process of observing and recording human attitudes and conduct and in accurately rendering what patients say. Unless one is very self-critical and skeptical, the exceptional things and the startling things get preserved while the ordinary, the unwelcome and the contradictory data are slighted, quickly forgotten or not even noticed.

Ability to design an experiment or to plan controlled systematic observations is more than a matter of general intelligence; it demands special knowledge and special skills. There must be a real question to investigate, one which can receive clear formulation, one which is susceptible of controlled study and is at least potentially answerable. Competence in setting up adequate criteria of validity and reliability presupposes special training in modern methods; and this is equally true of the task of handling and presenting psychological data in the most effective and intelligible form. Finally, interpretation of the data demands special attitudes on the part of the person who has collected them. It demands a scrupulous distinction between findings and inferences. It demands a readiness to admit that after the facts have been set out the rest is more or less clever guessing, that hypotheses are not final "discoveries," the plausible is not established fact, and reiteration is not proof. To be free to maintain such attitudes one must not have too much in the way of theory at stake. A somewhat loose and flexible group of hypotheses is best, one from which parts can easily be shifted or dropped, or new ones added. The man who is hog-tied inside a tightly-knotted system of immutable first principles and fixed ends cannot possibly manage it.

This brings me to the more indirect relationship between psychiatry and psychological research which I mentioned earlier, the way in which the results of investigation within *normal* psychology are able to play an important role in psychiatry. Several decades of experimentation and observation by psychologists in their own sphere have forced upon them, not only a reorientation toward their subject matter, but also some very fundamental changes in method and in interpretation over the whole field of human conduct. Nothing could be more striking than the contrast between the rigidly systematized mentalistic psychology of the early nineteen-hundreds and the flexible pluralistic normal psychology of to-day. The Watsonian revolt of thirty years ago against introspectionism and mental analysis was no mere academic soap bubble. Crude and inadequate as the early behaviorism turned out to be, it was at the time symptomatic of a sweeping change in attitude toward human action and reaction. As I have indicated, this change was forced upon workers, not by logiloquent speculation, but by the progressive decrease in dividends received from the investments of time and effort going into mentalistic research, and by the circular and redundant character of their terminology.

Do not misunderstand my allusion to Watsonian behaviorism; I am decidedly not suggesting a regression to that stage of scientific development. It started out as something crude, premature and extreme; it made extravagant claims; it indulged in gross oversimplifications. None the less it led to important advances. These advances have left behaviorism far behind for the same reasons they have left psychic theories far behind,—behaviorism and psychism rest on hypotheses that are no longer useful, and their fruits have become sterile.

I see a rough parallel between that evolution and the present situation in psychiatry. The fact we find difficult to recognize is that the psychodynamic revolt of fifty years ago has become the traditional and accepted mentalistic psychopathology of to-day. It is no longer revolutionary; it is at home even in the drawing rooms of our contemporaries; it has become respectable and complacent. Like behaviorism it has achieved its important mission; unlike behaviorism it has also succeeded in becoming established as a fixed system of explanation. I am of the opinion that the greatest single contribution to psychiatry we can expect from the results of psychological research will be a sounder and more modern basis in normal psychology, from which another fresh start can be made, and psychopathology further developed and advanced. If this comes, it will not come ready-made as another complete system of postulates, a new theoretical chassis to be rolled under the body of clinical psychiatry. It will have to be built up gradually on the foundations of modern psychology and biology, just as our current mentalistic psychopathology has been built up on those of nineteenth century psychology and biology. It will have to get its material for this job from the patient, from his biology and from his social environment.

Here again I shall have to confine myself to one problem as an example. For various reasons I have selected that of the relationship of mind to body. This question has preoccupied and vexed philosophers for centuries. In psychiatry the revival of interest in it that we are witnessing has grown out of the fact that our psychic theories have succeeded in getting us almost completely out of line with modern biology. We have come to realize the necessity for getting back in touch with the human organism with which the physician and the surgeon work; so we are now trying to implement our psychic world of realities by biologizing the psyche. This has found its most organized expression in the development of a discipline known as *psychosomatic medicine*. I think this development is a serious misfortune for psychiatry. The attractive new name is actually nothing but *mind-body medicine* rendered partially into Greek. It is only new upholstery for a rickety old piece of philosophical furniture; the old metaphysical structure is still there under the new covering.

Last week a very competent psychiatric clinician told me with considerable vigor and evident conviction that the mind-body problem is a very great and important one, and that it is absolutely insoluble. Putting it that way you have a conundrum, not a problem. Statements like that make me feel that we are letting ourselves be taken in by philosophical rationalists. It was the philosophers who long ago adopted the hypothesis that there are two distinct entities, a psyche and a soma. Now it is they who turn around and say to us who are struggling with our problems of psychopathology, "All right, let's see you bridge *that* chasm!" Our answer to that one ought to be, "You made it, you bridge it." As a matter of fact the only real chasm there lies between two conceptual hypotheses, which anyone is at liberty to believe in or to reject. It was made originally, of course, because the information about human conduct then available gave only very inadequate clues to the origins of behavior.

It is a difficult task to account for the fact that a man can and does react to his own responses, and so helps to initiate and control them. This was one of the unsolved genuine problems that led some among the older speculators to choose the easier way out by accepting the theological dogma of a special entity separate from the body, the mind or the psyche. This invisible and intangible psyche, distinct from its soma, was also conceived of as existing in a separate psychic world of reality, from whence it acted upon or through the soma, and was in turn affected by it.

There has always been a laudable tendency among biologically oriented men to question the efficacy of such a two-world arrangement with its action-at-a-distance. Attempts to get around this led to the inclusion of the psyche, as constructed by the philosophers, in the natural order. They brought this psyche into the organism and attempted to localize it there,—in the heart, the lungs, the genitals, the bowels, the brains, or in all of these.

The inclusion of this entity within the walls of biology was a serious mistake. The psyche has turned out to be a Trojan horse. Out of it has poured a company of well-armed and tricky propositions which have opened the gates of medicine to metaphysics and led to the fall of the biological citadel. To-day we find ourselves the perplexed hosts to an organized band of rationalistic problems which do not belong with us,—how the psyche affects the soma, and how the soma affects the psyche, what the psyche is made up of and how it ever gets around to contacting and learning about non-psychic reality. These also are conundrums rather than problems. They sound deep as the pit, but they are only verbal calisthenics. They belong to a philosophical game in which we need not participate unless we want to.

If, then, we start out with our own problems instead of theirs, we find that what is actually disordered in our patients is their mode of functioning,—their activities, their reactions, and attitudes towards others and themselves, the ways in which they interpret and use their environment. Part of their action and reaction is immediately accessible to us; we can see it, hear it or feel it. Much of it is hidden. Some of the hidden processes can be made accessible by the use of clinical instruments like the stethoscope, the ophthalmoscope, the x-ray and fluoroscope, the electrocardiograph and electroencephalograph. Much still remains inaccessible even to these instruments.

There is still another common indicator which increases the accessibility of hidden action and reaction to the physician. That indicator is the patient's responses to his own activities, in signs and spoken words. Internists use these verbal and other signals as diagnostic instruments all the time; surgeons use them; pediatricians use them when they can. The training in history-taking which the medical student and interne have to go through boils down to a course in guidance and practice in the skillful use of this verbal instrument. Of course it is often unreliable; and it can be downright misleading. Just because of this medicine has developed whole systems of checking, elaborating, supplementing and channeling the verbal report. Without it the accessibility to the physician of many important organismic changes is seriously reduced and, as in coma, may be practically eliminated.

When we turn to psychiatry we do not enter a new and different world. The psychiatrist is still the physician, an organism, working with a patient, another organism. They share and operate within a common social environment; they communicate by means of socially determined signs and sounds. These are the materials of medical practice as well as of psychology and psychopathology. Everyone knows that in psychiatry the dependence of the physician upon language behavior is very great. This fact is sometimes used as a rebuke to psychiatrists by the uninformed, as if what a patient says about himself were of no importance. Most of the malfunctioning with which he must work cannot, in fact, be made accessible to him as well by any other method. He has had to develop special techniques to increase verbal output and to free it from the restrictions of its immediate context.

Among psychiatrists the psychoanalysts have done more with language behavior as a diagnostic and therapeutic agent than any others have ever done. They cannot be held responsible for the division of continuous men, women and children into the discontinuous psyches and somas, of which I have spoken, nor for the subdivision of the disembodied psyches into conscious and unconscious compartments. We are all in this difficulty together because we still look upon our material in an antiquated fashion. It is only because of this that we have on our hands an over-systematized psychopathology which treats language behavior and emotional conduct as though they belonged in another world. We have already wasted years of effort in trying to work out the internal structure of a purely fictitious psyche and its esoteric love life, when we might better have been working out the dynamics of the organization, disorganization and reorganization of human behavior,—of action and reaction, of thinking, wishing, loving, hating, learning, fearing, forgetting, desiring, avoiding and hiding,—but all these studied as the activities of a social organism, not the dreams of a ghost. For these activities, too, take place in the world in which physicians and patients live and work. They see and hear, they think and decide, with their bodies; they say things and do things to and with other persons who are organisms like themselves.

The work of the psychotherapist, in spite of his title, is not more concerned with the psyche than that of other physicians; but it is more concerned with genetic and social influences and with social implications. Anxiety, for example, is the reaction of a socially integrated organism to a variety of conditions. Of these, the ones likely to be of most importance to the psychiatrist are social in character and origin. *I have a worry* is in the same category and the same world as *I have a pain*. They are both responses to something happening in the organism. The origin of simple pain can usually be localized within the organism; it may result from some pathological interaction between components of the organism; and it always has a biography. The worry is a reaction that takes place in exactly the same organism; but here the social environment by which human organisms live is usually a much more prominent factor. And the responses of the human organism to its own attitudes and reactions have to be given an important place in the account. Nevertheless the anxiety, or the fear, or the worry, is a reaction of the same biological organism in which the pain occurs and in which fever appears. Dragging in a mind or psyche at this point as an explanatory principle adds nothing but confusion to the account. Whether it be conceived as conscious or unconscious is immaterial; for the purposes of a modern dynamic psychiatry it is functionless; it amounts to so much excess baggage.

In summing up, I need say no more about the test procedures, the experiments and the systematic observations which make up most of the psychological research and practice within psychiatry. They seem to be proving their own worth wherever they are being given consistent and intelligent support. With a little nutriment and moderate sunshine I think their growth will take care of itself.

For the rest, I have given over a large part of this discussion to the psychological foundations of psychiatry, because I believe the need for a more modern orientation toward the problems of abnormal thought and behavior is becoming more and more widely appreciated. It is going to make a good deal of practical difference whether we continue trying to weave into current psychiatry the static introspective psychology of the eighteen-nineties and early nineteen-hundreds,—with its sensations, images and ideas, its psychic energies, its bodiless thought and thoughtless bodies,—or whether we try now to mesh in with whatever is relevant in the more objective and progressive psychology of the nineteen-forties.

Let me, before closing, draw an analogy which seems to me to represent the present status of psychopathology. Suppose that in medicine and surgery fifty years ago certain practitioners, in a revolt against the inadequate physiology and histology of that period, had deliberately and completely cut themselves off from all advances in those fields, and had spent five decades in elaborating their own private theories of health and disease out of materials taken from rationalistic philosophy. Suppose they had gradually organized centers where young surgeons and internists went through an intensive course of training and indoctrination in these theoretical elaborations; and imagine, finally, that such a system of hypotheses had been declared to be not merely descriptive, like traditional medicine and surgery, but genuinely *medicodynamic* and alone capable of explaining health and disease. If internists and surgeons had followed through on such a tack, they would probably by now have developed as anachronistic and unreal a system of explanation as we have in a good deal of our current psychopathology. The task for such medical Rip Van Winkles, once they had fully awakened, would obviously be that of re-establishing contact with their scientfic world and getting rid of their nineteenth century phraseology.

To some of you these comparisons will sound presumptuous. What right has anyone to expect the solutions of medical problems to be found in psychological research and, even more presumptuous, in psychological attitudes? The reply is that no competent psychologist expects them all to be worked out there, any more than well-oriented students of the internal environment expect to locate final and complete answers to psychiatric problems in the isolated organism, or on a slide, or in a test tube. There can be no doubt that the results and the techniques of modern psychological research, both in fields of normal behavior and within psychiatry itself, are beginning to make some noteworthy contributions toward solving our mutual problems.

To many psychopathologists the open-air objectivity of modern scientific psychology is refreshing. Its language uses the terms of this world. It dovetails with physiology in one direction and with the pragmatic and operational attitudes of the clinical man in the other. For their part, the psychologists need just as much the enlivening influence of clinical psychiatrists who deal with vital human problems on the hoof. Therefore it seems to me most certainly to our own and our patients' interests to put aside the old mistrust, to hasten the reconciliation and set up once more an *entente cordiale*.

Physiological Research in Psychiatry

By EDWIN FRANCIS GILDEA, M.D.

Professor of Psychiatry, Washington University School of Medicine

STIMULUS OF SKEPTICISM • PROBLEM OF MISDIAGNOSED HYPERTHYROIDISM • BASAL METABOLIC RATE • OTHER TESTS OF THYROID FUNCTION • DIFFERENTIATION FROM NERVOUS SYSTEM TROUBLE • BLOOD SERUM IODINE VALUES • CLINICAL AND BIOCHEMICAL METHODS OF APPROACH • SERUM LIPOIDS IN MANIC-DEPRESSIVE AND SCHIZOPHRENIC PATIENTS • PROGNOSIS • CONSTITUTIONAL ENDOWMENTS • LEPTOPHILIC AND PYKNOPHILIC POTENTIALITIES • STRUCTURAL PROTEIN AND LIP-
OIDS • NEED OF BIOCHEMICAL INVESTIGATIONS IN PSYCHIATRY

IN THIS talk I am going to make a plea in favor of supplementing clinical and physiological research with biochemical and physical methods of investigation.

As I heard Dr. Campbell speaking this afternoon on controversial subjects in psychiatry, I was reminded that much of the inspiration that led to my undertaking biochemical and physiological research in psychiatry was due to my experiences as a student and interne under his stimulating and wise guidance. Almost every formulation of a case history or theory which we presented to him would be met by several alternative concepts. I and many of my colleagues were tremendously stimulated by his skepticism.

At that time, 1926-28, one of the problems of concern was the determination of the amount of thyroid activity in emotionally upset patients. Dr. Bailey, in his talk this afternoon, referred to this problem. Patients who manifest symptoms of anxiety and have marked tremors and vasomotor symptoms were and still are misdiagnosed hyperthyroidism. Many physicians have the thyroids of such patients removed. Some of these patients came to us at the Boston Psychopathic because they continued to have the anxiety and the tremors and vasomotor disorders although they were now also myxedematous. We would also see other patients with their thyroids still in who looked as if they might have hyperthyroidism. Our staff and the medical and surgical consultants would be equally divided as to whether we should take out the thyroids of such patients or leave them in. Some of these patients had their thyroids removed and yet did not improve, or if they improved it was only to a slight degree.

Although much remains to be learned, the story of thyroid investigation is stimulating and should encourage us in our future investigation. As you know, we probably understand more about the thyroid, its disorders and how to treat them than about most diseases. We have a therapy, iodine administration, that improves a great many patients and if this does not work we take the gland out. Surgeons feel that this is one of their special fields. When they take out the glands of patients with high basal metabolic rates, the patients usually improve rapidly. They are well as far as the surgeon is concerned but later on many of these patients come to the psychiatrist on account of the persistence or exacerbation of their old symptoms. Although their basal metabolic rates may be down and their heart rate may be quite normal, they still have tremors and all the things that seemed to lead to the beginning of their disorder of hyperthyroidism.

For a time it was felt that the measurement of the basal metabolic rate was the most reliable means of estimating the degree of thyroid overactivity. Unfortunately when a person is excited, his basal becomes elevated regardless of how normal his thyroid may be. For this reason many workers have sought for other tests of the thyroid function. As you know, the lipoids and cholesterol were found to be in some way controlled by the activity of the thyroid gland. Unfortunately in the case of the lipoids, if there is enough disturbance of the nervous system, even though the thyroid is overactive, the lipoids may be high. If the nervous system is not markedly upset, as in relatively uncomplicated cases of hyperthyroidism, the increased amount of thyroid hormone will reduce the blood lipoids and cholesterol as much as half of the normal value. Yet in just the cases in which you want to know whether the symptoms are primarily nervous system in origin with very little disturbance of the thyroid or the reverse, the serum lipoids may be high or normal and thus of no assistance in the differential diagnosis.

A great many different physiological tests have been tried out on thyroid patients in an effort to differentiate those with nervous system trouble from those with thyroid disorders. In these studies the problem of the extraordinary individual difference in responses of patients has limited their value.

Early in the course of research on thyroid diseases it came to be known that iodine was intimately related to thyroid function, and a great many investigators attempted to measure blood iodine. The results were extraordinarily variable both in normal people and people with hyperthyroidism. The history of the development of the iodine methods is an interesting one which I cannot go into here. It now appears that practically all the conflicting results of various investigators were due to technical difficulties.[1] When these were eliminated by recently developed methods, normal individuals proved to have serum iodines with quite a narrow range of variation. In people whose thyroid had been taken out the iodine in the serum was practically zero. In patients with overactivity of the thyroid the serum iodines were two to three times higher than normal.

We have therefore a biochemical tool which helps to differentiate those patients who will respond with improvement after thyroidectomy from those who will not.[2,3] The experience we have had so far in a series of about fifty patients has been re-

[1] Riggs, D. S., and Man, E. B. A permanganate acid ashing micromethod for iodine determinations. I. Values in blood of normal subjects. J. Biol. Chem., *134*:193, 1940.

[2] Riggs, D. S., Gildea, E. F., Man, E. B., and Peters, J. P. Blood iodine in patients with thyroid disease. J. Clin. Investigation, *20*:345, 1941.

[3] Man, E. B., Smirnow, A., Gildea, E. F., and Peters, J. P. Serum iodine fractions in hyperthyroidism. J. Clin. Investigation, *21*:773, 1942.

warding. The patients who had high serum iodines responded dramatically to the removal of the thyroid gland. Some of these patients had marked emotional disturbances which led the staff to be uncertain as to the outcome following thyroidectomy.

This story illustrates the point that successful medical research usually requires many methods of approach. First comes clinical investigation which roughly lays out the field and gives clues as to direction for physiological investigations. Then when you have completed these steps you need to know what goes on under the skin, the biochemistry, in order that you may understand and control fundamental changes associated with these external appearances. This emphasis on biochemistry does not mean that I do not recognize that you can upset the internal chemistry by the effects of emotionally conditioned experiences. One need only consider the work of Cannon and his followers to emphasize this side of the problem.

You may remember that this afternoon Dr. Campbell quoted figures in a report from Burghölzli, the clinic of the late Dr. Bleuler in Switzerland, in which it was indicated that practically all their patients were schizophrenics with the exception of only two or three manic-depressives. We all know that if most of us here studied these same patients there would have been a great many more classed as manic-depressives. Consequently, as Dr. Campbell pointed out, we are at a loss as to how to reach an agreement on the differentiation of these patients. In New Haven we have the same controversies about patients manifesting these severe disturbances of emotions and output of energy, as well as in the organization of their thinking. Some patients have more illogical thinking and others less; others have more disturbances of mood, and you can see very little of what we consider schizophrenic thinking. Yet our colleagues with about the same training will work on the same patients and say, "Oh no, those mood disturbances are not important. Here I see all these schizoid symptoms, these queer ideas," and they will disagree flatly with our classification.

In our effort to solve these problems we have sought for differences in the underlying chemistry of these manic-depressive and schizophrenic patients. For reasons that I will not go into here we investigated lipoid metabolism. In our work at Yale we have found that in patients with either manic attacks or depressions of a relatively uncomplicated nature, the serum lipoids were high normal or above normal. On the other hand the patients with clear-cut symptoms of schizophrenia of a number of years duration had serum lipoids which were low normal or below.[4] Recently we were able to investigate the outcome of some 150 patients on whom we had made lipoid studies.[5] It was found that 85 percent of the patients who had had high lipoids experienced remissions that had enabled them to return to their former occupations and social activities. They were continuing to do well five or more years after the onset of their illnesses. In contrast, patients who had had low lipoids subsequently experienced poor or no remissions and were either in state hospitals or receiving special care at home. Thus it appears that the lipoids may be employed as an aid in prognosis. These findings are necessarily empirical and the underlying biochemistry of these remissions awaits clarification. Some order may be introduced into this problem by utilizing a hypothesis introduced some years ago by Kahn.[6]

According to this conception, people are endowed with certain constitutional potentialities which determine their development as regards physique, temperament, capacity for growth, output of energy, resistance to disease, ability to recover from disease, etc. Some of these may be recognized at present but others must await advances in the biochemistry of constitution for further definition. For the present there appear to be pyknophilic potentialities which are represented anatomically by pyknic body build; in terms of behavior by warmth of tem-

[4] Gildea, E. F., Man, E. B., and Biach, R. W. Serum protein, non-protein nitrogen and lipoids in schizophrenic and manic-depressive psychoses. Arch. Neurol. & Psychiat., 43:932, 1940.

[5] Gildea, E. F., and Man, E. B. Methods for estimating capacity for recovery in patients with manic-depressive and schizophrenic psychoses. To be published in American Journal of Psychiatry.

[6] Kahn, E. Constitutional aspects of personality type. Research Publ., A. Nerv. & Ment. Dis., 14:138, 1933.

perament, by high energy output, including sex drive, by strong resistance to disease and by remarkable capacity for recovery if overwhelmed by disease. That high lipoids may well represent a biochemical measure of pyknophilic potentialities is suggested by the studies just described where they were found in the pyknic people with high energy output and in the patients who proved to have a high capacity for recovery. Deficiency in these qualities may be considered the result of the predominance of leptophilic over pyknophilic potentialities. The presence of leptophilic potentialities is indicated by leptosomic physique, cool temperament, low output of energy, weak sex drive, low resistance to disease, and poor capacity for recovery and restitution. In line with this evidence low serum lipoids would constitute another evidence of leptophilic potentialities.

From what we know of body chemistry the structure of cells and tissues depends primarily on the structural arrangements of protein molecules. There is evidence, however, that the lipoids are in some way fitted into the intricacies of these patterns. Consequently, the amount and nature of lipoids in a tissue may well depend in part on these protein arrangements. Thus the serum lipoids may reflect fundamental constitutional qualities because of their intimate ties with the structural protein. And what we have been measuring gives us a reflection of the fundamental protein structure.

The work of Schoenheimer [7] suggests that we may learn a good deal about body structure by studying small samples of tissues including blood. Schoenheimer was one of the many scientists who have come to this country from Europe. You perhaps know that he suffered from mood swings and terminated his own life just last year in the midst of extremely brilliant and fundamental work. His work demonstrates that the whole chemical structure of the body is in a constant state of

[7] Schoenheimer, R. The Dynamic State of Body Constituents. Harvard University Monographs in Medicine and Public Health, 3. Cambridge, Harvard University Press, 1941.

flux although the form appears to be static. The elements that go into the protein structure as well as the lipoids are changing continually. This flux of molecules is modified by the food you digest, by the multiple activities of your body, and all parts are always in a state of continual change. Yet, within limits, a steady state of function is maintained. Schoenheimer established these principles by masterfully designed experiments in which he employed tracerisotopes of hydrogen, nitrogen, carbon and also radioactive isotopes.

From these considerations I would like to suggest that the next step in attempting to estimate potentialities for resistance to mental disease in biochemical terms lies in the direction of protein chemistry, and particularly in stereochemistry and in stoechio-chemistry.

Further illustrations could be given of the advances in knowledge made possible by biochemical investigations in people with mental disorders.[8, 9] In spite of the importance of biochemistry in giving us a measure of body structure and function, few departments of psychiatry are equipped with facilities for the pursuit of this kind of work. In closing, therefore, I wish to emphasize that biochemical investigations in psychiatry need to be encouraged and supported if we are to make substantial progress in the solution of the problem of mental disease.

[8] Cameron, D. E. Objective and Experimental Psychiatry. Second Edition. New York City, The Macmillan Co., 1941.

[9] Gildea, E. F. Biochemistry in relation to psychiatry. Yale J. Biol. & Med., 14:505, 1942.

Psychosomatic Research in Psychiatry

By FRANZ ALEXANDER, M.D.

Associate Professor of Psychiatry, University of Illinois College of Medicine; Director, Institute for Psychoanalysis, Chicago

THE MIND-BODY PROBLEM • NO LOGICAL DISTINCTION IN QUALITY • TWO ASPECTS OF SAME PROCESS • QUESTION OF PSYCHOGENESIS • PHYSIOLOGICAL BASIS OF PSYCHOLOGICAL PHENOMENA • HYSTERICAL CONVERSION • EMOTIONAL HYPERTENSION • FREUD'S RESTRICTIONS • SYMPTOMS OF VOLUNTARY NEURO-MUSCULAR AND SENSORY PERCEPTIVE SYSTEMS • SUBSTITUTE EXPRESSIONS • ABREACTIONS • SUBTITUTE INNERVATIONS • SYMBOLIC SUBSTITUTES • CONTRAST OF VEGETATIVE NEUROSES • PHYSIOLOGICAL CONCOMITANTS, NOT SUBSTITUTIONS • COUNTERPARTS • CHRONICITY AND MORBIDITY • PSYCHOGENIC ORGANIC CONDITIONS • PSYCHOGENIC DYSFUNCTION • SUSTAINED EMOTIONAL STATES • SPECIFICITY • SPECIFIC VEGETATIVE TONUS • EMOTIONAL SPECIFICITY • TECHNIQUE OF PSYCHOANALYSIS • SPECIFIC PERSONALITY FACTORS • SUBJECTS FOR FURTHER CLINICAL RESEARCH

IT WOULD be impossible in twenty minutes to review even briefly the work done in the field of psychosomatic research. I shall use the time allotted to me for a discussion of a few basic conceptions of psychosomatic research which require clarification. Although psychosomatic research is of recent origin, it deals with one of the oldest, if not the oldest, problems of scientific thought—with the mind-body problem. This may explain the heavy load of traditional concepts and assumptions which hamper its development. At first I should like to take up the concept of psychogenesis in general, then that of hysterical conversion in particular, and finally the question of the specificity of emotional factors involved in somatic dysfunctions.

The question of psychogenesis is linked up with the ancient dichotomy: psyche versus soma. When the journal *Psychosomatic Medicine* was started, our editorial staff felt that in the first issue some clear statement should be made about this confusing philosophical issue to discourage authors from writing endless discussions on this point. I quote from this introductory statement of the editors:

"Emphasis is put on the thesis that there is no logical distinction between 'mind and body,' mental and physical. It is assumed that the complex neurophysiology of mood, instinct and intellect differs from other physiology in degree of complexity, but not in quality. Hence again divisions of medical disciplines into physiology, neurology, internal medicine, psychiatry and psychology may be convenient for academic administration, but biologically and philosophically these divisions have no validity. It takes for granted that psychic and somatic phenomena take place in the same biological system and are probably two aspects of the same process, that psychological phenomena should be studied in their psychological causality with intrinsically psychological methods and physiological phenomena in their physical causality with the methods of physics and chemistry."

In spite of this statement, we still receive manuscripts in which the authors involve themselves in a hopeless struggle with this age-worn problem. For example, an author gives an excellent description of the effect of psychological factors upon some clinical condition, then becomes apologetic and tries to dodge the whole issue of psychogenesis by saying that one should not speak of psychogenesis but of the coexistence of certain psychological factors with certain physical symptoms.

It is important that the question of psychogenesis should be clarified, stating explicitly what is meant by it. First let us examine an example. In the case of emotionally caused elevation of the blood pressure, psychogenesis does not mean that the contraction of the blood vessels is effected by some nonsomatic mechanism. Rage consists in physiological processes which take place somewhere in the central nervous system. The physiological effect of rage consists of a chain of events —among them the elevation of blood pressure—in which every link can be described at least theoretically in physiological terms. The distinctive feature of psychogenic factors such as emotions or ideas and fantasies is that they *can* be studied psychologically through introspection as well as by verbal communication from those in whom these physiological processes take place. An automobile climbing a hill has no sensation of effort, tiredness, or of a goal to reach. In contrast to a man-built machine the organism climbing a mountain has an awareness of certain of its internal physiological processes in the form of effort, tiredness, discouragement, renewed effort, and so on. Moreover, man in contrast to the animal organisms is able to convey these internal sensations to others by verbal communication. Verbal communication is therefore one of the most potent instruments of psychology and consequently also of psychosomatic research. When we speak of psychogenesis we refer to physiological processes consisting of central excitations in the nervous system which can be studied by psychological methods because they are perceived subjectively in the form of emotions, ideas, or wishes. Psychosomatic research deals with such processes in which certain links in the causal chain of events lend themselves, at the present state of our knowledge, more readily to a study by psychological methods than by physiological methods since the detailed investigation of emotions as brain processes is not far enough advanced. My expectation is, however, that even when the physiological basis of psychological phenomena will be better known we will not be able to dispense with their psychological study. It is hardly conceivable that the different moves of two chess players can ever be more clearly understood in biochemical or neuro-physiological than in psychological and logical terms.

The concept of hysterical conversion also is closely related to the philosophical question of mind and body. The expression itself carries the connotation that a psychological process is transmuted into a bodily manifestation. Freud formulated the concept of conversion in the following way: "In hysteria the unbearable idea is rendered innocuous by the quantity of excitation attached to it being transmuted into some bodily form of expression, a process for which I should like to propose the name of *conversion.*" [1] Essentially a hysterical conversion symptom is nothing but an unusual innervation; it does not differ in principle from any other voluntary innervation or from such expressive movements as speech, laughter, or weeping. When we want to hit someone our arms are brought into movement; when we speak our ideas are converted into movements of the laryngeal muscles and of the lips and tongue. In laughter or weeping also, an emotion finds bodily expression. In a conversion symptom like hysterical contracture, "the leap from the psychic into the somatic" is not more mysterious than in any of these common motor innervations. The meaning of conversion symptom was originally very definite: a conversion symptom was a symbolic substitute for an unbearable emotion. It was assumed that the symptom relieved, at least to some degree, the tension produced by the repression of the unbearable emotion. It was considered a kind of physical abreaction or equivalent of an unconscious emotional tension. From the beginning Freud insisted that the repressed emotion ultimately can be always retraced to a sexual tension. Ferenczi made this even more explicit by postulating that a physical conversion symptom is always a kind of genitalization of that part of the body. I cannot enter into the discussion of the validity of the exclusively sexual origin of conversion symptoms at the present moment.

Repeated attempts have been made to extend the original concept of hysterical conversion to all forms of psychogenic disturbances of the body, even to those of the visceral vegetative organs. It was claimed that the essence of psychogenic disturbances is always the same. A repressed emotional tension finds expression through bodily channels. Whether it takes place in vegetative organs controlled by the autonomic nervous system or in the voluntary neuro-muscular and sensory percep-

[1] In the same article he states as the characteristic factors for hysteria the capacity for conversion, "and we may assume that the psycho-physical capacity to transmute such large quantities of excitation into somatic innervation is an important element of the disposition to hysteria, which in other respects is still unknown."

tive systems is a secondary matter. According to this concept emotional hypertension is the conversion of repressed rage or some other emotion into a physical symptom—the elevation of blood pressure. The adherents to this concept even went so far as to say that a peptic ulcer might be considered a conversion symptom. Some repressed emotion, let us say some biting fantasies, find somatic expression in tissue changes of the stomach. In previous writings I have tried to demonstrate the grave error inherent to such superficial generalizations. I pointed out that the original concept of hysterical conversion is still an excellent and valid one if it is restricted to these phenomena on which it was originally based by Freud. At the same time I introduced the concept of another form of psychogenic process which is observed in vegetative disturbances such as emotional hypertension or in psychogenic organic conditions such as peptic ulcers. Since these publications I have arrived at still more precise formulations which I should like to present on this occasion.

I still uphold my original suggestion that we restrict hysterical conversion phenomena to symptoms of the voluntary neuromuscular and the sensory perceptive systems and differentiate them from psychogenic symptoms which occur in vegetative organs, the functions of which are under the control of the autonomic nervous system.

The rationale of this distinction is about as follows: hysterical conversion symptoms are substitute expressions—abreactions—of emotional tensions which cannot find adequate outlet through full-fledged motor behavior. For example, sexual excitation, which normally is gratified by intercourse, if repressed may find expression in some other motor innervation such as convulsions imitating the muscular movement of intercourse. Or, anger which cannot find expression through yelling, shouting, accusing, hitting, might lead to conversion symptoms in organs which are used for the legitimate expression of rage—the larynx or the extremities in the form of hysterical aphasia or paralysis.

As Freud originally stressed it, these substitutive innervations never bring full relief; they are only attempts at relief; the symptoms express at the same time both the repressed emotion and its rejection. Just because they do not relieve the tension fully we have a pathological condition. The important issue, however, is that the emotional tension is at least partially relieved by the symptom itself.

We deal with a different psychodynamic and physiological situation in the field of vegetative neuroses although there are some similarities to the conversion symptoms. Here the somatic symptoms are not substitute expressions of repressed emotions but they are normal physiological concomitants of the emotion. For example, rage and fear are connected with a physiological syndrome consisting of such diversified vegetative processes as the stimulation of the adrenal system, mobilization of sugar, elevation of the blood pressure, changes in the distribution of blood which is squeezed out from the splanchnic area into the muscles, to the lungs and the brain.

These physiological processes are normal corollaries of rage and fear; they do not relieve suppressed rage but they accompany rage. They are the adjustment of the organism to definite tasks which it has to face in a dangerous situation, to fight or to flee. They are a utilitarian preparation and adaptation of the internal vegetative processes to a specific type of behavior which is requested from the organism. The elevated blood pressure or mobilization of sugar does not relieve the anger in the least; these symptoms do not appear in place of the emotional tension; they simply accompany the emotion of rage; they are an inseparable part of the total phenomenon which we call rage. They are the systemic reaction of the body to rage.

The chronicity of an emotional tension is what makes such a condition morbid. The non-neurotic individual is able to get rid of his rage by some legitimate expression. Some psychoneurotics can drain off the suppressed hostile feelings in compulsion symptoms or depressions.

The hypertensive patient's pathology consists in the fact that he is under a constant or frequent, not repressed, but unexpressed, emotional tension which is not drained either by psychoneurotic symptoms or by legitimate expression such as verbal or physical combat. He has not the relief that the angry man has of beating up his adversary or at least telling him what he has on his mind.

The difference between conversion symptom and vegetative neurosis is now obvious. A conversion symptom is a symbolic expression of a well-defined emotional content—an attempt at relief. It is expressed by the voluntary neuro-muscular or sensory perceptive systems whose original function is to express and relieve emotional tension. A vegetative neurosis like emotional hypertension is not an attempt to express an emotion but is the physiological concomitant of constant or periodically recurring emotional states.

The same conditions described in emotional hypertension can be applied readily to all other vegetative systems. Similarly a gastric neurosis consisting of a chronic disturbance of the secretory and motor functions of the stomach is not the expression or drainage of an emotional tension but the physiological concomitant of it. These patients want to be loved, to be taken care of, a wish to which they cannot give legitimate expression because of a neurotically exaggerated sense of shame or guilt; therefore they are under constant influence of these emotional tensions. The wish to be loved is deeply associated with the wish to be fed since the nursing situation is the first one in which the child enjoys parental love and care. Because of early emotional associations the chronic longing to be loved and taken care of is apt to stimulate the stomach functions. The stomach symptoms are the physiological concomitants of the passive state of expectation of receiving food. The disturbance of the secretory and motor functions of the stomach is not the substitute expression of an emotion but the physiological counterpart of an emotion, namely, of the desire to be taken care of. The wish to be taken care of may be repressed and transformed into the wish to be nursed. This is not a conversion, however, but the substitution of one psychological desire for another. Corresponding to this wish to be nursed are certain vegetative innervations which are not substitutes for the wish to be nursed but are its inseparable physiological sequelae. If the desire to be taken care of is satisfied, for example, through sanitorium treatment, the constant pressure of this wish may cease and with it the stomach symptoms may fully disappear. Neurotic stomach symptoms, however, are not conversions of a repressed longing for love into stomach symptoms; they do not appear in place of the emotions, but are the physiological concomitants of a chronic or periodic emotional tension. Bulimia, in contradistinction to a stomach neurosis, may be considered as a conversion symptom. Here the wish to be loved, to be given things or to take things is drained, that is to say satisfied, at least to some extent by incorporating food. Eating becomes both a satisfaction and a symbolic substitute for being loved or being impregnated or for a biting aggressive attack. It fulfills all the requirements of a conversion symptom. Asthma also has components of a hysterical conversion symptom since it can serve as the direct expression and partial substitute for a suppressed emotion such as the wish to cry. Breathing—although an automatic function—is also under the control of voluntary innervations. Acid secretion of the stomach, however, is not. Breathing is used in such expressive functions as speech and crying; stomach secretion may be a concomitant of an emotional state but is never used for its symbolic expression as is speech or crying.

Finally peptic ulcer is neither a conversion symptom nor a vegetative neurosis. In some cases it is the somatic end-result of a long-standing neurotic stomach dysfunction but in itself has nothing whatever directly to do with any emotion. It is not the symbolic expression of a wish or a self-punishment. It is a secondary physiological end-effect of a long-standing psychogenic dysfunction.

To summarize: it seems advisable to differentiate between hysterical conversion and vegetative neurosis. Their similarities are rather superficial; both conditions are psychogenic, that is to say, they are caused ultimately by a chronic, repressed or at least unrelieved emotional tension. The mechanisms involved, however, are fundamentally different both psychodynamically and physiologically. The hysterical conversion symptom is an attempt to relieve an emotional tension in a symbolic way; it is a symbolic expression of a definite emotional content. This mechanism is restricted to the voluntary neuro-muscular or sensory perceptive systems whose function is to express and relieve emotions. A vegetative neurosis consists of a psychogenic dysfunction of a vegetative organ which is not under control of the voluntary neuro-muscular system. The vegetative symptom is not a substitute expression of the emotion, but its normal physiological concomitant. We assume that corresponding to every emotional state there is a certain distribution of vegetative innervations. When we have to fight or undergo physical exertion the vegetative organs of digestion are relaxed, whereas the muscular system and the lungs are in a state of preparation. The emotional attitude accompanying food intake and digestion again is accompanied by a different distribution of vegetative tonus. In this instance the visceral organs become hyperemic, whereas the skeletal muscle tonus decreases and the concomitant drowsiness is the indication of a transitory anemia of the cortex. If these emotional states are chronically sustained the corresponding vegetative innervations also become chronic and assume the qualities of a symptom. The circulatory system of the hypertensive behaves all the time as if this person were ready to attack somebody at any moment. When the stomach neurotic breaks down under an excessive load of responsibility he recoils from his habitual overactivity and assumes the vegetative mood of the state that accompanies digestion, to which his alimentary tract reacts with a continuous hyperactivity.

This brings us to the last crucial problem of psychosomatic research, the question of specificity, which I can only briefly touch upon on this occasion. According to one school of thought there is no specific correlation; any emotional tension may influence any vegetative system. The choice of the symptoms may depend upon the history of the patient, on his constitution; if he has a weak stomach, he has a stomach upset when he gets angry; if he has a labile vasomotor system he might become a hypertensive under the influence of aggressions. Perhaps an early respiratory infection has made his lungs susceptible; then he will react to every emotional upset with an asthma attack.

The other heuristic assumption, which has guided our investigative work in the Chicago Psychoanalytic Institute, is that the physiological responses to different emotional tensions are varied; that consequently vegetative dysfunctions result from specific emotional constellations. As I have emphasized, we know from human and animal experiment that different emotional states have their specific vegetative tonus. The vegetative syndrome which corresponds to rage and fear is definitely different from that of passive relaxation during digestion; a state of impatience or of tense attentiveness has bodily concomitants in vegetative and skeletal innervations different from those in a paralyzing state of panic. The vegetative concomitants of various emotional states are as different from each other as laughter from weeping—the physical expression of merriment from that of sorrow. It is therefore to be expected that just as the nature of the chronic unrelieved emotional state varies, so also will the corresponding vegetative disturbance vary.

The results of current investigations are all in favor of the theory of specificity. Gastric neurotic symptoms have a different psychology from those of emotional diarrhea or constipation; cardiac cases differ in their emotional background from asthmatics. The emotional component in functional glycosuria has its own peculiarities and there is good evidence that the emotional factor in glaucoma has again its specific features. This emotional specificity can only be ascertained, of course, by careful, minute observation for which the best method available is the prolonged interview technique of psychoanalysis. However, briefer but careful psychiatric anamnestic studies conducted by well-trained observers often reveal the specific personality factors involved in different types of cases. To what extent this specificity determines the choice of symptom, to what extent constitutional factors influence the picture, and to what extent a pre-existing organic pathology or sensitivity are responsible are questions to be decided by further, careful clinical studies.

The Future in Psychiatry

By NOLAN D. C. LEWIS, M.D.

Professor of Psychiatry, College of Physicians and Surgeons, Columbia University; Director, New York State Psychiatric Institute and Hospital

PROBLEM OF GROWTH OF MENTAL DISORDER • PROPHECY FROM PAST ACCOMPLISHMENTS • FOUR QUESTIONS APPROACHING INDIVIDUAL PROBLEMS • PSYCHIATRY A BASIC SCIENCE OF PERSONAL RELATIONSHIPS • CRITICAL ANALYSIS • PERSONAL, FUNCTIONAL AND SOCIETAL MALADJUSTMENTS • WIDE RANGE OF INTERESTS IN CONTEMPORARY LITERATURE • ABUNDANT MATERIAL FOR PSYCHIATRIC RESEARCH • NEED OF BASIC SCIENCES • TEN ATTITUDES AND PROGRAMS DETERMINING THE PROBLEMS FOR INVESTIGATION • PRESENT RESEARCH TRENDS • PERSONALITY FUNCTION • THE ELEMENTS OF THE CONCEPT OF "CONSTITUTION" • THE CONSTITUTIONAL REACTION OF THE TOTAL INDIVIDUAL • GAPS IN KNOWLEDGE • COOPERATIVE WORK • ADVANCE IN CYCLES • CREATIVE IMAGINATION • UNCOMMON SENSE • MASS ATTACK OF QUALIFIED INVESTIGATORS • "FORKED ROAD" SITUATIONS • CHOICE OF MATERIAL • FIVE INDICATED PLANS

IN SOME respects this is a very difficult assignment. In approaching it I have the feeling of being lost which I used to have in my earlier days in psychiatry in connection with a certain schizophrenic patient. Frequently when I made rounds he would propound two questions. One was "What lies back of behind?" and the other, "How long is a long time?" I never tried to answer the first one, about what lies back of behind; but sometimes I would answer, "Ten years could be considered a long time." He would always reply, "The answer is not satisfactory!" I am here confronted with a question of a similar degree of obscurity as to what lies ahead instead of behind us. We know what is behind us in psychiatry better than we know what lies ahead. However, the trick of the professional prophet is to make his predictions in such terms that he is always right regardless of the final turn of events.

I am in doubt as to whether I should confront you with threats or promises. We know that we are up against the threat of this enormous problem of mental disorder which is growing monthly and yearly, and that we have to do something about it if only for self-preservation. We can advocate further study, and we can advocate research, among other things, but something will have to be done in addition to present activities if we are to survive as biological phenomena. I was impressed this afternoon by the remarks of Professor Sturgis in his outline of the research attitudes and procedures in general medicine, and I thought how, with very little modification or pointing up, they are very applicable to this whole psychiatric problem. During the course of the day we have heard descriptions of different procedures and research ideas. We have seen quite a number of "windows" opened, so to speak, through which one can look at psychiatry or look out at it. It takes a very long-necked observer to see the whole firmament out of one window. Therefore I have decided to look at some of the different windows which are available and have served as background or as a basis from which we have to move toward and into the future. I do not know how one can prophesy in science in any other way than to use past accomplishments as a starting point.

We have in psychiatry four questions with which individual problems are approached. The *first,* a very general one, is: why does one individual rather than another develop a mental disorder? The *second:* why does a person break down at some particular life period rather than at some other period in life, earlier or later? The *third:* why is there a difference of reaction pattern among individuals? The *fourth:* what is the meaning or the significance and what are the diagnostic and prognostic values of each expressed symptom or reaction or part-reaction? In our attitude toward the special problem and the individual patient we attempt to learn what it is that confronts us.

Although I am fully aware of the arguments usually offered against this statement, as far as I am concerned psychiatry is a basic science. It is a science of personal relationships, and while it is not a science of which every aspect can be subjected to laboratory experimentation to obtain the facts, we do have the facts of experience which are equally important and which we can handle in a scientific manner, substituting the experiment of the laboratory with the tool known as critical analysis. The phenomena of mental disorders are natural events, functioning in conformity with the laws of the material world. Some of these laws have been revealed through the application of methods of science, which encourages a continued use of these methods in an attempt to discover other and still more important mechanisms concerned with natural events. Those who seem to have the best grasp of the mental disorder problem welcome all the aid they can obtain from morphology, physiology and chemistry, but so far are inclined to admit that they find the bulk of their pertinent facts in the personal, functional and societal adjustments and maladjustments. We need the disciplines of developmental morphology, neurophysiology and biochemistry in order to understand the manner in which the individual is integrated, since these factors play a definite role in determining in turn the way in which a person becomes adjusted to his family, life work and society.

A glance at contemporary psychiatric literature reveals a wide range of interests. There are studies in general biochemistry, brain chemistry, physical chemistry, endocrinology, heredity, morphology, experimental therapy, psychology and psychometrics, psychoanalysis, criminology, drug addiction and alcoholism, the influence of emotion on bodily functions and numerous problems suggested by epileptics with their biochemic, physiologic and psychologic components. Among these investigations we find descriptive, analytic and laboratory approaches which reveal much information of practical value as well as of theoretical interest. It is rather obvious that there are problems in organic constitution and in function structure, in addition to the paramount psychological expressions in mental disorders, and that psychiatry cannot be reduced to a simple study of any one set of developments. It is indeed a broad field and one finds some difficulty in attempting to take its actual measure at the present time.

The material for psychiatric research is to be found everywhere in human society. Opportunities are always present. Psychic disorders appear as such at the clinical level, and psychiatrists, like students of cancer, need the basic sciences to guide them in the determination of fundamental constitutional factors which create the background and the conditions under which these disorders arise. The modern attitudes and programs which influence the trends of research and determine the problems for investigation are—and I should like to itemize these briefly—first, the analytical and interpretative attitudes which consider the individual as a biological unit; second, the opinion that the personality organization from infancy to adult life must be thoroughly studied to understand the normal and pathological mental states and reactions; third, the careful investigation of heredity and environment, and the adjustments and balances between these large groups of factors; fourth, the evaluation of physical illnesses, and the search for possible organic brain lesions and alterations in function; fifth, the attempt to reveal the mechanisms and the particular meanings of behavior and ideas exhibited by psychotic and neurotic patients; sixth, the child guidance clinics and the study of problem children for the detection of early mental disorders, personality defects and changes, odd dispositions and characters; seventh, the social aspects of mental disorders, particularly those leading to juvenile delinquency, criminal careers, and so on; eighth, the special aims toward the prevention of mental disorders in a community; ninth, the education of the public by surveys, lectures and conferences (and here I believe the bulk of the activity should be directed, more than in the past, toward educating the educators, i.e., the doctors, clergymen, school teachers and newspaper editors, those persons in the community to whom others go with their problems when they do not go to the physician. The newspaper editor should know the facts and become oriented in this field in order that we can obtain more accurate expositions of the subject, as so many people get almost all their information about everything in this world from the newspapers); and tenth, the types of medical and nursing education pertaining to the specialty of psychiatry.

Research in the field of psychiatry now consists of the investigation of brain potentials and conduction phenomena in the central nervous system; in searches for detailed pathological changes in the brain and other organs, in the physical and chemical variations in the blood, spinal fluid, and other constituents of the body; the study of the precise nature of the instinctive drives and urges, the delineation of the elements entering the organization of the personality, the various patterns of personality reaction including the disorders; the significance of the human environment in the home, the school and in economic and other social adjustments; and the search for any medical and psychological resources which can be utilized for therapeutic adjustments. These are some of the windows through which we look and through which we try to work.

From the variety of approaches in psychiatric thinking and research just mentioned, it is apparent that no single discipline is in a position to claim exclusive domination over the whole field of psychiatry. However, they should all follow and extend their conceptions and techniques as far as they will reach. Most of them have achieved success in illuminating some parts of the complex problem which psychiatry presents, and they may reasonably hope to make additional contributions in the future. Any formulation attempting to embrace all of the concepts of psychiatry in a generalization must be projected into the future and it is improbable that any one of the avenues of research now known and utilized will ever succeed in solving some of the major problems. At present we are justified in looking to the neurologist, the physiologist, the chemist and the psychologist to contribute all that it is in their power to produce, and we must accept the inevitable result that their various interpretations will not blend into a coherent picture for many years to come. Finally, it will probably be found that, in keeping with the history of the past, the efforts of the workers along these divergent paths have contributed to the building of the structure of knowledge by supplying some of the elements which compose it.

Psychiatry is a complex and important representation of psychobiological integration having as its principal object the understanding of personality function. Its work tries to comprehend the human being as an organism or unit in action, and this attitude must be maintained by all who enter this field expecting to add anything to it. The professions of medicine in general and of psychiatry in particular are so embedded in the social forces of time that they become part and parcel of sociology. The structure and integration of the personality with its particular normal and abnormal features, both transitory and permanent in nature, can be fully understood only through the investigation of personal relationships with those at home, at school, at work, and in other personal contacts. However, a great deal of work has been accomplished already relating to these particular points, but in the minds of some thinkers it seems that the attempt to seek the causes of psychological events by studying other psychological events has advanced about as far as possible for the present and that the advances of the future must be sought in other fields. This attitude will lead to failure or to only partial success, unless the functions of the personality and its attempted adjustments are correlated.

All physicians must accept the psychiatrist's extension of the concept of "constitution" as such if they are going to contribute to this problem. The elements which compose what every physician includes in the constitution are the factors of heredity, the effects of the environment on growth and bodily development, and the effects of diseases. The psychiatrist also considers the constitution as including those factors but adds the traditions, the influence of the parents, the contact persons and the identifications, in other words the human environment which is a notable part of the reaction pattern of the individual. The individual himself knows that these human factors are part of his constitution. He knows that his early training, his concept of society, and his conscience which is the representative of society will allow him or will not allow him to behave in certain ways. To repeat, the early family traditions, the social contacts, the experiences with parents and teachers, and the emotional identifications which he makes with other people are part of the reacting constitution. If these are included, then psychosomatic problems will be seen as part of the constitutional reaction of the total individual. In these days we seem to be thinking in these terms and that is why I am inclined to prophesy that this will be one of the worthful future developments in medicine.

All of our classifications of knowledge, including those of mental disorders, are man-made and not spontaneously arranged by nature. Therefore, they may not be valid and at best only temporary in significance. There is no distinction in nature between organic and functional. This concept is man-made and is the result of gaps in knowledge. There is a greater gap in our knowledge of correlations between "anatomical" and "physiological" than between "physiological" and "psychological." Just how does anatomy perform its physiological activities? The sense of it is this: that each science for its own purposes simplifies by abstracting, by "essential neglect," as it is called. It is this which separates the sciences. If the body of knowledge which the sciences together compose is to be seen as a whole, as a totality, these abstract simplifications must be put together again. This is definitely one of the tasks of the future, that is, the synthesis of the knowledge already known in several biological sciences.

A coordination of the work resulting from the different unit investigations by those who use the electron as the unit in their work, those who use the atom, those who use the cell, those who use the organ system in physiology, and those who use the individual as the unit becomes increasingly urgent. No one man can think in all of those terms, because it requires a different type of orientation and thinking to study the total individual as a unit and the problems of society than it does to work with the molecule as the unit. Therefore, the scientists representing the various branches of research can, by pooling their special knowledge and by cooperative work, produce results heretofore hardly dreamed about. Research in the future will probably grow along these lines and will be conducted by diverse specialists who attempt deliberately to correlate their findings.

Many scientific workers are afraid to indulge themselves in a little loose thinking (not wishful thinking) lest they be considered unscientific. There is no harm in loose thinking if one knows what one is doing; a little wild thinking may stimulate creative trends. This wild thinking must not permanently displace facts or be interpreted as such. These extensions of thought which are not scientific but speculative and imaginative must be followed by more rigid thinking to establish the basic facts of a background on which to advance and create. But, if one studies the history of science, one will find that every science has been characterized by two aspects; viz., a loose thinking period followed by a strictly rigid one, the whole moving forward in repetitions of these two in cycles.

The factor of the creative imagination, out of which working hypotheses and techniques are constructed, is important. Many are too fearful of making mistakes, which reminds me of what was said about the great Danish sculptor, Thorwaldsen, who when found weeping by the side of his latest statue was asked the reason for his sorrow. He replied that he could detect no fault in the creation, it was perfect and therefore he knew that his imagination was in decay.

We need much common sense but do we want so much common sense in research? Why not some uncommon sense once in a while? I doubt whether common sense discovers anything very astonishing. It is a great help, it cuts out a lot of underbrush of wildly growing thoughts, but it is the uncommon sense which should receive some encouragement.

We must obtain more qualified people to work in psychiatry, and to think about our problems. Perhaps there is something to be said in favor of the project type of research versus the talented individual who goes his own way. I am aware of the arguments in favor of the genius and the talented individual worker who is said to be worth a dozen of the average type, the one individual who makes the discoveries and leads the way. However, there might be some virtue in a mass attack such as is used in industrial research where skillful men adequately supported are obtained to attack a given problem. They are not sparing of funds in some of the large industrial organizations to solve mechanical problems. Granting that this kind of a problem in physics or chemistry is different because variables are usually less numerous than in biological problems, the method might nevertheless work more often in biology than we have suspected. The biological scientist is not particularly receptive to the idea of this mass attack, of mass research, but provided the right men are obtained for the given task I fail to see why it should not be applied to some of our puzzling questions. As before mentioned, biological research requires a different orientation, a different approach, and a different variety of thinking from those applied in physics and chemistry where the variables are less numerous. Moreover, statistical analysis is less effectively operative; many statistics built up in experimental psychology and psychiatry are composed of doubtful experimental material. When the material is doubtful, statistics can be of little help. Statistics now help us only in terms of the units. Groups of individuals will not be handled very well in psychiatric statistics until we have much more information on personality types.

We are always looking for and trying to take advantage of "forked road" situations. We now have such an opportunity in the study of the different varieties of shock therapy which are being applied to all kinds of psychiatric patients. Some treated patients improve, others recover temporarily; in some the usual period of disorder is shortened, while others show no improvement. These varied reactions create a "forked road" situation for research which should give us the opportunity to study and attempt to ascertain whether these results indicate differences in physical constitution, differences in early experiences, training, personality organization, or some other group of factors. Full advantage has not been taken of this opportunity although some investigations are being made along these lines in certain centers, but among sets of workers there is as yet no concerted effort and no uniformity in the selection of material, in the application of the techniques, nor in the criteria set up to estimate the final results. It is characteristic of psychiatric research for someone to select a group of patients grouped under a collective name like "schizophrenia" on which to conduct a piece of work. The results obtained are doubted by someone else who selects for himself what seems to be a similar group of patients and obtains different results. They are in fact not using the same material. Their focus is on the group diagnosis and they neglect the more important individual differences within the group. That is one reason for a lack of accord in psychiatric research, but it is something that can be easily corrected with a little cooperative effort and with a clearer recognition of the difficulty.

Psychiatrists are frequently criticized openly for the manner in which they approach their problems, for the methods they use in obtaining their facts, and for the way in which they interpret their findings. Usually these criticisms are not in keeping with the facts and are made by those who are unaware of the nature or size of the riddle to be solved.

In conclusion, it may be said that there are indications that we should proceed in psychiatric research with some attempt, first, to synthesize and coordinate the facts already known in the different fields of biological science; second, to have a more painstaking selection of those working objectives which will allow the application of more than one type of scientific discipline to a specific problem; third, to train properly a selected personnel; fourth, to promote the basic sciences in order that they may expand their knowledge at the peripheries of their respective interests; and last, but by no means least, to organize adequate financial aid with which to support the efforts.

There are already some signs that the future evolution in psychiatric research will progress in these trends and eventually contribute toward lightening the burden imposed upon society by the ever-increasing disorders of the mind.

PART III

PSYCHIATRY IN THE TRAINING, EXPERIENCE
AND EDUCATION OF THE INDIVIDUAL

Introduction to Part III

By ORUS R. YODER, M.D.

Medical Superintendent, Ypsilanti State Hospital. Member of the Committee on the Conference on Psychiatry

PSYCHIATRY IS no longer the art of observing and directing people who are suffering from some serious mental disorder, but it has gone from the mental hospital to preventive programs in child guidance, school and college health clinics, family adjustment centers, into courts and even into the churches.

This Session (Part III of this volume) deals with that phase of psychiatry which is a matter of personal relationship and enables an individual to get along with his fellowmen in the school, the church and the home.

A healthy mind and an unhealthy mind both have the same source. It is not difficult to educate an individual to use a mental disorder to solve his social problems.

The personality of the child is the combination of his heredity, his intelligence, his physical condition and his environment. These are the tools he has with which to reach his goal.

Parents carry on an educational program until the child is about the age of six. During these years he develops a pattern of thinking and feeling. When he is old enough, the teacher assumes a certain amount of responsibility in directing this personality. We hope the teacher will have a program not only for his collective group but also for the individual. The teacher will find some with an emotional life which has been badly twisted by a poor home situation or an unhealthy and improper educational plan instituted by the parents.

With a marked increase of juvenile crime during this war

149

period, the message of the church must not be forgotten. Many homes are broken down, school facilities are over-taxed, recreational and social programs are abandoned. What we need in addition to an education program both in the home and in the school is a return to the practice of religion.

The most important thing a psychiatrist, a teacher, a clergyman, can do is to make an earnest effort to secure a sympathetic understanding of the relationship between the conduct of young people and their environment, this environment having been created by parents and a society in which they must find their happiness. If we can do this it will go far in helping men and women become mature, self-reliant and efficient human beings.

Psychiatry and Education

By TEMPLE BURLING, M.D.

Director, Providence Child Guidance Clinic

PSYCHIATRY AND PERSONALITY AND INTERPERSONAL RELATIONSHIPS • RELATION OF
PSYCHIATRY TO SCHOOLING • TRAINING OF SKILLS • ACULTURATION • GROWTH
OF PERSONALITY • DIVIDING LINE BETWEEN PSYCHIATRY AND EDUCATION • AMPU-
TATIONS OF PERSONALITY • PSYCHIATRIC PRINCIPLES IN SCHOOL SYSTEM • CAUSES
OF BEHAVIOR • BY-PRODUCTS OF EDUCATION • UNCONSCIOUS INDOCTRINATION •
TECHNIQUES IN CHILD MANAGEMENT IN CLASS ROOM • PROBLEM CHILDREN •
PROBLEM TEACHERS • OCCUPATIONAL HAZARDS OF TEACHING • AUTHORITARIAN
ATTITUDE • THE TEACHING PROFESSION • METHODS OF TEACHING AND SUBJECT
MATTER • THE GROWTH OF THE TOTAL CHILD

THIS TITLE is open to many interpretations since both terms are used in widely different meanings by various practitioners in both fields. We can narrow psychiatry to mean merely the treatment of the mentally ill, particularly in mental hospitals. Such a meaning would afford little that has significance for education though it is true that a mental hospital is not unlike an educational institution, as is attested by the frequency with which patients speak of the hospital grounds as "campus." If we broaden the meaning to include the prevention of mental illness, its connection with education is closer.

We have some knowledge and considerable pertinent speculation as to the causes of the major mental illnesses, but I think it would be a very bold psychiatrist who would say that we are yet in a position to prevent mental illness by any educational program. We can trace back with a patient the forces in his home which have made him what he is today, but we can only through therapy of the parents prevent similar parents from producing similar injuries on growing children.

Psychiatry, however, has a much wider aspect than simply

151

the prevention and treatment of mental illness. The very titles of the papers at this Conference are evidence that to this group, at any rate, the field is much larger. I take it that we are all agreed that the psychiatry we are talking about is a body of knowledge of the growth of personality and of interpersonal relationships, and the application of that knowledge to the amelioration of the disturbances to which they are subject. It is about the relationship of that psychiatry to education that I want to talk.

It is also necessary to be clear as to what we mean by education, for it also has as many different interpretations as does psychiatry. In the first place education is both formal and informal.

One can consider under the term all the influences which adults bring to bear upon youth either purposefully or as a by-product of their other activities. Or one can focus one's attention on organized, purposive activities, particularly schooling. One would so quickly get lost in the wilderness if he attempted to cover the former that I shall focus my attention on the relationship of psychiatry to schooling though I recognize that one cannot make any hard and fast line between what goes on in the classroom and what goes on elsewhere.

Even after narrowing "education" to schooling it still has widely varied meanings. It can be looked upon as training—the development of manual and intellectual skills which presumably will be needed in adult living. This is a very important goal of education and one which in recent years has been somewhat neglected. The complaint of our Army leaders that the service men coming to them are not adequately trained in mathematics for participation in modern warfare is one evidence of this neglect. One reason for such neglect is that educators in recent years have tended to place more and more emphasis on another aspect, the controversial one of indoctrination. A more polite term is aculturation, the implanting in children of the customs, beliefs and ideals which are held to be important by adults of the culture group. A large part of this, of course, is done unconsciously in informal education but the schools have always attempted to participate in the effort, with, it must be confessed, rather indifferent success.

A third way of looking at education, which is not an alternative to these two, but which includes them in a wider perspective is that education is the sum of the forces favoring the growth of personality. This growth is forwarded principally by two things, providing intellectual and aesthetic nourishment for the growing child, and providing group associations appropriate to his stage of development. Perhaps those two are really one.

This last definition of education arrives on common ground with the definition of psychiatry which I like to use, for both deal with the growth of personality through interpersonal relationships. In fact, with these definitions it is impossible to draw any dividing line between psychiatry and education. Their goals are identical, to enable immature personalities to reach maturity. Or, to put it another way, both psychotherapy and education have as their purpose the curing of children of their childishness. Psychotherapy attempts to cure children who are chronologically adult, whereas education deals with children whose chronological and personality ages are approximately equal. Psychotherapy is needed where there has been some hitch in the growth processes and barriers to growth need to be removed, whereas education attempts to facilitate a normal rate of growth in individuals who have not met with frustrations. But no two personalities grow at the same rate and there is no definable standard of normal rate of growth. It is fair therefore to say that education is one end of a continuum and psychotherapy the other.

I am talking about education as an ideal—what about education in reality? Its purpose is to supply the optimum conditions for personality growth. Do our schools really do this? What follows may at first blush sound like severe criticism of our teachers, but it is not. In the first place, children are the product of their total education, and not merely of their schooling. In the second place, as you will find if you bear with me to the end, I am criticizing the social climate which prevents the schools from performing their function, rather than the teachers in the schools. And in the third place, the shortcomings of education are a reflection on our own failure to make our professional insights widely effective in improving many aspects of interpersonal relationships—a failure to meet our professional obligation of citizenship. There are several causes for this failure, such as the satisfaction of being practitioners of a mystery and an ivory tower attitude which has kept us from real awareness of the way the mass of society thinks and feels about human nature, but the most important cause is that when we attempt to influence the behavior of groups we make just those errors which we so quickly criticize in the efforts of others to modify the behavior of individuals. We exhort and we admonish and we even scold and we ignore the dynamic interplay of personalities which is just as significant in the group as in the consulting room. We have developed our tact so highly in one unique sort of situation that in a group we become conspicuously tactless.

To go back to the question, do our schools really reach their goal? By and large they fall very short of the objective. Anyone who visits even better than average schools, going from kindergarten and stopping in each classroom up through junior or senior high school, cannot fail to be struck with the steady loss in color and spontaneity which he observes as he ascends the grades. Instead of growth in personality, in too many cases we see amputations of personality. If one allows himself to recognize the contrast between the potential wealth of personality which is housed in the school building with what actually is finding expression and a chance to grow within those walls, a visit to even a better-than-average school is a most depressing experience. After such a visit I have more than once found myself muttering "After six thousand years wouldn't you think that we could have found something better to do with children than to put them into school?"

This loss is very decidedly the concern of the psychiatrist, for we are more and more setting ourselves up as guardians of personality. Does our profession have anything to help the schools fulfill their functions more adequately? We can contribute in two ways, through psychiatric principles and through the actual presence of psychiatrists in the school system.

When I put down the psychiatric principles which can be helpful in the classroom they seem so platitudinous that I almost hesitate to bring them to you. But in spite of all our own propaganda efforts, they are ignored over and over again in the classroom. The first is, of course, that behavior, whether desirable or undesirable, has discoverable causes and is not the result of spontaneous generation. This has become so much a matter of second nature in our reactions that it is almost impossible for us to realize that the majority of people who deal with children still think of badness as an entity. If they could learn to think of it as a process it would be a long step forward, and if they could recognize that it is a process in interpersonal relations, and not within the child, it would be revolutionary. The second principle is equally obvious, that one should always endeavor to discover the causes of undesirable behavior, and treat them rather than the symptoms themselves. A slight shift in the point of view brings out a third principle, that the goals, both conscious and unconscious, for which the child is striving, are of greater significance in deciding how to handle him than the particular behavior he engages in. The illustration of the effort to gain attention through a temper tantrum is hoary with age, and yet I have more than once in recent months seen it come as a sudden illumination to intelligent people.

A fourth element which should be common to both psychiatry and education and is so important that I give it a paragraph by itself is a deep respect for personality.

A fifth principle which is not quite so painfully obvious as these, is a recognition of the importance of the by-products of education, a realization that whenever two or more personalities inter-react a great deal happens outside the main thread of action. For example, a very important factor in education both for good and bad has been the association of the children themselves on the playground and in the classroom, but until relatively recent years this was simply a by-product of the fact that it was cheaper to gather children together and put them under one teacher than to attempt to tutor them all individually. And in many schools the fact that children interact is still regarded as an annoying complication of the educational process rather than a vital part of it.

Another by-product which teachers fail to recognize, or recognize only occasionally, is the role of unconscious indoctrination. A few years ago there was quite a furor over the question as to whether or not schools should indoctrinate. And the whole subject was fought out on the assumption that teachers could make a choice. The fact that unconscious indoctrination inevitably is going on all the time was almost lost sight of in the debate. A third by-product of which teachers are very little aware is that with every successfully implanted positive attitude an unconscious negative attitude is also implanted. A full realization of this truth would turn education upside down.

A sixth psychiatric principle which would be helpful to the classroom teacher is the realization of the dynamic nature of all interpersonal relationships. Where education is looked upon as training it is too often assumed that the teacher's skills are somehow detached from the teacher himself and that they in turn act on a child who is, during the training experience, divorced from his own personality. The fact that his personality crops up when all he is supposed to be doing is learning long division is regarded as more or less reprehensible on his part. The dynamic element in the classroom interpersonal complex most overlooked is what corresponds to counter-transference on the part of the teacher. One phase of this, the teacher's pet, has always been recognized. But it is much more important for the teacher to realize that the personalities of her children cannot move toward maturity unless she truly desires them to. If she does, everything else will automatically follow, and if she does not, not all the progressive techniques in the world, no substitution of chairs and tables for screwed-down desks, no activities program, no nature walks, or rhythm orchestras, or any of the rest of it, will set her children free.

These are the things which a psychiatrist feels would be

most helpful, but they are not the things which teachers ask for first from a psychiatrist. The first of the teacher's requests, and it is a legitimate one, is some systematic theory of personality. This has its dangers. When a teacher first acquires one or another of the rather heady theories of personality structure, she is in danger of riding a hobby, but the theory can be a useful tool in organizing her thoughts about the children whom she is caring for.

The other thing which teachers ask for, and which we psychiatrists as a group are extremely reluctant to give, is techniques in child management. Teachers have a right to ask this of us, particularly of the psychiatrist in the school system, for sooner or later they will see him take to his office a child who has been quite impossible and in some mysterious way modify his behavior, not only with striking completeness but with striking suddenness. They have a right to ask how it was done. The answer that the psychiatrist is able to work this apparent miracle through his use of his total personality, guided by his entire psychiatric knowledge, is not calculated to satisfy the teacher. She still wants to know what he did. Dr. Gilbert Rich of Milwaukee, in a staff conference, once said a very wise thing about giving specific advice for handling concrete, untoward behavior. He presented a very unruly, unpleasant youngster and at the conclusion he said, "I gave the mother a few simple rules for modifying the boy's behavior. Of course, I recognized that his behavior is based on the fact that he has a sense of rejection—the thing that will cure him is to be loved. But I do not think he can be loved until he has become lovable." Some guiding rules for the handling of children will help the teacher more quickly to develop enough confidence to enable her to give her children a sense of freedom.

The psychiatrist who is called upon by teachers for techniques in dealing with children should do two things to guard against his advice doing more harm than good. In the first place, he should always earnestly attempt to make clear the principles back of the technique, and in the second place, he should recognize that handling a child in the presence of twenty to thirty other children is a very different matter from handling the child alone in an office. The things that he can do the classroom teacher cannot possibly do and until he is very thoroughly familiar with classroom problems he would best avoid giving advice at all. I think that is one of the places where psychiatrists when called on for help in education have made mistakes over and over again. They have attempted to translate the techniques of the consulting office directly into the classroom with only the vaguest notions of what classroom problems are.

The psychiatrist who is connected with a school system has other contributions to make. Of course, the first one is obvious—the direct treatment of problem children. This is of value but it just scrapes the surface, and if that were all the school psychiatrist could do, it is doubtful in my mind that schools would be justified in employing one. Psychotherapy is more analogous to major surgery than it is to vaccination, and schools do not supply surgical treatment for their children.

Almost equally obvious, and a role that has been emphasized in recent years, is the treatment of problem teachers. When the function of the psychiatrist is presented to the school in that way, of course the possibility of his doing anything is almost nil. I once worked with a superintendent who continued, in spite of all my efforts, to call teachers into his office and say, "I think you'd better consult Dr. Burling." I did not make much progress with those cases. However, it is possible for a psychiatrist who becomes genuinely a part of the school system to implant points of view and interpretations in the course of his casual contacts. In a sense what I am advocating is that the psychiatrist attached to the school use purposefully what is ordinarily unconscious indoctrination. As time goes on, the psychiatrist becomes more and more able to do this. He is an embodiment, a living symbol to the teachers of the psychiatric point of view. When problems are presented to him, he automatically begins attacking them from this point of view and, in consequence, the teachers imperceptibly learn to think in similar terms.

After the psychiatrist has become a real part of the school system, he is in a position to discuss with the policy-making members of the faculty many aspects of the school program which are not at first sight of psychiatric significance but which in one way or another will facilitate or impede the growth of children.

I have postponed mentioning until now what I think is the most important contribution of the psychiatric point of view to the whole school program and that is a clear recognition that the personality of the teacher outweighs everything else for good or bad in the classroom experience of the child. I know of one teacher who, by all standard practices, should be super-annuated. She is very fuzzy in her thinking. She is dowdy and her classroom is in a degree of disorder which would set many teachers' teeth on edge. But she has never lost her enthusiastic surprise at the capabilities of children. She loves them and she respects them and a year in her room is a year in growth. But she is unusual—she has not succumbed to the occupational hazards of teaching. These hazards are serious ones and I believe it is in them that the inadequacies of our school program are to be found. Though partly inherent in the classroom situation itself, they are aggravated by community attitudes and the social setting of the schools. There is little that we as psychiatrists can do about them directly. But they are things which all citizens interested in youth should be aware of.

The first of these is a hazard that we have been hearing much of in other situations, the lack of a loyal opposition. The classroom teacher is in an authoritative position. She is backed by the school law and the attendance officer and behind them is the State Reform School. It takes a person with a very deeply rooted respect for personality not to succumb to the temptations of this position and to use authority in inappropriate situations. I have found teachers over and over again hampered in their efforts to work out a cooperative program with parents because they find it so easy to slip into a dogmatic authoritarian relationship toward them. In talking with the teachers themselves and endeavoring to get them out of that attitude,

I have more than once said something like this, "When a teacher has an opportunity to discuss a child with a parent and comes to me to get advice, the question that she invariably puts to me first is 'What shall I tell the parent?' When a social worker is in a similar situation, her first question is, 'What more do you want me to find out?' " I once asked a member of the faculty of a school of social work how they succeeded in training social workers who are relatively free from an authoritarian attitude. She said, "Well, in the first place, one who has a dictatorial trend is more apt to go into teaching, whereas one who wants to work cooperatively on a problem is more apt to to go into social work. In the second place, we social workers find in very short order that if we take a dogmatic stand we do not have any clients, whereas the teacher can do it every day in the school year and the truant officer brings her charges back."

The second occupational hazard is association with immature minds. This could be very greatly ameliorated by a change in community attitude but by and large teachers have altogether too little opportunity to compensate for their working-day job of furnishing almost all the stimulus and receiving very little in return, by contact with invigorating intelligences in their hours free from duty.

Teachers are a group apart and it is very difficult to break the barriers down. One reason is that adults carry over into adult life something of the fear and discomfort which they once felt in the presence of their own teachers, and they compensate for that by laughing at teachers and thinking of them as a bit queer. Another reason is our traditional attitude that teaching is what one does until one does something else. Formerly, when we used more men, one taught until he could establish himself in a profession. Now one teaches until one gets married, or one gives up hope and goes on teaching. Teaching a short time is a stop-gap; teaching a long time is an acknowledgment of having missed the bus. In all too many instances as a result teachers enter the profession with very little enthusiasm, or lose it very quickly. The refusal of many school boards to employ married women aggravates the situation. There are, of course, some real social and organizational objections to the employment of married women. But refusal to employ them has two harmful results which, in my thinking, outweigh all other considerations. The first is that by and large marriage removes just those women who have the richest personalities to give to the pupils. The second is that it crystallizes and makes explicit the social attitude that teaching is not really a profession but is just the next best thing.

Another occupational hazard is the lack of a sustaining professional ideal and philosophy. Educational leaders would challenge that statement fiercely. The large educational conventions and the periodical literature of education are filled with discussions of educational goals and the philosophy of education. But the fact remains that this has not permeated the rank and file of teachers. A very large proportion of them is just teaching. The truism that they are handling the most precious of our national resources somehow has not been made living to them. The leaders in educational thought are brimming over with enthusiastic pride in their profession and its opportunities but somewhere this stream of enthusiasm just trickles away into the sands.

The fourth hazard is of relatively recent origin and we ourselves are probably partly responsible for it. It is more serious in the secondary schools than in the primary. It is the emphasis on methods of teaching to the neglect of subject matter. After all, one important goal in teaching is that children be taught things. And there are too many teachers well-grounded in pedagogic methods but only half-informed about the subjects which they teach. This has unfortunate results, beyond the mere fact that children come out of school half-trained and misinformed. It also stunts their personalities. Much of the growth of personality which is the fundamental goal of education is better achieved by indirection than when aimed at directly. It is well that educators be consciously aware that their concern is with the total child and his growth. But too frequently that is translated practically into efforts which are analogous to stimulating the growth of a plant by weights and pulleys designed to lengthen the stem. A teacher who knows his subject thoroughly and is on fire with enthusiasm for it is more stimulating to the total growth of the child than one who has been so busy learning about education and complexes that he has not had time to learn physics or geometry or to be carried away by the intoxication of poetry. A by-product of enthusiasm for subject matter is almost always an enthusiastic respect for the young minds which are engaged in absorbing it. The ideal of the child-centered school has been a very valuable one. Certainly everything which is done in the school must be justified by benefits to the children. But when this touchstone is honestly and intelligently used, it will emphasize the fact that if subjects were better taught children, too, would be better taught.

Psychiatry in the Training, Experience and Education of the Individual: Infancy, Pre-School and Elementary Schools

By LESLIE B. HOHMAN, M.D.

*Assistant Visiting Psychiatrist and Dispensary Physician, Phipps
Psychiatric Clinic, The Johns Hopkins Hospital; Associate
Psychiatrist, The Johns Hopkins University*

PHILOSOPHY OF EDUCATION • POSSIBILITIES OF TRAINING AND CHANGING HUMAN
MATERIAL • ADULTS A PRODUCT OF EDUCATION • NEED OF CONSCIOUS DIRECTION •
PRINCIPLE OF INTEREST • SKILL READINESS • DOCTRINE OF STATIONARY INTELLI-
GENCE QUOTIENTS • HABIT TRAINING • THE HARD WORK OF TEACHING AND TRAIN-
ING • NEW TECHNIQUES OF EMOTIONAL EXPRESSION • "SOCIAL GAINS" PHILOSOPHY
• THE BENEFITS OF WAR • IDEALS OF USEFULNESS • BETTER PEOPLE IN A BETTER
WORLD

T HE CENTRAL theme of my theory about child training is
that as the twig is bent so is the tree inclined. I believe that
the bending is done by the environmental milieu, and that we,
the adults, are most largely responsible for what happens to
our future adults. I hold that habit training is of paramount
importance in all phases of childhood development and the
transformation of childhood patterns into adult patterns. I
hold this to be true for emotional and total personality reactions.

Each theorist finds evidence for his own point of view. The
anthropologists seem to me to be presenting material now
which lends great force to my position. Boas has pointed out
that cultural attitudes can be transformed so radically that
you could convert the most war-like of Norsemen into the

peace-loving Norwegians without any change in blood lines. Margaret Meade has clearly demonstrated that the aggressiveness or passivity of populations can be seen as the result of a definite training program beginning very early in infancy. She has said that ten infants of ten different cultures would be indistinguishable to her at birth, but that by the end of six months she could tell you by merely handling the infants to what tribe they belonged. Her observations on the training of very young, primitive children in jealousy, or passivity, or aggressiveness, is to me just as strikingly reproduced in our more complicated structure.

May I state early that because I believe that habit training is of prime importance, I do not wish to deny differences in native endowment and inborn differences in emotional dispositions. I believe that the inborn equipment sets limits to trainability but does not limit the possibility of very wide transformations of native endowment. I do not wish to be understood to deny the instinctive creativeness or spontaneity of individuals but I do believe that we can, by the control of the forces which play on children, force this forward-going impulse into early and effective flowering or choke it so that it dies in the bud.

It seems to me implicit in any philosophy of education that there is enormous and varied possibility of training and changing human material, or else why do we have schools and keep struggling for better schools? It is because all of us know that how we educate children is going to determine what kind of adults we are going to get.

Without being able to define accurately the historic causes of individualistic philosophy, I am convinced that we established an overwhelming fear of being caught in the role of director of human life. We became so fearful of repression and stifling of impulse that we neglected a very simple but very important piece of knowledge. When we do not consciously direct or train, training and direction forces are being beamed at the child just the same. We may not be forcing religion on a child, but cynical parental, or societal, attitudes are training the growing child just as effectively as if they were consciously used. The lack of positive attitudes in directing only leaves the field to negative and unrecognized and unorganized influences.

This doctrine of no directing has led us into curious and, I think, dangerous educational theories. The principle of interest as the guiding influence in education seems to me to be part of this individualistic non-interfering philosophy. I frankly do not trust interest as a safe principle. Interest too frequently means immediate interest, and what good is interest if it is not implemented securely and soundly by tools and work habits? How many people like to do the hard and difficult thing? Yet the hard and difficult techniques which are necessary for the living out of later interests must be learned many years before the interest arises. It is too late at twenty for the garage mechanic to get the tool subjects for the late arising interest in airplane or automobile designing. Every day I see men with grammar school education about to enter the new army, wanting to be airplane cadets. By endowment they have much more than grammar or high school capacity but interest came too late to have been properly implemented. Hard work, drill, must be taught at least in part when interest is lacking.

Furthermore the development of skills by the hard way is in itself a stimulus to interest. All one has to do to prove the point is to watch nursery school children, when they have been limited in following out their casual or random moment-to-moment shifts in interest and forced or helped to build or construct something which requires work. The joy in the learned new skill is clear demonstration that we come to be interested in what we have accomplished the hard way. The ensuing reward of interest is as important as, or more important than, the original interest. And only in this way can you establish the attitude or habit of doing those things which necessarily require dull drill and techniques.

We have a somewhat sorry spectacle today of what pure interest direction provides in the way of childhood avocation.

Movies, radio serials, and comic strips are where childhood immediate interest directs children and that is where they go. Nobody wanted this for children, but nobody seems to want to force children into learning to do the things which will teach them to entertain themselves. The overuse of the interest principle seems to me to fail in another respect: interests in children are often multiple and conflicting. The adult must help children to limit interests to those which have been deemed worthy by adults. Still another marked difficulty of the interest philosophy is that the child tends to do only what it tends to do well. But this easily leads to very lopsided and distorted education. The pre-school child says, "I don't like to do that," and if left alone does not learn to catch or throw a bean bag. He may be interested, especially if he lacks native skills, in continuing to make jelly pies in the sand box. Before long, however, he is not part of the group, because at the moment he was not interested in learning to throw a bean bag. He refused to do that which he was not interested in learning to do, and perhaps had little native skill for. Nevertheless he is not part of the group because he lacks learned skill. The same child may be interested in talking and may be able to compel the interest of adults in sophisticated talk, but before long he is disliked for his incessant talk and his inability to get along in school where only talk does not get him ahead with his school work.

The general talk about skill readiness is part of the same fallacy. When the child is interested in reading, he will begin to read. So runs the story. When his interest dictates, he will learn arithmetic. So says the theory. This is true only if he wants to learn reading and arithmetic at about the same time that most children are doing it. Otherwise he drops behind and before long he loses the late emerging interest because he is in the second grade while his friends are in the fourth grade. He must get his place in the sun by competing in other fields where he can meet his age group on equal grounds, and we are likely to see him developing big-shot leadership, or playing hookey, or developing his skills in athletics, because he lacked the present interest in learning the skills which would keep him abreast of his age group.

Interest readiness ties in with some present day ideas of growth which I think tend to stultify our attitude about trainability. When we discovered that childhood capacities of one sort or another cannot be trained until a certain degree of growth and maturation has been reached, we began to believe that maturation itself was the guiding principle for education. This child is not ready to read because his reading ability must wait on maturation. Johnny is left alone at six or seven because he does not learn to read as readily as his next-door neighbor. Too many children are ready all too late to learn reading or arithmetic. This seems to me not to be a signal to wait for Johnny's readiness, but is good reason for giving early and more intensive training in reading. Without tool subjects Johnny is lost. What good if he is interested in history or social sciences if he cannot read the book which will instruct him?

We have assumed that growth limits the amount of intelligence a child can have. The doctrine of stationary intelligence quotients is being constantly refuted, and yet too many educators, because of an I.Q. are unwilling to give a child a chance. A parent recently was told that his son was not Latin material. Yet six weeks' coaching put this boy well up in his Latin class and he now maintains his Latin position in the upper third of his class. The same boy was at the age of ten discharged from a very fine boys' school because he was, by the diagnosis of the school and its very good psychiatrist, an incurable psychopath. He may have been a psychopath, but his stepfather has made the community in which the boy lives admit that he is one of the best boys in his school. This stepfather did not accept the dictum that growth was stopped and constitution limited. He decided to use habit training. He rewarded good behavior and punished bad behavior, and he found the appropriate rewards and the appropriate punishments. The training was only as rigid as the circumstances demanded. He accepted the idea that he would force interest and readiness without waiting for maturation which he was told was never coming.

I believe that early childhood is the best place to work on the transformation of patterns which appear poor or unhealthy as they begin to emerge. We had an interesting example in our nursery school—aggression in a three and one-half year old boy, who came to us with much charm, good interest, and forcefulness which he was using as first class ability to bully. In the nursery school group he used his bullying for what he thought effective purpose. But we saw to it that no child had to yield to this bullying. Without our presence he would have forced the issue and would have won with it, and would have gained the temporary rewards of success. But after a short period when nobody would play his games, because they did not have to accept his force, he turned on the charm and his capacity to interest the others, and before long became the leader of the group. What we did was to force him to convert his whole approach. We let him use his energy only in leadership and blocked it as pure aggression. Once in a while he would assert the ugly aggressiveness, only to have it met by failure. When he found he could not get a kicking foot loose, he turned on the charm and then we made it easy for life to become interesting again. Even his mother was persuaded to stop letting tantrums get rewards.

Parents are constantly being blocked in their training by believing that growth has progressed more slowly than it really does. Mothers are never able to recover from the startling fact that Jane can unbutton her coat. She is always surprised to learn that Jane is now ready also to button her buttons. Edith has never fed herself a mouthful at home but she comes to the nursery school and feeds herself completely without any help. These are tiny fragments of behavior but they are to my mind the stuff out of which the big ones are made.

Over and over one sees children stuck at the level of repetitive activity and not encouraged to turn this repetitive impulse into more complicated and constructive work. Color designs in beads and blocks are done to the amazement of the parent who did not think that the child could understand. The child frequently insists that it does not understand, because he gets satisfactions in other directions, and the parent is convinced that he must wait for growth. This static attitude about growth lets us limit unnecessarily the learning of little children. The world is too ready to admit the limitations of growth and accepts mediocrity in development because teaching and training, as Dr. Burling has just pointed out, are hard work and cannot be made as comfortable and easy as letting the child drift.

We feel that emotional patterns can be converted, and can be made to grow or wither by the same process of habit training. Tommy, aged three and one-half, is a very sensitive, intelligent, over-serious and hard working, but a somewhat unhappy little boy. Whenever anything untoward happens, Tommy's face puckers up and tears are near the surface. Tommy's mother is so anxious to have him sent in the right direction that she is miserable that something is wrong when Tommy looks unhappy. She promptly sets about trying to correct it. We are less sympathetic and do not regard Tommy's kind of sensitiveness as desirable. We do not try to make the world over for Tommy but we ask Tommy to make a new attitude toward untoward events. No reward of sympathy for tears or solemnity. Each day Tommy is asked who is a happy boy and Tommy is asked to smile. In not too many weeks whenever we look at Tommy we get a smile and we get Tommy's joking statement "Tommy's a happy boy." Tommy is a serious person but he is a much less unhappy person. He is learning new techniques of emotional expression. If Tommy's cooperative mother continues to follow our lead, Tommy will stop using sensitiveness and will use smiling joyousness instead of ready tearfulness.

And now to the influences of war on these little folk. If we do not have bombing, I think the effect upon young children is going to be the one bright spot of the terrible world catastrophe. The post-war cynicism with its abandonment of all kinds of patriotism, its rampant individualism, empty entertainment, the philosophy that nothing counts or matters, is disappearing from the cultural pattern. Democracy is ceasing to be only a word which nobody thought worth anything. "Social gains" philosophy, with the idea that everybody in our society is important has come alive as a principle of our democracy. Children are learning from the attitudes of parents that something in the world is again worth fighting for. Piddling and frittering away time and energy are stopping. Working has again become a good ideal. Children are going to be again allowed the right to work in their own homes and take on some family responsibility. They cannot be transported any longer all over creation to a movie or a dancing class or a theater party, etc. Children will learn how to entertain themselves and make their own pleasures. The many drives such as those for scrap collection, and saving money for war stamps for the common good will give children a sense of importance in participating in the work and effort of the whole group. Errand running and table setting and dish washing will come back into fashion and work habits and a sense of responsibility will be the children's gain.

They may soon learn much from the fact that those who need will receive from the group rather than those who can afford. That will help build ideals of common need and common service. All the talk in the world would not be as effective as these lessons the children are going to be learning day by day through hard necessity and example and attitude of parents and teachers. Children are likely to develop much better eating and food habits. "I don't like that," or "I don't want this," will yield to hunger for the available foods. Parents will learn that children have much more capacity than they ever suspected. The shortening of the time left for education now that school will probably terminate at eighteen, will probably make all education proceed with greater earnestness and more work. We may even get to the place that Italian Renaissance children achieved, of being really educated at sixteen. We have tended for some years to infantilize children and the coming adults. The war will stop that. Children will probably be more sober but they will again have the ideal of usefulness. I am so convinced of the indelible and lasting effect of habit training, both in the emotional sphere and acquisition of skills, and general personality development that I feel that these young ones today may be better people in a better world—when through the terrible travail we have again won the battle of democracy.

Psychiatry in the Training, Experience and Education of the Individual: Secondary Schools and Colleges

By FREDERICK H. ALLEN, M.D.

Medical Director, Philadelphia Child Guidance Clinic; Assistant Professor of Psychiatry, University of Pennsylvania

POSITIVE EMPHASIS IN PSYCHIATRY • BROADER SCOPE INCLUDING CHILDHOOD AND ADOLESCENCE • CONFLICTS, PROBLEMS, DILEMMAS OF YOUTH • PSYCHIATRIC PERSPECTIVE • POTENTIALITIES OF YOUTH FOR HEALTH • PLACE IN ARMED SERVICES • MOLDING OF THOUGHT AND SOCIAL ACTION • REALITIES OF LIVING • SPONTANEITY OF THE PERSON • FULFILLMENT OF A SELF • MORE POSITIVE AND CREATIVE PSYCHIATRY IN SERVICE OF YOUTH • BELIEF IN CAPACITY OF YOUTH • PLATO'S ALLEGORY OF THE CAVE • CAVERNS OF THE PAST • THE ILLUMINATED WORLD OF PRESENT EVENTS AND REAL PEOPLE • PSYCHIATRY A POSITIVE SOCIAL FORCE

PSYCHIATRY HAS passed through many phases in its development as a medical and social science. It has moved away from the early preoccupation with constitution and structure but carried into its later period the value of these interests without, however, being shackled by them. Growing from this broadened base, this discipline flourished as a more human science in our mental hospitals where there has emerged a wider understanding of the pathology of human nature and the influences that cause sickness. From this emphasis which has given a more dynamic understanding of emotional pathology, psychiatry has been moving on to a more positive interest in human nature and the means whereby individuals achieve healthy and responsible patterns of behavior. With this more positive emphasis, psychiatry has developed its services for children and youth.

172

This widening sphere of psychiatry was inevitable. In one sense this broader scope, which included youth and the adolescent period, is the result of greater enlightenment in our whole culture; in another sense psychiatry has created much of this enlightenment. The wider contributions of various schools of psychological thought, psychoanalytic, Gestalt, behavioristic and the scientific humanitarianism of pioneers in the modern era of psychiatry made it inevitable that psychiatry would have a broader service in the field of childhood and adolescence.

In pondering over what emphasis to give to the very broad scope of my title, I wondered what new orientations we are ready for and would be essential to enable this, the most human of scientific disciplines, to take its proper professional place in influencing the directions and accomplishments of the youth of tomorrow.

I have tried to answer for myself and to present to you, what psychiatry had to offer, not just to the individual who needs help, but to our schools, to our colleges, to industry, to teachers and educators who play such an important part in shaping the direction of the lives of boys and girls who are on the threshold of manhood and womanhood. Being no longer a child and yet not an adult focuses and accentuates many of the natural growth dilemmas, universal for this period of human development, which are brought to the clinical services,—the means of psychiatry through which its practitioners are brought into professional relations to the stresses and strains of this period. Here we see youth in conflict with authority and yet at the same time wanting and requiring a firm hand; youth maintaining an air of self-sufficiency in the face of anxiety and uncertainty; youth experimenting with newly developed functions; youth wondering what he will become and be in his new interpersonal relationships which come at this period, and how to maintain some of his idealisms and enthusiasms in a world of trouble and realness; youth holding to the home ties and trying at the same time to break away, youth intolerant of others and of "old-fashioned ideas," and yet maintaining a rigid type of conservatism. We see in these reactions, youth at the cross-road of his development with an awareness of having two selves; the one carved from his own experiences and reactions, the other shaped and related to the mother and father and other impinging cultural forces. Every adolescent, even more than in any other period of life, is confronted with the need to feel and affirm his own value as a person, a value that gives meaning to the various facets of his life.

Psychiatry in the position created by its professional knowledge and responsibilities does become a symbol in the eyes of those who need its services, of the enlightened world of the new for which youth is reaching. The question we must all face quite realistically is whether psychiatry has incorporated into its philosophy and professional practices a point of view about human nature that enables it to become such a symbol, not only for the individual but for a society that needs a more positive understanding of the adolescent period rather than one that merely points out the dangers and the uncertainties of this period of life.

What then are the elements in our psychiatric theory and practice which need a greater emphasis in order that this more positive note is to gain the ascendancy? Certainly there is an awareness of the need for these services as shown by the expansion of work in schools and colleges. The need is the evidence of wanting and requiring of psychiatry something more than a concern with the pathology of human nature, something which does more than explain the mental mechanisms operating to produce disturbances, which does more than merely understand and classify the pathological manifestations and just point out what is wrong.

Psychiatry has contributed a great deal to the knowledge of how and why young people get disturbed in their adolescent period, and real advances have been made in understanding the physical and emotional causes of the adolescents' difficulty. The very fact that psychiatry has made a contribution to the understanding of children and youth is evidence that it has moved out and beyond this emphasis which focuses too exclusively on what is and has been wrong. We realize particularly in our therapeutic activities that no one has ever been straightened out just by the fact that a psychiatrist knows what is wrong. It is what youth can be helped to do in his relation with a person having this knowledge and understanding that can lead to a more responsible utilization of their assets. The psychiatrist must be interested in what a patient *can* do and not just in what he cannot do, if he is to become an effective therapeutic influence. We need to shake ourselves loose from the narrower outlook which emerges when there is a too exclusive emphasis on the sickness of youth and gain the broader perspective which is concerned with the potentialities of youth, even as they are revealed in the disturbances that many show.

A simple illustration will bring this out in what I want to emphasize. An intelligent and physically mature, healthy girl from an intelligent family decides to go to college. She goes to a college of her own choice and within the first week writes panicky and anxious letters home saying she cannot stay. This is a common clinical situation with which every college psychiatrist is called in to work.

Psychiatry here has the opportunity to take two directions in the service to such a girl. A study of her background would have revealed that she had had a difficult time in making her place in high school, that she had been sheltered in a home which tried to help her by shielding her from some of the undue strains natural for the period; would have shown that she had had a close relation with her mother and had avoided making many new friends, because friendships "entangled" her in relationships she did not feel capable of handling. We would discover that she had a good high school experience in the end through borrowing on the confidence of family and sympathetic teachers. All this and much more has valid importance in the understanding of the background of a problem of this type. Where does it lead to and how does it affect the therapeutic services around the present problem? Is she to be seen only as a disturbed girl frightened by the separation from the "ties that bind," or is her disturbance also to be seen as her own effort to reach out for the new? Both factors are there, but psychiatry should come in through the opportunity which her distress has created and be the means through which this girl can gain a clearer and more confident feeling about the very strengths she is trying to get at. Her anxiety can be understood not just as the outgrowth of her past, but the evidence of her reaching out for a new use of herself. The question then is not so much as to whether this girl should stay in college or go home, but more one of helping her to arrive at a clearer and more confident feeling of what she is and wants. Even going home, with that emphasis, can become for this girl a way of gaining strength and not merely a returning to the old, and retreating into some of the things she is trying to move away from. Psychiatry needs this emphasis which has its understanding and orientation directed toward the potential strength of the individual person which may be obscured by the distress. Then it can stand as a symbol of the new for which youth is reaching. With the more positive emphasis, psychiatry can direct its services toward the reaching out, and not just to the evidences and causes of failure.

There is an immediate need and opportunity for psychiatry to make a positive professional contribution in the field of youth, and that is based not just on knowing what is wrong, but an interest in how things can become right. That is the matter of the eighteen- and nineteen-year-olds and their place in the armed services. The real issue here is *not* whether they should be drafted. The really professional responsibility here is to make available our knowledge about the nature of this period with its potentialities, its limitations and its wide variations, in order that our government may be helped to use, develop and preserve these abilities selectively, and help to define and utilize the conditions which will make this possible.

A sound professional contribution to this large social problem cannot be made by stressing the immaturity of youth and the danger of breakdown through premature separation from home ties. Nor can there be any further clarity through statements or points of view or emphases which say that because of their enthusiasms and quickness of thought and action they would make ideal soldiers. In this very split, one stresses their weakness and the other exaggerates their strength. Neither approaches or meets squarely the professional responsibility involved, which is to use our knowledge to define the needs and conditions most favorable, under the circumstances of war, which will enable these boys to become strong, and will help them develop their skills essential both for the individual and for the government.

This is where psychiatry can take its professional place as a molder of thought and social action, and would be an indication that the discipline has reached its own professional maturity and is ready to help the individual stand in his own territory and affirm his potentialities.

In this area of youth, psychiatry comes very close to the everyday realities of living. Working directly with children and adolescents while they are going through these periods, helps us to see what they are and not what they have been through retrospections of a disturbed adult. So much of our early knowledge in this field came from knowing adult neurotics and psychotics. Valid as some of this material is, it hardly gives a balanced and true picture of childhood and adolescence. These periods have been understood too much from the point of view of the pathology of human beings, an emphasis which has colored so much of the earlier clinical activity in our work with youth. In too many ways it still does. The question which has gained and still holds the most prominent place in diagnostic efforts has been "What is wrong with this person?" and has not always been balanced and illuminated by the equally important emphasis which asks "What are the potentialities and what does the pathology really reveal as to the person's efforts and ability to achieve a solution of his own life problem?"

Several years ago Dr. Meyer in writing on the all-important

subject of spontaneity, made this highly provocative statement: "The spontaneity of the person—that which he can do and actually does do, on his own, and in his own way, without external prompting or coercion, is what interests us above everything else."

It is this emphasis which needs a fuller and richer opportunity to be imprinted on our therapeutic services with youth. It contains the essentially positive interest and will help psychiatry to move away, as it has done before in other ways, from an over-emphasis on the pathology of human nature to an interest and concern with a living person whose capacities for spontaneity and responsibility have been shrouded and obscured by distress. It is an emphasis which needs a greater expansion as the evidence of our belief in the creativeness of human nature. Youth, even more than any period, needs that type of service. It is needed particularly in our professional training both for the psychiatrists and other professional people who are placed in a responsible position of helping children and youth to a fulfillment of a self they have and which they are learning to own and use. Too frequently psychiatrists only see in the hostile boy or the shy girl the potential schizophrenic, rather than understand these behavior reactions as an attempt to effect an adjustment. This does not mean the first is replaced. Instead, it would mean a more sensitive, discriminating use of the concepts contained in certain diagnostic terms. Too frequently they are prognostic and fatalistic.

Brief mention of another case will bring out these two emphases I have been discussing. A high school girl of fourteen had, according to the history, in her daily contacts, particularly at school, evinced an increasing shyness and a tendency to draw away into herself. As the family and school tried to push or draw her into activity normal for her age and ability, she tended to resist and draw further into herself. Finally, she would not go to school at all and she was brought to the attention of a psychiatrist.

Now with just this much detail, many of you may have already reached the speculative evaluation of this common problem and have thought of a possible early schizophrenic process. Our knowledge of the pathology of this process would so warrant. In the procedure set in motion by the family's concern and the natural pressure of school, the girl was diagnosed as an early schizophrenic and sent to a hospital for observation, where the impression was supported by other observations. The family, however, were not willing and ready to go ahead with the recommended plans for hospitalization and sought the help of the Child Guidance Clinic.

In the reports there was nothing technically wrong. But at no place in these earlier contacts was there any interest in the girl and the potentialities which they might reveal for coming into a more livable contact with reality. It was clear, however, that she was studied and diagnosed only as a sick girl and the conveyor of a pathological process rather than as a girl who was, in her ineffectual way, trying to find a way of living and a way of being well. With that emphasis which dominated the diagnostic procedure, there was neither interest in nor opportunity to know what this girl's potentialities for health were. She had no opportunity to reveal this other side of herself, and the psychiatry operating in that type of way failed to create the opportunity.

This girl was a fourteen-year-old high school girl whose behavior indicated that she was disturbed more than that. It represented her efforts to solve her life problem. Psychiatry is concerned in understanding, first, the meaning of these efforts, not just as sickness but as an attempt to be well; and secondly, what use this girl can make of any new experience or any new relation which a psychiatrist might help to create for a different type of spontaneity, for a different use of her potentialities, which in their present expressions takes her away from relationships. This can still be a very important part of a diagnostic procedure which has a very dynamic element in it.

The girl had several interviews in a setting in which this broader emphasis was exemplified in the attitude and technique of the therapist, who could start with that girl where she was. He was able to help her bring to this new relationship her fear of anything new, her withdrawing shyness and her determined silence. These reactions represented more than evidences of sickness; they indicated what that girl was able to do and be at the moment. The psychiatrist created the opportunity for a new reaching out if the girl could make any use of it. There was no assumption that she could, but what was more important, there was no preconceived assumption that she was sick and could not.

In these few interviews significant trends were revealed. The protective wall of silence and shyness began to be a less excluding one. She began to reveal in words and behavior a waking up, and in the last hour that she had there was a new expression of her spontaneity as evidenced by her wanting to carry out an interest in drawing and painting. She was beginning to use this relationship to share rather than to withdraw.

I use this material to re-emphasize what I believe must be the cornerstone of psychiatry in its future developments and contributions to the services of youth.

The principles of this more positive and creative psychiatry which can symbolize for youth in its professional practices a belief in his capacity for responsible and illuminated action in a real world, are not new. But these principles can be and must be revitalized in each new generation and given more effective application by the very fact that psychiatry is founded on a basis of knowledge which gives reality to a belief in the creativeness of human nature. This is not a blind faith nor a pious wish, but one which rests upon the solid foundation of clinical experience. It is a point of view which sees in youth not mere recapitulation of a past and a precipitate of forces impinging upon him, but active participation in the shaping of his own destinies.

Psychiatry built upon this foundation can become the symbol of an illuminated world which many youths, caught in the meshes of an outlived past and confused by the realities of a world they want but cannot quite reach by their own resources, will need.

I stated these principles are not new. They probably are as

old as man. But it remains for our present day to clarify them and build them into our professional practices and philosophy. Recently [1] I used some material from Plato to illustrate certain principles of therapy which were beautifully described in his allegory of the cave. In closing, I would like to refer again to that material because of its significance for this age period and the problems which need psychiatric help.

You may recall that in this allegory Plato compares the natural condition of man so far as education and ignorance are concerned, to a state of affairs such as the following:

"Imagine man living in a cavern, shackled to a seat from birth, facing a distant beam of light and a bright fire burning way off, with an elevated roadway passing between the fire and the prisoners, with a low wall along it. Then figure to yourself a number of persons walking behind this wall and carrying statues of men and other things with passersby—some silent and some talking. Could persons so confined have seen anything of themselves or of each other beyond the shadows thrown by the fire? And is not this knowledge of things carried past them equally limited? And if they could converse with one another, do you not think that they would be in the habit of giving names to what they saw? And if the cavern returned an echo whenever a passerby spoke, to what could they refer the voice if not to the shadow which was passing? Surely such persons would hold the shadows of the manufactured articles to be the only realities.

"Now picture what would happen—and here we come to the therapeutic emphasis in this material—if one was released from his fetters and compelled to stand and walk with eyes open toward the light. And let us suppose there is pain in this movement and that the dazzling splendor renders him incapable of discerning those objects of which he used formerly to see the shadows. What answer would you expect him to make if someone were to tell him that in those days he was watching foolish phantoms, but that now he is nearer reality and is turned

[1] Allen, F. H. Psychotherapy with Children. New York City, W. W. Norton Co., 1942, 297.

toward things more real? Should you not expect him to be puzzled and regard his old visions as truer than the objects now forced upon his notice, and would he not shrink and turn away to the things which he could see distinctly and consider them to be really clearer than the things pointed to him?

"And if he were dragged violently out of the cave into the dazzling light of the sun, would he not be vexed and indignant and be so dazzled by the glare as to be incapable of making out so much as one of the objects that are now called true?"

Hence, I suppose habit will be necessary to enable him to perceive objects in the upper world. At first he will discern the shadows, then the reflections of men and other things in water, and afterwards the realities. Last of all, I imagine, he will be able to observe and contemplate the nature of the sun, not as it appears in water, but as it is in itself in its own territory.

We can utilize this allegory, written 2300 years ago, to illuminate the contribution of a psychiatry which symbolizes for many a puzzled and troubled youth, who is reaching out for a reality of which he has only seen the shadows. He will be impelled to reach out for the new, either through his own cravings and the naturalness of his own growing or by those who want a different life for him. A psychiatry which can see in the reaching out, a craving for a different reality, will know the new will be seen and described in terms of the shadowy world he is trying to leave behind. But psychiatry is less concerned with the shadows, the pathology, than with the movement and the ability to move out into the illuminated world of the present in which it functions.

Too frequently, psychiatry in its concern with sickness, goes back into the caverns of the past and becomes interwoven with the shadows. Psychiatry cannot serve youth, or anyone else, when it loses its place in the illuminated world of the present where it can stand ready to help young people to find their place in a world of events and real people.

Many of our youth will reach out for what psychiatry can stand for. Some will sustain their efforts through the pain and anxiety the readjustment will cause; others will slip back and resume their place in the world where realities depend upon darkness. But we, as psychiatrists, cannot help them by going back in the concern of this past, because the values of a positive psychiatry can flourish and exist only in a real and illuminated world of real people.

In conclusion, psychiatry, I firmly believe, can do again what was essential in its early period—move away from the past and broaden its base of thinking and acting. Just as psychiatry has previously loosened its bond from a rigid emphasis on constitution and revitalized the value of that emphasis by its concern with the living individual, so again psychiatry must move away from an emphasis on the pathology of human nature and revitalize that emphasis by a broader interest in the potentialities of human nature to achieve wellness and responsibility. It will be this more positive note in our philosophy which will make psychiatry a vital factor in the direction and training and education of youth.

Just as youth can be free from the past through affirming in himself the values of what he has gone through as he moves into new realities with new directions, so psychiatry can grow as a science of human nature by moving away from earlier and outworn emphases. We, as its practitioners, can become a symbol for youth of a faith and belief in human nature as it exists. With the attainment of this emphasis which clinical services with children and youth is accelerating, psychiatry will assume its rightful place in our society, not just as a clinical service to the distressed, but as a positive social force.

Psychiatry in the Training, Experience and Education of the Individual: Courtship and Marriage

By ANDREW H. WOODS, M.D.

Professor and Head of the Department of Psychiatry, University of Iowa; Director, Iowa State Psychopathic Hospital

HUMAN PRODUCTIVE PROCEDURES • FRAGILE HIGHER CEREBRAL MACHINERY • PHYSIOLOGICAL OR PATHOLOGICAL • WAR ROMANCE • PRE-EMBARKATION EXPERIENCES OF SOLDIERS • REPRODUCTIVE CONJUNCTION IN ALL FORMS OF LIFE • SELECTIVE MUTUAL ATTRACTION • CHROMOSOMES, ORIGINAL GERM CELL, AND BLUE PRINTS FOR DEVELOPING ORGANISM • THE COURTSHIP PROCEDURE • SIGNIFICANCE OF MARRIAGE • NUTRITIONAL MACHINERY • MAN THE CONVEYOR OF CHROMOSOMES • THEIR TRANSFERENCE MOST IMPORTANT ACCOMPLISHMENT OF MAN OR WOMAN

CRITICS OF the cosmic order, the way things are run, point to serious faults in human reproductive procedures. A literary woman, amid the discomforts and inconveniences of early pregnancy, could see no sense in the whole business. Why all this bodily intimacy, mixed up sensations, explosive emotions, that leave one feeling like a fool after they pass? A simple thing like begetting a child, if it must be done, ought to be got through with on an impersonal basis—as one would plant and scientifically care for an acorn until it became an oak and could look out for itself.

Hypo-hormonic old bachelor, Thomas Browne, relieved himself as follows: "I could be content that we might procreate like trees without conjunction, or that there were any way to perpetuate the world without this trivial and vulgar way of

184

coition; it is the foolishest act a wise man commits in all his life, nor is there anything that will more deject his cooled imagination."

From the moment the human bisexual foetus is forced by hormonal influences to take on the duties and responsibilities of one or the other sex, until the late period of life when its sexual machinery is dismantled, the whole organism is liable to tides of uncontrollable feeling. Most of us manage to steer our barks through the turbulent waters and into safe anchorages, but many suffer damage; not a few are sunk.

Whether in war or in peace, psychiatrists note that the higher cerebral machinery is liable to disorganizing processes of peculiar severity during and following sexual activity. The most recent (philogenetically) equipment of the human brain, which is the part concerned in those disorders, is composed of the most delicate and fragile of all nerve cells. It seems probable that our finer shades of feeling result from the action of the ultramicroscopic elements within those cells, for detecting derangements of which we have no adequate techniques. Accordingly, for the present, we have to side-step the pathological problems presented and be content with the paradoxical utterance, "purely functional."

Whatever name is applied, the affect disorder appearing when sexual love misfires may be the most demoralizing, destructive of efficiency and deflating to enthusiasm that man can suffer. It has gotten so mixed up with poetry, romance and sermonizing that science is loth to recognize it. A physiologist in an ecstacy of love gets confused between brain and heart as the seat of his experience, but stoutly refuses to think of it as physiological. A pathologist, baffled in a sexual affair, considered his trembling, sweating and palpitation as abnormal, but refused to call it pathological.

War is always accompanied by effervescence of romance. In times of military or religious excitement, sexual activities are unduly stirred. Girls and women ordinarily of strict conventional habits feel obligated to grant to their heroes every possible comfort and indulgence. Resulting babies, jealousies, dis-

illusionments and forced marriages then complicate lives there-
tofore serene enough. To the soldier may accrue bizarre inco-
ordinations of movement and emotion or attacks of anxiety as
he faces combat, and often these are found to have emerged
out of a background of loneliness and sexual rumination, traceable to his unassimilated pre-embarkation experiences. One of
the most disrupting emotional illnesses known to me occurred
in both the man and his ambulance-driving sweetheart, after a
week-end party in which the coincidence of menses and sexual
ardor led to self loathing and several years of incapacity for
work.

Most of you are familiar with the varied galaxies of symptoms that follow when the course of true, or false, love fails to
run smooth. It will, therefore, be more profitable for us to
consider these pathological conditions only in view of their
biological background.

We know well that, as far back as man's reactions are
known, situations involving peril have evoked painful, highly
disturbing responses, which involve both the higher brain cells
and those of all the vegetative organs. The individual must be
saved from immediate destruction. It will appear that a yet
stronger reason exists for strenuous reactions throughout the
entire organism when the individual errs in doing his part to
insure continuance of the race.

We are asked to consider these phenomena as they occur
particularly in courtship and marriage, among lower animals as
well as in human beings.

Biological Significance of Courtship

Uncle Remus is better reading in these troubled days than
most of the high-brow magazines. He made no claims to scientific knowledge, but in his story of creation he hints at our early
bisexuality. The earliest models, he assures us, consisted of
one male and one female united back to back. The design was
not popular, so the Good Lord cut the two apart. If you don't
believe it, just feel the sawn ends of the bones under the skin

of your back. But the two, in each case, felt lonely and to this day keep running around the world looking for each other.

From the motile zooids of vorticella up through all levels of multicellular forms, reproductive conjunction with a mate is the most persistent quest of living things. Color changes and suggestive movements act on visual receptors; odors, sounds and gustatory stimuli start action in other reflex systems. Finally, higher integrating brain machinery effects secretory and motor coordinations that bring numbers of potential partners near each other. Responses of each further excite the other. Groups of eager males and females come together until maximal mutual stimulation operating between pairs of individuals bring them to the finals. The complicated activities of coitus follow.

The objective of this process, however, is not merely the consummation of coitus with just any mate. It is definitely selective. Even in the non-sexual conjugation of single cells, definite selectivity is apparent. The motor process of a nerve cell will struggle past impediments, refuse other unions and, if distance and obstacles are not too great, will finally implant itself in its own predestined muscle. In the race of a million or more spermatozoa from even the external skin to the waiting ovum, various purely physical conditions and the relative vigor of the competitors may determine the winner, but the problem remains unsolved as to whether the selective mutual attraction, predicated by Kappers as neurobiotaxis in the conjugation of nerve cells, is not the important influence that brings sperm and ovum together. However that may be, it is certain that in unicellular forms, such as vorticella, sexual conjugation does not occur between the zooid of one cell and a cell of an entirely different order. Some arrangement within each keeps them from coming together. In higher forms, the sperm of fish, for instance, does not fecundate the ova of frogs.

In animals in which the motor and secretory coordinations of coitus are necessary, the stimulation for the effecting of those reflexes fails between mates of different species. The emanations from a rutting cow stimulate the superficial receptors of a stallion, but that receptor activity does not arouse his higher nervous centers so as to lead to coitus; possibly they produce reactions of disgust.

In human beings there are various levels of higher cerebral controls that initiate and regulate sexual action. The cruder emanations, potent among beasts, act also between man and woman, and in individuals of simple make-up sexual action may at once be started. But as civilization has become more complex, the conditions for successful stimulation of the higher enforcing neural centers and for neutralizing inhibitory regulators have become correspondingly intricate. Allowing full credit to the charms of Potiphar's wife, perhaps it was pictures of the menacing sword of Potiphar that put the brakes on Joseph's activities. The full panoply of Venus' incitements, even when reinforced by the nearby chance performance of his eager steed with an avid mare, aroused no motor or hormonal responses in Adonis. Angelo, in *Measure for Measure,* unaffected since boyhood by the scents, legs, tints and songs of women, after exposure for only an hour to the ingenuous charms of Isabella, went into action from garret to cellar, apostrophizing Nature as amazing, "that to catch a saint, with saints doest bait thy hook."

Selective mating between man and woman is effected through the matching of a complicated stimulus-response pattern. When the patterns fail to coincide, the hormonal, motor, glandular and circulatory reactions do not occur; there is no motivation through feelings; even the mechanical procedure of coitus is impossible when erectile tissue and lubricating devices refuse to play their part. When mutual stimulation is adequate, barriers that could not be blasted away are easily melted down. Modesty, shyness, aloofness, fastidiousness, revulsion from intimacy, fade away; down fall those stubborn bastions made up of racial, religious and ethical standards. Then, with the defenses gone, there must still be presented positive stimuli that arouse trust, admiration, enjoyment, affection. Ideals as to manliness and womanliness must be satisfied; and, be it remembered, those ideals represent qualities desired by men and women in their offspring.

We have no knowledge that chromosomes in ova or sperms have any influence upon the cells of the individual's somatic or nervous organs. They are commonly looked upon as virtually foreign bodies, incidentally carried in ovaries or testes until ejected, though occasionally they may manage to combine with similar bodies to produce embryos and determine in those new organisms all important structural and functional characteristics. We assuredly have no knowledge to warrant the supposition that the sperm of a given man, although capable of uniting with an ovum in a particular woman so as to produce the greatest musician of all time, could in any way act upon the brain of that man to produce feelings, movements or secretions that would lead up to such a union of chromosomes. There is, however, an important relationship between the chromatin of brain cells and that of the sperms and ova of the individual who carries them.

Here we enter a field of speculation, not absurd but of the kind that stimulates thought. The nuclear chromatin of every cell in our bodies is a direct derivative of the chromatin of the original fertilized ovum from which all that individual's cells developed including those of the nervous organs and the sperms or ova later to be produced by the testes or ovaries respectively. As far as our methods of investigating chromosomes supply information, the set of chromosomes in the nucleus of every brain cell is identical with that of the original germ cell from which the individual developed. If, then, the chromosomes of that original germ cell contained the blue-prints for detailed structure and function of the developing organism, it may eventually be found that each cell nucleus of that organism contains plans and specifications directing it as to its cooperative part in the whole undertaking. The anlage of the lachrymal gland is directed to produce that special kind of secretory cells, and later those cells are made to produce tears and not saliva. Our conscious states, psychic reactions, are produced by brain cells.

It is rather to be expected, then, that those cells determine not only the individual's motor and secretory reactions, but also the psychic reactions, that are called for in order to continue the longitudinal (generation to generation) series in which that individual is but the current link.

However, it is to be physiologically explained, the fact is that the treasures of human chromosomes, inherited from past ages of ancestry, are biologically the most important possessions of an individual man, and they are subject to special provision against indiscriminate intermixture with those of others. They are guarded by locks with intricate cylinder-patterns that can be opened only by keys of corresponding intricacy. As is true in all the provisions in natural selection, as we dimly see it in the course of evolution, the pattern-matching in sexual mating is far from fool-proof. Nevertheless, courtship has emerged as the procedure by which the severed mates that, according to Uncle Remus, belong together, are currently, for the past million or so of years, being brought together.

Orientals and, to a considerable extent, British and continental European parents feel that age and experience enable them to select marital partners for their children more successfully than the children themselves could do it. Crude tests like "bundling" reveal only compatibility for coitus. Selection by parents overweighs matters of finance, family social standing and the tastes of the parents themselves. Courtship takes into the account the essential elements of mutual feelings and places responsibility on the ones directly concerned.

Biological Significance of Marriage

Among both lower animals and mankind instinct provides for longer or shorter periods of partnership between parents for the protection of the mother and her offspring. In subhuman species parents are in this way kept together and go through forms of behavior that bring the young to mature independence. In some instances males cling to their mates through many breeding cycles. In various ways the mothers are protected while unable to fend for themselves; the young are brought to birth, fed and trained until their inborn capacities for gaining food, escape, defense and mating are effective. The eagle still, as in the days of the Hebrew journalist, builds its nest, feeds and fights for its young; then tears down its nest, throws them out, watches the first flying reactions stimulated by falling, darts under and catches them when their own efforts seem to fail. It is noteworthy that brooding birds take the business as a full time job. No time for bridge and the club.

The home established by human parents is not a chance product of custom and convenience. It is the evolutionary development of the nest of lower animals. Homes, marriage laws and customs change as to details through the generations, but the human home is the modification of the nest as worked out by the instinct-plus machinery of man's brain. It takes longer to make a battle-ship than a raft. Instead of the few weeks for maturing an eaglet, a human child's elaborate organization calls for fifteen to twenty years before it is ready for the competition of modern life. In view of our present discussion, it is pertinent to note also that the completion of a battle-ship calls for more complicated machinery and instruments of precision than the saw and hatchet needed for a raft. Serious and costly damage results when things go wrong with the machinery of shipbuilding.

The most successful homes may not have involved expensive material equipment, but they possessed a subtle atmosphere made up of such ingredients as loyalty, honesty, kindness, affection and the mutual feelings and relationship that determine partnership, the sharing of burdens and responsibilities. Let any one of these elements be absent, or permit bitterness between parents, distrust and self-seeking to bring acridity into the atmosphere, then emotional disorders, abnormal social attitudes, distorted character development, result.

So, Why the Emotional Involvement?

Perhaps the dynamite is added to insure energy. Certain it is that with dynamite goes risk of explosions.

Man's feelings are themselves driving forces, or are associated closely with other brain activities that press to action. A busy man may overlook shaving but he is fixed so that he cannot neglect eating. First, unrest; then inexorable hunger; finally, his whole machinery goes into action to get food. He labors, fights, sweats for it. As he eats, each step is reinforced by pleasant states of consciousness stirred through taste and smell receptors. Having eaten enough, an entirely different feeling supervenes; satiety appears and the machinery is turned off.

More than that: the reflex responses to gustatory and olfactory receptors are selective; they determine what food is to be eaten. New-born calves, without instruction, are pressed into sucking activity by the odors and taste of milk alone. A few weeks later, new arrangements of their brain mechanisms alter responses so that grass and grain will be eaten. Goose livers and champagne fail as stimuli.

In general, our functions above the level of automatic, coercive instinct, are regulated and energized by appropriate affect states. When an individual is to act in the interests of succeeding generations, stronger and more compelling feelings urge him on and direct his effort. Here, I think, we have the significance of conscience and remorse. Man's neural machinery presses him to act now, influenced by yesterday's experiences, so as to attain greater advantage for himself or the race tomorrow, or ten years hence. This is total brain action. When effective, it brings the finest rewards in the form of the subtlest feelings. He can, even when urged by hunger, refuse food that might have been poisoned or food that belongs to another. He can even give the food to one who needs it more. On the other hand, he can eat gluttonously. His machinery accelerated by immediate pleasure during the feast, unregulated and uninhibited by past experiences, continues to work through the night. We undoubtedly suffer for slips in our nutritional machinery—colic, dyspepsia, jitters and melancholy.

Much more do we suffer when the controls and regulators of reproduction go wrong. Throughout the long process of evolution, the individual appears to be secondary, a mere carrier of chromosomes. Let him convey them safely, then combine them with others so as to beget an organism of higher excellence, and he has served his turn. The long process has as its primary objective the making of a better race. If the individual slips in caring for his own nutrition, colic may whip him into line; or he may even eliminate himself through inanition. But he must reproduce or run the risk of severer remonstrances.

Bearing and rearing children is no easy business. Pregnancy is uncomfortable; parturition, painful, also dangerous; rearing offspring is exacting, expensive. If those steps had to be taken in cold blood, motivated only by reason and duty, few children would be born. Hence, to insure the continuance of the race, each step has attached to it the most alluring sensory and emotional rewards. The thalamus outdid itself in devising pleasures to go with the conjugating act itself. Crowns are sacrificed, kingdoms lost, life imperilled to secure the hour of approach and the final ecstacy, purely as ends in themselves.

However, with reproduction as with nourishment, the regulating devices, perhaps because of their intricacy, are often out of order. Mating is consummated for merely the immediate pleasure; children, if born, are neglected; parents tire of each other and separate. Men and women try to beat the game; they take the reward but refuse to deliver the goods. Even in what looked like the most hopeful setting, the machinery slips, cogs grind, bearings rattle. The best integrated personality, after the age-old sequence of ingenuous trust, prolonged sexual intimacy, then disillusionment, may continue a long life devoid of spontaneity, incapable of enthusiasm, with the entire energy-generating equipment burned out.

So, I take it, the most important accomplishment of an individual man or woman is the transference of a collection of chromosomes, done in such a way as to produce a better individual in the transfer. Each is guided by an arrangement of feelings which regulates the pertinent behavior. When all goes well, according to the degree of excellence of the individual's personality, high satisfactions accrue. When the regulators fail, derangements of all degrees of gravity ensue.

When the whole of the brain works well, the individual at

the lowest level protects himself, gains nourishment, grows. At the cooperative level, that is the social life, he gets on well with his fellows, adds to his own effectiveness and theirs. At the highest level, that of race-building, the individual mates, reproduces and rears children in such a way that the apparent goal of myriad ages of living organisms comes measurably nearer to attainment because of his life.

Medical scientists are the engineers who keep this machinery up to its best attainable working level. Not an easy job; but, as mankind goes through harassing stages like that of our day, it is of especial moment, and, if well done, the most gratifying work that man can undertake.

Psychiatry in the Training, Experience and Education of the Individual: Family Life

By ARNOLD GESELL, M.D.

Director, The Clinic of Child Development, Yale University School of Medicine

FORCES WHICH IMPROVE THE ORGANIZATION OF HUMAN PERSONALITY • FAMILISM • WAR AND IMPORTANCE OF DOMESTIC HOUSEHOLD • TOTALITARIAN KULTUR • DEMOCRATIC CULTURE • PRECONCEIVED IMAGES • EXPECTANT PARENTS • PRE-PEDIATRIC GUIDANCE • SELF-REGULATORY MECHANISMS OF INFANTS • INTERNAL DISCIPLINE • SELF CONTROLS • MORALE AND SECURITY • FAMILY LIFE AND CHILD MORALE • INSTITUTIONAL AND CONGREGATE CARE IN WAR TIME • PICTURE OF A COMMUNITY NURSERY • REDUCTIONS AND DISTORTIONS OF BEHAVIOR PATTERNS • PSYCHOLOGICALLY ORPHANED INFANTS • THE INSTITUTIONAL SYNDROME • JUST DISTRIBUTION OF DEVELOPMENTAL OPPORTUNITIES • THE PROTECTION OF FAMILY LIFE

IN THESE days of confusion and chaos, one begins to look around for eternal verities. Where are they? Medical science and conferences like this should enable us to identify the psychological forces which are most likely to improve the organization of human personality. Family life releases and creates such forces.

There is a quaint word in the dictionary: *familism,* defined as "the disposition to create families and the tendency to make the family a social unit." *Familism* may well be one of the verities. To be sure, in the heyday of behavior*ism* it was questioned (by a leading behaviorist) "whether there should be individual homes for children, or even whether children should know their own parents." Watson, however, conceded that the family institution is with us—inexorably with us. We shall have to make the best of it!

The war has already demonstrated with tragic impressiveness that the domestic household is indeed the most fundamental unit of a democratic culture. The household is the cultural workshop in which the folkways of democracy are renewed, reshaped, transmitted. A totalitarian Kultur subordinates the family completely to the state, fosters autocratic adult-child relationships, favors despotic discipline, and relaxes the tradition of monogamy. It unmistakably degrades women and children. It is not concerned with the individual as a person.

A democratic culture affirms the dignity of the individual person. It exalts the status of the family group, favors reciprocity in parent-child relationships, and encourages humane discipline through guidance and mutual understanding. Psychologically speaking, a family consists of two personalities (to say nothing of next of kin!) who presumably respect each other, and who desire to create the best conditions for the growth of a third personality—another individual.

This democratic truism comes to its first test even before the child is born. Husband and wife choose each other, but they cannot choose their children. Parents cannot determine in advance the kind of child who will be born of marriage. This is another truism, but one which does not operate automatically. Many parents harbor, more or less consciously, an image of the kind of boy or girl they wish to rear. The image may be held with abnormal intensity and with extreme specification, prior to and also after birth. Such fixation impels the mother or father, or both, to attempt too strongly to make over the child in terms of a preconceived image. Matters grow still worse if the father has one ideal and the mother another.

Nothing can resolve these tensions except an acknowledgement that every child is a unique individual with some traits which are beyond cultural moulding. This demands a liberal form of tentativeness in the parent-child relationship, prenatally and postnatally. The supervision of the obstetrician tends to limit itself too much to the birth episode alone. The expectant parents would greatly benefit by a pre-pediatric type of guidance designed to build up wholesome attitudes of tentativeness, a philosophical readiness to rear the child in terms of his unique growth needs.

If more attention were given to these emotional orientations prior to birth, the methods of infant care would benefit greatly. Incidentally, there would be a striking increase of breast feeding during the first few months. The mother would be interested to understand her baby as an individual, as a person. She would be more intelligently alert to the behavior-language of the baby—his crying, fretting, anxiety, quiescence, satiety, smiling and self-activity.

The new trend in pediatrics is away from authoritarianism to individualization. Iron-clad schedules, rigidly imposed in accordance with clock-time, may be actually harmful. Mother and physician alike are acquiring more faith in and insight into the self-regulatory mechanisms of the infant. The infant is in such close league with Nature that he knows a great deal about certain fundamentals: (a) when to eat, (b) what to eat, (c) when to sleep, (d) when to wake up, (e) when to be sociable, (f) when to play, alone, (g) when to obey, (h) when to resist. A flexible infant care schedule takes account of the baby's needs as expressed in his behavior. Culture must, of course, guide and direct; but it cannot overlook the innate "wisdom of the body," which is also the wisdom of the baby's mind. Self-demand schedules, under medical supervision, promote mental as well as physical welfare.

Self-regulation is a principle of natural development which applies not only to feeding and sleeping, but to the whole gamut of growing behavior. It is a democratic principle in the sense that it acknowledges the central factor of individuality. It is not an abstruse principle; because it comes to unceasing expression in the every-day care of the child—in the development of upright posture, prehension, manipulation, bladder control, bowel control, language, and the whole wide range of personal-social behavior. Family life in a democratic culture must put this principle into operation from the very beginning. Even the infant (if we respect his demanding cries and his expressed resistances) can participate in the working out of a schedule of his behavior day. Society can give increasing scope to self-regulation in the nursery school, kindergarten, and through the educational system. This does not mean license or indulgence. It means guidance. The child, of course, must do his own growing; the ultimate controls come from within as products and mechanisms of growth. This is the psychological essence of the democratic ideal. The ideology of democracy and the concept of individual development are inseparable. The antithetical totalitarian concept places *its* faith in the child mind as a malleable fragment, which is organized through habit formation, reflex conditioning, and indoctrination. It makes a fetish and an enormity out of external discipline.

The mechanisms of self-demand and self-regulation, on the contrary, lead to internal discipline, and to greater *self* controls. They also build up that inner sense of security which psychiatry regards as the essence of mental stamina. Only by individualizing our methods of psychological care, can we meet the organic needs of the infant promptly and fully. By meeting them with certainty, we multiply those experiences of satisfied expectation which produce an increasing sense of security. This "sense" is a patterned product of individual mental growth. It comes from within; it cannot come from without. It cannot be engendered in a vacuum. It needs the nurture of a family group.

Security lies at the basis of morale. What every child wants most is a feeling of security in his own home. A healthy family life is all but indispensible for the development of child morale, and doubly so in times of violence and war. Now, as never before, we must be on the alert to avoid the deterioration of home ties which come from institutionalization and injudicious forms of congregate care. We shall need child care centers to provide for the pre-school children of mothers taken out of the home to serve the demands of war; but we shall pay a heavy psychological price for these arrangements if we do not preserve the patterns of family life.

Let me try to picture the psychological effects of a community nursery, an over-institutionalized nursery. It is a bright, sanitary nursery; the caretakers are in neat uniform, they are kind and industrious. There is a mural of Red Riding Hood on the wall. The playroom has a clean, polished, expansive floor. Sun is streaming through the windows. At first blush all looks well.

But closely observe the behavior of the children. There are a dozen or more infants on the floor. And they are getting in each other's way, or occupying islands of isolation; the play objects are promiscuously exploited in a fragmentary manner; there are no cohesive, continuing small groups with an adult and a baby as a focal center of the group. There are no stable focal centers at all; the centers are ever shifting; the activities are scrambled and almost aimless. Toys and possessions are communal. This is in fact a loosely organized chaos so far as patterned personal-social behavior is concerned. The major activity is motor activity; the vacuums of tedium ‘are constantly being filled with stereotyped circular-repeat-reactions. Here is one infant, tired of hitching about, who sits in the middle of the floor with a rubber toy and sways back and forth for minutes at a time as though doing some incantation. Two or three children are standing, but not still; they are weaving back and forth with incessant rhythm, reminiscent of the head rolling acquired during lonely hours in the crib. This too is environmental stereotypy. Another child is transfixed in a bent-over stance, similar to that of a football center about to pass the ball. But the child is poised for inaction; he peers through his legs again for minutes at a time—a bit of almost cataleptic perseveration again. Other children are indulging in unwonted, persisting, chewing movements, a sterotypy of the mandible.

To a discriminating observer there is only one child in the entire group who seems to be behaving really normally. He is a newcomer just arrived, for emergency reasons, from his natural family home, where he learned to be communicative under the organizing influences of family life. He is talking to one of his creeping colleagues, and offering him a toy, but there is no language response. In time the prattling visitor will also adopt the institutional silence.

The institutionalized child is not so much oversensitive to strangers as he is socially stupid with respect to their advances. He has not had much training in the subtleties of social advance and retreat. Nor can he meet halfway the overtures of speech and gesture when they come from another child. He has learned to be indifferent to many of the activities of an institution, because most of them are not personally directed toward him. He has had both too much and too little privacy. So many of his spontaneous initiatives have been unobserved and unheeded, that they were virtually stillborn. Many will not be born at all—why should they?

Such are the mechanisms and the circumstances which in institutions choke the growth of speech and muffle social interchange, with all its give and take of humor, of echoing back, of repeating over and over again, of laughter, praise, of mock surprise, of dramatic play, and of expressed affection which are part and parcel of a mono-baby-centered home. Lacking all these repercussions, the pluralistic institutional child often acquires an impassive face. His facial muscles have not been adequately animated by social behavior; his countenance becomes rigidly bland.

These depressed and distorted reactions constitute a clinical syndrome, which can be diagnosed early by a developmental examination of the infant's behavior status. We examine the infant while he is lying in his crib, or is seated in a supportive chair before a table top on which diagnostic test objects are presented. We have ample norms which tell us how normal family-bred infants react under comparable conditions.

If the infant has been institutionalized from birth, we begin to detect reductions and distortions of normal behavior patterns as early as the age of eight weeks. There is diminished perceptual and social interest, reduced reactivity and lowered integration of total behavior.

By sixteen weeks there is excessive preoccupation with strange persons. Between the ages of sixteen and twenty-eight weeks, the psychologically orphaned infants often react better in the supine test situations than they do while seated at the test table. They are accustomed to lie on their backs, over-accustomed, in fact, for they have acquired exaggerated, circular forms of hand play, hand and mouth play, head nodding and head rolling. Such activity becomes congealed into stereotypy, into blind-alley behavior patterns which have not been sufficiently sloughed off or displaced by normal developmental elaborations. Even hand inspection, which should be dropping out of the picture between sixteen and twenty weeks, may usurp in such a child other forms of activity and assume an unnatural dominance at twenty-four weeks. Why not? The child has spent an unnatural preponderance of time on his back and has become an over-expert hand inspector—hyperplasia rather than morphogenetic differentiation.

In the seated position he shows his limitations still more clearly. He may not even look at the cube on the test table; but instead gazes inordinately at the examiner or looks recurrently at his own hand, with semi-automatic jerks of attention.

Why, he doesn't do as well as an ordinary twenty-week-old baby, you say to yourself; and it is true, for even a normal twenty-week-old baby will avidly bring eyes and hands to bear upon the cube in an effort to corral it.

The retardation of the twenty-four-week-old, institutional baby may be only slight, but it is significant. It becomes increasingly serious if that same baby stays in the same institution for a half year or a whole year more. Environmental retardation works by attrition as well as by impoverishment. Effects tend to be cumulative in susceptible infants.

The very acceptance of a restricted environment may reach an abnormal degree of intensity. The baby becomes overweaningly attached to the institution; not so much from sheer love of the place as from ignorance of other places. By the age of one year he may be terrified to be taken somewhere else; he resists strangeness; he clings to the attendant; he cries. The new situation is altogether too much for his limited experience and for his atrophied adaptability. The social ineptness which began to show itself at twenty-four weeks thus comes to its developmental issue.

Contrast the behavior typical of an average one-year-old child in a developmental examination. He has been brought up in ordinary home surroundings; and he may show shyness in this new situation (we rather like to see him show it); but presently he thaws out, he sizes up, he adjusts emotionally. Confidence mobilized, he bends to the tasks of the developmental examination with eagerness. There may even be a burst of protest as he is about to leave the examining crib. He enjoys new experiences; he profits by them; he gets them in abundance. He helps us to understand the origin and nature of the institutional syndrome.[1]

The cultural impacts of family living are so important during the first five years of child development that we must safeguard the functions of the family home even in times of emergency. After freedom from want and fear have been achieved, we shall still be under the necessity of enriching the psychological patterns of domestic households. This can be accomplished through (a) a broadened health supervision, embracing both physical and mental child development, (b) through nursery schools of a guidance type, (c) through parental and pre-parental education.

Even in a technological civilization there is danger of educational want in the early years of growth. Only through a democratically conceived system of developmental supervision can we attain a more just distribution of developmental opportunities for infants and pre-school children. It is probable that the

[1] For more detailed discussion of the institutional syndrome, see Gesell, A., and Amatrude, C. Developmental Diagnosis. New York City, Harper and Bros., 1941, Ch. 16.

principle of universal education will be extended in the post-war period to include the pre-school ages. This will be done through nursery schools. We may hope that in America these nursery schools will function as auxiliaries to the home, as guidance centers for parents, and as induction centers for pre-parents. Otherwise the educational provisions for pre-school children may become unduly institutionalized, and we shall create more problems than we solve. The home will long remain the true threshold of a democratic culture.

We are fighting a war in order to protect family life in a democratic culture. We cannot make democracy a genuine folk-way, unless we bring into the homes of the people a developmental philosophy of child care, an informed philosophy, which thinks of *growth* as a concrete, living process, rather than a mere label. The growth of the mind is a series of actual events governed by laws and forces just as real as those which apply to an internal combustion engine. It will be a major social task of post-war science to familiarize parents and preparents with the concrete nature of these psychological forces. We live in a technological age; we know something of the precision and beauty of engines and machines. The people will readily absorb a science of child development which acquaints them with the mechanisms of growth, with the machinery of behavior. That will be sound self-knowledge. Such realistic science will give form to our spiritual aspirations. It will certainly make them more sensible and workable. It will alter the attitudes of parents and the temper of households.

To sustain a culture, at once highly technological and democratic, we shall need a type of family life which protects the individualities of its children through the mores and the science of developmental concepts.

Psychiatry in the Training, Experience and Education of the Individual: Religion

By the Reverend OTIS R. RICE

Religious Director, St. Luke's Hospital; Instructor in Pastoral Theology, General Theological Seminary, New York City

MEETING GROUND OF RELIGION AND PSYCHIATRY • RE-TRAINING, RE-EDUCATING OF INDIVIDUALS • SALVATION, ADEQUATE ADJUSTMENT • RELIGIOUS EDUCATION AND PSYCHIATRY • THE TRAINED RELIGIOUS TEACHER • CONTINUITY OF IMPACT OF THE PASTOR • RECOGNITION OF DANGER SIGNALS • CONTRIBUTION TO ADEQUATE MENTAL HYGIENE PROGRAM • THE PASTORAL COUNSELOR • HIS PART IN THE FIELD OF EMOTIONAL EDUCATION AND RE-EDUCATION • PSYCHIATRISTS IN THEOLOGICAL SCHOOLS • THE MATTER OF ADJUSTMENT AND SELF-UNDERSTANDING OF THE MINISTER • PRIVATE AND CORPORATE WORSHIP • "TOGETHERNESS" AND "BELONGINGNESS" • PERSONAL RELIGION AND RELATIONSHIPS • PHILOSOPHY OF LIFE • MUTUAL NEED OF MINISTER AND PSYCHIATRIST FOR EACH OTHER

Introduction

THE FACT that you have invited a parson to meet with you this morning, is, I think, significant. Perhaps it is an indication that the disciplines of psychiatry and pastoral theology are effecting a rapprochement which may not only be amicable but also mutually valuable.

You could scarcely have chosen a better ground on which religion and psychiatry may meet than the topic of our present discussion. For both disciplines are deeply concerned with the training, experience and education of the individual. Unfortunately most of us, psychiatrists and ministers alike, must admit that until recently many of our endeavors should be described as the *re*-training, *re*-interpreting of experience and

204

the *re*-education of individuals. We have both been engaged in a patching-up process; patching-up those who should have been educated otherwise. That this is so may be ascribed by the theologian to "original sin" in his parishioner or by the psychiatrist to the "immature emotional development of parents," "environmental or situational conditions" or "adverse hereditary factors" of his patient.

Yet I take it that despite obvious important differences our aims today are not so divergent. We both look forward to the time when our efforts may make possible for many more individuals a continuous development from infancy to maturity of such a character that re-training and re-education will be unnecessary. The theologian may describe the end result as "salvation"; the psychiatrist as "emotional maturity" or "adequate adjustment." But the individuals thus described would be strikingly similar. At any rate we on the theological side are most of us frankly more eager to help produce the "once born" individual whose religious and emotional development represents unhurried but steady growth, rather than the spectacular "twice born," who is more than likely to be thrice or even more frequently born—and may indeed end up by having his associates wish he had been stillborn!

I would like now to present a few notes on the relation of religion to psychiatry.

I. Religious Education and Psychiatry

Today the intelligent religious educator recognizes that religion and the emotional life are closely interrelated. He accepts the fact that a sound religious attitude and sound emotional maturity are together achieved through the developmental life of the individual. He knows that the person who is disturbed or emotionally maladjusted can warp or misuse his religion precisely as he misuses his personal relationships, his vocation, or his pet dog. A person may be so emotionally disturbed or so mentally ill that he may not for a time be able to accept what religion has to give. On the other hand, one is quite frank to admit that grotesque or unsound religion may upset the delicate emotional balance of some individuals and do incalculable damage to personality. There is a form of religion which over-stresses a feeling of guilt and cultivates this feeling of guilt. There is also the religion which a Bishop has described as: "All the world is lovely and I am lovely too." Sweetness and light are quite as dangerous from our point of view as an over-emphasis on guilt and sin. Therefore, you see, *our* study is to examine as critically and as objectively as is possible our religious beliefs and practices as they affect the emotional life of men; and also to encourage and incorporate in our programs of religious education those techniques, understandings and attitudes which psychiatry tells us make for adequate emotional growth.

Inasmuch as many young children attend church schools a year or so before they enter public schools, the social and experiential opportunities in the gift of the trained religious teacher are obvious. The hours spent in religious education and religious activity groups can be creative, *if* directed by informed and well-adjusted leaders. The contact with parents of very young children through pre-school departments of our parishes, sometimes called "cradle-roll departments," and parent study groups can also be extremely valuable.

II. The Pastoral Ministry and Psychiatry

The faithful pastor touches the lives of his parishioners in an intimate way; and there is a continuity of impact which psychiatrists may well envy. *You* have to be called in to undertake a case but *we* enter life situations as a matter of course. We do not have to await a summons.

When a baby is born we are often the first to call, whether we are there to arrange for his baptism, to extend our congratulations to the parents, or to offer prayers of thanksgiving for the safe delivery. Then for several years we follow intimately the life of the growing child through our own pastoral visits, the medium of the "cradle roll" relationship in the parish and by parent study groups.

Again, we meet the family and touch the life of the child

when he is brought for the first time to our church school. We later see him when at adolescence we prepare him for confirmation (full membership in the church). When he is ready for college or his first job away from home he comes to us for a letter commending him to some other minister's pastoral care, thus preserving the continuity of the pastoral contact.

When this same individual is to be married, we give him premarital counsel; then solemnize his marriage. I sometimes think psychiatrists do not realize what an opportunity the pastor has in this matter of premarital counseling. Perhaps it is not so much in what we can actually do in advance for the couple whose marriage we are to solemnize as it is the fact that we open the way for easy access to us after marriage, when problems arising in marriage are brought to us. Frequently we are the guinea pig on which the young husband tries out his wife's first experimental apple pie! Young couples who have had difficulty in the early months come to us with problems of impotence, frigidity, hostility, guilt and problems relating to "in-laws." We are then in a position to refer them to adequate psychiatric attention. Indeed, in some instances we are able to help them ourselves as they face problems.

We are with the individual in illness; we go to him in times of special stress; rejoice with him in his days of triumph or happiness; and serve him and his family when he passes through the normal crisis of death.

Do you see what an unmatched opportunity we have to observe and to serve as a personality develops? Think of what it will mean as more and more pastors come to recognize the "danger signals" of serious emotional disturbance, see the difference between a religious and an emotional problem, know how to seek adequate psychiatric assistance, learn how to make referrals, train ourselves to place in your hands observations and records that can implement your treatment of such referred patients!

Think what can transpire when preachers, by the kind of sermons they preach, by the way they preach them, contribute to an adequate mental hygiene program and make "remote preparation" for their own pastoral or your psychiatric ministrations!

It goes almost without saying that the minister's intelligent cooperation with the psychiatrist and the psychiatric institution can be genuinely helpful. He can do much to encourage a decision on the part of parents or relatives to refer or commit patients who need treatment or hospitalization. He can assist appreciably in removing the fear, mystery and stigma which still so frequently surround mental illness and its management.

The understanding pastor is sought after by his parishioners for counsel, advice and help. Between him and them there has existed for centuries a privileged relationship (privileged in both the legal and traditional sense), quite akin to the similar relationship between physician and patient. I need not point out to this gathering the dynamic importance (either for good or ill) of this rapport. Where the pastoral counselor knows his own limitations, possesses himself an adequate adjustment, shuns the giving of advice and deciding for others, and especially forbears from passing judgment upon them, he is in a position to help greatly in the emotional education or re-education of individuals.

III. Pastoral Training of the Clergy

Whether you as psychiatrists like it or not people will continue to seek help from their ministers; and parsons will continue to counsel them. Therefore an impressive number of the clergy are realizing their own limitations in this area and are turning to other disciplines to implement their own techniques and approaches. Mind you, they do not seek to be amateur psychiatrists. Rather do they strive to make their own proper ministrations more effective and to prevent themselves from being guilty of malpractice on human souls.

In general this is what we ministers want to learn from you: enough of developmental psychology to know how people grow; enough about mental and emotional mechanisms to give us a clearer understanding of human behavior and attitude; a deeper knowledge of ourselves and our own emotional "blind spots" so that we can the better avoid emotional involvement; a familiarity with the "danger signals" of mental disturbance; what we can do to assist psychiatry in referral and therapy. Finally we must know something of the trustworthy psychiatric resources available in our community.

We also need especially to ally ourselves with psychiatrists who themselves have a knowledge of religion and who have known the problems of the clergy and their opportunities, who will tell us what we as ministers of religion can do to assist in this whole field of emotional education and re-education.

As some of you know, many of our seminaries and theological schools are already seeking to provide some of this data and experience for our embryonic parsons. I see several of you in this room who have been pioneers in sharing your own insights and knowledge with properly qualified students and young clergy in our graduate schools. Others of you have assumed leadership in the program of clinical training given many of our Seminarians in summer courses offered in some of the best mental hospitals.

There is hardly a theological school in this country which does not now call in psychiatrists or other trained teachers to give courses and supervised experience in such subjects as pastoral psychology, mental hygiene and child psychology.

But we do not think this is enough. The parson's own emotional adjustment is of paramount importance in his effectiveness or peril in dealing with people. I know of no profession (with the possible exception of psychiatry) where a man's own adjustment and self-understanding play more important roles than in the ministry. Therefore, we seek to accept as candidates for this sacred calling only those whose own emotional maturity promises real effectiveness. In some communions, admission for candidacy is granted only after a thorough psychiatric examination. Some of you here have been more than generous in helping us with this problem.

Moreover, during their theological education or soon after ordination many men are themselves seeking some form of psychiatric counseling in order that they may the better handle their difficult work with people. It is really surprising how many ministers have themselves welcomed and made constructive use of psychiatric assistance and therapy.

IV. Religious Resources and Opportunities

Before the discoveries and achievements of psychiatry we ministers must be very humble. You have shown us our wasted opportunities, our most unfortunate failings, our dangerous blindnesses. Yet at the risk of being guilty of sinful pride I must say that I feel we parsons need not be too humble before you. We, too, are interested in, and devote our lives to, the individual. Ours, too, is a respected relationship (perhaps older than yours) and if sometimes we have gone astray it is not the fault of our religion but of our own egocentricity.

In any case I cannot close this brief presentation without mentioning some of our resources, perhaps not adequately used, perhaps not fully recognized, but resources nevertheless for the more adequate and mature development of individuals.

I have already spoken of our normal pastoral relationships with our own charges in our own parishes and communities. I have spoken of our relationships in the usual and the abnormal crises. I have spoken of our impact through religious education and through preaching.

We have in addition the important functions of private and corporate worship by which the individual relates himself to a reality outside himself, and by virtue of this common loyalty, to other individuals engaged in the same worship and bound to a similar goal. There is a "togetherness" in worship which gives meaning to individual worth. There is a feeling of "belongingness" which comes from participation in a ritual, an observance, a group experience, which transcends individual loneliness and isolation.

Religion also has much to say about the individual, his own worth and his place in the universe.

Religion, moreover, has something to say about relationship and the quality of relationship. Religion holds out to the individual a cause or a goal by which he may orient his life. Organized religion offers resources in time of normal and abnormal crises: the sacraments, the rites of religion which can be used by the believer to bolster his courage and to give him strength in times of special stress. Religion provides the believer with a philosophy of life, a framework in which he can fit himself and a framework which gives meaning to his universe.

Now we who are ministers and priests and rabbis want to learn from you who are psychiatrists. We need your help as we go about our pastoral duties day by day. You have already helped us by directing our attention to many of our opportunities. I wonder if it would be fair for me to say that perhaps you need us; that as intelligent cooperation develops between the clergymen and psychiatrists, we may both be setting forward the cause of well-adjusted, mature individuals. I know I speak for my fellow clergy when I say that we want to become better trained pastors and teachers. We are eager to learn more about our opportunities and also about our limitations in dealing with individuals; on the other hand, we would like to be helpful to you.

Psychiatry in the Training, Experience and Education of the Individual: Communities, Rural and Urban

By GEORGE H. STEVENSON, M.D.

Professor of Psychiatry, University of Western Ontario; Superintendent, Ontario Hospital, London

DEFINITION OF PSYCHIATRY • FACTORS IN MENTAL HEALTH • ENVIRONMENTAL SITUATIONS • FUNCTIONS OF MENTAL HEALTH CLINICS • PUBLIC EDUCATIONAL PROGRAM • GROUPS AND ORGANIZATIONS INVOLVED • COMMUNITY FACILITIES • A PSYCHIATRIC WARD IN EVERY GENERAL HOSPITAL • COURTS • THE STIGMA OF MENTAL DISEASES • AN INFORMATIVE MOTION PICTURE • HIGH STANDARDS IN A HOSPITAL

I LIKE TO define psychiatry as general practice in its broadest terms, broader than the physical only and including in the health of the individual the mental aspects as well. The variety and extent of psychosomatic relationship prevent a separation of mental and physical. The duty of the psychiatrist is to see that the mental aspects of health and disease are thoroughly considered along with the physical.

The practise of psychiatry is divided into preventive and curative techniques. Every individual has an interest in the preventive features, the methods by which he may keep mentally fit. Only a fraction of the population has a personal interest in the treatment features, a fraction which we hope will become steadily smaller as mental hygiene procedures become better known and more available.

The maintenance of good mental health depends on more than the learning of mental hygiene precepts. Quite apart from intervention by mental hygienists, it depends on being well born, on good pre-natal, obstetrical and post-natal care, on good home life, on good food, on good physical health, on opportunities for development; on a reasonable economic basis, on good social relationship. The gross psychopathic symptoms seen frequently in children and to a lesser extent in adults when there are serious disturbances in one or more of the foregoing environmental factors and the speedy relief of symptoms which occurs with melioration of the environmental situations, indicate that cause and cure of some mental symptoms are dependent on factors entirely or in large part external.

The mental hygienist (the preventive psychiatrist) needs therefore to know these stressful external factors and to associate himself with all movements that make for a better environment—good housing, slum clearance, adequate diet, social agencies, the schools and the churches.

While working hand in hand with all agencies that make for better health, the preventive psychiatrist has duties and responsibilities which only he can perform; and to increase his effectiveness he is usually found as the director of a mental health clinic, assisted by psychologists and social workers. The activities of the mental health clinic in the community are numerous. Perhaps its chief function is the examination of children and adults who may be referred to it by physicians, schools, social agencies and the courts. These individuals for the most part will be showing minor mental deviations which it is hoped can be corrected before they can become serious problems. It is suggested that the clinic be located in the outpatient department of a general hospital or in close association with a general hospital in order to have ready access to consultants in all other fields.

Preventive psychiatry should of course establish contact with people while they are well and before even minor deviations are present. This means some sort of an educational program whereby people may learn the rules and techniques for keeping mentally fit. Obviously a single psychiatrist in a city or county can be effective only to the extent to which he can get the cooperation of various groups and organizations.

Some of these contacts might be listed as follows:

1. The physician of the city or district by personal contact, by addressing medical meetings, attending staff meetings at general hospitals and taking part in discussions. Mental hygiene literature should be sent periodically to them.
2. Medical students. Every good medical school should offer its students suitable opportunities to learn both the preventive and therapeutic aspects of psychiatry. This is not the place to go into details of the content of the teaching but its importance can not be over-rated.
3. Nurses. Endeavor to see that student nurses receive theoretical and practical instruction in mental hygiene and the care of the mentally ill.
4. Teachers. Teachers and school principals should be contacted frequently, supplied with mental hygiene literature, given reading references and addresses at their annual conventions. The school nurse and certain school teachers might be invited to attend the mental health clinic. Reports given to teachers and physicians should be explicit, non-technical and emphasize the points where mental hygiene violations occurred.
5. Parents. Similar instruction by addresses to organizations and especially to parent-teacher groups.
6. Students. Principals of high schools might arrange for short practical mental hygiene addresses to the students.
7. Clergy. Every effort should be made to take such information to the clergy. No group has closer contact with adults and their cooperation should be sought. The clergy will be very receptive to such approaches.
8. The press. A sympathetic press which once a year will print a series of short authoritative mental hygiene articles can be of the greatest value.
9. The rural public. The fall fairs or similar functions can

be used to advantage for mental hygiene exhibits and the distribution of mental hygiene literature.

10. Paroled patients. Through the social worker or visiting nurse the preventive psychiatrist aids in the successful re-establishment of former mentally sick patients. Continuous follow-up helps to keep these recovered patients in good mental health.

So much for preventive psychiatry. What facilities are there in the community for the person who has actually become ill mentally?

We are apt to think immediately of the mental hospital but I would suggest that we think of the mental hospital last. Not that the psychiatric hospital is not the best place immediately for some of the mentally ill but in the majority of cases other facilities should have prior consideration.

1. The psychiatrically trained physician. Ideally this should mean every general practitioner, internist, surgeon and pediatrician. The individual practitioner or the medical clinic should see that the patient receives a thorough physical and mental examination, missing nothing. Many patients may be treated successfully by office practice.

2. The mental health clinic. The clinic director and his staff now become a part of curative psychiatry. They offer a consultant service to the family physician, assist with the diagnosis and actually undertake treatment in certain cases. They may have charge of the psychiatric ward in the general hospital and assume full responsibility for treatment of patients under care in this ward.

3. The psychiatric ward or service in the general hospital. Too few general hospitals provide such facilities but a general hospital is not a complete hospital and is denying its facilities to many sick people if such ward or service is not available. Ebaugh's recent book *The Care of the Psychiatric Patient in the General Hospital* goes into this feature with great detail. We should work for a properly equipped psy-

chiatric ward in every general hospital of fifty beds or more
and this should be accomplished within the next ten years.
Such wards should not only be diagnostic centers but should
also have full treatment equipment. They should be as freely
used as any other divisions of the general hospital and with
equally good results.

4. The courts. One hesitates to include any discussion of the
courts in this outline. However, many people may be charged
with offences as a result of an abnormal mental state. Hence
the necessity for the mental examination of many prisoners
for a better understanding and treatment of the offender.

In some states, also, the mentally sick persons are
"charged" with the "offence" of being mentally ill and must
be tried in a law court as to their sanity and may be committed by a court to a mental hospital. This procedure may
have been designated originally to protect the individual
from unscrupulous or unprincipled relatives but it has long
since lost its value. It is resented by patients and their relatives. Sick people should be cared for by physicians, not by
court officials, no matter how humane and considerate they
may be.

5. The state mental hospital. Every community in the United
States and Canada is served by a public mental hospital. It
should accept those patients who cannot be cared for satisfactorily at home or in the ward of the general hospital, or
where the mental illness is likely to be protracted or to require the special treatment facilities available only in this
type of hospital. Such hospitals are more readily used than
formerly but the dread and fear of mental illness too frequently carries over to the mental hospital, almost by a
process of identification.

We recall that cancer and tuberculosis for long had associated with them a so-called "stigma." A program of enlightenment has removed this stigma and sufferers from these diseases can be treated more efficiently as a result. We have not
yet entirely removed the so-called "stigma" from mental dis-

eases and many people who might respond quickly to mental hospital care still hesitate to place themselves in such institutions. As aids to making the mental hospitals more acceptable to the mentally sick one would suggest that such hospitals cultivate cordial relations with the press, with the medical and nursing professions, with social agencies, with the other hospitals in the district. The general public should also be made more aware of the activities of mental hospitals by mental hygiene campaigns of information.

The use of motion pictures has been found useful to acquaint the citizens generally with such activities. The film which is a part of this presentation is in constant request by clubs, lodges, ministerial associations, young people's organizations, service clubs, etc. Our film is entirely in color, takes thirty minutes to show, and the member of the staff making the presentation gives a running comment and answers questions as they may be asked. Such comment could be used on a sound track if desired. Our film starts with general views of the grounds and buildings, the nurses' home and nursing school activities. Interior of wards, dining rooms, recreation rooms, industrial sections, farm and garden, follow.

We then show a patient being admitted (posed by staff) and follow this patient through all the diagnostic and treatment facilities of the hospital. Considerable film space is devoted to occupational and recreational therapy. The patient is then followed into family care, from family care to her own home where she is shown being visited by the social worker, and the activities of the mental health clinic are here introduced. Printed explanations appear on the film whenever indicated.

One might add, in conclusion, that these educational efforts are secondary to the operation of a hospital by the best standards and ability. The medical standards must be the highest; qualified consultants and every diagnostic and treatment facility should be available; the physical condition of the hospital should be good, and overcrowding should be avoided. High standards in a hospital are its best advertisement.

The Relationship of Psychiatry to Sociology and Criminology

By WILLIAM HEALY, M.D.

Director, Judge Baker Guidance Center, Boston

SOCIOLOGY THE POSITIVE SCIENCE OF HUMANITY • THE OFFSHOOT FROM PSY-
CHOLOGY • CONSTITUTION AND THE WORKING OF THE MIND • THE INDIVIDUAL,
SOCIAL DIFFERENCES, SOCIAL RELATIONSHIPS • DEFINITION OF SOCIOLOGY, OF PSY-
CHOLOGY • SOCIAL PSYCHOLOGY • PSYCHIATRY AND THE CAUSATIVE SOCIAL SITUA-
TIONS • EMOTIONAL INTERRELATIONSHIPS • PSYCHIATRIC SOCIAL WORKER •
SCIENCE OF INTERPERSONAL RELATIONSHIPS • STUDY OF SUICIDE • POSITIVE PRE-
DISPOSITIONS TO SOCIAL LIFE • THE ORIGINAL NATURE OF MAN • MAN IS BOTH
HERO AND VILLAIN • STUDY OF TWINS • POSSIBILITIES OF EDUCATIVE PROCESSES •
TEACHING THE STRUCTURING OF PERSONALITY CHARACTERISTICS • THE PUBLIC AC-
TIVITIES OF CERTAIN ABNORMAL PERSONALITIES • THE DRIVING FORCES OF MAN-
KIND • LEADERS WITH CHARACTERISTIC PARANOID ENERGY • THE PRUSSIAN PARA-
NOID GROUP • SOCIOLOGISTS AND PSYCHIATRISTS AT THE PEACE TABLE AND IN POST-
WAR PLANNING • CRIME A SOCIAL DISORDER • A VOLITIONAL ACT WITH DIRECTING
MENTAL ACTIVITY • STUDY OF PRECURSORS BELONGS TO PSYCHIATRY • DUTY OF
SOCIOLOGISTS • THE ENGLISH BORSTAL METHODS • GROWTH OF SELF-RESPECT •
BEST PRINCIPLES OF APPLIED SOCIOLOGY AND PSYCHIATRY • A YOUTH-CORRECTION
AUTHORITY • TRAINING AND TREATMENT OF YOUNG OFFENDERS

FOR YOU at this luncheon meeting when very properly you have need for relaxation between the formal sessions of the Conference, I propose to speak rather discursively and informally. Someone has said that in a sense a novel must inevitably be autobiographical. The novelist can reveal only his own remembrances of experiences, his own thought-life or his own phantasies. And the papers of this Conference, except reports of facts gathered, show just that self-revelation. So, too, this address of mine.

I am not aware by what strange divination the program

committee knew that I had ever had even a minor interest in sociology. But it is true, though I am sure that any sociologists present will recognize the limitations of my knowledge in their field. It came about in this way: I had a boyhood affair with biology. I wanted to know about life and growth in plants and animals, but after a time these did not seem to be related enough to human living. Then one fine day I ran into Auguste Comte, introduced to him by the philosopher, George Henry Lewes, the husband of George Eliot, a lady who had been my friend for years. Sounds a trifle anachronistic, does it not? But then, those who have written well are real persons long after they have passed away. This Auguste Comte, there was the man for you. He had named a new science "Sociology" and proclaimed it to be The Positive Science of Humanity. In the enthusiasm of late adolescence that phrase hit me hard. But somehow behind the façade of words I seemed to find little that really was human, or scientific. Then I met up with Herbert Spencer and his "First Principles" and his two volumes on the principles of sociology and two volumes on the principles of psychology and what not. Well, during the years that I was scraping up enough money with which to go to college, Spencer was my tutelary saint. But once within the gates of Harvard, where I arrived in the early gay nineties, I found that Spencer was thoroughly discredited by the eminent philosophers there and that my noble science of sociology was relegated to a very inferior position. The brilliant courses on political economy were explaining man's relations to man.

But some ideas derived from Spencer, who was so largely responsible for enlarging the concept of the new science, I could not shake off. Stated in short they were: (1) For the welfare of mankind, sociology is the most important science. (2) Its subject matter is the social organism, which exists for the benefit of its members. (3) Like other organisms it continually shows evolutionary progress. (4) There is such a thing as social inheritance and this is the foundation of social progress. (5) Sociology as a science cannot advance except hand in hand with advancing psychological science.

Outside the sacred precincts of Harvard Yard but among the Cambridge illuminati of that day was a bulky figure whom older people here will perhaps remember, John Fiske, the eminent historian and philosopher. He put into plainer language and more succintly what Spencer had spread out in pages. Said he, "We must regard Sociology as an offshoot from Psychology, specialized as the introduction of inquiries concerning the relations of many percipient and emotionally incited minds to each other and to the common environment." With all its implications for sociology, instead of "psychology" he might well have said "psychiatry" if that word had been in use in those days.

Omitting what many other sociologists have stated in this connection let me quote two or three. McDougal comes out flat-footed with these statements: "The science which formulated the body of ascertained truths about the constitution and working of the mind must be the foundation of sociology." "The springs of human action, the impulses and motives that regulate conduct are what sociology must take into account." And then a more recent writer, Lindeman: "The minutest observation of what a man is doing can never reveal the precise purpose or motive which fully accounts for his actions." "Psychiatric technique is able to arrive at explanatory inferences because this does not rely upon objective observations or accepting the individual's rationalizations." Or Odum: "The individual is the key to social studies. Their aim is the knowledge of what sort is the individual, how do individuals differ, and what social differences are there that make or mar the individual and influence him, in turn, in his social relationships."

For this occasion and an audience composed of others than psychiatrists or sociologists, I am going to dwell a minute on definitions and comments concerning these sciences. Perhaps the best definition of sociology is that it is the science which deals with the phenomena of collective living or collective behavior.

Psychology, as it has been developed, is the science which

deals in more formal fashion with mental processes. And what a chance it missed earlier by remaining academically minded when it might have joined the medical sciences for the study of all phases of mental life!

Social psychology is a recently developed union of psychology and sociology which takes note of much that modern psychiatry has to offer. It definitely represents study of the mental processes involved in and sometimes causing phenomena observable in the behavior of human beings living collectively.

Psychiatry, which formerly confined itself to study and treatment of the individual from the standpoint of his immediately discoverable physical and mental functioning, has been forced by virtue of being presented with a wider and wider range of problems concerning human behavior to deal with causative social situations as well as with the individual himself—and just this for the sake of therapy. Nowhere is this seen so clearly as in what may be termed preventive psychiatry as practised in child guidance clinics. There the development of a case history must take account of much that might be subsumed under the head of sociology, or social psychology. Particularly in the family life, in the primary social unit as Cooley of Michigan called it, a deep study of emotional interrelationships is frequently indicated. This, of course, is what a psychiatric social worker is especially trained to do. Explicitly, a good case study is largely an investigation of what man in social relationships has made of man. Indeed, psychiatry can almost be defined as being the science of interpersonal relationships. It is how the individual behaves in social relationships that is the point when he becomes the subject of psychiatric investigation. Man does not live or behave in a social vacuum; the most important feature of his environment is social.

Out of all this we can easily discern that for the best development of both sociology and psychiatry we cannot put a fence around either one of them and exclude the other. Nor, for that matter, can either exclude allied scientific fields, notably psychology, social psychology and anthropology.

A favorite illustration of the part that psychiatry and sociology can play together is in the study of suicide. Sociology undertakes to give us facts for the incidence of suicides as they are related to time, place, age, general population, types of population and so on. Psychiatry looks at the subjective motives, constitutional predispositions, emotional states, internal conflicts, reactions to personal experiences in family life.

As throwing light upon the contention that psychiatry and sociology as sciences can only advance hand in hand, let us come to a problem that for theoretical and practical considerations deeply concerns both. What is the essential nature of the human being? Or, putting the question in other words, what is the raw material of human nature that cultural pressures mould into the shape of the human being whom we know mainly through observation of his social behavior?

One of the most used text-books of sociology indulges in some challenging phraseology. While insisting that, "It is with social forces and human nature that sociology is mainly concerned," we are called on to realize that "Man is not born human." "Human beings as we find them are artificial products." If this leaves us puzzled about the meaning of the term "human nature," we must add that Park and Burgess proceed to discriminate between *human nature* and *original nature*. And thereby hangs a tale, for we may well do quite a bit of thinking about what in its natural state constitutes the original stuff that is gradually shaped and patterned by social contacts and social institutions so that the individual comes to behave like a human being.

Does a child come into the world with anything more than an inheritance derived from purely biological sources? Has it traits and tendencies that have been patterned by ancestral social experiences? That is a nice question for you, and one that has little to do with Spencer's social inheritance or Korzybski's time-binding aspects of the history of the human race. Baldwin, the sociologist, was quite convinced that "The individual comes into the world with the impulse of the history of the race behind him. He has not only individualistic and egoistic impulses, but also positive predispositions to social life." Proofs offered are blushing, jealousy, shame, and so on, which seem to reveal ancestral conditions of collective life and habit. Such traits or predispositions Baldwin says "may be termed quasi-social or gregarious impulses."

To this problem I would invite serious thought: whether or not created or patterned by ancestral experiences, is it or is it not true that certain predispositions or qualities of great social value are definitely part of the matrix of the original nature of mankind?

Nowadays we are immensely impressed—sometimes I wonder if we are not almost over-impressed—by the inimical under-the-surface nature of man. For psychiatrists I need hardly speak in this connection of unconscious, instinctive drives or of unconsciously active repressions, projections, identifications, reaction-formations, and so on, to say nothing of anxieties, regressions and fixations. Contemplation of these goings-on within the inmost life of the individual led earlier psychoanalysts to state that man is "lived" by unknown and uncontrollable forces. Although it would seem to have been safer to say "partly lived" and "uncontrolled forces," yet evidently that early formulated deterministic idea still has its adherents. Sociologists and anthropologists, as some of them are doing, may well join with psychiatrists in trying to answer the question of to what extent, if any, this undercover mental life has been brought about by social living, by exigencies that have confronted the individual in his life situation in any particular culture. We should very much like to know what part of what man does is necessitated by his original nature.

If we rely on observations of infancy to tell the story, the entire story of the original nature of man, we forget that some innate drives and potentialities are not yet apparent. Whole systems of nerve fibres are not yet medullated; millions of connections between brain cells are not yet made. And are not the hidden potentialities and urges to develop and unfold new characteristics and powers part of original nature? Study it as we may, the unfolded bud does not reveal the nature of the flower. Considering how little we comprehend as yet of human nature in terms of neuro-psychic or other body-mind relationships, does it behoove us grandiloquently to pronounce on what man really is in his fundamental make-up?

If it is argued that man is constructed in such dastardly fashion that deep down and in any ultimate sense he is altogether controlled by the irrational and unsocial impulses of the Id, whence come his often astonishingly powerful drives and urges to exercise certain higher powers? For example, the strong impulse to reason, to respond to reason, and to some extent at least to live by reason, does not this arise from the original nature of man? Quantitatively still weak, not only the capacity but also the drive to exercise reasoning powers are very early displayed. And from whence do appreciations and abilities in the arts come, with all their cultural implications, except from the original nature of human beings which, in these particulars, is not evident until neuropsychic mechanisms have been structured at a later date than infancy?

I wish all of you might read C. Judson Herrick's spirited essay, *A Neurologist Makes Up His Mind*.[1] Basing his optimism on the fact that through the natural structuring of man there are many millions of unused brain cells which could conceivably be put into action, Herrick asserts that there is a great future possibility for better and more reasonable control of ourselves and of our social living.

You will easily note that I have very considerable skepticism as to whether we have as yet dug up enough in the fields of anthropology, sociology, psychiatry or psychoanalysis to fill out a complete picture of the fundamental nature of man. I ask, are we yet equipped either to say this is what man is, in and of himself, or this is what collective living has made of him through the ages during which he has been influenced by many social institutions including language constructions, some of which have afforded ennobling ideas and ideals as well as restraints? Until we have grown more mature in our knowl-

[1] Herrick, C. J. A neurologist makes up his mind. Scient. Monthly, *49*:99, 1939.

edge of such things what right have we to take the attitude that we are pawns of fate, in the long run powerless to combat what may be socially before us?

To my mind it is only this incompleteness of our conception of man's nature that could lead the brilliant psychoanalyst and former sociologist, Zilboorg, to produce a recent essay wherein he writes with dire foreboding of the future of human affairs. His thesis is that within the frame of his cultural existence man has a biopsychological endowment which, apparently forever, through return of the repressed renders him a menace to civilization. It is ignorance of this fundamental fact that leads to the common "megalomaniac belief that it is man who makes history with his own hands." Even scientific psychology and sociology dare not face the truth of the deep-lying conative psychology of man.

On the way here I read Alexander's just published book, *Our Age of Unreason*. Here is an entirely different point of view. In a challenging discussion of Pareto's philosophy of violence, Alexander insists that human nature can be influenced and modified. "Freud took the first step toward converting the ideal of the Greeks and Locke, the rule of reason, into a scientific reality." "The reign of reason should be established by the scientific study of personality." In this work I find agreement with my own opinion that the essential nature of man includes both noble and ignoble qualities. As Alexander says, a man is both a hero and a villain, and this "is a fact which still awaits popular recognition."

Still another set of ideas concerning the nature of man and its meaning for culture and civilization, past, present and future, is contributed by Otto Rank in a book, *Beyond Psychology*, which, after his many writings, is his last will and testament. For Rank all orthodox psychology is poor stuff because it does not recognize the irrational forces active in the life of man, inciting not only his destructive tendencies but also his creative impulses. He strongly disagrees also with much in the Freudian psychology. For example, the superego which restricts the primitive instincts has not, or at least, has not entirely grown into being as the result of external prohibitions derived from social living. There is "a self-inhibiting impulse inherent in the individual which creates protective limitations against the irrational self." Well, for civilization, Rank asserts, "the only remedy is an acceptance of the fundamental irrationality of the human being and life in general." Granted this dynamic functioning of the irrational "we have the basis for the emergence of everything of which mankind is capable in personal and social capacity for betterment." However, which in the long run will turn out to be the stronger, the rational side of man—evidently also inherent in his nature—to which Rank vehemently appeals with his own reasoning, or the dynamic functioning of the irrational? I leave that for your own calculations.

If we wonder about what present-day sociologists are thinking with regard to sociology and psychiatry working together hand-in-hand, we may obtain some information from a review of recent trends in social psychology by L. L. Bernard in the *American Journal of Sociology* for July, 1942. For one thing, he says, "No one but the psychoanalysts any longer give credence to the theory of control by instincts, and even they would appear to consider their basic instinct patterns to be the result of experience rather than of direct inheritance." Right or wrong? Though Bernard notes that the most important trend in the field of social psychology seems today to be in the direction of development of new lines of interpretive insight, he thinks that "we must study what men do in order to discover what patterns they live by and what we may expect from them." Of course the psychiatrist might counter: What do you mean by what men do, just what you can see? Is not what they do within their unexposed-to-view mental and emotional life of the greatest importance for knowing what patterns men live by and what to expect of them?

In thinking of research possibilities, if psychiatry and sociology join hands, I am reminded of the highly promising work of our Russian friend Luria, psychologist and psychiatrist, whom some of you know through his method of eliciting the existence of emotional conflicts. In Moscow in 1935 we found a finely equipped institute devoted to work on the old problem, what is nature, what is nurture—a question of paramount importance for the Russian ideology. Luria with thousands of rubles for research, but nothing for a good pair of shoes, had the OGPU round up for him sets of twins. He had under observation about one thousand pairs of non-identical and two hundred and twenty pairs of identical twins. In many cases one of the twins was being brought up apart from the family, with special physical, social and educational training in nursery schools and elsewhere, in order to observe what special types of conditioning and training could or could not accomplish. Study of possibly induced mental and emotional responses was part of the plan of research, while for comparison investigations of the characteristics of the family life and of the responses to them of the other twin who remained at home were being made. What a pity that this important experiment has had to go by the board!

In this period of horrific affairs among the peoples of the world, we are all thinking of what the future may be. Judging from history we can well doubt whether the repartition of nations or the redistribution of economic balances or even the extension of so-called democracy will result in any greatly bettered social ordering of life—in the large or in smaller group relationships. Then let us have some thought about the possibilities of educative processes—slow processes to be sure, but it is a long future to which we must look forward and the social institutions of mankind have not been formed in a day. However, we can learn something of the potentialities of education through what has been accomplished in a relatively short time in the dictator countries and most notably in Russia. I directly ask whether the time is not ripe for psychiatry to take the lead in formulating plans for educating human beings to know more about themselves for the sake of their own better self-direction in social interrelationships.

Sociology and the other social sciences continuously present the facts of disastrous group adjustments but, through not having been developed as therapeutic disciplines up to the present, they find themselves timid about offering solutions. To be sure, Ward and Ross have demanded that sociology should point the path to better ways of living, and Lynd in his *Knowledge for What?* shows his dissatisfaction with sociology as merely a normative and informative science. It is rather instructive that a certain committee of sociologists meeting in conference some few years ago decided that sociology should be very careful about declaring for any practical philosophy of social life—not enough is yet known, it was thought. For me sociology would still be the noble science if it would come together with psychiatry and plan to do things instead of merely talking about them.

What can psychiatry offer? The main point is that human beings need above everything for right social living the indoctrination of new conceptions of themselves, about the facts and origins of their irrationalities, about the nature of fundamental drives and urges and, even more important, about their potentialities for more rational social behavior. It was the latter that Dr. Allen emphasized this morning when he was speaking about psychotheraphy for the individual. It is a striking commentary on the educational process at even the college level that psychiatric insights into human nature are not dealt with as a part of the prescribed curriculum. What could be more valuable in the furtherance of civilized progress? And am I wrong in my phantasy that much could be accomplished already at the high school age by teaching something about the structuring of personality characteristics? I know of some apparently successful attempts to do this, though not undertaken with this wording. Among other results, wide education for the understanding of underlying and often unconscious motives of behavior, and promulgation of information about the energetic reiterative public activities of certain types of abnormal personalities might go far toward preventing acceptance of a lot of zany ideas that now lead to socially inimical group activities. What should be understood, for example, about a Huey Long, a Pelley, a Talmadge of Georgia, or an Elizabeth

Dilling—all of whom have been able to get groups behind them?

Now about some even wider issues. The latest publication of a learned economist, Peter F. Drucker, seems to be quite devoid of the knowedge that psychiatry can give concerning the driving forces of mankind. In *The Future of Industrial Man,* he pooh-poohs the idea that Naziism is at all the product of the particular characteristics of "the German mind," whether represented by Nietsche or any other Teutonic ideologists. The present world struggle is entirely based on economic and industrial issues. What does sociology or social psychology, or psychiatry say to that? I use the example of Drucker's style of thinking as a foil in calling your attention to a very different point of view.

A persuasively interesting and highly important study of the paranoid trends to be found in a long-prevailing German culture has been made by one of our colleagues, Dr. Richard M. Brickner. He has amassed an astounding amount of historical and literary evidence to the point, and gives us in the last number of the *American Journal of Orthopsychiatry* [2] a professional preview of a forthcoming book addressed to a more general audience. It is quite unlikely that a victory by the United Nations will render null and void these internationally unsocial personality attributes of the German people, so we may give heed to Brickner's, or any other, ideas about the possibilities of a better post-war ordering of the world we must live in. Brickner says: First, of course, get rid of those leaders who with characteristic paranoic energy so infect and influence others. Second, disperse and infiltrate the German people so that in any given social setting there may not be too many of the Prussian paranoid group. Third, educate and re-educate for the sake of developing new insights on the part of large proportions of the German people. Here, as you see, psychiatry comes into play by making interpretations of collective behavior and offering suggestions for sociological planning.

Is it too much to hope that at the peace table and in post-

[2] Brickner, R. M. The German paranoid trend. Am. J. Orthopsychiat., *12*:611, 1942.

war planning broad-gauge sociologists and psychiatrists may find a place?

Since the subject assigned to me includes the relationship of psychiatry to criminology, which of late has been rated as a branch of sociology, I turn for the remaining few minutes to that topic. In earlier days attempts were made to develop a science of criminology by a physician, Lombroso, a police official, Huns Gross, and various others who were not sociologists —and then sociology took over. Perhaps this was because crime is a social disorder and, like other social phenomena, our knowledge of it must remain very incomplete unless all sorts of relevant social data are gathered by fact-finding techniques. Then sociologists with their opportunities for research while on the side-lines can survey a wide field of life wherein crime plays a part.

Where does psychiatry join in? One might make a long story of this, but the main points that I would make are as follows: if one takes any fundamental attitude with regard to criminology, it must be acknowledged that in almost every instance the commission of a crime is a volitional act, and consequently that immediately antecedent to the crime there is a directing mental activity. This may be in the form of ideas or of mental representations, often with strong emotional components, and always involving a lack of inhibiting concepts or automatically active inhibiting impulses. The study of the nature and causes of these activating factors within the mental life as well as of the causes of the absence of inhibiting impulses which are potent for the behavior of non-criminals, is a job which belongs to psychiatry. And this does not discount in the least the value of sociological data concerning crime. The mental elements that are the precursors of crime are the most immediate factors in the production of the volitional activity—that is all.

One of the great strides forward in sociological research has been made by taking over from psychiatry the technique of case studies. Notable in this respect are the criminological studies of Clifford Shaw. But I submit that what is missing in

these case studies are facts that modern psychiatry would demand and interpretations that psychiatry could offer. For example, in *Brothers in Crime* we have very good accounts of
the environment, of the overt facts of the family life, and,
so far as they go, the "Own Stories" as told by these young
criminals ring true. But what we miss is factual material and
interpretations concerning the emotional reactions provoked
by interpersonal relationships, particularly the father-son relationships in these cases, the significance of the lack of an
ego-ideal and of frustrations and hostilities developed within
the family circle—all these so overwhelmingly important for
the formation of patterns of personality structure and behavior, including criminality.

My work and observations over the years have led me to
become far less interested in sterile sociological and psychiatric theories of the genesis of crime than in planful efforts to
deal constructively and therapeutically with criminalistic behavior—whether in its beginnings or its later continuance. Indeed, so far as knowing anything about the various factors of
crime causation is concerned, I argue that, as in medicine, we
may come to learn much from evaluating the results of different types of therapy. This, if we ever arrive at the time when
scientific treatment is applied in this field.

It is the duty of psychiatry to do much more than it has yet
done, first, in competently diagnosing and loudly calling attention to the abnormal personalities among those who commit
crime; second, in unearthing, for the purpose of individual or
group therapy, the various sorts of mental and emotional an-
tecedents of criminal behavior; third, in planning, particularly with sociologists, for the introduction of scientifically
based re-educative training and treatment of at least youthful
offenders.

It is the duty of sociologists, with all their accumulations of
the overt facts concerning crime, to give more attention to
underlying motivations of this form of human behavior. Also
their opportunities for influencing young men at the college
level should lead them to be able to inspire a certain propor-

tion to become professionally interested in the prevention and cure of crime. In this country there has been almost entire neglect for the need of men of ability and training to cope with the problems presented by our young and treatable criminals. On the other hand, in England where such treatment is vastly more effective, men of very unusual qualifications are willing to enter this type of public service and are highly esteemed for doing so. Can we imagine one of our reformatories being headed by two Groton and Harvard men? Yet only that would be the equivalent of what I found in the Borstals visited—in one both the governor and his deputy were Eton and Oxford. This is enough to indicate a public attitude that differs widely from our own.

As perhaps some of you know, we have published our careful studies of the English Borstal system—*Criminal Youth and the Borstal System,* 1941. If that remarkable system of dealing with offenders between the ages of sixteen and twenty-three is summed up in short, it would be about as follows: In the first place, the social implications of the treatment process are never lost sight of. If sociologists will make themselves acquainted with the details of what has been experimentally developed for re-education in collective living they cannot fail to have admiration for Borstal methods. Secondly, though not specifically designated as such, the varied programs of the ten different Borstal institutions are oriented according to the best principles of mental hygiene. For example, even the great emphasis that is placed on physical training as taught by their experts in the Borstals has the common sense idea back of it that the development of strength, good posture, and bodily skills plays an important part in the growth of self-respect that is a first step towards reformation. And here I would insist that the arduousness of the program that is representative of a Borstal day is so utterly in contrast to the softness of life in our reformatories that there is no comparison; our young fellows would think they were being killed. Yet the program is so varied and so recognizably upbuilding that very soon after admission it is usually accepted with good grace and later many express gratitude for what the training has done for their personality development. Besides other features of the regime, such as vocational training and academic instruction, what may rightfully be termed psychotherapeutic interviews are extensively utilized. Housemasters and governors are constantly on the lookout for emotional disturbances and from the very first take pains to develop such friendly, confidential relationships that they, working by psychiatric principles, come to know much of the inner lives of the young men and to aid them about many troublesome matters. Again this is a tremendous contrast to our reformatory methods; here the prevailing rule is that officials should not mix into the personal problems of prisoners. Taking it all together, the Borstal system represents an outstanding achievement, embodying some of the best principles of applied sociology and of psychiatry.

In connection with this, I should hope that all of you will become acquainted with what the American Law Institute has done in framing a model act for a Youth-Correction Authority. Any state might modify this act for passage by its legislature, but the central idea is to make possible the scientific treatment of youthful offenders. In a wide sense this is a sociological undertaking, and a very important one for our given culture where crime is so prevalent. It was contemplated that even though, of course, psychiatrists enough could not be found to deal with the inner needs of all offenders, yet psychiatric principles of treatment could filter through to all who would come in contact with them, whether as educators, guards, or administrative officials. To this end, the personnel probably should gain for themselves pretty much the point of view and to some extent the training of the modern, effective, psychiatric social worker. I hope this contemplated enactment will receive all your backing. An immense amount of time has been spent by a group of experts in considering the framing of it from the standpoints of legal requirements and procedures and the practical possibilities of vastly bettered forms of training and treatment for young offenders.

PART IV

PSYCHIATRY AND THE WAR

Introduction to Part IV

By THOMAS J. HELDT, M.D.

Physician in Charge Division of Neuropsychiatry, Henry Ford Hospital.
Member of the Committee on the Conference on Psychiatry

THE ALL absorbing concern of the Conference on Psychiatry at this time is how we can be of assistance, individually and collectively, in directing the processes of thought and action to the proper solution of a devastating social catastrophe—a global war.

The primitive and biological motivations of man have been offended and disrupted. The characterological attitudes and values gained through civilization have been cast aside like so much veneer. Geographical, ethnological and sociological differences have been magnified beyond reason. Disregard, disrespect and total indifference for the freedom of religion is commonplace. Bondage and abuse of conquered peoples are carried out in open defiance of international law. Freedom of speech is turned to dire account in malicious rumor and propaganda. Employer and employee stand in fear of each other. Want is a matter of expediency and an unstable end-result of conflicting social misjudgements.

In such a state of national and international turmoil, a small group of medical adherents with special interest in human behavior and the causes for its alterations in certain settings has turned to psychiatry and this Conference to pool considerations, analytical, synthetical and, we hope, remedial.

The Conference thus far has dealt with the philosophy of psychiatry, its scope, its aims, its principles and its advancements, as well as its values and its potentialities in the problems of research and investigation. The psychiatry of the individual has been considered, as seen in his training, his experience and his education reviewed in terms of analysis and synthesis; the relationship of psychiatry to sociology and criminology has been reviewed.

All of this has provided a background upon which the problems peculiar to psychiatry because of the war may be more satisfactorily presented, as well as an approach from a broad psychiatric viewpoint to the problems of the war.

Psychiatry in the Army

By COLONEL WILLIAM C. PORTER, M.C., U. S. Army

Director, School for Military Neuropsychiatry, Lawson General Hospital, Atlanta

THE NEUROPSYCHIATRIC SERVICE IN THE UNITED STATES ARMY • THE MILITARY MISSION OF THE MEDICAL DEPARTMENT • SELECTION OF VOCATIONALLY FIT AND ELIMINATION OF CASUALTIES • CHANGING STANDARDS • ACCEPTING MENTAL RISKS • USEFUL MEN REJECTED • BENEFITS OF SERVICE • MENTAL DEFICIENCY AND SPECIAL TRAINING UNITS • CLERICAL OR MANUAL SKILLS • BANK CLERKS AND MONKEY WRENCHES • MENTAL HYGIENE UNITS AT REPLACEMENT CENTERS • NEUROPSYCHIATRIC SECTIONS IN FIXED HOSPITALS • PREVIOUS EXPERIENCES OF PSYCHIATRIC STAFFS • NECESSITY FOR COMMON STANDARDS • TIME FACTOR IN TREATMENT • ELEMENT OF RISK • LINE OF DUTY STATUS • ARMY REGULATIONS • PRIMARY OBLIGATION TO MILITARY SERVICE • ACUTE SCHIZOPHRENIA OF MILITARY SERVICE • ACUTE ANXIETY STATES • THE MILITARY PSYCHIATRIST

WE HAVE been greatly edified by the addresses on the philosophy of psychiatry, on the needs and opportunities for research and for the application of psychiatry to special problems. I bring you a pressing problem, which is in the terrible present, having significance to each and every citizen of the United States and especially to this Conference. I refer to the Neuropsychiatric Service in the United States Army. My remarks will not apply in every particular to the other armed forces, but the same principles apply and will be amplified by the representatives of the other branches.

We in the armed services are not unmindful of the need for research and of the great opportunities which the war gives us to deal with large numbers of human beings and to use them for research and experimentation in the field of human behavior, but the demands of war make impossible research into many of the problems by those of us who are performing the military mission which is placed upon us. One must be mindful of what that mission is before discussing what we as psychiatrists or what we as medical officers should do in our present situation. The mission of the medical department is to make men fit for combat or for servicing combatant troops and, failing that, to remove casualties from the army. That is the sole mission. We have no other major directive. The psychiatrist has the problem of selecting individuals who are vocationally fit for service in the armed forces; and having accepted him, to assist him in preserving his mental integrity; and failing in that, to eliminate him from the service. He has no long therapeutic program facing him. There are other branches of the government, both state and federal, as well as private agencies whose duty it is to care for the ex-service man. Our duty is to carry on such therapy as will restore him to a combat or a supply status and, failing that, to make him as fit to live with as possible for the length of time that he remains in the military hospital and then eliminate him from the service and dispose of him in an orderly humane manner.

The duty of the psychiatrist starts at the selective service echelon—now known as the induction recruiting station—at which time he applies such training, aptitudes and technics as he has, to the selection of men for the service. We emphasized, especially during the training period, prior to the onset of the present war, that military service constitutes a type of vocation for which all men are not fitted. That is obvious and is well known. However, since the declaration of war and as the man power reservoir has been depleted, the considerations of standards for elimination must be modified to some extent. In other words, we cannot apply exactly the same standards of selection at this time as we could during the training program. The War Department and the Selective Service have already dipped into the substandard physical classes. Whether that is wise is not, of course, for me to say. It is being done. Class 1-B's are being taken. It is true that no specific directive says that mental substandard risks should be accepted. In fact, it says quite the contrary, but when you are taking a substandard physical class, it is easy for selective service boards and induction boards to let a few mental risks slip in, which they would have not taken had the standards remained on the level of Class 1-A.

Another question has lately been raised. Have we as psychiatrists rejected men who would have succeeded in the service? Of course, the answer to that is not immediately apparent. However, from one or two research projects which have been under way, there is some indication that we may have to revise our opinions somewhat in the selecting of human material. These projects tend to show that certain men who are on full duty and give performance which is quite acceptable to their unit commanders and to everyone concerned, have not seriously complained of anything, have not appeared with undue frequency on sick report, are apparently getting along all right, these men show many deviations from normal in the association tests and in various other psychological tests, to the same degree as individuals who have broken and who are in the hospital. So this raises the question whether we have not rejected some individuals who would be of use in the national effort inside the military service. Indeed, there are some psychiatrists who say that some psychoneurotics get along pretty well in the service, that there is a type of psychoneurotic who is actually benefited by military service. He is given protection and makes an adjustment which would have been impossible for him in non-military life. I have known certain simple schizophrenics who have served three enlistments of three years each, have received honorable discharges, and did very nicely under various unit commanders as long as they were not put under conditions of stress to which they might be vulnerable and as long as no sudden changes were made in their mode of living. However, in time of war I would not advocate that we take psychoneurotics indiscriminately or that schizophrenics generally should be taken into the service for therapeutic or other reasons. We know that many mentally deficient individuals who are below the ten-year level get along pretty well in military service. In fact, we have reached the stage in the clinical program in the disposition of

cases where we do not discharge a man solely because he tests
below ten years on a psychometric scale of any variety. We
wait until he has shown some emotional difficulty, until he
shows some behavior deviation in addition to his mental deficiency before we attempt to eliminate him. In fact, at the
hospital with which I am connected, a mentally deficient person must be referred by a unit commander or by somebody
who has observed something which has brought him to attention as a behavior deviation problem before we will dispose
of him on the basis of his mental deficiency.

There are some mental deficients who cannot learn general
orders and who cannot learn the ordinary rudiments of military knowledge, so they automatically bring themselves to
the attention of the unit commander by that lack of ability to
learn. However, there are now special training units to which
these individuals may be transferred where they are placed for
a period of observation and training for from one to three
months under skilled personnel directors, psychologists and
psychiatrists, to ascertain whether or not there is anything in
them which can be made useful to the service.

At the reception centers, where the men have their initial
classification, there are tests and interviews given by psychologists of the Adjutant General's Office, who determine
aptitudes in a rough way between clerical and manual skills,
and who further determine the type of skills to which they
are adapted and enter the results upon the classification personnel record of the individual. This record accompanies the
man throughout his army service and should guide those in
authority over him in the selection of the tasks to which he
is assigned and of the unit to which he should be assigned. The
theory is good and in practice the system will work one hundred percent if the personnel directors and unit commanders
have confidence in its integrity. That in time will be demon-
trated. At first, there have been some mistakes made. Bank
clerks have been assigned to handling monkey wrenches in a
tank unit. But after all, that may not be so bad and in most

instances it has actually worked out to the advantage of the individual.

The man may stay a short time or a long time at a reception center awaiting requisition from a unit training center or from a replacement training center. At the replacement center he is trained for about thirteen weeks in the combat branch or the supply branch in which he has shown general aptitude or has expressed interest. At that echelon there is a large opportunity not only for singling out individuals who have already shown behavior deviations, but also for mental hygiene, preventive psychiatry, by an individual not in any way connected with the therapeutic or administrative end of the psychiatric program. At several replacement centers mental hygiene units have already been set up and are functioning. The medical officers acting as mental hygienists are generally divorced from therapeutic and administrative functions at station hospitals and are assigned to the branch of the service under which the camp is operated.

Station hospitals and general hospitals are what we call fixed installations. They are fixed hospitals. They serve a command or a geographical territory and are located in buildings either of cantonment or permanent type construction. That is true in the zone of the interior, that is, anything back of the combat area or the theater of operations. In those hospitals it is customary to have set up neuropsychiatric sections with a capacity up to a maximum of five hundred beds. We have one general hospital which is devoted exclusively to psychotic cases. The general hospitals afford a particularly good opportunity for neuropsychiatric service. However, we remember that our function is not long-term care. We receive psychiatrists for duty from all sorts of sources, with all sorts of training and aptitudes. We have men from teaching institutions; we have those who have been doing mental hygiene work or health officer work; men from state hospitals and men from private practice. The variety of individuals working on a neuropsychiatric section makes it necessary to find a common denominator in formulating diagnostic and therapeutic standards.

The new medical officer soon learns that any type of therapy which he has practiced in the past requiring undue time is not applicable to military practice. He finds also that any therapeutic procedure to which there is attached an element of risk is not applicable to the service. The first is true because time does not allow any one patient to be retained in a hospital for a long-term therapy which he may receive from private, state or federal agencies. The second reason is that the "line of duty" implications are very potent. A man who has a condition which, under the regulations, is held to be constitutional in nature and which arises within the first six months of his military service is not in line of duty for military purposes. That does not necessarily mean "for pension purposes" or for any purpose, except War Department purposes. The compensation and the hospitalization by the Veterans' Administration is adjudicated by that agency and not by the army and is done after the man leaves the military service. Therefore, it is our duty, except in an emergency or to save a life or for some special purpose, not to undertake a type of therapy such as psychosurgery or shock therapy, unless we are fairly sure that there will be no complications which will throw that man from a "not in line of duty" status into a line of duty status for which the government is liable. So we are very loath to embark upon some type of therapy which many others have found to be beneficial, but which is still in an experimental stage. However, with more than ordinary caution, we do use shock therapy in selected cases, but we are probably much more selective than would be the case in a non-military hospital.

Many psychiatrists come into the army without any knowledge of the military setting in which they must work. The army abounds with customs and precedents, with many ways of doing things which the non-military man finds rather irksome at first. He is confronted with a formidable set of regulations, regulations not only for the army, but for his social conduct and for the official setting in which he works and for the medical installation in which he is operating. He is confronted with this formidable set of documents and may feel that they are irksome and are preventing him from performing the functions for which he entered the service. However, he soon learns that army regulations and other regulations are friendly and helpful. As soon as he grasps the philosophy back of the regulations, he will find that instead of being preventive, they are helpful in accomplishing the mission which he has to perform.

The newly activated military psychiatrist has other habits to overcome. I have already indicated the difference in goal that confronts him in the way of therapy and in disposition. He must forget that his primary obligation is to his patient or to society generally. His obligation primarily is to the military service and his objective is either to return men to combat or supply, or to remove elements in the forces which will destroy the spirit and morale of other men.

I have often heard it said that there is no difference in the types of mental disorder seen within or without the military service. That conclusion is not strictly true. I have had considerable experience in both fields, and this observation and belief is corroborated by many of my associates who have been in both fields. There is a type of acute mental disturbance, acute schizophrenia, which occurs in the military setting and which is peculiar to the military service and to prisons. It is an explosive type of reaction with a tendency to recover quite rapidly. The recovery begins to take place almost as soon as the individual is hospitalized with no special type of therapy having been given. The only rationalization on the part of the patient which is necessary is the belief that he is on his way home, or is on his way toward discharge, or is on his way out of the situation which presently confronts him.

Then we have the acute war neuroses, notably the acute anxiety states which in themselves carry no unfavorable prognoses. The factors of fatigue, discouragement, feeling of defeat in the presence of military reverses and of lack of ability to retaliate are those which lead to acute anxiety states, which promptly subside under sedation, restorative therapy and perhaps some narcosis or suggestion under hypnosis. The rebound is quite complete within a comparatively short period of time and with no prognostic implications as to the future. The only individuals who do not react favorably are those who have had a habit of psychoneurotically reacting in their pre-military life, those who have a psychoneurotic constitutional make-up. We are particularly concerned about fatigue states, but as I have already indicated, they are fairly benign, fairly short in their duration, manifesting themselves in many bizarre fashions, and promptly recover under restorative therapy.

Therefore, we feel that the military service does present some problems which are not common to the practice of the non-military psychiatrist. There are not many, it is true, but it does require a stable type of individual. It is unfortunate that the psychiatrists, who by definition and by their choice of discipline and therapeutic approach, should themselves sometimes be unstable and be inadequate to meet the needs of the war situation. It is unfortunate that we have so many medical officers who do not appear able to stand the gaff or to make adequate emotional adjustments. However, we in the army feel that the medical profession in general and our fellow neuropsychiatrists in particular should be highly complimented for their unselfish and painstaking efforts in Selective Service, on induction boards, and finally as medical officers within the armed forces.

Psychiatry in the Navy

By CAPTAIN FORREST M. HARRISON, M.C., U. S. Navy

Head, Division of Psychiatry, Office of the Surgeon General of the Navy

NAVY PSYCHIATRY AND SERVICE REQUIREMENTS • LIFE AFLOAT IN THE NAVY •
HAZARDS OF DAILY DUTIES • ATMOSPHERE AND EXPOSURES • CONCENTRATION OF
MEN • RIGIDITY OF DEMANDS • PROBLEM OF READJUSTMENT • INCIDENCE OF
MENTAL DISEASE • INVALIDING RATE • TYPES OF MENTAL DISORDERS • ANXIETY
STATES • HYSTERIA • ACUTE SCHIZOPHRENIA • MANIC-DEPRESSIVE PSYCHOSIS •
EMOTIONAL INSTABILITY • CONSTITUTIONAL PREDISPOSITION TO MENTAL DIS-
ORDERS • PRECIPITATING FACTORS, TRAUMA • INSTINCT OF SELF-PRESERVATION •
ELIMINATION OF MENTALLY UNFIT • ENLISTMENT OF PSYCHOPATHS AND NEU-
ROTICS • HIGH INTELLIGENCE, GREAT ABILITY AND UNSURPASSED MORALE OF THE
NAVY • NEUROPSYCHIATRIC PROCEDURE WITH RECRUITS • INSTRUCTION IN
MILITARY PSYCHIATRY • POSTGRADUATE WORK IN SAINT ELIZABETH'S HOSPITAL •
NEED FOR EXPERIENCED PSYCHIATRISTS • METHODS OF HANDLING MENTAL
PATIENTS, DISPOSITION • RED CROSS SOCIAL WORKER • STATE VOCATIONAL
REHABILITATION BOARD • U. S. EMPLOYMENT SERVICE • PROPHYLAXIS • STRESS
AND STRAIN • REST CENTERS • VOCATIONAL APTITUDE • CLASSIFICATION OF
OFFICERS AND MEN • ADMINISTRATION OF DISCIPLINE AND PSYCHIATRY • HOMO-
SEXUALITY • MORALE AND FITNESS • THE ENGINEERING OF MORALE • CONTROL
OF FEAR • LEADERSHIP • THE UTILITY OF PSYCHIATRY IN THE NAVY, AS A
MAJOR SPECIALTY

Introduction

FOR THE past three years we have been watching the evolution of a gigantic conflict, which has involved people all
over the face of the globe. We too were caught in the mael-
strom, and forced into the struggle. The angry clouds of war
continue to hang heavily over us, and they show no signs of
lifting. We are confronted with a great crisis. Forces are at
work which are rocking the very foundations of our civilization. It is not surprising that patriotic impulses, stirred by the
dangers of these critical times, should seek methods of expression. Psychiatrists, both individually and in groups, are com-

ing forward, offering their experience and skilled services. The many suggestions they have already given us have been very helpful indeed.

We in the Navy have much to learn about psychiatry from our civilian associates in this field. On the other hand, if the various psychiatric organizations throughout the country are to continue their constructive assistance, they must have a clear conception of the fundamental issues involved in Navy psychiatry, and a definition of our service requirements. There is no corrective equal to a discussion with others. The participation of the Navy, therefore, in the proceedings and deliberations of this Conference will be more than justified, if our coming together increases our mutual understanding and enlarges our stock of common knowledge.

Navy Environment

First of all, let me pause by the way, so to speak, and call your attention to certain aspects and features of our service environment, in order that you may have a more intimate knowledge of the setting and background in which mental disorders develop in the Navy.

When a recruit is accepted for enlistment, he is sent at once to one of our large training stations for indoctrination and instruction. Upon his arrival there, he is immediately surrounded by the necessary regulations and restrictions. His hours of sleep, drill, work, liberty and recreation, are all fixed. Discipline is strict, but it must be instilled, along with habits of obedience, promptness and cleanliness. After a brief period of training, he is sent to the Fleet, where the process of making an efficient fighting unit of him is continued.

Life afloat in the Navy is abnormal and unnatural in many directions, even under the most favorable conditions. A modern battleship is perhaps the highest type of concentrated mobile power ever developed by the mind of man. It is a veritable mass of machinery controlled and operated by steam and electricity. Both officers and men are engaged in hazardous duties and occupations at all time, night and day, such as handling boats in bad weather, working in the engine and fire-rooms, drilling with guns and turrets, firing target practice, oiling ship, stowing ammunition, and performing the thousand and one things which go to make up their daily lives. Then, too, the personnel lives in an atmosphere of constant noise, bugle calls, loud speakers, vibration, artificial light and ventilation, and irregular hours, all of which are nerve racking, to say the least. In addition, the frequent contacts of Navy ships with foreign ports the world over, where health conditions are dangerous, mean that everyone in the service is often exposed to all sorts of diseases, which may have some bearing on the development of mental disturbances.

The environment at our training stations and on board ship is fixed, unvarying and non-flexible, and is much more uniform than that of the average civilian community. This has a tendency to mold to a likeness all of the activities of the individuals who compose the organization. There is, in addition, a marked concentration of men, which is necessary in order to satisfy military requirements. The intensity of human intercourse is naturally increased by this density of population. The officers and men, therefore, are subjected to exceedingly close social contacts and relationships. There is probably no branch of the armed forces which imposes such rigid demands on its personnel as does the Navy.

It is easy to see that an individual upon entering the Navy must readjust himself to an entirely new and complex environment. The ease and completeness with which he makes this adaptation has an important bearing on his future welfare, and also upon his value to the service. He has perhaps gotten along quite well in civilian life in familiar surroundings and in a job to which he is accustomed. Upon being introduced, however, to the routine of the Navy, he often runs into difficulties, especially during war, and if the strain becomes too severe, he may be overwhelmed and react with a neurosis or a psychosis.

Incidence

One of the problems in which Navy psychiatry is intensely interested is the incidence of mental disease in the service. We shall not bore you with statistics. Suffice it to say, the average annual admission rate for neuropsychiatric disorders in the Navy for the past thirty years has been approximately three per thousand. In this connection, it is very gratifying to note that since the opening of hostilities on December 7 last, the incidence of the neuroses and the psychoses in the Navy has been below expectation. There has been an increase in the actual number of cases, proportionate to the expansion in personnel, but the admission rate per thousand has not been as high as originally anticipated. This is undoubtedly due to the effective measures for eliminating the mentally unfit which we have been using, and which will be discussed later on.

Invaliding Rates

While the incidence of mental disorders in the Navy is comparatively low, the story is quite different when it comes to the invaliding rate.

Neuropsychiatric conditions represent the most frequent of all causes for disability discharge from the service. The number of sick days, which they build up, and which each case averages, is enormous. The high invaliding rate results from the fact that once a definite diagnosis of a mental disorder is made in an officer or man, his separation from the Navy ordinarily follows. It has been found by experience that such individuals do not do very well when returned to duty, and their symptoms are likely to recur, if they are subjected to the same stress and strain which precipitated their original breakdown.

Types of Mental Disorders

It is but natural to suppose that certain types of mental disorders are commonly seen in the Navy, while others are not so frequent, and that the circumstances of war tend to produce characteristic reactions. This is true to a large extent. It must be emphasized, however, that one encounters all sorts of neuropsychiatric disabilities in the Navy, and they present essentially the same symptomatology and clinical course as they do in civilian life.

Since our entrance into the present struggle, the most frequent neurosis seen has been anxiety states, followed by hysteria, neurasthenia and psychasthenia, in the order named. The general manifestations of hysteria in the Navy are so numerous that it would be impossible to describe them without being kaleidoscopic. Anxiety neuroses in the Navy are either acute or chronic, the latter being more frequent. They vary in severity from a mild exaggeration of the normal fear reaction to panic and utter demoralization, which subside in several hours or a few days. The so-called psychosomatic disorders, such as effort syndrome, peptic ulcer, functional gastro-intestinal conditions, enuresis and others, are additional manifestations of a deep-seated anxiety state. As a rule, they are not properly diagnosed as neuroses, because the physical symptoms over-shadow those of the underlying mental disorder. Neurasthenia and psychasthenia show the same general trends in the Navy as they do in private practice.

As far as the psychoses are concerned, dementia praecox causes more admissions to the sick list than all the rest of them combined. Generally speaking, our cases of schizophrenia are more acute in onset, occur at a relatively more superficial level, are more easily modified, and respond to treatment more rapidly than they do in civil life. Manic-depressive psychosis is the next most frequent problem. These are particularly trying cases to handle, especially aboard ship. Dementia paralytica is third on the list, but this disease does not give us as much concern as formerly because of new and improved methods of therapy. Other types of psychoses are quite rare.

Among the constitutional psychopathic states, patients with emotional instability predominate, although the inadequate personalities are a close second.

Psychopaths are a constant source of annoyance and trouble, and they make up the bulk of the absentees, the discontented, the inefficients, and the inmates of the brig.

Of the remaining neuropsychiatric conditions encountered in the Navy, mental deficiency has been practically eliminated. Curiously enough, the military services seem to possess a fascination for epileptics. They are constantly trying to enlist, and they remain a decided problem to us.

Etiology

As far as the etiology of mental disorders in the Navy is concerned, constitutional predisposition, whatever that is, plays the most important role. The majority of our cases occur in individuals who since childhood have exhibited ineffective ways of dealing with their conflicts and handling the minor difficulties of life. As a matter of fact, quite a few of our patients give a history of having actually had a definite neurosis or psychosis before enlisting. It has been our experience that the average man in the Navy, unless he is constitutionally predisposed, will not break down with a mental disease, even when he is exposed to the most extreme hardships, both physical and psychological, of service life, and to the most harrowing and terrifying circumstances of modern warfare.

The usual precipitating factors operate in the production of mental disorders in the Navy, both during peace and war, just as they do in civil life. Trauma probably never causes a psychosis or neurosis in the Navy, unless the injury is an insignificant one, and the patient has an unconscious desire for some gain, such as evacuation from a combat zone, or discharge from the service. Almost never do we see mental disorders in individuals who are also suffering from severe physical wounds. From a psychological point of view, the psychoses and neuroses occurring in the Navy during war depend almost entirely upon the coming into play of the instinct of self-preservation. There is certainly no longer any reason to endow all of the symptoms and manifestations which our cases present with a restricted sexual significance.

Elimination of the Mentally Unfit

Perhaps the most essential psychiatric problem in the Navy is the elimination of the mentally unfit. In the great task of selecting the human material out of which to construct our service personnel, the psychiatrist has a particularly useful place, as we shall presently see.

The detection of the mentally unfit individual is always a very perplexing problem, especially in the recruiting office. Men with marked feeble-mindedness and clear-cut psychoses are eliminated rather easily, but the highest grades of defect, the psychopath and the neurotic, show very little to the examiner, and they are often well developed, physically perfect, bright looking and mentally alert. With only a narrow cross section of the applicant at the disposal of the examining medical officer, it is evident that he cannot hope to detect mental obliquities in a few minutes which would show up plainly in a longitudinal section covering a month or more. When the applicant presents himself for enlistment he is governed by his desire to enter the service, and naturally is not expected to divulge much information which would assist in his exclusion. In other words, he is putting his best foot forward, and the burden of proof is with us. Then, too, during periods of national emergency and war there is always a rush of volunteers, a demand for man power, and a natural desire on the part of recruiting officers to reach their quota as quickly as possible. Under these circumstances, the examinations are not as thorough as in times of peace and less time is devoted to each applicant. This results in the passing of many mentally unfit individuals who would otherwise be rejected in normal times.

In spite of these obstacles, however, large numbers of gross defects have been eliminated, and what is perhaps more important, with the present system of recruiting, a very high type of enlisted man only is being accepted. All of this, of course, makes for a Navy of high intelligence, great ability and unsurpassed morale, as well as a much more pleasant and wholesome environment for everyone in the service.

It is impossible to eliminate all of the mentally unfit at the recruiting office. This is particularly true in the case of individuals who may have latent defects in their character or temperament which will become evident only under conditions of stress. Realizing this, and facing a rapidly expanding Navy, the Surgeon General, in order to meet the needs of the situation, inaugurated a definite neuropsychiatric procedure during the national emergency, to be followed at all training stations for picking up the mentally unfit who had escaped detection and slipped by the recruiting office.

Reduced to its basic principles, this procedure involves: (1) a preliminary psychiatric survey of all incoming recruits, during which those who make an unfavorable impression or who seem to be of doubtful material for retention in the service are set aside for further examination later on; (2) a detailed study by the Psychiatric Unit of all recruits referred to it by company commanders, and others in administrative authority, and all those picked up as a result of the preliminary psychiatric survey; (3) indoctrinational lectures by psychiatrists to those officers having charge of personnel in which the major psychiatric conditions leading to maladjustment are outlined and the types of individuals to be referred are described; and (4) psychological examination of recruits when indicated in order to evaluate their abilities and determine their temperamental and emotional characteristics.

It will be seen, therefore, that on December 7, 1941, at the opening of hostilities, the Navy had a very definite psychiatric program and organization for the detection and elimination of the mentally unfit from the service, which had proved its worth from a practical standpoint. All that was needed when war was declared was to expand the existing organization and augment the psychiatric personnel engaged in this work, which was done. This program has continued to function and there has been no deviation from the basic principles originally laid down.

Reports received in the Bureau of Medicine and Surgery from the different training stations throughout the country indicate that this procedure is accomplishing the desired results. A large number of recruits with neuropsychiatric disabilities is being detected and eliminated early in the period of training and before they are sent to the Fleet.

Psychiatric Training and Personnel

It is hardly possible for the average naval medical officer, speaking generally, to acquire a sufficient knowledge of psychiatry to become expert in eliminating the mentally unfit, in spotting the prodromal signs of psychological breakdown, and in solving various other psychiatric problems. The Bureau of Medicine and Surgery recognizes, therefore, the need of special instruction of its medical officers in the subject of military psychiatry, and provision has been made for their systematic training in this field.

For a number of years, all officers entering the Medical Corps of the Navy have been required to attend a course of instruction at the Naval Medical School where psychiatry is a major subject. The student officers are given a series of lectures on the modern concepts of psychology. In addition, the methods of psychiatric examination are presented to them and the clinical pictures of the more important mental diseases. This does not make psychiatrists of them, but at least it gives them some idea of how psychiatry can be used to the best advantage in the Navy.

It is also necessary to provide for those medical officers who have had their interest drawn towards psychiatry, and who desire to specialize therein. From time to time, therefore, a certain number of them have been assigned to Saint Elizabeth's Hospital for post-graduate work. There they have received excellent basic training, and as a result there are always a few psychiatrists available in the Navy for the key positions.

Early during the period of the national emergency, with

a terrific expansion going on in the Navy, it became evident
that the small group of regular psychiatrists was not sufficient
to meet the psychiatric needs of the service, and that it would
be still more inadequate if war were declared. The procurement of trained psychiatrists, therefore, became one of our
cardinal problems.

This situation was met by increasing to the limit the number of medical officers undergoing psychiatric training, but
they could not be turned out fast enough. We were forced to
look to civilian psychiatrists who were engaged in peaceful
pursuits to supplement the nucleus of regulars in the Navy.
Reserve psychiatrists were enrolled in large numbers and
ordered to active duty for the most part at training stations
and marine recruit depots to function especially in connection
with the program of eliminating the mentally unfit.

With the opening of hostilities, the need for experienced
psychiatric personnel became even more acute. Training of
regulars is still being pushed. The procurement of reserve
psychiatrists has continued apace. The latter have entered
the service with splended enthusiasm, and they are doing excellent work.

Reserve psychiatrists on being ordered to active duty are
now being sent in groups to the National Naval Medical Center, Bethesda, Maryland. There they become acquainted with
the psychiatric problems of the Navy, and they get some idea
of the customs and etiquette of the service. After this course
of indoctrination, they are assigned to various activities requiring the services of a psychiatrist, and they are kept busy
doing useful professional work in their chosen specialty.

Methods of Handling

This brings us to a consideration of the methods of handling
and hospitalizing patients with mental disease in the Navy.

When a patient develops a psychosis or a neurosis aboard
ship, he is placed in the sick bay, where his treatment is begun
immediately. The quarters assigned to the medical department
on our larger men-of-war are ample, well arranged and thor-

oughly equipped. There are no facilities, however, for taking care of the mentally ill. If the patient is disturbed or excited, and if he is a menace to others, it is often necessary to place him in the brig for safe keeping, which is undesirable, of course.

An endeavor is made to transfer all mental cases arising in the Fleet as soon as possible to a hospital ship, which has facilities for taking care of these patients and, in addition, the services of a trained psychiatrist. When cruising at sea, this is not always practicable. Then, too, it is almost impossible for the hospital ship to accompany all of the task forces in the Navy at one time. Each vessel, therefore, must be prepared to care for its nervous and mental cases as an independent and self-sufficient unit until assistance can be obtained later on.

The Navy has several large hospitals located on the Atlantic and Pacific Coasts, which maintain neuropsychiatric services with staffs of trained psychiatrists. All mental cases which have been collected by a cruising or hospital ship are transferred to one of these hospitals as soon as contact is made. Patients with mild mental disorders and borderline conditions are kept in the hospitals to which they have been transferred until they can be discharged from the Navy and safely turned over to a responsible relative, or until they are well enough to go home by themselves. The grossly psychotic patients are eventually institutionalized, having first appeared before a Board of Medical Survey for the purpose. Navy patients are not adjudicated unless for some reason or other it becomes necessary. After about three months, they are discharged from the Navy and retained for further treatment. Those men who have the required service are usually held on the active list until they have completed sixteen, twenty, or thirty years in the Navy which entitles them to retirement.

In times of war, this whole problem is very difficult. Very frequently units of the Fleet and task forces are operating at some distances from their bases and they remain at sea for long periods of time. Mental cases developing aboard a ship after an engagement may be weeks in being returned to a hospital in the United States. Every possible effort is being made, however, in the Fleet and elsewhere, to get neuropsychiatric casualties into the hands of a psychiatrist at once. With this in view, psychiatrists are now attached to mobile hospital units, advance base hospitals, isolated stations, aviation activities, and on ambulance ships, which are located at strategic points. It must be remembered that our fighting fronts cover a tremendous area, and distances are great, to say the least, particularly in the Pacific.

The necessity for formulating plans for handling and hospitalizing mental cases is ever before us. Their prompt evacuation from combat zones, their transfer to institutions, and their final disposition is under constant study in order that all this may be accomplished expeditiously and with the maximum efficiency, and that existing methods may be improved.

Disposition

With the urgent need for man power at the present time, the question immediately arises as to what disposition should be made of the individual who has been discharged from the Navy because of a neuropsychiatric disability. The incentives for the development of a mental disease, especially a neurosis, should not be increased by making it a well known and respectable way of avoiding work. Nor should such an individual be absolved from all forms of national service. If he has broken down or proved incompetent to cope with life in the Navy, he can contribute to the war effort in other ways. He should not be left to find employment, because he may lose out due to excessive competition. His own capacity and the needs of the country must be evaluated. Suitable opportunities should be planned for him, and he should be assigned to non-combative military duties or civilian projects connected with the war effort. This method is one for the psychiatrist to handle.

For several years, the Navy has made an attempt, at least, to place its mental misfits in positions in civil life in which they can be useful. When a man is brought before a Board of Medical Survey or an Aptitude Board for discharge because of neuropsychiatric disability, he is instructed to report to the Red Cross Social Worker. She in turn refers the man to his State Vocational Rehabilitation Board, to the United States Employment Service, and to other agencies which might be of help. In this way, the economic problems of many of these individuals are taken care of, and the way is paved for their return to the home community.

Treatment

As far as the treatment of mental disorders in the Navy is concerned, all of the accepted forms of therapy are used in our hospitals, but emphasis is placed on prophylaxis. This is instituted largely through the exclusion of the mentally unfit, which we have already discussed. In addition, we are constantly trying to improve the conditions under which the personnel must live and fight, and to remove irritating influences, as far as possible. These measures tend to lessen the inevitable stress and strain of service life, especially during war. The Navy has also established rest camps and recuperation centers where exhausted fighting men may be sent for an indefinite period to recover from their fatigue. Upon reporting to one of these activities, they are interviewed by a psychiatrist whose function it is to detect the psychoses and neuroses in their incipiency. In addition, he assists the men in regaining their normal efficiency, and in overcoming fatigue, and gives advice as to its prevention. Before being returned to duty, they are given a thorough examination to determine their fitness for the same. In this way, breakdowns are prevented, and fighting men are kept out of hospitals.

Vocational Aptitude

The economic use of manpower, or vocational aptitude, which constitutes another one of our major problems, is becoming increasingly significant in the general scheme of things. It has both psychologic and psychiatric implications. Selecting the right man for the right job has become more imperative in industry, as machines and factories have grown more complicated. It is equally important in the Navy, if not more so, to classify both officers and the enlisted personnel, and relate their special abilities to specific tasks, so that each individual may be placed in a position of maximum usefulness.

In the early days of the Navy, when the ships were small and not so complicated, every member of the crew was supposed to be able to carry out any task required of him, regardless of whether or not he happened to be fitted for it. With the gradual increase in the number of special ratings, however, more attention was paid to the element of selection. Men were tested psychologically and mentally during the last war for such important duties as gun-pointing, fire control plotting, anti-submarine listening, and the lookout service. Since that time there has been a decided trend towards an even more intelligent handling of this whole problem. Under the direction and supervision of the Training Division of the Bureau of Personnel, educational, achievement and aptitude tests have been given since 1923 to all candidates for the various special trade schools in order that personnel not suitable for instruction might be eliminated. These are proving to be eminently successful.

Delinquency

One of the most striking developments in applied medicine in recent years has been the trend toward managing delinquency along psychiatric lines. It has been firmly established that a considerable number of the individuals in the armed forces who constantly break the rules, who do not profit by punishment, and who are in trouble over and over again, are mentally unsound. In the Navy, therefore, it is being more and more appreciated that within the framework of military law, the administrative solution of problems of discipline and justice requires the aid of psychiatry.

The Navy Regulations made it mandatory for the medical officer to make a physical examination of any person recommended for trial by general court martial. This is construed as including a determination of his mental condition. The commanding officer is furnished with a report of the findings. This has prevented in many instances the trial and punishment of irresponsible individuals.

Plans are being also formulated looking toward a more intelligent and humane method of dealing with the problem of homosexuality in the Navy. The procedure under consideration involves forced resignation of the officer, and inaptitude discharge for the enlisted man, who commits a homosexual act, instead of a general court martial as heretofore.

Morale

This presentation would be incomplete if it did not mention the subject of morale in the Navy. The present war has caused all intelligent people to think and talk a great deal about morale, and we are hearing of its different phases on all sides. Dealing as it does with human instincts and emotions, psychiatry is in an excellent position to make valuable contributions to the problem of developing, improving and maintaining morale in the Navy during periods of emergency, mobilization and actual warfare.

The meaning of morale is not always clear. No two conceptions of it are alike. Its ultimate source is the great evolutionary urge itself. When and where it is strongest, it makes the individual fit for any task. Morale in the Navy is the fruit of leadership which inspires confidence, trust and enthusiasm in every member of the organization. Without morale, masses of men, guns, ships and planes are of no avail. Morale is the very soul of the Navy and its presence or absence will determine the success or failure of the Fleet in battle.

The study of the tremendous, important factor of morale in war must be undertaken in times of peace and preparation, so that its accepted principles may be firmly and scientifically applied when the enemy strikes. Morale can be created, planned and deliberately engineered, even though our knowledge of its psychology is meagre.

This is accomplished in the Navy in a number of ways.

Each commanding officer is made responsible for the morale of his unit. Athletics are encouraged and opportunities for healthful recreation are promoted. All possible physical comforts in quarters aboard ship and in barracks ashore are provided for the officers and men. Health of the personnel, which is a prime requisite of morale, is protected and maintained by periodic physical examinations, vaccinations against various diseases, daily setting up exercises and frequent inspections. Good food also conditions morale. It has always been known that starving troops could or would not fight. The Navy ration is the best the market affords, and it is prepared and served in a meticulous way. Rest and sleep are insisted upon at all costs. Provision has also been made for the families of both officers and men to be treated in Naval Hospitals and at Naval Dispensaries, while the Navy Relief Society looks out for their welfare. This prevents a great deal of worry over these matters on the part of the personnel when they are away from home. Then, too, arrangements for the frequent deliveries of mail, and periodic leave when practicable, are also contributing to the morale of all hands. These are not psychiatric measures, but Navy psychiatry is well aware of their importance and is continually bringing them to the attention of the proper authorities.

One of the most important factors in developing morale during war, and one which has definite psychiatric implications, is the control of fear. There are many ways in which this may be done, but we can only enumerate a few of them. When a ship is anticipating contact with the enemy, courage can never long survive if the attention of the crew is focused entirely upon the peril. Diversion is the best mechanism possible under such conditions. Any kind of activity which takes the thoughts of the men away from danger helps to relieve the strain. Another corrective of fear is example. Here, the role of the officer is the most potent of all. Often every eye is upon him to see if he flinches, waivers, or hesitates. The officer must be an individual to whom his subordinates turn instinctively for a clue. Probably the most practical factor in the conquest of fear is familiarity. Frequent trips through the war zone, repeated engagements and contacts with the enemy, and witnessing the casualties of battle about him, give the individual a certain immunizing callousness to it all. He becomes hardened to the conditions of war, and he accepts the fact that he might be the next victim with growing equanimity.

Conclusion

In conclusion, let me emphasize the fact that the primary function of psychiatry in the Navy, in peace or in war, is to keep the personnel of the Fleet at the topnotch of mental health at all times. The only excuse for its existence is that it shall accomplish results in this direction. If the events of the last World War and the present one are to be taken as criteria, the utility of psychiatry in the Navy has been clearly established. Psychiatry has developed tremendously during the last quarter of a century, not only in the number of trained psychiatrists, but also in the deeper knowledge of etiology, examination techniques and treatment procedures. The Navy has kept pace with this expansion, and has been utilizing psychiatry in all its phases throughout the service. Whatever may be its shortcomings, psychiatry has made good to such an extent that it will always be a major specialty in the Medical Department of the Navy, and it will forever occupy a prominent and permanent place therein.

Psychiatry in Aviation

By BRIGADIER GENERAL EUGEN G. REINARTZ, M.C.,
U. S. Army

Commandant, The School of Aviation Medicine, Randolph Field, Texas

PREVAILING INCIDENCE OF NEUROPSYCHIATRIC DISORDERS • TYPES OF INDIVIDUALS
DRAWN TO FLYING • PSYCHOGENETIC DIFFICULTIES DEPENDENT UPON PERSONALITY
TYPES • FEAR • GREATER CONCENTRATION AND FREQUENCY OF NEUROSES •
SHOCKS IN AVIATION • THE SELF-PRESERVATIVE INSTINCT • CUMULATIVE EFFECTS
OF SUBCONSCIOUS NERVOUS TRAUMA • AERONEUROSIS, SYMPTOMS AND ETIOLOGY •
WORRY ABOUT ECONOMIC INSECURITY • INCIPIENT AERONEUROSIS • CLINICAL
PICTURE AND TREATMENT • FLYING STRESS OR OPERATIONAL FATIGUE • TREAT-
MENT • ANOXIA • AEROEMBOLISM • THE BLACK-OUT AND THE GRAY-OUT •
COMBAT FLYING AND FEAR • LONELINESS • COLD • ADEQUATE SELECTION OF
FLYING PERSONNEL • CARE AND TREATMENT

I AM HAPPY that I have the opportunity and the privilege of discussing before this Conference the psychiatric, neuropsychiatric and psychoneurotic manifestations incident to military aviation. The factual data that are available up to the present are unfortunately most meagre as regards our own Air Forces and even though meagre are of such nature as to preclude the publication of statistics. Statistically, one should be able to visualize fairly well what the problems of the future will be by studying the statistics of the past.

In the draft accompanying the last war 48,888 individuals were rejected by reason of psychoneuroses, psychoses and other acquired mental disorders as well as a larger group who were congenitally and constitutionally deficient or defective.[1] It is presumed that an equal proportion, if not greater, of those appearing before the Selective Service Boards at this time are so afflicted; greater, possibly, because of lack of disci-

[1] Ireland, G. O. Neuro-psychiatric ex-service man and his civil re-establishment. Am. J. Psychiat., 2:685, 1923.

pline exercised subsequent to the last war by parents of those who are now in the lower brackets of military age.

Some idea of the scope of the government's activity relative to the care, treatment and rehabilitation of the American disabled of the first World War may be gathered from the quite generally known fact that 6,000,000 casualties and disabilities were directly or indirectly traceable to that World War. It is of interest that more than 525,000 persons have applied for compensation in accordance with the War Risk Insurance Act. About one-third of these (30%) comes within the purview of the neuropsychiatric group.[2]

It is regretted that data concerning the proportion of neuropsychiatric casualties of the Air Service in the last war are not available. However, it is to be presumed that this branch of the service had its proportional share of those who were incapacitated and needed rehabilitation.

It may be well to state some of the conditions in connection with aviation which create the psychiatric response, and to mention some of the types of individuals drawn to it, who by their mental make-up are among those to create the problems for the solution of which this Conference has been called.

It shall be my purpose to limit my remarks to flying personnel, as the non-flying personnel, being Ground Forces, will be subject to the same stresses and strains as those of the other branches of the Army must endure—privations of all types, absence from home, hunger, thirst, heat, cold, regimentation. However, to these, for flying personnel, must be added the additional hazards of their particular profession, which immediately projects them into a new medium with all of its devastating assailments.

It might be well to detail the types of individuals, in the writer's experience, to whom flying appeals. These are the extrovertive nomads who go out to meet reality and enjoy the exhilaration of flying, and the introvertive types who by reason of their introversion attempt to compensate for their deficien-

[2] Kindred, J. J. Neuro-psychiatric wards of the United States government; their housing and other problems. Am. J. Psychiat., 1:183, 1921.

cies by attempting to excel in a profession to which much glamour has been attached.

The compensated introvert is the one generally found in the make-up of flying personnel.

The stable thinking and feeling type is the ideal for flying. It is the type which lasts well and wears well through the stresses and strains incident to flying.

With flyers, it is found that their difficulties are, for the most part, psychogenetic in origin and their reactions will be dependent upon their personality type. Because of this fact, it is readily understood why some will break down by reason of regimentation, religious, economic, occupational and now the added military stresses with which they are confronted.

A great many of the difficulties experienced by the beginning flyer are based on a conscious or unconscious fear. This may manifest itself in conversion syndromes such as hysterical paralyses, amauroses, contractures, aphonia, deafness or manifestations of disease.

Since sickness from time immemorial has always been the one and only accepted excuse from work, so individuals engaged in flying when they break, fly into disease. If their personality type is such as to preclude this manner of reacting, they may respond by a withdrawal.

The same problems are encountered in the services as are found in civil life. However, the manifestations seen may well be compatible with mundane existence while their development in flying personnel would be incompatible with flying.

There are those who take their flying training in stride and weather all the stresses imposed on them by this new method of transportation and by this instrument which has become such a potent weapon for the waging of war.

With the exception noted by Colonel Porter, the sharp breaking schizophrenic episodes seen in Army service, and with which exception I am fully in sympathy, it is stated that any psychiatric entity occurring during peace time may appear during war. It is an important fact that war and the exigencies of military service beget no novel or unique psychological phenomena, although comparative incidences of syndromes will be altered. The only difference would seem to be that war offers opportunities for the development of neuroses in much greater concentration and frequency than do the conditions of peace.

In the Air Forces much stress is laid on the psychological selection of those who will ultimately constitute the air crew. To the degree that the unstable individual is ruled out, to just that degree, will the problems of maintenance of flying personnel be minimized and the development of neuropsychiatric conditions lessened. Time alone will determine how successful the classification of those now being trained will be.

There are few occupations which subject those engaged to such marked shocks as does aviation. Serious airplane accidents occur to pilots with years of flying experience; and even though there be no physical injury a crash invariably produces profound psychic shock. The total effects cannot be accurately evaluated but there can be no doubt that there is an effect on the central nervous system. The witnessing of crashes and death of one's friends in the most violent type of death known, often complicated by a seething inferno of gasoline flames, in which the victim writhes in his death agonies, leaves a searing, deep, lasting, emotional scar and gives actual physical pain. Such an experience is not soon forgotten, and yet, in order to fly, such experiences must be repressed and in the repression, if not entirely successful, new conflicts arise.

In flying, the self-preservative instinct is continually called into play. This is one of the most deep seated of instincts and when stimulated may, and frequently does, arouse profound emotional disturbances. The instant one leaves the ground, this instinct is brought into play, as the individual is then projected into a new medium and the sustentation to which he has been accustomed, by reason of being a terrestrial animal, is removed. This arouses an instinctive fear which must be repressed successfully before an individual is able to learn to fly. If not successfully repressed, the fear manifests itself in tenseness and tenseness leads to "wash out" or possibly to a crash. Even though the fear engendered is repressed, it is the opinion of the writer that each pilot experiences the subconscious nervous trauma with its attendant emotional factor each time he goes into the air. Furthermore, it is believed the effects of such trauma are cumulative and have their distinct bearing on the development of later aeroneurosis among those not so well equipped as their fellows to withstand these traumata.

The very nature of a pilot's duties is such as to carry with it all the elements producing mental fatigue, the principal and all-important factor again being mental conflict. The concentration and attention constantly required in flying is probably greater than in any other occupation. One needs only to watch beginning students of flying or flyers of longer experience, after a long or arduous mission, to appreciate the attendant exhaustion, and the overpowering desire for sleep.

For years Flight Surgeons have recognized a condition occurring in aviators known as "aeroneurosis." [3] It was known by such names as "staleness," "flying sickness," "aviator's neurasthenia." It is defined as a chronic functional nervous and psychic disorder occurring in aviators and is characterized by gastric distress, nervous irritabilities, minor psychic disorders, fatigue of the higher voluntary mental centers, insomnia and increased motor activity.

The principal exciting etiological factor in this disease is emotional stress.

Pilots early in their careers realize that by reason of increasing age, minor accidents and disease, their careers are in jeopardy. They constitute sources of worry which reach their climax at the time of the regularly scheduled physical examination. While waivers for minor physical disabilities are recommended and granted, these only stave off the evil day. The fear of economic insecurity, often for a period of years, increases the pilot's burdens and lowers his nervous resistance.

A pilot's salary with flying pay is sufficient to give him financial security, but if his salary is jeopardized by his re-

[3] Armstrong, H. G. Principles and Practice of Aviation Medicine. Baltimore, The Williams & Wilkins Co., 1939, p. 340.

moval from flight status, it necessitates readjustments and the reduction of his standard of living. This he thinks brings with it a "loss of face" professionally and socially, as he feels he cannot well associate with flying personnel nor compete with those whose salaries are one-third higher than his.

The first change that takes place in a pilot, directing his attention to his uncertain economic status, is when he shows minor physical defects which temporarily suspend him from flying. He begins to realize that physical perfection is no longer a gift but something which from that time on must be maintained. A second change occurs when he marries and assumes the responsibility of a home and family. The conservatism of age adds to his problems, for now he has more at stake and must protect and provide for others as well.

The onset of this condition is insidious and no specific time for its beginning can be set. The pilot himself is unaware of its onset and it may be weeks or months before symptoms or signs are sufficiently pronounced to bring the individual to the attention of the Flight Surgeon. Many cases of incipient aeroneurosis are detectable by a Flight Surgeon when flying with his borderline cases. Having flown with all of his personnel, he will know of their reactions in the air. The changed, tense attitude of a pilot in the air, who is unknowingly developing aeroneurosis may be recognized, by an experienced Flight Surgeon. In this way, the disease can often be detected weeks before it would otherwise be recognizable.

The symptoms of the disease may make themselves manifest in any of the bodily systems, and are generally subjective in nature. Depending on the psychological make-up of the individual, he will react with a neurasthenic or anxiety syndrome or by the development of conversion symptoms.

The subject is restless and irritable and rather than believing himself sick, he will complain of overwork. Everything and everybody irritates him and his conduct in his home is evidence of the release of his pent-up emotions. Apprehensiveness and a feeling of miserableness dominate the picture. Sleeplessness disturbed by unpleasant dreams and by so-called nightmares involving crashes is one of the commonest complaints. Consequently, his condition seems worse in the early part of the day, with improvement as the day wears on. There is a diminution of attention and difficulty of concentration due to preoccupation. In most cases there is also the development of mild paranoid tendencies, the patient believing others are taking advantage of him or that he is being discriminated against. Headaches are also complained of, but these must be evaluated in the light of other possible causative factors such as glare, obstructed nasal passages, carbon monoxide, anoxemia, tight fitting earphones and the crash of static in radio phones.

Gastric symptoms which express themselves as a gnawing pain in the epigastrium and not unlike the ulcer hunger pain are universally present and are usually the expression of a conversion syndrome, the Alvarez stomach of general practice. There is no loss of appetite nor does the individual complain of nausea, vomiting, eructation, or distention. Later hypermotility of the stomach and intestines can be demonstrated under the fluoroscope. This is accompanied by a diarrhea. As might be expected, no pathology of the gastro-intestinal tract can be demonstrated.

In advanced cases, there may be an increased pulse pressure, lowered exercise tolerance and a tendency to neurocirculatory asthenia.

The prophylactic treatment is one of the Flight Surgeon's greatest problems and from the side of the flying and emotional strain involved, he can do and has done much. The correction of the social and economic problem is outside the medical domain, and yet Flight Surgeons are doing their utmost to correct this hazard as well.

Active treatment is best accomplished by complete removal from flying and things flying, provided additional economic strains are not entailed. If caught early, the individual, following his return from a period of removal from flying, is avid for flying and has completely rehabilitated himself. However, there may be those who have progressed further and may show improvement for a time, only to relapse, and who finally must be relieved from the responsibility of piloting aircraft.

During the present war, there is found developing a syndrome known as "flying stress," "flying fatigue," or "operational fatigue." While the aeroneuroses are found in normal individuals who are subjected to stresses and strains over a long period, they are not necessarily entirely due to flying, as indicated previously. They have their most fertile field in those unstable individuals who have adjusted sufficiently to meet the normal vicissitudes of life, but who retreat in the face of stresses which to them are overwhelming. It is the exceptional individual who is involved. On the contrary, flying stress or operational fatigue is used to describe a condition that may be observed as an *abnormal* flying strain being placed on a *normal* individual. It is particularly found in those members engaged in battle flying. These well-coordinated individuals, presumably because of the care used in their selection for specific assignments, free from psychogenic disorders, can break only on exposure to overwhelming stresses. The assumption is that, at some level of pressure, the most firmly integrated individual will succumb. It is seen in both pilots and air crews alike and frequently appears in them simultaneously. Its characteristics are varied and various but in every case there are sufficient symptoms and signs, no matter how they may be grouped, to arrive at a diagnosis.

It is one of those conditions in which one makes the diagnosis by awareness of the symptom complex and by making an evaluation of the situation, as a whole, instead of by the detection of individual symptoms. For this reason, the total behavior changing somewhat, the squadron commander will most likely be aware of the condition as quickly as will the medical officer. The liaison, therefore, between the commander and the Flight Surgeon must be close if cases are to be recognized early.

The condition is characterized by symptoms which begin slowly, but once having begun, develop rapidly with deterioration and disintegration of the mental and physical constitution of the victim. They "crack up" so to speak. It is the sum total of symptoms raising themselves above the diagnostic threshold which brings the individual to the attention of medical personnel. It is the duty of the doctor, therefore, to reduce this diagnostic threshold to the lowest level.

Some or all of the following symptoms will manifest themselves in each case.

Lack of enthusiasm becomes pronounced with an increasing listlessness in one who has been active, lively and eager. Physical energy and active vitality are replaced with indolence and lethargy. They are continually tired and from this tiredness there is no relief.

There is a loss of power of concentration no matter what the activity. Reading books or newspapers can be tolerated but a few minutes. Letter writing is out of the question. Even though the pilot knows that the performance of a certain duty is pressing, he will avoid it. He roams from room to room and place to place in search of diversion to occupy his mind, without avail. He becomes solitary where previously he had been a gregarious individual—he sits alone, avoids his friends, hides behind a newspaper, sits idly in his room without occupation, and if drinking is indulged in, becomes a solitary drinker.

His enthusiasm for flying and things flying is replaced by a detestation for their sight and sound. He shuns all articles published concerning aircraft nor can he view them in motion pictures.

Confidentially he will tell his medical officer that he is haunted by a sense of guilt and feels he is a slacker leaving work to others which he himself should do.

There is invariably a loss of appetite. In smokers there is a great increase in the amount smoked—they become chain smokers and smoking not infrequently replaces meals. Drinking occasionally increases but is not the rule. It is not uncommon for several highballs to be taken before retiring to induce a stuporous sleep.

The nature and habits of sleep are changed in almost every instance. He feels tired but fears his bed realizing that each night is an added burden to him. He puts off retirement because of the insomnia he experiences. His sleep is light, restless and disturbed with terrifying dreams which invariably have as their "core" aircraft or aircraft accidents. When he arises, he has the feeling that he is more tired than when he went to bed.

He is aware of his heart beat and may complain about it.

Digestive disturbances often in the nature of duodenal pain are manifested. They are not outstanding symptoms yet when investigated they are found to be more real than imagined. Either diarrhea or constipation may be present. Vomiting before or after breakfast especially, may be associated.

There is a distinct inability to fly to altitudes formerly routine. His "ceiling" gets lower and lower. When attempting to fly above the level to which his condition has limited him, he feels stiff and has a heaviness of his limbs; he feels tired and fearsome lest he, by reason of his diminished reaction time, jeopardize his own life and the life of his crew, to say nothing of his inability to complete his mission. He not infrequently feels that he simply must terminate his mission somewhere, anywhere, but immediately. He may feel as though he were about to faint and knows that he "blacks out" more readily than was his wont.

It is seen from the description, that the above enumerated symptoms could easily be missed by an observer unless he was well and intimately associated with his pilots. The symptoms are furthermore, not such as to bring the patient to the doctor and certainly not in the early stages. Pilots and crews with a strong sense of duty will hide their disability and will not report sick until they are definitely ill, thereby making it difficult to detect their early symptoms for the application of remedial measures. The doctor usually has to find the patient and then unfortunately it is often too late for rehabilitation and the victim may be lost to his flight, if not permanently, certainly for a period of many months.

As the case progresses, the appearance of the patient is characteristic. His posture is apathetic, his shoulders droop, his face is pallid and lined with shadows under the eyes. Mobility is markedly lost. No movement is made unless it is entirely necessary. The condition has been described as though the individual has been "pithed." It might almost be likened to beginning encephalitis lethargica although the patient frequently states that he "feels all right." The blood pressure shows a reduction of from ten to twenty points below that which has been the individual's normal. The heart action shows some irregularity following exertion. Prophylactically much can be done and is being done.

The active treatment of this condition must vary at least to some extent with the type of individual and the severity of the condition. In most instances, the treatment which can be given by the Flight Surgeon at the station is inadequate. A period of sick leave is not enough. The mildest cases may be treated by a reduction in flying activity. If within a week improvement is not manifest then the case is not one to be treated by the local medical officer. In moderate or advanced cases, the individual should be removed to an appropriate hospital at once. If the individual is permitted to remain with his squadron he only becomes worse. This condition is among tired men and, like panic in a crowd, is infectious. The patient must be informed that he is bodily ill and the necessity for his immediate hospitalization explained to him.

The conditions which have been described, aeroneurosis and operational fatigue, are the two named entities recognized as diseases, the etiological factor of which is flying; however, any of the manifestations of neuropsychiatric conditions can be and are encountered in flying personnel from the mildest form to the most malignant.

Judging from the experiences of the last war, it would seem that while the psychoses and mental deficiencies are the most frequent causes of initial rejection, in actual warfare the psychoneuroses are a far more important cause of disablement.

Practically every condition with which air crews come into contact is such as to produce effects which lead to psychiatric trauma. The condition of anoxia or oxygen deprivation has assumed great practical significance, particularly since the air war at almost unheard of altitudes has assumed such large proportions. The symptoms of anoxia are increased respiration and pulse rate, cyanosis, muscular and mental incoordination and loss of memory. In order to function properly, the nervous system must have an adequate supply of oxygen. Anoxia of increasing duration or repetition seems to be followed by graded severity of damage to the nerve cells in the brain and brain stem. It is our opinion, based on experimentation, that no prolonged period of significant oxygen want leaves the brain totally unscathed.

In aeroembolism, the collection of nitrogen bubbles in the cerebrospinal fluid causes increased intracranial pressure, mental depression, obfuscation, amnesia, headache, slowing of psychomotor function, etc. Electroencephalographic changes also take place. None of the changes is permanent and complete recovery is believed to follow. Yet who at this time can predict the ultimate results from such repeated traumata?

What is the end result to be envisioned in combat pilots who in operational flying at terrific speeds are continually being subjected to the gravitational forces applied in battle maneuvers, the so-called "G" which when positive forces are applied causes an anemia of the brain, the black-out or its lesser manifestation, the gray-out?

Who can say what the continual stimulation of the adrenal glands will bring in its train, by reason of the numerous situations in which flying personnel find themselves? This stimulation is on a basis of fear and anoxia. Fear is one of the most easily and constantly evoked of the biological reactions, since it is the emotion which appears whenever an individual's life or activities are threatened in one way or another. When so jeopardized the reactions of stimulation express themselves in the tensing of muscles, quickened respiration with hyperventilation, marked quickening of the pulse and profuse perspiration. There are numerous occasions while flying where fear in some form is experienced. This is especially true in combat flying where at the same time it furnishes the necessary stimulation for the supreme effort. If the effort is long continued, fatigue sets in, and fatigue creates a fear of incapacity, fear of failure and a fear of inferiority. Depression flourishes in the soil of fatigue. Pilots and crews who have spent a sleepless night arise with a feeling of exhaustion, lack initiative and do not care to fly.

When flying at extreme altitudes surrounded by a harsh environment, the pilot becomes lonely. Loneliness, too, engenders fear. Being gregarious animals, pilots crave companionship. The JU 88 is said to have the crew positions extremely close for the purpose of maintaining morale.

Fear is the emotion reserved for the unknown. When an air crew takes their ship to an altitude of 35,000 or 40,000 feet, they are certainly in an unknown environment. Fear is also identified with the inscrutable, as when a pilot is searching for an enemy in the dark of the night, knowing that he, too, is being sought by one who has but one object in mind.

The effect of cold on flying personnel causes all manner of symptoms to arise. Heavy flying clothing, which is not effective, adds to the pilot's burdens by the handicapping of his movements. Some of the most serious effects of cold upon the pilot are those in the psychic field and are due to the physical discomforts experienced. These bring in their train mental distress, loss of self-confidence, the feeling of "is it worth the price?" and an overpowering desire to bring an end to the mission. If a pilot is subjected to such an environment beyond this point, he will be the subject of an overpowering lethargy which will steal over him quietly, quickly, and certainly, and will end in stupor and death.

It must, therefore, be concluded that the stresses and strains incident to aviation, and their effect on the psychic constitution of those engaged in this branch of the military service are probably greater than in any other branch of the service. This may be thought an overstatement, but, the hazards which continually face flying personnel from the time of take-off till a successful landing has been made, are such as to jeopardize their mental and physical well-being. Everything a pilot must of necessity do to maintain his equilibrium, maintain contact with his environment, and bring his plane and crew safely to a landing must be done correctly in the first instance as there is but rarely the opportunity for afterthought or second choice. This is routinely true, without adding the battle hazard with which all operational units are now faced. Life is continually in jeopardy and the pilot is continually faced with dissolution.

This then is a partial statement of the problem and it would seem that the more adequate the selection of flying personnel, the less will be the number of those breaking under the terrible strain of the cataclysm which has engulfed the world.

The neuropsychiatric problems arising out of the present war will be the most significant military and economic problems with which the Government will have to deal. The earlier the treatment is instituted, the less the number of cases; and every effort should be made to organize medical centers where such treatment may be given during active service. This as far as the Army is concerned, is already in effect and it is presumed to be so in the sister service. Furthermore, careful consideration will have to be given to the problem of rehabilitation at this time and after the military activities have ceased.

In view of the stupendous price paid by the people of the United States as a result of the psychiatric conditions consequent to the last war, it would seem that the approach to the care and treatment of those already so afflicted and those yet to be afflicted should be made along practical, economically sound lines, devoid of sentimentality, and yet not with the ruthlessness practiced in Germany. The recommendations made by this Conference should be based on the tragic lessons of the last war in an attempt at lessening, for future generations, the burdens which we have had to carry.

Psychiatry in Civilian Defense

By LEO H. BARTEMEIER, M.D.

*Michigan Representative, Committee of Public Information,
American Psychiatric Association*

WHOLESOME DEVELOPMENT OF PSYCHIATRY • EXPANSION IN WAR IN BEHALF OF CIVIL POPULATION • RIGHTFUL PLACE IN EVERYDAY LIFE OF MANKIND • CIVILIAN PROBLEM OF REGISTRANTS REJECTED FOR MENTAL HANDICAPS • PSYCHIATRIC SEMINARS FOR INSTRUCTION IN CIVILIAN DEFENSE • NEW ROLE AS OFFICERS OF PUBLIC MENTAL HEALTH • VOLUNTEER WORK AN OCCUPATIONAL THERAPY • SELECTION OF AIR RAID WARDENS • FIRST AID TREATMENT OF NERVOUS AND EMOTIONAL CASUALTIES • MAINTENANCE OF FAMILY AND HOME • EMPLOYMENT OF MOTHERS • PLANS FOR DAY NURSERIES • INCREASE IN MENTAL DISORDERS AND DELINQUENCIES • DEARTH OF PSYCHIATRISTS • QUALITIES OF PROFESSIONAL COMPETENCE • SEMINARS FOR PSYCHIATRISTS • TEACHING OTHERS • PUBLIC EDUCATION

WE KNOW from our clinical experience that if our work is to be effective, we must attempt to maintain an awareness about ourselves as well as about the person with whom we are working. It is equally true that in discussing the utilization of psychiatry for the preservation and promotion of civilian morale and defense it behooves us to understand our problem from this same double aspect. I will attempt to picture the significance of this problem for psychiatry and what it may mean for our fellow man. Anything short of this cannot be worthwhile.

The very title of this presentation attests to the wholesome development of psychiatry. From a discipline which formerly confined itself exclusively to the diagnosis and treatment of mental disorders it gradually applied itself to the fields of education and to industry. Now, in the catastrophe of total war, it reaches out to make a practical application of its prin-

278

ciples in behalf of our civilian population and our social structure. This tremendous expansion of psychiatry is in some respects somewhat premature and we must admit that, while we may not feel as well prepared to cope with the destructive processes which now beset our society as we should like, we are face to face with the very kind of human distress which our particular training is best suited to remedy, and the responsibility is ours. In this connection, we need to be mindful of our prejudices and our resistances to changes and to that which is relatively new in the realm of our personal experience. It is only through such awareness about ourselves that we can sense that the social needs of today also carry with them the opportunity for psychiatry ultimately to take its rightful place in the everyday life of mankind.

In addition to our ordinary professional responsibilities, many of us are working in our communities with various problems connected with civilian defense. These efforts are of some benefit to public mental health but they are so necessarily limited in their scope that they comprise only a small fraction of what should be done and what must be done if any reasonable degree of morale is to be maintained. This fact becomes more serious as our numbers are reduced through enlistments in the armed forces and as our services are increasingly required by the mentally sick. From this, it becomes evident that if those of us who are to remain in civilian life are to perform a truly worth-while service in the preservation and promotion of public mental health during the present crisis, we need to work together in order to evolve a better direction of our efforts, techniques for therapy for a larger number of the population and effective methods for the solution of specific problems which have developed out of the war. Consideration should be given to the advisability of psychiatric seminars for instruction in civilian defense similar to the excellent seminars conducted by Sullivan in behalf of Selective Service. The organizing of psychiatrists for eliminating those who are mentally unfit for service in the army, has been of inestimable value in the war effort and this organization continues to perform its highly useful function in the induction centers. In this connection, however, those who are rejected because of mental handicaps present a problem for civilian morale which requires our immediate attention and intelligent management. I mention this problem of the rejected registrant and the repercussions arising from his rejection among the people who make up his world because it is one example of a variety of situations for which we might well establish a uniform method of procedure through seminar discussion. The practicability of instituting such seminars seems an appropriate topic for discussion.

What I especially have in mind in this connection may be summed up very briefly. Within recent time, a considerable amount of literature on the topic of civilian defense and morale has appropriately appeared in our technical journals. It is doubtful whether this, by itself, constitutes adequate preparation for our new roles as officers of public mental health. Certainly, we did not learn what we know about medicine and psychiatry solely by reading the literature and it is equally true that our competency for making fairly adequate examinations of selective service registrants at a saving of considerable time was markedly enhanced by the psychiatric seminars and the distribution of Medical Circular Number 19. Inasmuch as civilian defense and morale are of equal importance to the military arm in the situation of total war, it seems imperative that American psychiatry be mobilized for the protection and the participation of the civilian population. We know a good many of the laiety who give us the impression of being indifferent, apathetic and wholly lacking in a sense of reality about the possibility of an invasion by air, the dangers from subversive groups and other questions in connection with civilian defense. It is equally important that we maintain an awareness about our own sense of reality regarding these matters about which it is so easy to rationalize because the war has, in fact, placed heavy demands upon our time and our energies.

When we direct our attention to the psychiatric aspects of

civilian defense, we may feel encouraged by the large numbers of our people who are engaged in volunteer activities. With some few exceptions they have not been selected for their various duties in the event of an air raid or any other emergency. They are functioning quite satisfactorily from the viewpoint of the authorities. We know, however, from our daily experience that many of these people have been energetic in becoming air raid wardens, for example, just *because* of their neuroses about which they consult us. We have all had some opportunity to witness the temporary salubrious effect of such air raid work upon the daily lives of some of these people. We may observe how it has provided them with a feeling of being useful and being acceptable to their neighbors. We note in other instances how their new interest has served to distract them from their preoccupations and how it has somewhat lessened their anxieties. For the people I am speaking of, such volunteer work constitutes good occupational therapy and unless there is imminent danger of an actual air raid they need not be removed from their work. They are *not*, however, psychologically prepared to avoid panic reactions in a real emergency and in fact *because* of this they might well precipitate mass hysterical reactions among their neighbors. We do not yet know whether there will be any possibility of eliminating those air raid wardens whom we, as psychiatrists, would regard as being unfit for such service, but certainly all those interested in such work should undergo some degree of personal investigation. If this is not done, we cannot believe that our civilian defense will be adequate if the occasion arises when the population really needs to defend itself. In contrast to the acceptance of all who volunteer, there is the consoling thought that in some districts air raid wardens have been carefully selected on the basis of some plain and sensible qualifications. To become an air raid warden in such a district, I understand, one must have lived in his home a long time, must be well known to his neighbors and must be a person who has their respect and their confidence. We can only wish that selection on such basis might become nation-wide. In the interim, however, we should consider well the advisability of formulating a clear, concise statement for general distribution describing the potential danger to which I have been referring.

It may be of interest to note in passing that a well-planned pamphlet entitled *First Aid Treatment of Nervous and Emotional Casualties during War Time,* which was drawn up by Himler and his Mental Hygiene Committee here in Washtenaw County, met with an unexpected response. I am informed by the executive secretary of our Michigan Society for Mental Hygiene that some twenty-five thousand copies have been requested by various factories producing war materials, by libraries, by agencies in Minnesota, Wisconsin and Massachusetts and that this material has been accepted by the American Red Cross for inclusion in one of its first aid courses. Permit me to read a few excerpts from this pamphlet which consists of suggestions to air raid wardens, auxiliary police and firemen so that you may see how excellently it has been done. "Be tolerant, kind, but firm. Handle the patient sympathetically but undramatically, as you would a routine job for which you have been given full responsibility. . . . Be positive in giving directions, but don't argue, lose your temper, or assume an attitude of contempt or impatience. . . . Treat the nervously upset patient, as you would a frightened child, or as you would guide a terror-stricken person away from a forest fire." We may imagine that carefully prepared suggestions to the air raid wardens about themselves might prove to be equally acceptable.

In the great drive for manpower and war materials there lies the grave danger of a gradual though definite increase in mental disorders and delinquency with their consequent effects on civilian defense and morale. As mental hygienists we need to publicize in plain language some of the basic relationships between personal satisfactions and mental health. We should especially emphasize the necessity of maintaining the family and the home throughout the period of war time in as far as this is possible, so that the children are not subjected to drastic changes which come about when their mothers take employment in factories or leave the home for other equally remunerative positions. The increase in delinquency should be of greatest concern to psychiatrists interested in civilian defense and the future solidarity of our social structure. The removal of the father's authority through his having to go to war is unpreventable and often gives rise to serious disturbances in the lives of children at puberty and the early adolescent period. It is the unnecessary dislocation of the mother's influence, however, which should cause us to speak out firmly in behalf of the future lives of the children. The value of unnecessarily breaking up the mother-child relationship for increasing income is highly dubious from the psychiatric standpoint. Conversely when the shortage of manpower requires the mother entering industry, it is highly advisable to have well-matured plans in day nurseries in which the better aspects of child psychiatry will have their place in managing the children. If, instead of day nurseries, the children are to be cared for in other homes, the choice of these homes is not to be left to sheer chance. The British experience has already shown that if the setting is too dissimilar from their own homes, a sharp increase in problems occurs.

With these examples in mind, it may be well to consider the rough outline of a practical program. The first consideration in practical programs is the dearth of psychiatrists. The question then becomes: What contributions by psychiatrists are absolutely necessary to some program of civilian defense? How can the utility of each available psychiatrist be best augmented? And lastly, what activities in this general direction should be started immediately?

There is no magic in being a psychiatrist and the psychiatrist himself may profit greatly by a careful analysis of the new task confronting him—not in any sense because he is more limited than any other psychiatrist. One may well speak of the man on a state hospital staff for the last fifteen years. This man is concerned with the administration of hospital service for persons gravely disordered in mind. A psychoneurotic patient on his wards is really a nuisance, a person in the wrong place. The institutional psychiatrist will be happy to discharge such a mildly disordered patient on the first signs of his willingness to leave. Entirely aside from the many other influences which dictate this course there is the factor of the psychiatrist's lack of interest in the personal problem represented by this patient.

To take this institutional psychiatrist from his job and place him without any indoctrination as a psychiatrist examining on an Army Induction Board would be quite unsatisfactory. He would be looking for psychotic registrants and would be bored and annoyed with the seemingly fraudulent extravagances of some of the psychoneurotic registrants who ought certainly to be excluded from the armed forces. The discrimination between an alcoholic who has shown conclusively an inability to handle intoxicants by recurrent loss of jobs or social standing and the heavy drinking young man who still avoids socio-economic disaster seems to an institutional psychiatrist rather a frill or a foible. He thinks in terms of delirium tremens or alcoholic psychosis.

What has been said about the draft board or the induction station could be said of a great deal of the psychiatry of national service. Our institutional psychiatrist without indoctrination can scarcely be expected to handle the nuances of family relationships in child guidance or in exciting favorable influence upon the school. He certainly finds himself unhappily out of his element in industry and in administrative positions concerned with the dissemination of information, the combating of hostile propaganda, etc.

Yet, as was true in the development of selective service psychiatry, the experience and the qualities of professional competence which make this man a good institutional psychiatrist can easily be re-oriented so that he becomes highly useful in any one of these previously foreign fields of psychiatric work.

The first step in our program would therefore seem to be the organization of another set of seminars for psychiatrists in which emphasis is placed on the several aspects of defence work, their special requirements and the criteria of mental health and its absence which are particularly significant.

But unhappily we cannot stop with this easily feasible step. There are not enough psychiatrists. Psychiatrists properly indoctrinated as to the new tasks should be teaching the other members of the medical profession the facts of psychiatry in the national defense, which are of importance in the doctor's practice and in his special efforts in war work. True, not every psychiatrist can teach. True also, a good many psychiatrists discourage some general practitioners by attempting to teach before they have formulated their subject matter. This is a difficult field but its importance, as the most practical way of augmenting psychiatric skill, demands its achievement.

We may be inclined to turn to one particular group of the community and by-pass the medical profession. I refer here to the social worker. It is all too true that the social worker by training and experience is rather more accessible to psychiatric indoctrination than are many physicians who left the medical school a good many years ago. It would be absurd indeed to imply that the social worker is not already a great help to the psychiatrist. It is decidedly unwise, however, to expect these already heavily burdened workers to carry out a phase of essentially medical treatment. The social order gives the doctor a role which he should be able to perform. In so far as we can, we must help him in the art of psychiatry.

The third great step requiring immediate attention would seem to be that of public education to the realities of personality gratifications as related to success and failure, in particular, vocations and recreational activities. I scarcely need to stress to this audience the benighted state of public information in this field. I have to stress slightly the advisability of adequately organizing work looking to public education and the careful formulation of the information which we seek to communicate.

Psychiatry in National and International Relationships

By JOHN W. APPEL, M.D.

Psychiatrist, Pennsylvania Hospital, Philadelphia

THE ATTITUDE OF INDUCTEES • NEED OF PSYCHOLOGICAL CONDITIONING • PSYCHO-
LOGICAL PREPAREDNESS THE DECISIVE FACTOR IN WAR • THE MORALE OF THE
TROOPS • EVERY PSYCHOLOGIST AND PSYCHIATRIST IN THE WAR MACHINE • AMERI-
CAN ADVERTISING METHODS AND NAZI PROPAGANDA • TRAINING OF YOUTH • BOM-
BARDMENT OF IDEAS • EXCLUSION OF IDEAS • A REVOLUTION OF IDEAS • MEIN
KAMPF • RUSSIAN INTEREST IN IDEAS • JAPAN • THE PICTURE IN ENGLAND •
PROPAGANDA AND MORALE IN THE UNITED STATES • HISTORY OF THE IMPORTANCE
OF IDEAS • THE KNOWLEDGE OF STIMULI AND THEIR POLITICAL USE • STRUGGLE
BETWEEN MEN ARMED WITH MACHINES • KNOWLEDGE OF HUMAN NATURE • MAN'S
INDEPENDENT WILL • THE WILL TO FIGHT • ABLE TO FIGHT AND WILLING TO
FIGHT • WEAPONS OF PSYCHOLOGICAL WARFARE • HOW TO CREATE AND HOW TO
DESTROY THE WILL TO FIGHT • CONFIDENCE IN ABILITY • REASON FOR FIGHTING •
ROLE OF PSYCHIATRISTS IN THIS WAR OF IDEAS • THE PROBLEMS OF THE NORMAL
MIND IN ABNORMAL TIMES

THE TITLE of this paper is PSYCHIATRY IN NATIONAL AND
INTERNATIONAL RELATIONSHIPS. Such an all-embracing
subject first attracted my attention some two years ago. Living in Philadelphia at that time was a Swedish psychologist
named Von Koch. For the preceding five years he had been
a member of the staff at the Goering Institute in Berlin. This
Institute, which I understand is run by a cousin of Marshal
Goering, is one of the foremost psychiatric centers in Germany. Von Koch told me that during his stay there the Nazi
Military Headquarters was in constant communication with
this Institute at the rate of four to six telephone calls and
conferences daily. Naturally enough, the question arose in my
mind, why? The Institute of the Pennsylvania Hospital is a

good psychiatric institute, and I was a psychiatrist on the staff. What in heaven's name would I have to say to an army general?

I knew that in the last war one-seventh of all casualties in the United States Army were neuropsychiatric (110,000) but this problem alone would hardly account for four to six conferences daily between psychiatrist and military leaders over a period of five years.

Obviously, war was a matter of guns, tanks, bombs, tactics and strategy about which I knew absolutely nothing. In what way could my knowledge of psychiatry and practical psychology be of any interest to a military commander?

Having asked this question, a whole series of things began to strike my attention with new significance.

What served to change my interest in this point from a casual academic interest to a practical urgent one was my experience as examining psychiatrist at the army induction center in Philadelphia. I was examining fifty to one hundred inductees a day with the object of rejecting those who were psychologically unfit for military service. Regarding these men in the context of mental disease the problem was not too difficult, at least one was able to detect and eliminate obvious pathology. But then looking at these men, not in the context of present mental disease, but in terms of psychological preparedness for military life and the ordeal of war, it began to dawn on me that very few of the men I saw were prepared. The most typical attitude about going into the army was, "If you gotta go, you gotta go." The spirit was one of resignation. Not once in the first one thousand men I examined did I encounter the spirit of aggression or anger at the enemy. The only individuals who were anxious to get in the army were those who said, "Sure I want to go into the army. I can't get no work and I'm tired hanging around." The men were in sound mental health, but it seemed to me they would need an enormous amount of psychological conditioning before they would be able to stand up under threat of death and mutilation, separation from family, loss of jobs, without developing serious nervous reactions. I reflected that the psychological conditioning of the entire country for the last twenty years has been directed toward pacifism. The sudden reversal toward militarism had produced confusion and instability in the average inductee.

Was this perhaps the problem which was discussed in the conferences between the phychiatrists at the Goering Institute and the Nazi Military Headquarters?

Then I saw a pamphlet put out by the Committee for National Morale called *German Psychological Warfare*. In it was a bibliography of over five hundred articles written by German army officers, psychologists and sociologists, attempting to apply the knowledge of psychology to military and governmental problems. There were titles such as "Psychological Rearmament," "Psychology of Combat," "Weapons of Psychological Warfare," articles on "Fear," "Morale," "Fighting Spirit," "Rage," "The Importance of Will." And there were some very interesting statements which I shall quote: General von Clausewitz, ". . . psychological preparedness and proper estimation of morale is the decisive factor in war." A radio commentator with the Nazi troops during the Polish campaign of 1939 writes, ". . . tremendous morale force which drove the Germans to victory in their first blitzkrieg. Technological weapons would have meant little without that morale force." Colonel Foertsch, reputed to be the "brain" of the German general staff, says, "The final word regarding victory and defeat rests not on arms and equipment nor on the way in which they are used, nor even on the principles of strategy and tactics, but on the morale of the troops." The deputy director of the psychological laboratory of the German army writes, "The ideological conditioning of soldiers is considered of equal and often greater importance than technical training." A German military handbook says, "War itself is a struggle of opposing morale forces in which genuine victory depends on the breaking down of one or the other's morale equilibrium."

Another point of interest is that in addition to being in constant touch with the Goering Psychiatric Institute, the Nazi army not only had two hundred psychologists on its payroll, but had mobilized every psychologist and psychiatrist in Germany to take his place in the German war machine.

From an article in the Saturday Evening Post, we learn that just as Germany borrowed from us the idea of the dive bomber, the parachute trooper, the submarine, some eight years ago a group of Nazi officials came to this country to investigate and become trained in the use of American advertising methods including graphics, movies, press, radio.

We note that since that time not only the whole German population, but the whole world has been deluged with Nazi propaganda. Posters, pictures, "war films," newspapers, radio broadcasts issue from the Nazi headquarters in a steady stream. One hears of mighty short-wave broadcasting stations implanted in strategic outposts the world over pouring out ideas, facts, truths and untruths twenty-four hours a day in over a hundred languages, bombarding every race, color and creed on the face of the globe.

And then one hears that the Nazi government "gets 'em when they're young." It focuses its attention on children, organizes them into youth groups, junior storm troops, and with control of schools, school books and instructors, fills their heads with ideas and beliefs preparing them for their future place in the Greater Reich and perhaps if they are lucky, fits them for the glorious role of dying for their Fuehrer. And in contrast to this vast program of bombarding the German people with ideas, we note that there is an even vaster program designed to exclude ideas. A ruthless Gestapo snoops, spies and ferrets out the innermost thought of every man, woman and child. Secret listening devices and informers prevent a man from expressing his ideas even in the bosom of his own family. Rigid censorship is clamped down on every medium of expression. And we see men tortured and sent to concentration camps and killed, not for expressing ideas, but for merely listening to ideas. It is to be noted that the Nazi government attempts to withhold facts and figures from its enemy just as zealously as it withholds them from its own peoples.

Then we hear that the entire Nazi movement from its very

origins in Germany itself has been a revolution not of force but of ideas, that the Nazis gained control not so much through the power of weapons as through the power of ideas. The American Revolution in this country was a long and bloody battle with guns being fired and people being killed. The Nazis came to power, it is true, with individual acts of violence and many threats of brutality, but actually without pitched battles or actual physical warfare. The milestones of Hitler's rise to power in Germany were not military decisions corresponding to those of George Washington, for instance, but a series of speeches, long one and one-half, two and three hour speeches which bombarded the German people at regular intervals. The chief symbol of this revolution was perhaps not a sword or a gun, but a rather thick book called, "Mein Kampf."

We note that of the four top men in Germany to-day, three of them are devoted almost exclusively to influencing ideas of the German people: Hitler and Goebbels bombarding, Himmler censoring—and even Goering devotes a good deal of his energy to this project.

Turning the attention to Russia, we see that there, too, is the same keen interest by the government in the ideas, not only of Russians but of all the world outside Russia. Here, too, we see powerful radio broadcasting stations bombarding friend and foe alike; pamphlets, speeches, plays, books, movies and leaflets and posters exposing ideas to man, woman and child. Here, too, is an iron censorship implemented with secret police, concentration camp and blood purges. And up until two weeks ago, we note that the entire Russian army was invested with a system of political commissars, otherwise known as morale officers. Each line officer from platoon leader to general was accompanied by a double, a man of proven ideological loyalty to act as custodian of ideas, both of officer and troops and with the authority to countermand any order of the line officer as a means of implementing this role.

In Japan, too, the same phenomenon is to be observed, a powerful propaganda machine bombarding inside the country and out, a rigid censorship—American and English newspaper men being tortured and killed for having expressed unwelcome ideas.

Looking toward England the picture is different. But we note the importance of the Churchill speeches in preventing the dissolution of the British Empire just two years ago. We note that the most serious threats of political upheaval were in connection with censorship of facts, figures and ideas, and that man after man was forced to resign as Minister of Information.

In the United States the picture is also different. Perhaps the chief point to be noted is that in the last few years the two words "propaganda" and "morale" have become prominent in daily conversation, editorials, magazine articles, committee meetings and conferences. Here, too, perhaps the most serious criticism of the government has been in regard to the issuing or withholding of facts, figures, or ideas.

In the middle of the eighteenth century, Voltaire said, "The pen is mightier than the sword." Machiavelli before him wrote a book saying much the same thing. Since that time the sword has grown mightily; technological developments have increased its power of destruction many times. However, the pen has grown even more. In the middle of the eighteenth century even books were few and far between, magazines, the press, posters, movies, radio and telegraph, telephone and mail, and transportation facilities as we know them to-day were nonexistent. In Voltaire's time it might take an idea ten years to reach even a few thousand people. Nowadays a man can press a button and in ten seconds an idea may reach a few billion people.

Looking back through history at the influence of ideas on man's behavior, we see with Sir James Frazer that for many centuries man engaged in the most extraordinary behavior as the result of ideas. "Among the high mountains of a certain part of the orient, there is a district in which if the rain has not fallen for a long time, a party of villagers goes in a long procession to the bed of a mountain torrent, headed by a priest who leads a black dog. At the chosen spot they tether the beast to a stone and make a target for their bullets and arrows. When its life blood bespatters the rocks, the peasants throw up their weapons and lift up their voices in supplication to the dragon divinity of the stream, exhorting him to send down a shower of rain." Here is behavior which to a meteorologist, at least, would seem extraordinary and wasteful. The peasant behaves in this manner because of the idea that he thereby will bring rain.

A glance at the horrors of the Spanish Inquisition also shows extraordinary and destructive behavior of man arising from an idea, the idea that by behavior of this sort, mankind would be benefited.

The effect of religious ideas upon man's behavior has been a major one throughout history. One notes with particular interest that in Germany, Russia and Japan there has been a frank attempt to substitute worship of state and leader for worship of church and God, a frank attempt to divert powerful emotions and energies away from religion and into use of the state. In Germany a man's greatest glory is to follow, not the will of God, but the will of der Fuehrer. In Japan the emperor is worshipped even more than is Lenin in Russia.

At the present moment we are faced with the spectacle of a new kind of war. The weapons in this war are radio, press, graphics, pamphlets, movies, speeches, books, rumors. The ammunition is ideas. A war of ideas. The Nazis bombard the German people and the outside world with ideas: "The destiny of the Greater Reich; the Jew guilt of the last war; Lebensraum; the New Order; Communism is dangerous and must be destroyed; Roosevelt is a war-monger and must be destroyed; the United States is a weak democracy run by self-seeking capitalists." Japan bombards the world with other ideas: "Asia for the Asiatics; the Chinese incident; the divinity of the emperor; the glory of a military death." Germany bombards Russia with propaganda; Russia retaliates with counter-propaganda; and Germany returns with counter-counter-propaganda.

But how about this war of ideas, this propaganda, this censorship, this speech-making, this rumor-mongering, this flood of leaflets, pamphlets, posters, movies, etc.? How important is it? The time has come for action, not talk. Wars are won by bullets and bombs, by fighting soldiers and factory workers, not by some orator shouting into a microphone.

If you take a certain nematode worm and place him at the bottom of an inclined plane and on his right place an electric light of a certain candle power and on his left a light of also a certain candle power, the worm will start crawling. Because the worm is positively phototropic and negatively geotropic, it is possible to write a formula based on distance, candle power and other factors which predicts the exact course the worm will take on its passage up the inclined plane. Now if I am forced to concede that man is not a worm, I nevertheless believe that he, too, though in an infinitely more complicated manner, tends to respond to certain stimuli in a certain way. As a psychiatrist, I earn my living by my ability to predict a man's behavior under a given set of stimuli and to influence a man's behavior by exposing him to various types of stimuli. The thought occurs that this knowledge and the means of bringing stimuli to bear might be available to the Nazi government and might be being used to influence the behavior of the German people and of their friends and foes: the psychological knowledge of stimulus and response in human beings turned to political uses.

In this machine age, in this machine war, one important fact is apt to be forgotten and that is: machines are run by living men. No matter how formidable the fire power of a gun, it is utterly useless as a weapon unless there is a man to pull the trigger. Regardless of new weapons in the technological sense, living man is the first weapon of battle. War is not a struggle between machines, but a struggle between men armed with machines.

Tactics, strategy, technical knowledge, are essential for army commanders. Of equal importance is knowledge of human nature. Napoleon did not gain the position he did so much by a study of rules and strategy as by a profound knowledge of human nature in war. An officer spends countless hours learning the dynamics of a gun, a tank, a plane. It is perhaps of even greater importance that he learn certain simple fundamentals in the dynamics of his most essential weapon—living man, the soldier.

The importance of this knowledge becomes apparent immediately in the light of one simple point, a point so obvious it is apt to be ignored; namely, that a soldier is possessed of an independent will. Just because a soldier *can* fight, it does not follow that he *will* fight. Any other weapon of war, a gun, a tank, a plane, responds inevitably with maximum power merely by the pulling of a trigger or the pushing of a lever. A living soldier, on the other hand, even though he be armed to the teeth and well trained in warfare, may either fight with maximum power, may fight half-heartedly, or in the final analysis may refuse to fight at all. Because of this fact a completely disarmed soldier may have more fighting power than a soldier with a gun who will not pull the trigger. At the extreme logical conclusion a completely armed soldier may be destroyed by the bare hands of an unarmed boy so long as he refused to fight or even defend himself and the boy has the will to kill.

The significance of this fact becomes apparent on considering the fundamental factors involved in winning a fight. The purpose of fighting is to render the enemy harmless. This may be accomplished by killing him, disarming him, or by *making him unwilling to fight*. When two small boys fight on a street the battle is over when one or the other says, "uncle" or "gives up." The fight is over when one or the other cannot fight or will not fight further. In other words it is not necessary to kill the opponent or even to disarm him; the battle will be won if the opponent can be made to "give up." Thus a battle can be won in two ways: (1) by rendering the opponent unable to fight, (2) by rendering him unwilling to fight. That this principle applies to warfare as well as street fights has been clearly demonstrated by Hitler in the present world war.

Germany conquered Austria without firing a shot or killing a single man. He accomplished this by rendering Austria unwilling to fight. Austria possessed guns and soldiers trained to use them. Austria could have fought but she was rendered unwilling to fight. The same thing happened with France. After brief contact with the German armies, though she still possessed guns, machines, trained soldiers and was able to fight, France became unwilling to fight and the war was over. The same pattern has been reproduced in other countries. In still other countries, notably Yugoslavia, the armies' ability to fight was largely destroyed, yet the fight continued because the will to fight remained.

When one man in the enemy ranks is shot and killed, the chief accomplishment may be not the death of that particular man but the destruction of the will to fight in the men at his side. From this standpoint it can be said that guns, tanks, planes, are merely weapons of psychological warfare, obviously by far the most effective weapons, but nevertheless in this category. Strictly speaking, a war fought on the basis of ability to fight versus ability to fight would not be won until every man on one side or the other had been killed, literally a fight to the death. Actually history shows that relatively few wars, battles or even fights, have been fought on this basis. Most fights end, not when one side or the other has been destroyed, but when it "gives up." The loser could fight further, but he has no will to do so. Frequently only a small segment of a regiment or company need be killed to cause the entire unit to cease fighting. There is evidence that if the casualties in any combat unit reach as high as twenty percent, the whole unit will lose its will to fight and retreat or surrender.

From an historical perspective the most important phenomenon in the present world conflict is the discovery and use of psychological knowledge in affecting human thought, feeling and behavior. The Germans, Japs and Russians have discovered that the will to fight is of equal importance to the ability to fight. The French, British and Americans have conducted war on the outmoded formula of ability to fight versus the enemies' ability to fight. The Axis and the Russians have discovered that the formula of war is ability to fight *plus* the will to fight versus the enemies' ability to fight *plus* the enemies' will to fight. The Allies have been concentrating their efforts, both in training their troops and in attacking the enemy, on the ability to fight and leaving the will to fight up to chance and the eternal verities. The Axis and the Russians have not left the will to fight up to chance. They have concentrated equal effort and thought on the will to fight, and on the ability to fight. They have discovered how to create the will to fight and how to destroy the will to fight. The Nazi army engages the services of every psychologist and psychiatrist in Germany in a scientific program to arouse and maintain the will to fight in the Nazi army and civilians and to destroy the will to fight in the enemy. In their own troops they give as much attention to the letter the soldier receives from home as to the instruction in marksmanship he receives from his commanding officer, because they know it has equal if not greater importance in affecting his behavior in war.

What is this will to fight? There are several words in daily use which refer to it. The most common one is "morale." This, however, is a much misused word which has become painful to the ear. It has the added defect of having become associated in people's minds with entertainment and recreation which deflects the attention from more vital aspects of aggression and self-sacrifice. "Esprit de corps," "discipline," "sense of duty," "team work," are words also used in reference to the will to fight, but they, too, fail to connote more fundamental factors. The will to fight must include the willingness to die. It includes the willingness to kill and the willingness to be killed. To be effective the will to fight must be stronger than the will to live. This does not just happen merely because a man is drafted into the army, given a gun, and told to use it.

A psychiatrist knows that for a man to have the will to fight he must first have confidence in his ability to fight, confidence in his weapons, his skill, his strength. The forces of his super ego or conscience must be mobilized. He must have a reason to fight which satisfies his conscience. Whether this be to protect his family or his country, to survive, to do his duty, to preserve freedom, to follow the will of his leader, depends upon the individual. The powerful energies of his id or emotions must be not so much aroused as directed toward fighting. His anger and aggression which in peace time flow out toward any number of objects, must be gathered together into anger at the enemy. There must be fear of not fighting, fear of the consequences of defeat. There must be confidence in his fellows—that they will do their part if he does his. There must be confidence in his leader—that his leader shares his goal and has the ability to achieve it.

The war of ideas is aimed at these factors, to create them and maintain them on the one hand, to destroy them on the other. Do psychiatrists have a role in this war? They know something of why individuals fail to function in peace time; can they diagnose why masses of people fail to function in war time? Could psychiatrists help to formulate the questions in Gallup poll public opinion surveys used to diagnose the status of the will to fight both in soldier and civilian? Could psychiatrists help in interpreting the results of these surveys? How about treatment? Mobilization of the will to fight both in soldier and civilian is being done by newspapers, speeches, radio broadcasts, pamphlets, posters. Psychiatrists are not skilled in the use of these media, but could they not help formulate the propaganda programs? Should they be directed at the conscience? Should they appeal to duty, to patriotism? Should they attempt to arouse anger and fear of the enemy?

Turning to the offense, daily, powerful short-wave broadcasting stations in the United States and England bombard the German people. What do they say? Do psychiatrists have any suggestions? They often know what to say to prevent a man from committing suicide. Do they know what to say to cause a man to commit suicide?

Who actually is running this war of ideas at the present time? Who is making the diagnoses; who is formulating the propaganda and psychological strategy? It is my impression that psychiatrists are not. To my knowledge, there is no psychiatrist on the staff of any governmental agency engaging in this problem.

To summarize, in this paper I have attempted to present the following points:

1. There is a new force abroad in the world. Because of immense technological developments in means of communication and rapid growth of psychological knowledge, ideas have gained power to affect human behavior as never before in history.

2. In warfare the will to fight is of equal importance to the ability to fight.

3. Clever and ruthless enemies have recognized these two points. They have engaged this country in a war of ideas. It seems to me we are not using our best energies and facilities in fighting this war.

4. Whether the problem is regarded as one of preventive psychiatry, of preparing soldiers and civilians to withstand the ordeal of war, or whether it is regarded as the application of knowledge of the mind to the war of the mind, I believe psychiatrists have a responsibility to contribute.

Therefore, in conclusion, I agree with William Lawrence of the *New York Times* who said, "It is time for the psychiatrist to turn his attention from the problems of the abnormal mind in normal times to the problems of the normal mind in abnormal times."

Post-War Psychiatric Perspectives

By LAWRENCE KOLB, M.D.

Assistant Surgeon General in Charge of Mental Hygiene, United States Public Health Service

SANITY AND SECURITY OF THE PEOPLE • MENTAL AND NERVOUS DISORDERS AFTER THE WAR • GOVERNMENT'S REHABILITATION PROGRAM • CARE OF MERCHANT SEAMEN BY PUBLIC HEALTH SERVICE • MENTAL EFFECTS OF WAR AMONG CIVILIAN POPULATION • NO INCREASE IN MENTAL DISEASE • SYPHILIS AND ALCOHOLISM • THE GREATEST OF ALL HEALTH HAZARDS, THOSE TO MENTAL HEALTH • MENTAL HEALTH CONSERVATION PROGRAM • PSYCHIATRIC EDUCATION • NUMBERS OF PSYCHIATRISTS • CHILD GUIDANCE CLINICS • INSTRUCTION OF PUBLIC HEALTH NURSES • FEDERAL FUNDS FOR A FIELD PROGRAM • GRANTS-IN-AID OF SOCIAL SECURITY ACT • WORK FOR CRIPPLED CHILDREN • THE HOUSING MOVEMENT AND EMOTIONAL HEALTH • PHILOSOPHY OF THE SOCIAL SECURITY ACT • ENEMY ALIEN PROGRAM • ALCOHOLISM A MENTAL DISEASE • CRIME A MALADJUSTMENT • STATE MENTAL HOSPITALS • COMMITMENT LAWS • DESIGN FOR A GOVERNMENT INSTITUTE FOR RESEARCH IN MENTAL AND NERVOUS DISORDERS • PSYCHIATRY AND THE FUTURE OF HUMANITY

SANITY AND security are two exceedingly wholesome words to hear in this chaotic world. These two words formed the keynote of the opening of the annual meeting of the National Committee for Mental Hygiene in that fateful 1940. "The sense of security of mankind is at stake," Dr. Adolf Meyer reminded the assembled men and women of psychiatry, "and it is our share and our duty to contribute to the sanity and security of our own people." The importance of that contribution has grown with every succeeding month.

A poll of American public opinion on the war's after-effects, for which we must willingly pay in money and in services, would bring out a widespread acceptance of responsibility for the mental and nervous disorders of the people who return from the war. Men, women and even the children of this country are aware of the ordeal through which our armed forces are fighting their way. The gods of war are hard on their personnel. Combat forces have to make a complete readjustment of life habits in an atmosphere of physical danger, under conditions of hunger, fatigue, exposure to inclement weather, and infections incident to the gathering of persons in intimate contact.

The last war was only a localized affair compared to this one, and it left us with a bill for mental and nervous disorders which we are still paying. The Federal Government alone has paid out close to $1,000,000,000 for the care and pensioning of neuropsychiatric veterans of the last war.

When our present Selective Service went into operation, psychiatrists were called in to help weed out the unfit among the draftees. In the examination of the first million men, neuropsychiatric conditions were fifth among the causes of rejection. Nobody knows, however, how many of the young men going into the war are predisposed to mental illness and under the stress of war will break down sooner than would ordinarily have been the case. Nobody knows how many of the less predisposed will break down temporarily. Nobody knows how many who apparently come out unscathed will need the services of mental hygiene. A flier in the last war wrote in his diary that back in civilian life once again he "roamed the streets by day and by night alone with his nervous system." These, the ones for whom it is an ordeal to be alone with their nervous systems, also need the protection and help of psychiatry.

The post-war problem of the mentally ill is already manifest in admissions from the Army and Navy to Saint Elizabeths Hospital and veterans' hospitals and in claims for disability for mental and nervous conditions.

The Federal Government is shaping up the rehabilitation program which we shall owe to those who are giving themselves to winning the war. Companion bills have been introduced in the Senate and the House to provide for the vocational rehabilitation of individuals suffering from "war-connected or other disabilities." The bills are written to include not only members of the armed forces, but industrial workers who with their labor fight the war on the production line, and other people connected with the conflict.

The type of casualty of which the public hears very little is that occurring daily among our merchant seamen. These seamen without benefit of uniform or the title of fighting men keep the supplies moving to our forces, our allies and to ourselves through exceedingly troubled waters. Twenty-three hundred of them have lost their lives since the war started. Hundreds have been shipwrecked and have arrived on land in great need of medical and hospital care. Among these have been numerous psychiatric casualties. They have suffered from shock similar to that so common among soldiers at the front, shock due to harrowing experiences, exposure to wet and cold for days in open life boats, and to deprivation of food. These men are greatly in need of assistance, and the War Shipping Administration has arranged for it through the medical facilities of the Public Health Service. A special psychiatric service has been set up to deal with these cases in the Marine Hospitals, in special hospitals, and in convalescent homes where under the guidance of psychiatrists the merchant seamen will recuperate before returning to sea.

Our most anxious thoughts today are quite properly for those who are running the greatest risks. Psychiatry's clients, however, are the entire hundred and thirty million of the population. Psychiatry's mission is to foster sound minds to go with the sound bodies for which the public health movement has worked so long.

What the war will produce in the shape of special problems among the civilian population no one can predict. We do not have statistics war by war upon the mental effects of war among civilians. What data we do have lend no support to the view that wars cause an appreciable increase in psychoses as a whole. In Britain numerous psychotic casualties were anticipated and extensive preparations were made to take care of them, but the raids came and nothing unusual happened to the mental health of the people. All our reports from England indicate that the civilians are standing up well to the war of nerves, the air raids, the threat of invasion and all the dislocations war has brought into their personal lives. Crime has decreased there as it did in both Britain and the United States during the last war. This last statement does not hold true for the child population, for juvenile delinquency in England shows an alarming increase.

The news from Spain is similar to that from Britain. There were some psychotic casualties among predisposed civilians, but, as in Britain, some neurotic individuals were improved by their preoccupation with the war.

It is beyond the power of analysis to strike any prophetic balance between the people who are going to give way and those who are going to benefit because of the war, but the evidence of the past, incomplete as it is, seems to suggest that the aggregate of mental disease is very little affected by wars, peace, depressions or prosperity. The most reliable reports which we have from the Civil War both during the conflict and afterwards seem to indicate that there was no increase in mental disease because of the war. The same applies to the Spanish American War and World War I.

In Massachusetts, a state which has had an adequate mental hospital system and reliable psychiatric data for years, first admissions to mental hospitals decreased sharply from 1917 to 1920. The same thing to a less striking degree happened in New York and other parts of the country. It is significant that the drop in first admissions in Massachusetts during the last war exactly paralleled the drop in alcoholic psychoses.

Suicide rates tell the same story. In 1941, the rate among the policy holders of the Metropolitan Life Insurance Company dropped sharply from that of the previous year. In England, there was a decided fall in the number of suicides in the last three months of 1939, the opening scene of the war. The rate fell in 1940 and again in 1941.

When the tumult and the shouting dies, and the strain is

over, and the war duties are done, we will nevertheless have a considerable psychiatric problem to solve. Syphilis and alcoholism may increase during the war, and these are two of the more potent specific causes of mental diseases. The economic switchback from war production to production for peace is going to mean a dislocation involving millions of people. It may be a catastrophic dislocation in so far as the emotional and psychic elements of the problem are concerned.

Whatever the war and post-war conditions produce in the line of special problems, we still have the old constant problem, the appalling incidence of mental illness. The hazards to mental health are apparently the greatest of all our health hazards.

In 1940, 163,556 patients were admitted to hospitals for mental disease and defects—only 10,000 fewer than the number of persons who graduated from college that year. This comparison has an imaginative as well as a statistical value. The person who steps forth with his new sheepskin is prepared in his mind to conquer the world. The person who leaves the world to enter the doors of a mental hospital has gone down in defeat.

In dealing with mental diseases we started far up the line— with the end results. Psychiatry has not only a treatment responsibility but an epidemiological responsibility, to find the early cases, to ameliorate the conditions which breed cases. It is only through a national program that we can prevent the end results and the appalling bill which we pay for them.

The public reaction to the homecoming of the inevitable psychiatric casualties of this war will be favorable to the development of a far-reaching mental health conservation program and we should be ready with it.

The program should include:

1. Better psychiatric education of physicians.
2. An increase in the number of psychiatrists.
3. A wide distribution of mental hygiene and child guidance clinics.

4. More attention to mental hygiene in colleges and schools.
5. Attention to mental hygiene in industry.
6. Provision of measures to reduce juvenile delinquency.
7. Psychiatric assistance to courts and to discharged prisoners.
8. A saner approach to the problem of alcoholism by the police and courts.
9. Provision of treatment for chronic alcoholics including hospitals, clinics and consultation bureaus.
10. Better state mental hospitals.
11. A wide development of psychiatric units in general hospitals.
12. The establishment by all the states of sane, humane commitment laws as free as possible from judicial procedures.
13. The development of mental hygiene-public health activities in state health departments.
14. And above all a far-reaching development of research into nervous and mental diseases.

The country has now only about one psychiatrist for every 57,000 of the population. More than half of these are ordinarily employed in mental institutions where they are for the most part unavailable for early treatment designed to prevent hospitalization. No wonder the majority of first admissions to mental hospitals has never seen a mental specialist until they arrive at the hospital seriously ill. A wider interest in psychiatry and better support of mental hospitals will automatically increase the number of psychiatrists, but it is more important still that every medical student in the course of his education should receive sufficient psychiatric background to enable him to meet, in a common sense way at least, the numerous psychiatric problems with which he will inevitably be faced.

Many authorities rank child guidance clinics of supreme importance in the prevention of mental disorders. About twenty-seven of our larger cities have such clinics. However, in small cities and in rural areas such preventive service is almost nonexistent. Clinics for child guidance and mental health are doubtless very useful, but perhaps the more helpful way of carrying on preventive mental medicine would be the more subtle one of making mental hygiene activities an integral part of the services of public health departments. Studies are now being made in the Eastern Health District of Baltimore, Maryland, and in Williamson County, Tennessee, which are designed to set a pattern for mental hygiene-public health activities.

Dr. Julius Levy, Director of the Bureau of Maternal and Child Health of New Jersey, is carrying on a program which seems to be especially effective. All the public health nurses in this department are instructed in mental hygiene. They begin in a subtle way before the child is born to indoctrinate women with the principles of mental hygiene. From there on, without benefit of any loudly proclaimed program, they follow through with common sense mental hygiene measures administered along with their other health services. These measures are exclusive of treatment; they are limited strictly to prevention.

Mental hygiene is well over the threshold among our social efforts. Even in those favored communities which have mental hygiene clinics, however, the services are far inadequate to the needs. In our complex modern civilization, a program of mental hygiene like any public health program must have the backing of Federal and State Governments to carry out its mission properly. The President's Committee on Medical Care, reporting in 1938, recommended that Congress make available increasing amounts up to $10,000,000 a year for a field program of mental hygiene similar to the special annual appropriations for venereal disease control. While this recommendation has not been carried out, it may be described as a strong prevailing wind of opinion.

There are other indications that psychiatry is about its business and will eventually have the proper backing. The Public Health Service has made a psychiatric consultant available to the states in expanding public health programs through the grants-in-aid of the Social Security Act. The Children's Bureau hopes to put on a psychiatric consultant to work with the states in the program for maternal and child health. State health officers one after another are accepting responsibility in mental health and are calling in the psychiatric consultant to help incorporate mental hygiene in their public health programs. None of the money available under the Social Security Act as grants-in-aid to the states has ever been earmarked for mental hygiene purposes. Nevertheless for the fiscal year 1942, twelve states managed to readjust their budgets to include this activity. Before that time only four state health departments had mental hygiene programs.

When we reach a stage in our attack on mental disorders comparable to our attack on other diseases, psychiatric services will be widely accessible to the population. They will be as accessible as the x-ray of the lungs and as the blood tests that we hear so much about these days.

The influence of mental hygiene runs through all our health and welfare activities. Psychiatric training for professional workers who are carrying out programs in tuberculosis control, in venereal disease control, in maternal and child health, in industrial hygiene and all other programs of health or of welfare will help to knit the separate efforts in mental hygiene eventually into a strong national program.

The Children's Bureau has promoted institutes for psychiatric training for nurses among the states.

All the work for crippled children has a great psychiatric bearing upon their lives as adults. President Roosevelt has asked Congress to authorize a special wartime appropriation, not to exceed $7,500,000 the first year, for expanding Federal aid to states for the care of crippled children and child health and welfare services, all of which, of course, will include mental hygiene. The President stressed the special needs of mothers and children arising from war conditions.

The whole ideology behind our housing movement is mental hygiene. Winslow has said that poor housing shows its effects to the greatest degree in accidents and in poor emotional health. In England, the national housing program from the very beginning was under the Ministry of Health. In our country, the housing movement started as a low-rent proposition to get people of limited means out of unwholesome slums and into dwellings that would contribute to their self-respect and therefore their self-management. The war has turned it temporarily into a movement for war workers. The cooperation of local health departments is sought in providing public health services on the Federal housing projects. Housing and health programs are joining forces in our social structure. And throughout the housing literature written today you will find first of all the thinking of mental hygiene.

This philosophy likewise underlies all our activities under the Social Security Act. The genealogy of this Act goes back to those ugly blue laws under which administrators of the public funds for welfare must make sure that the pauper was duly servile for that which he received. The ideology prevailing in the administration of Social Security provisions is that the assistance should build up the self-confidence of the person receiving. Our Social Security people are good mental hygienists. They believe those receiving aid should feel they are accepting that which they have helped to provide for themselves, and that they are therefore still masters of their destinies.

The Social Security Board has inaugurated an Enemy Alien Program to provide for dependents of aliens and thus not only relieve distress but eliminate any reasons for resentment and consequent mental and social difficulties.

All of these health and welfare activities attest constantly to the mental hygiene disposition of this country.

In our quickening sense of the broad field in which mental medicine should function, we cannot overlook the necessity for taking alcoholism out of the category of crimes and treating it as a mental disease. It is evidence of an appalling lack of appreciation of essential principles that the arrests for drunkenness per unit of population in a large proportion of cities of the United States are from twenty to eighty times higher than arrests for drunkenness in New York, and that, as a rule, in these cities of high arrests less is done for the alcoholics than in New York. We shall never get anywhere with solving this problem until alcoholism comes to be generally regarded as a disease, the sufferers from which need careful study and attention. Neglect, indifference and punishment have never provided any solution.

The problem of crime should be approached from the psychiatric angle. In our broadened conception of mental medicine, it would be treated as a social or personal maladjustment. This treatment would not involve the abolition of punishment but would rather widen our approach to include the more saving efforts of prevention and rehabilitation.

In the Federal prison system, the Public Health Service operates the hospitals as psychiatric hospitals. The psychiatric approach to the crime problem has been adopted in some of our large cities. Follow-up work for discharged prisoners and probationers by means of psychiatric clinics attached to courts in all large judicial districts, Federal and State, and a wide adoption of the Briggs' Law principle are goals to be worked for.

Many years ago the National Committee for Mental Hygiene started its campaign for the improvement of State mental hospitals and brought about great advances. The work was later on taken up by the Hospital Survey Committee and is now being done by the Public Health Service. Conditions in some states are still appalling. By educating the public in these states to the unfortunate effects of political control and financial neglect of their institutions, we may expect the hospitals everywhere to be brought up to the standards adopted by the American Psychiatric Association and now maintained in several of the states.

The commitment laws in many of our states are still antiquated and as administered work severe hardships on the mental patient and his immediate family. We may hope that a broader interest in the mentally ill will stem from the war. This greater interest will inevitably result in so changing the laws that in every state admittance to and discharge from mental hospitals will be as cheap, as easy, and as painless as it is possible to make them.

Most important in our post-war psychiatric perspective is an advanced interest in and an increased public support of research into nervous and mental disorders. The problem is alarmingly great, but the research has been relatively neglected. It has been allowed to linger on and to receive incidental benefits from research into other conditions, but no great amount of effort has been directed toward psychiatric goals. Even though the psychiatric field has been comparatively neglected, it has been the scene of some brilliant achievements during the past forty years. When we look at the incidence of mental disease we must admit that these achievements hardly scratch the surface, but they do point the way to further advances especially in relation to the large group of mental diseases that we call psychogenic. We are more or less helpless in the practical application of preventive and curative measures for these diseases. This suggests that our knowledge of them must be woefully inadequate.

To remedy the situation, I have for several years been advocating the establishment by the Government of an institute to carry on research in mental and nervous diseases. The design for this institute is such that every field of science which has a bearing upon mental disease would be extensively studied. The necessity of and possibilities for research in some of these fields have been ably discussed in this Conference. Research would not be limited to the central institute. The institute would utilize talent and facilities throughout the country by subsidizing hospitals, clinics and universities to carry on projects that would be approved by a central board. The improvement of the mental hospitals envisioned as part of the post-war development will broaden the base for research. Potential research talent now going to waste will develop in many of them and where this happens the institute will furnish the needed financial assistance. By such a program of research we may hope eventually to get closer to the heart of some of the baffling psychiatric problems so that it will be possible to apply effective preventive and curative measures.

Psychiatry can play a tremendous role in shaping the future of humanity. We plan for the future with the double realization that we need more knowledge and need to apply to a greater degree that which we already have. A multitude of psychiatric problems are in the making for lack of a good scheme of prevention. The finer obligation of psychiatry as of all medicine is to prevent rather than to patch up. Our post-war perspective to be true perspective must include not just the victims of mental disorder but the hundred and thirty million.

Preventive Psychiatry

By GEORGE S. STEVENSON, M.D.

Medical Director, The National Committee for Mental Hygiene

CAUSE OF MENTAL DISEASE • NUTRITIONAL CONDITIONS • LIVING, WORKING, EDU-
CATIONAL CONDITIONS • PUBLIC HEALTH ACTIVITY • GENERAL PRINCIPLES OF PRE-
VENTION • PRESUMPTIVE PREVENTION • PREVENTION BY EARLY TREATMENT, BY
ESCAPE FROM EXPOSURES • REMOVAL OF CAUSES • RELIGIOUS INFLUENCES • EX-
PECTANT EMPIRICAL METHODS • PREVENTIVE OPPORTUNITIES • PREVENTIVE
STRATEGY • THE FOCUS OF PREVENTIVE EFFORT • EUGENICAL MEASURES • OB-
STETRICAL AND PEDIATRICAL CARE • SAFEGUARDING PHYSIOLOGICAL PROCESSES •
GENERAL MEDICAL PROBLEMS • THE PSYCHOLOGICAL LEVEL • CHILDREN AND
PARENTS • THE PRESSURES OF WAR • NEW BEACONS FOR PREVENTION

I WISH FIRST of all to express my appreciation to McGregor Fund for the opportunity to come here and to meet with those who are working or are otherwise interested in this field.

The beacon by which psychiatry has steered its course in its search for more knowledge of the causes of behavior and personality disorders is the hope that this knowledge will not only help cure them but will prevent them and enhance human living. But in charting its course, psychiatry is again and again disturbed by the question "But what is the cause of mental disease?" Its experience with actual people shows consistently that there is no single cause; there are instead a multiplicity, a combination, a conspiracy of causes. The demand for "a cause" often recalls merely the last straw, the last factor, the last experience, under which the patient broke and yet this need by no means be the main or even an important cause.

It can be seen that through this multiplicity there is a wide range of things for preventive psychiatry to do, things which may sometimes appear to be contradictory, but which actually are not. Thus the nutritional condition of a person may be improved, fatigue and insomnia overcome, emotional pres-

311

sures bearing upon him reduced, by change of location, change of business, or by a change of attitude; or the eradication of infections may turn the tide in his favor.

The fact that there is this wide range of causes also gives us wide opportunity to affect community influences or causes which exist on a large scale, causes which burden many people, such as poor living conditions, insecurity, occupational and educational misplacements, or untreated syphilis. In attacking these causes we have a real public health activity in the field of mental hygiene.

The term prevention has been used in such a variety of ways that it is necessary to be clear as to a particular meaning whenever we use it. Otherwise we get into endless and meaningless arguments. Probably the most frequent attempt at prevention could be called "presumptive prevention." It is assumed that if we bring under control a condition which frequently precedes a mental disturbance we will have forestalled the disturbance itself. For example, the shut-in personality is said to precede dementia praecox, but without waiting for absolute proof that this is causative or an essential stage in the progress of the disorder we deal with it with such facilities as child guidance clinics. The effort is presumptive because it is never possible in a case which has been treated successfully to say what might have happened if no treatment had been given. In reporting on a preventive effort of this sort one psychiatrist, Dr. H. L. Levin,[1] writes as follows: "Although the four problem children [whom he was studying] seemed to have been definitely started on the praecox route, psychiatric intervention appeared to have vitiated some of the malignant elements in the environment and brought about, for a period now of from two to four years, an apparent arrest of the praecox process. The question is raised whether similar intervention during the childhood of the four adult praecox cases [which he had been studying] might not have been the

[1] Levin, H. L., Role of child guidance in prevention of schizophrenia (dementia praecox). New York State J. Med., 33:808, 1933.

means of preventing chronic, if not lifelong, psychoses." The process of presumptive prevention is justified. Sometimes it is the only opportunity to do something, even though it is an uncertain thing. By doing it we gain a new orientation on some aspects of the problem. We have always to realize that something is happening to a person in any case. We can seldom be neutral.

Some attempts at prevention are only relatively preventive. Early treatment of a condition is relatively preventive since it is recognized that treatment at an early stage is preventive of later developments, and that is the meaning sometimes given to the term "preventive." We are doing this sort of preventive work in treating alcoholism and in giving special attention to persons who shop from doctor and doctor, those who exhibit delinquency, laziness, moodiness and overscrupulosity.

Kasanin and Veo [2] found that in about half the cases of later dementia praecox early signs of this disorder were apparent to the school teacher and gave a warning for early treatment.

Dr. Adolf Meyer clarified the real focus of many of our so-called preventive efforts as follows: "We are at times made to believe that all our mental hygiene work and effort aim largely at the prevention of 'insanity and crime,' just as the early advocates of psychopathic hospitals made it look as if, through the creation of a psychopathic hospital in each state, the existing state hospital care would then be made less expensive and perhaps in part unnecessary. To be sure, early work means a heading off of some of the disastrous depth of aberration and deviation and much unnecessary blundering. But the chief goal is much more direct; it offers prompter and more and more enlightened help both to patient and family and to the community in respect to really new problems, largely left to themselves before; it is a direct service to the positive needs and opportunities of the community in behalf of what I re-

[2] Kasanin, J. and Veo, L. A study of school adjustment of children who later in life became psychotic. Am. J. Orthopsychiat., 2:212, 1932.

emphasize as health, happiness, efficiency, and social adaptation.[3]

Another method of relative prevention is to circumvent causative factors which in themselves may not be modified. The person may be removed from the conditions which trouble him. Penology prevents crime by extirpating the criminal from society. The person under great emotional pressure may take time out for a vacation or otherwise escape long enough to reassemble his forces.

The acme of prevention, of course, is the removal of clearly proved causes or the application of processes which have been scientifically validated, even though we do not understand how they work. In the case of syphilitic or toxic mental disorders we have a clear opportunity for sound scientific prevention through the prevention of syphilis or of the misuse of drugs, although in actual application such prevention necessitates the control or influencing of human behavior in other respects in a way which throws us back to the presumptive level.

The empirical approaches to prevention, approaches whose value we can assess even though we cannot understand them, include the often sudden and startling changes which occur under religious influences, e.g., Alcoholics Anonymous and the Salvation Army. There is abundant evidence that these empirical efforts produce results. They should be studied that we may discover the principles and reasons behind this result, but even without this understanding we are on solid ground in applying the method empirically with expectation of some success.

Preventive psychiatry, if it is to be effective, cannot submit to slavish routine. It must observe a strategy or else find the effort dissipated or misplaced. This effort must be directed toward realms of human function which are capable of modification, to causes accessible and vulnerable. It must be practical.

[3] Meyer, A. Individualism and the organization of neuropsychiatric work in community. Mental Hygiene, 9:675, 1925.

Some prevention falls definitely within the range of psychiatry, but the family doctor, the lawyer, the minister, the employer, the nurse, the social worker, the teacher and the public health functionary, all meet with preventive opportunities as a part of their daily jobs. The royal road to prevention is traversed by those persons working as far as possible in unison, but each one of them as a part of his daily routine has an opportunity to carry on his job in a way which will enhance the mental health of those with whom he is dealing.

Preventive strategy requires that factors be weighed carefully to reveal their importance and that those attacked be accessible and vulnerable. We cannot undo the death of a loved one, but we can support a healthier attitude toward the death. We can also see that sometimes one must be quite opportunistic, particularly where we are dealing with a chain of causes—factor A may lead to B, B to C, C to D and D to A again. The interruption of the chain depends on finding any weak spot for attack. We do not need to know which came first. In fact the original major factors of a mental deviation may disappear but the problems continue on through the entrance of later influences. For example, an unfortunate attitude may start from ignorance, but may persist through what we may call pride in the face of later knowledge. The giving of information may not any longer interrupt the progression of these attitudes whereas it might have stopped its beginning.

It might be said briefly that the causes of mental disorder are so diverse and aftermaths of any one factors so different that prevention cannot usually be stipulated specifically for a certain illness. We face the apparently paradoxical fact that one does not prevent mental diseases by setting out to prevent them, but he rather achieves this as a result of promoting the best positive development for a person in terms of his survival, satisfaction and productivity. We play because it is fun, not to prevent something, but in playing we prevent a lot.

So much for the general principles of prevention. Now for the focus of preventive effort. Prevention is necessarily directed toward the phases of human function related to mental disorders, insuring to persons the best possible endowment at birth, the soundest possible functioning of the body organs, the development of useful habits and attitudes, and the provision of a wholesome environment and experiences.

Eugenical measures include the control of marriage, sterilization, the limitation of conception and the interruption of pregnancy. Marriage has been left largely to individual judgment, although laws do obstruct precipitous marriages and protect from parenthood many of the socially and mentally incompetent. Sterilization for one specific problem has been supported by the Supreme Court of the United States in the case of Virginia. The great difficulty is that these measures are hardest to apply where the problems are the greatest, i.e., the borderline case of mental deficiency. The limitation of conception is subject to legal regulations varying state by state up to the extreme of completely tying the tongue of the doctor. More important are the individual moral regulations which carry this matter beyond the range of scientific decision. Similar problems of law and morals may arise in the case of the woman whose mental disturbances occur with each pregnancy and for whom the avoidance or termination of pregnancy presents the most promising solution.

Prevention of prenatal accidents and birth injury so important to psychiatry is becoming a legitimate concern of good obstetric practice and the use of large doses of x-ray on the pregnant mother is now a matter for serious second thought because of the dangers it holds for the child.

Recent studies have emphasized the importance to the mental health of the coming child of the attitudes of his mother before his birth, attitudes which determine how she will care for him afterwards. The development of this preventive possibility is still a task of the future, but pediatrics is developing a greater appreciation of this in its handling of the mother and her child.

Now let us turn to prevention through safeguarding physiological processes. Some physiological functions are very general in their effects. Fatigue, insufficient sleep, poor nutrition, variations in atmosphere, smoldering infections, inadequate convalescence from illness, disordered metabolism and oxygenation, vitamin deficiency, endocrine imbalance, allergies, alterations of blood content, circulatory disorders and disturbances of smooth muscle function, all have their concomitant disturbances of behavior and these may at times be major considerations. Unfortunately these physiological disorders often exist at sub-clinical levels which are not taken seriously by the physician because they do not involve acute or very evident incapacity. The consideration of these subtle influences needs to be given more serious attention in medical education if the best preventive opportunity is to be grasped—a clear task for our medical schools.

Better appreciated than these subtle influences is the need for efficient functioning of the muscular (motor) and sensory nervous apparatus. It is well recognized that deprivation of hearing and sight may result in a disorder resembling mental deficiency and that crippling frequently results in seriously distorted personalities. Preventive activities are, accordingly, within the scope of those handling such problems. Disorders of brain tissues are so frequently associated with general medical problems—syphilis, meningitis, encephalitis, accidents, poisons, pellagra—that their prevention becomes a part of good medical care. Caution in the use of drugs, encouragement of regular health examinations, the preventive and treatment programs in the field of industrial hazards, sight, hearing, venereal disease, public safety and alcohol, therefore, are an important part of preventive psychiatry.

Let us now look at the possibilities of prevention focused on the behavior of persons rather than their organs. This classification of the eugenical, physiological and psychological is useful chiefly for getting a perspective on the various processes and not at all for actually dealing with people; for seldom can our efforts be limited to one of these categories alone. On the psychological level we attempt to safeguard the development of healthy attitudes and habits. Fear, bigotry, suspicion, prejudice, fanaticism, moodiness, shyness, stupidity and many other disabling personal characteristics are legitimate starting points for preventive work.

Careful guidance in the formative years is particularly important. There is evidence that cuddling a baby and giving him full opportunity to suck is conducive to his development. The child and youth need affection, particularly today when other expressions of worth, such as in work, are less available.

In infancy many transitory behavior phenomena appear which call for wise guidance rather than stern interruption. There is still as a rule an inherent adjustability in the child on which we may rely as long as we "keep an eye peeled." The anxieties of the parent which precipitate him into hasty action are an opportunity for all who are helping the family in its guidance of the child—the doctor, the minister, the nurse and the teacher—to ease the tense situation. Frequently the best thing to do is to do nothing until the tension has subsided. This is particularly true in cases involving sex deviations. Much time has been spent in improving the sex orientation of children, often ignoring the fact that the undescribable feeling aspects of sex are the critical issue. Any preventive effort with children must face the fact that they are confronted with a continuity of experience unpredictable and uncontrollable, some helpful and some otherwise, and that it is the experience of the child in meeting and solving problems as they come along rather than outside help with these specific exigencies, which becomes the strength of the child.

Automatization of behavior is essential to security and tranquillity, as also is a margin of safety between the capacity of the individual and the demands made on him both in school and in work. It is a part of growth and strength to play, not only to exercise muscles but to try one's capacities for coping with problems and to build up a feeling of one's own resources.

Emancipation at best is a gradual progressive process beginning at birth and not one which begins with the high school senior. A vocational goal is an integrating core about which experience is unwittingly organized, and thus becomes useful.

A philosophical construct, religious or otherwise, similarly gives experience something about which it crystallizes and takes on meaning.

Emergencies and pressures such as war and imminent danger are especially potent in magnifying weaknesses and may be useful in revealing needs and opportunities for preventive work which would otherwise escape detection. It is for this reason that Selective Service, employment and personnel systems, economic stress, school tests, examinations and competitions often bring problems to light. Insight may have preventive value, insight into one's own peculiarities, insight timed to the readiness of the person to use it. Improperly timed insight may become destructive.

If one looks between the lines of what I have said about the general aspects of prevention and the preventive opportunities through eugenics, physiological safeguarding and psychological care, it will be evident that an immense preventive opportunity is to be found in the melioration of the surroundings of the person, his home life, work, public health forces, religious resources, play facilities, economic opportunities, friends and the law. All have their plus and minus values in helping or hindering mental health. It is hopeful that among the leaders of each of these fields are prophets whose leadership if successful will carry us far. When I look about me at the present time and see a common interest in preventive psychiatric work in those fields which deal with people in need or in trouble, I cannot but be encouraged. Looking purely at the war situation, from Red Cross, USO, army chaplains, company officers, technical instructors in the armed forces, the morale division, and spots of dense civilian occupation under Army auspices, I meet common questions: How can we come to know the signs of need for special attention? What can be done to bring the proper help in the right way to those who need it? What do these things tell us about the needs in our own fields? These questions are being asked. Therein is our hope and therein I think we have new beacons for prevention.

Psychiatry in Industry

By ERNEST E. HADLEY, M.D.

Executive Secretary, The William Alanson White Psychiatric Foundation

IMPORTANCE OF NUMBERS AND PERSONAL EFFICIENCY OF MANPOWER IN INDUSTRIAL WAR WORK • SMALL NUMBER OF PSYCHIATRISTS • NEED IN FIELD OF PERSONALITY PROBLEMS • HELPLESSNESS OF THE GENERAL PRACTITIONER • CONTRIBUTION TO MEDICAL EDUCATION AND THE PSYCHIATRIST • INDUSTRIAL SUPPORT ORGANIZATION AND FIGHTING ARMS OF THE GOVERNMENT • PSYCHIATRIC SELECTION OF MANPOWER • REHABILITATION OF WAR MENTAL CASUALTIES AS USEFUL INDUSTRIAL WORKERS • PSYCHIATRIC FIRST AID • PLACEMENT OF MANPOWER • SELECTION FOR PROMOTION • SUCCESS AND FAILURE • PSYCHIATRISTS NOT WELL PREPARED TO TURN TO PROBLEMS OF INDUSTRIAL WORK • TRAINING CENTERS • EVERY DOCTOR A NEW SENSE OF RESPONSIBILITY • MENTAL HEALTH OF ONE OUT OF EVERY FOUR AMERICAN CITIZENS

MANY OF you will recall how in his *Twentieth Century Psychiatry* William Alanson White envisaged the practical utilization of psychiatry in industry. The field of industry impressed him as a peculiarly distinguished area for psychiatric study and he foresaw the development of an industrial psychiatry which amounted to a special scientific discipline in itself. Nothing could be more timely than his thoughts pertaining to the significance which would attach to psychiatric studies of actual industrial set-ups both as self-limited organizations and as parts of a social whole.

Any consideration of the place of psychiatry in industry today must take cognizance of the national emergency and the period of world reconstruction which must follow victory of the United Nations. With the armed forces to be expanded to the neighborhood of nine million men, the most conservative estimate would indicate that over one hundred million people will be occupied in industry and other activities indispensable to the conduct of the war. This means that the productivity of nearly every three out of four persons is significant for victory and reconstruction of a better world.

If one can grasp even the simplest implication of this staggering fact, one has to see that it implies the unprecedented importance of personal efficiency in contrast with the waste of human resources and the cultivation of personal nuisance values.

Since industry is one of the major fields for employing manpower in winning the war, any contribution psychiatry can make to greater personal efficiency and productiveness is far too important to be neglected in the war effort.

The pioneers in industrial psychiatry—notably Dr. Lydia G. Giberson of the Metropolitan Life Insurance Company—have shown incontrovertibly that mental and personality disorders have a large place in accounting for absenteeism, serious accidents, pranks, vandalism, generally unfavorable relations between worker and supervisor, and the difficulties which arise from misunderstandings and disappointments, including almost everything from lowered efficiency and labor turnover to deliberate sabotage.

I need not stress the monetary significance of this complex of factors to impress you with the urgent desirability of a frontal attack; the only part which clearly needs laboring is the practical matter of what psychiatry can actually accomplish under existing and probably immediate future conditions.

As the White Psychiatric Foundation has been at great pains to publicize, there is an extreme dearth of psychiatric competence. It is extravagant to assume that there are five thousand people in these United States who are able bodied and well trained to meet psychiatric problems which would be encountered in any large aggregation of people. The recruiting of psychiatric specialists for the armed forces may be expected to call to the colors not less than sixty percent of the able bodied and competent males actually trained in this specialty. One needs no particular flair for mathematics to see that psychiatrists—men and women—who remain in civilian life can be supplied to industry, or to any other part of the civilian war effort in far less adequate ratio. It is not unreasonable to assume that the most pressing question confronting psychiatry today arises simply from this consideration. The question is: how can the psychiatrist retained in civilian capacity in the home base area contribute most adequately to the winning of the war and world reconstruction? One of the answers which can be found may be distasteful to a great many of the medical men concerned. But before I discuss this answer, let me digress, seemingly, to the inadequacies of the medical profession to do the work which an enlightened population expects of them.

It is self evident that a population enjoying the benefits of such thorough grounding in the natural and biological sciences, as is assumed in the case of every child of ordinary intelligence in these United States, should look to the physician for the treatment of difficulties which he had been taught to regard as physical or mental. The psychiatrist does not need to be told that a great majority of the people who are suffering mental disorders, mild or severe, believe themselves not to be ill and in need of medical aid. Equally, blatantly obvious is the fact that it is a rare physician today who has anything helpful to offer the patient whom he does not find to be *really* sick: that is, the patient requiring psychiatric assistance. Psychiatrists thus find themselves confronted by the absurd situation in medicine that, while doctors ordinarily require the support of specialists only when they encounter problems of managing unusually complex medical problems, they require —knowingly or even more deplorably—a psychiatric specialist to take over any and all problems in that field.

Continuing on this seeming digression, let me adumbrate to you the implications of some cross sectional studies of American manpower in its most productive years. I think I need not argue the industrial utility of persons between eighteen and thirty-five as compared with their seniors. The unwillingness to employ older workers has even in peace times reached the proportions of a great socio-economic problem. Now, therefore, when a group of psychiatrists working with a set of standards, both rather clear and rather reasonable, find the distribution of personality handicap in the eighteen- to thirty-five-year cross section to exceed two hundred and fifty per thousand—one in four—is it not clear that the most urgent of all medical problems is the helplessness of the general practitioner in the field of personality problems?

Now I come sharply back to a consideration of psychiatry in industry. Wherever there is a physician primarily concerned with maintaining maximum productivity, there is a person with the education of whom the industrial psychiatrist should be acutely concerned. Vastly the greatest contribution which any psychiatrist could make to winning this war would be in the field of medical education. All this follows automatically from the indications about the frequency of personality problems in the general population. All this must be clearly in mind when one thinks practically of what can be done in utilizing psychiatry in any phase of the war effort and the world reconstruction.

I must hope that I have said enough in this preliminary note on the unhappy state of medicine. I turn now to a hurried survey of the field in which I am asked to speak.

Because total war is now clearly seen at least numerically to involve almost everyone, because *we* as *a people* have never seized on the clear social responsibility implied by the coincidence of opportunity and ability, and because, as is perhaps only a national consequence of the latter, *we* are far from a highly sane, realistic, and personally efficient body of people, the problem of psychiatry in promoting the war effort looks much the same in any field of endeavor where concerted and coordinated efforts of many persons are required for the achievement of results. It is by no means unreasonable to consider the industrial support organization in much the same way that one considers the more highly disciplined and closely regimented fighting arms of the government.

As the White Psychiatric Foundation has been at pains to indicate, the first useful function of the psychiatrist is the classification of men with respect to their vulnerability to the circumstances which will inevitably confront them in the service for which they are being considered. Gross psychiatric selection of manpower for industry is closely related to psychiatric selection for the armed forces. It is tragically beside the point to assume the attitude that only the mentally healthy should be admitted to employment in industry. This attitude with respect to the armed forces does some violence to experience, but it must be evident that the circumstances which a person will encounter in the factory will seldom or never be identical in their implied stresses with the circumstances commonly encountered in the Army or Navy.

Clearly there is a field for competent discrimination among persons somewhat handicapped by personality difficulties in selecting the perhaps small proportion who will remain effective in the armed forces and the much more significant proportion who can function with worthwhile efficiency and comparative personal safety in industry. There is every reason to believe that a great many of the unsuitable persons already and presently to be mental casualties in the armed forces can be rehabilitated as useful citizens engaged in industrial aspects of the war.

I cannot hope that this will follow automatically from its possibility. I cannot but fear that it will for a long time be conspicuously absent from the policy and procedure governing psychiatric functions connected with the Army; but we will come to it.

However lamentably medicine has failed in the development of skill in psychiatric first aid, it would be unfair to expect every psychiatrist to show good judgment in correlating his technical skill in the placement of manpower. There is great need for translation and expansion of the principles in Selective Service *Medical Circular No. 1* to the industrial field and there are also wide differences of opinion as to the significance of minor personality handicaps in this field as in the military avocation. These deficiencies have first to be recognized before they can be remedied just as the limitations of experience and of outlook of the particular psychiatrist may be very properly contemplated as a preliminary to industrial practices.

Gross selection of manpower is by no means the greatest contribution psychiatry can make to industry. The great virtue of selection lies in its preventive aspect which is much more significant for all concerned than is its role in its treatment of full blown difficulty. Beyond selection and beyond early recognition of impending difficulty and wise intervention to prevent its developing, there is a great and untouched field in which psychiatry as the science of interpersonal relations can be used in the selection of persons for promotion —particularly to positions entailing leadership and its function in exploring the causes for relative success and failure, and the management both of trouble-making workers and of general discontent.

Now, synthesizing these various considerations one can only say that psychiatry despite its unparalleled development in the past twenty-five years, in part by the momentum gained with Thomas M. Salmon in the last World War, psychiatrists as a whole are none too well prepared to turn from personal practice or institutional staff positions to the wise application of their uniquely valuable insights in the problems of industrial work. Just as the armed services find it practical to indoctrinate their specialists to prepare them for the special demands of military service so, too, a wise and foresighted administration might well concern itself with the organization of training centers for psychiatrists entering all these phases of total war.

Beyond all this I must repeat that everything cries for the sensitizing of the general physician, that every doctor who is assuming a new measure of responsibility in promoting the war effort, become acquainted with the rudiments, by no means recondite, of psychiatric diagnosis and treatment. It is not enough that this truth be recognized by the few; the national safety demands that it be recognized by the public itself. Psychiatry as science and as art cannot be ignored in this time of national crisis and stresses which will increase along predictable and wholly unknown lines for years to come. No conservative attitude of many medical educators and no archaic superstition about psychiatry of many of its administrators should be permitted to endanger the mental health and personal efficiency of one out of four American citizens. By the same token, no discipline in medicine has had so great a responsibility unless it be the relatively well prepared fields of epidemiology and Public Health.

Psychiatry and Morale

By HARRY STACK SULLIVAN, M.D.

The William Alanson White Psychiatric Foundation

PSYCHIATRY AND SOCIAL PSYCHOLOGY • THE FIELD OF INTERPERSONAL RELATION-
SHIPS • PERSONAL INTERREACTION PSYCHIATRY • ABERRANT TYPES AND THE GREAT
MIDDLE GROUND • MORALE • ACUTE DEMORALIZATION • PANIC • PSYCHONEUROTIC
DISABLEMENTS • CHRONIC DEMORALIZATION • DISCOURAGEMENT • DESPAIR • MASS
DESPAIR AND THE COLLAPSE OF FRANCE • THE CERTAINTY OF DIVINE LAW AND ULTI-
MATE JUSTICE • THREATS OF INSECURITY • SHRILL NOISES • FATIGUE • CON-
STRUCTIVE PREOCCUPATION • THE ENEMY'S PSYCHIATRIC STRATEGY • THE
MOBILIZATION OF LEADERSHIP • NATIONAL MORALE • THE ARMY AND THE NAVY •
THE MERCHANT MARINE • A STUDY IN MORALE • MORALE AMONG PSYCHIATRISTS
• AGRICULTURAL COMMUNITIES • INDUSTRY • NEGRO COMMUNITIES

THERE IS a reason for psychiatrists having to deal with
many relatively interesting and important topics other
than patients suffering mental disorders, and I think I am
justified in taking a moment to discuss this reason. The study
of man and of all things cultural, man-made, has in the science
and art of medicine fallen to the lot of psychiatry, as in the
field of social sciences it has fallen to the lot of social psychology. The chance of anyone's making an adequate discrimination between social psychology on the one hand and modern
psychiatry on the other seems to me to be rather small. The
most one can say is that they sound very different and they
do not like each other very warmly; perhaps chiefly because
the social scientist comes along an academic path which seldom touches the biological disciplines closely, whereas the psychiatrist comes along the path of medical education which is
rather strikingly biological in its roots, and, at least until
recently, sadly lacking in any attention to social-scientific data.
The facts are that the two disciplines are very closely related
in subject matter and as the years pass will quite certainly

become more and more closely related in the type of theory, experiment and conclusion with which they are occupied; and in the formulations and advisory statements about important matters occasionally demanded, as for example, that asked of the psychiatrist now addressing you.

Of course, morale, whatever it means to you—and I shall spend no time on that—is important. We had a profoundly shocking instance of its importance in our recent conversion from a country wonderfully wishful in the belief that we could get other people to fight our war into a people frantically at the business of preparing to defend itself against the most dangerous enemy which has appeared in the history of the western world.

It would be a waste of time to struggle with a definition. Let me content myself simply with discussing how the psychiatrist attacks the problem of morale. As a number of the essays in this remarkable Conference on Psychiatry has indicated, psychiatrists tackle a good many problems because there is no one else to tackle them and because they do in their way fall rather clearly in the broad and fundamental field of interpersonal relations. This means the way in which people live together, deal with each other, and come to have the beliefs, convictions and attitudes, real or imaginary, which they are constantly manifesting to friends and enemies, neighbors and distant correspondents. Just because psychiatry includes the only body of scientists who are clearly aware of a primary concern with the field of interpersonal relations which has only quite recently been recognized as the really proper field of social psychology, in so far as this is the science of personal interaction, psychiatry is called on to deal with a good many things far indeed from the alienism in which it perhaps had its birth in this phase of culture.

Psychiatry, when it tackles a problem, distinguishes itself from its sister discipline of social psychology by looking for the most aberrant types of interpersonal relations which have some bearing on the problem, while social psychology, traditionally social-scientific, is apt to seek the great middle ground for its data. In the problem of morale, I think that the psychiatric approach seems the fortunate one. When one looks for major aberrations in the field of morale they stand out clearly. Demoralized people, on the one hand, and the people who survive really desolating experiences with unimpaired drive, coherence, coordination and collaborative abilities, those are the aberrant poles that the psychiatrist has to study in attempting to make sense of morale. He studies the abnormal, and gradually expanding the field to the less abnormal, discovers that he has crossed the normal without noticing it and has covered the ground.

The study of demoralized people as a way of approaching the problem of morale is somewhat illuminating. We and you—because you must remember that psychiatrists and others have much the same experience—certainly know people who have been acutely demoralized and probably know people who are chronically demoralized.

A degree of acute demoralization which is practically beyond the true meaning of demoralization, which is related to it as lightning is to any other celestial illumination, is panic. Now "panic" is unhappily both a technical term and a word which appears in the newspapers. So let me say that the panic I speak of is an exceedingly ghastly experience which usually passes over and into the kind of blind terror the newspapers mean by the term. When one is in panic one does nothing. In blind terror, one rather blindly seeks a scheme for action, for escape. Below this intensity, the degree of fear which we call blind terror, there are various levels of fear to be observed in states of acute demoralization in which one is horribly afraid and tries to escape, more or less purposively and effectively. Still lower in intensity in this same series and a part of the picture of acute demoralization, is the fear and anxiety from which arise what we may call the psychoneurotic disablements. In these, a person who is acutely demoralized, neither panic-stricken nor a victim of blind terror, but very much afraid, rather abruptly is relieved of a large measure of that fear by the occurrence of some apparently organic disease.

Some of the war neuroses are striking instances of this: the threadbare example being the boy with none too good a background for mental health, who had been drafted and sent overseas. He had been delayed a terribly long time on his way to the front and had finally been there about two weeks when word came that his battalion was to go "over the top" that night. While he had the usual symptoms of very real fear, the first barrage came and ended and he was still among those present and ready to go over the top. But a little before the zero hour he had a painful seizure in his right arm and it was found that his index finger was paralyzed. That unfortunately reduces the usefulness of a marksman to zero. In other words, being right-handed and depending largely for effectiveness on using a gun and having lost the use of his trigger finger, he suddenly became what the services call "ineffectual."

There are some people, I suppose, even in such an intelligent audience as this, who are impressed by the singularly purposeful character of this disablement and are inclined to look down the nose at this soldier and say, "Huh, not a very honorable performance." Let me assure you that psychoneurotic disablements which relieve the fear and anxiety that would otherwise drive one to perhaps most disastrous attempts at escape, are no more the voluntary choice of the person who suffers them than is your eye color an instance of your deliberate selection. They are not psychoneurotic disablements if you select them and cook them up and stage them as a dramatic performance; then they are usually rather transparent fraud. They are psychoneurotic disablements when they come without calling, notwithstanding the fact that they come very conveniently.

A thing much more commonly encountered in acute demoralization of mild degree is what is meant when one speaks of getting rattled. A famous example I remember from the days when I practiced in New York City, was the case of a gentleman who had just acquired his first automobile, who, while driving, spotted a dear friend in a car going the other way, reached for his hat to greet her and drove his car straight into the other. He was rattled.

Then there is the mild stage of demoralization which we do not ordinarily recognize as such but the appearances of which the psychiatrist sees through realizing this is the most probable explanation, an occasion when one flies into a rage. Often in mere anger one is angry because something has tended to demoralize him. So much for acute demoralization.

The picture of chronic demoralization is quite different from that of acute demoralization. The time factor in acute and in chronic demoralization is important, perhaps unusually important. Acute demoralization is always a brief affair. There are some acute conditions which are sustained or which recur, and demoralization can recur, but it does not ordinarily go on. It is almost always sharply time-limited; and what follows is something else. Thus, our psychoneurotic soldier has his finger paralyzed while he is demoralized, but then, after the paralysis, suffers a psychoneurosis, a so-called war neurosis, without any particular demoralization. Chronic demoralization, in contrast, can go on for months or years. There are two great polar manifestations of these conditions. One is *discouragement*. By discouragement I do not mean that you decide you really are not interested in something and give it up, but I mean being discouraged to the point that a psychiatrist might mistake you for a regression. You do not do much of anything. You do not think of much of anything but you are not depressed chiefly because the victim of a depression does think of something, a circling of the same thought "I have committed the unpardonable sin. God will never forgive me. I am lost." This goes on. A discouraged person thinks as little as possible, but such thinking as he does is *progressive* or *retrogressive* preoccupation with gloomy evidence of failure and not merely circling. Now and then there may be a moment of spontaneity and he thinks of attacking the thing again; then comes a flow of gloomy recollections of when he tried that before and it failed and how many other things have failed, and so on.

The other polar contrast in chronic demoralization, still not so different, is *despair*. Now "despair" may seem to some of you just a beautifully dramatic word which should appear in romantic literature. When it is renamed *disorganization apathy*, it sounds pretty impressive. If I remind you that the inculcation of mass despair was the great success of the German psychiatric strategy in the early days of the blitzkrieg and that it was the widespread dissemination of this mental state that contributed most vividly to the sudden collapse of France, then you may take despair as something more than a dramatic word. The person in despair is reduced to a vestigial state of humanness. What goes on in the mind is almost entirely accidental and goes on to no particular purpose; and what goes on as behavior is a matter merely of what has been begun. If a person in despair were standing at the top of the aisle here and someone gave him a firm push he would walk at a fairly steady rate, probably stumble around the corners, come down here and I suppose wind up looking blankly at the curtain behind me. They keep going; not anywhere in particular and with no evidence of enthusiasm or purpose. They have very little in mind. They are quite incapable of grasping anything which requires concentration or immediate, alert response. The blitzkrieg succeeded in filling most of the roads any good for the transport of troops, tank supplies, etc., in France, with hordes of peasants, demoralized—already chronically demoralized—to the point of despair. They wandered blindly along these roads, making little or no effort to get out of the way of troops, getting hit or run over—and the troops could not stand it, and did not go ahead.

This is something of what the psychiatrist finds when he attacks the problem of morale. He sees the picture of demoralization and having realized this and having filled in many more details than I can do here, he comes to the problem of what the circumstances are under which people become demoralized, and what the circumstances are under which some people avoid demoralization when the average person would logically be demoralized. Study shows that demoralization in various degrees follows when some implicitly trusted and very significant aspect of one's universe suddenly collapses. Your universe and my universe are not the same. I am not talking about the physical universe but about the universe in which you live. To some of you, the greatest of all values and certainties in your universe is the certainty of divine law and ultimate justice. If that part of your universe suddenly fails rather dramatically, under circumstances which bring its failure to you quite abruptly, you will pass into acute demoralization. The principle is so true that it holds for all sorts of situations. If you were used to walking on a certain sidewalk, which you crossed twice a day, and it suddenly sank under you, you would be acutely demoralized—how gravely, depending on your past experience. I mention these two examples to suggest to you that if something always trusted, never doubted, is swiftly wiped out, if it suddenly proves wholly inadequate to support you in some way or other, then demoralization follows immediately. The state as it is experienced, in so far as one experiences anything, is of suddenly becoming a prey of utter insecurity. No feeling of security remains, whether it is trust in the ultimate character of divine law or trust in the sidewalk. When one is demoralized all one's security has disappeared.

Next to this in the causing of acute demoralization are any grave threats of insecurity. In other words, any rapidly appearing, pretty convincing suggestion that you will be made deeply insecure in any field is quite apt to provoke acute demoralization. In some cases where you suddenly find that you are in a position where all your major satisfactions can be cut off, then, too, you can become acutely demoralized. These threats fail under one circumstance to be demoralizing and this is very illuminating. If the threat to your security, or in the rarer case the threat to all your important satisfactions, appears gradually enough and under circumstances when you are in fit condition so that you can engage in what is called rational analysis of the threat and achieve an understanding of how it has come upon you—I need not tell you how far from logically perfect your analysis may be or how relatively empty your understanding may be—then acute demoralization does not follow. But if you are tired, or at a great disadvantage from some social reason when the threat impinges on you, you are reduced to a state of acute demoralization. These are the outstanding illuminating instances of the occurrence or nonoccurrence of acute demoralization.

The psychiatrist is used to seeing certain acute mental disorders progressing into chronicity. My distinction between acute and chronic demoralization is somewhat different. Chronic demoralization does not necessarily or even usually begin as acute demoralization, but gradually grows under circumstances different from the ones which are acutely demoralizing. The striking instance is where one rather expectedly fails to perform something, while sure that he knows just how to do it; checks on his technique, and goes on trying and trying and trying and it does not happen. In other words, what, according to the best information he can get, should work, does not work. Gradually one slips into the state of discouragement and under certain circumstances, if the goal is important enough, becomes desolate and beyond any constructive effort.

Again, if one encounters any devastating experience and discovers by experimentation, by effort, that he cannot improve his situation, that he can do nothing about it, he becomes demoralized. And if one discovers that this is the result of the enmity or the lack of affection of others—in other words, if one just does not have any friends or if one has enemies who stand firmly in one's way—and one finds one can do nothing about it, yet one's security depends on these people's performance, then one demoralizes as rapidly as one's self-deceptive fantasies about the situation are broken down. A special case which does not pertain particularly to the war is when you find out that a person entirely necessary to your satisfaction or security actually has no respect or affection for you, is just being polite or something of that kind. Under those circumstances demoralization is apt to occur and to become rather profound.

I have given you a sketch of the type of interpersonal situation in which demoralization happens. You will see that other people have a good deal to do with it, but it would be unfortunate if you took this to be the whole story. There are other important factors, sometimes no more complex than mere physical matters; physical conditions which impose great strains on our bodily organism can and do facilitate the occurrences of demoralization. Moreover, there are certain types of stress which are, you might almost say, directly demoralizing; to a great many people, shrill noises are an example. That is the reason for shrieking bombs and so on. There are people who will probably through the very long war be somewhat demoralized whenever the air raid siren goes off. A shrill progression of sound increasing in pitch is apparently directly demoralizing. I do not know how much this is the case because it preoccupies the hearing apparatus and thereby closes off one of our contacts with the world.

I am going to suggest the next factor by mentioning that obscure states of the organism which we call fatigue and exhaustion have a place in explaining the occurrence of particular instances of demoralization. The onset of so grave a thing as *schizophrenia,* the more modern name for what was called *dementia praecox,* can be delayed for a day or two by giving the person a good night's sleep, which is simply a matter of attacking the element of exhaustion. Other physiological aspects of the organism and demoralization could be dealt with, but I must pass on to my current topic.

Let us consider the person who in an ordinarily demoralizing situation is not demoralized. This is the other extreme in the interest of psychiatry. What do we find about him? In general, we find that he maintains an unusually alert attention to the situation which might ordinarily be demoralizing and that when he encounters one of the generally demoralizing interpersonal situations to which I have referred, he reassures himself by quickly demonstrating his ability to do something about the situation. A variant of this is seen in children who might be demoralized by an unsympathetic adult. While the boy or girl is not able to do anything directly to ward off the demoralizing onslaught, he immediately makes himself a nuisance in some way. He becomes thoroughly unpleasant. While this does not remedy the situation that is causing him distress, still he is showing that he can do something; he can be somebody, even if merely a nuisance. This saves him from being demoralized. From instances of this kind it is easy to demonstrate that, along with alert attention to the situation, there must go a constructive preoccupation. The strange thing is it does not matter much with what one is constructively preoccupied. It may be something highly irrelevant to the situation. Sometimes hopeless situations are survived merely because one plunges into an irrelevant but constructive preoccupation.

These are the general statements of instances when one could become demoralized but does not. I might add that in all these operations the real menace that hangs over the person who escapes or avoids demoralization is still fatigue. If the alertness to the actual course of events, which is essential to an understanding of what is going on, has to be continued very long, or if efforts to keep oneself reassured that one can do something about something have gone too long, then we see these phenomena which are almost as definite as particular types of poisoning, in that one's attention shrinks in spite of anything. One's ability to maintain a perspective on the situation dies out. Fatigue, boredom, or a state of exhaustion set in. Under the circumstances, the protections that these people have against demoralization fail them and they become demoralized—incidentally to the fatigue.

Now what does all this teach us? I have attempted elsewhere to demonstrate how these considerations underlie a good deal of what we call psychiatric or psychological strategy, which Germany has developed to an extraordinarily high degree and which I surmise Russia has carried even further.[1] From these principles and from our analysis of the enemy's

[1] Sullivan, H. S. Psychiatric aspects of morale. Am. J. Sociol., 47:227, 1941.

psychiatric strategy, we can work out certain measures of counterstrategy. One of the things that stands out, which seems necessary to implement my recommendations, is the production of a national community or solidarity. I cannot give much attention to the methods. So I will refer to an editorial entitled "Completing our Mobilization" (in the May issue of *Psychiatry Journal of the Biology and the Pathology of Interpersonal Relations*) where I have indicated the major operation necessary for the production of a community or national solidarity, namely, the mobilization of leadership. I must refer the interested to these two articles because I wish now to talk on what may be called the morbid in discussing morale.

We hear a good deal about the national morale. I am unable to find any meaning in that expression. I know it points in a general direction but indices do not always mean that there is reality at the other end of the arrow. If a psychiatrist has to do anything about morale, I am sure he will be barking up the right tree instead of getting lost in a largely imaginative forest if he realizes that he must deal with persons and discoverable groups of people instead of with great generalized entities which are supposed to represent some curious kind of addition to all these people and groups. We do find some very large groups of people in the United States about whose morale we can perhaps make meaningful remarks. I assure you, however, that in general, the larger the group the less meaningful the remarks. If I were to talk about the morale of our Army I would come so near to talking about nothing that I am not going to say anything about it now. I am very much more than interested in any discussion about the morale of the 86th Division of our Army, or of a particular company or a particular installation. Why? Because the people concerned in these units show morale and demoralization in the face of concrete events which the large entity can scarcely be conceived to experience. Only at the disastrous end of a decisive battle could a whole field army be subject to gross demoralization. Even then, I surmise, there would be companies who would fight to the death if they were not trodden on by their retreating companions.

The Navy is somewhat different, but to talk about the morale of the Navy in general is a little bit beyond the limits of reason. The significant difference between the Army and Navy lies in the fact that many of the Navy units are almost incredibly self-contained. The organization of a battleship, for example, is not only a strikingly isolated community but an intensely compact and intimately interdependent community with very highly differentiated duties and highly cultivated sense of personal responsibilities and, over all, an intense realization that in a crisis the life of everyone may depend on the life of anyone. The utter closeness and recognized interwoven, mutual security in many of the naval units make them among the world's best laboratories for the study of morale.

I wish I could add something about the morale of another body of people who are waging this war, of which I was so happy to hear Assistant Surgeon General Kolb speak this afternoon. I refer to the Merchant Marine. Unhappily, if I did, I would be even more absurd than in talking about morale in the Army and the Navy, because the Merchant Marine is not a highly organized national arm, with highly developed public relations. They are scarcely mentioned in the press. They are a lot of people who expose themselves often with reckless abandon to the most appalling risks in performing an absolutely necessary war work of transport and supply. The way that these people come through the experience of having a ship torpedoed under them, getting out of it into a sea of burning oil, having a few pot-shots taken at them, drifting perhaps days before being rescued, and then, after they rest for a little while, taking on another ship which is apt to undergo the selfsame experience—that is something for the student of morale.

Now let us come to what I conceive I am supposed to talk about. The communities which make up the United States are the places where morale or its absence, its height or its lowness, is to be studied and, if possible, improved. These communities are many and interpenetrating. For example, the morale of American psychiatry has occasionally demonstrated itself to the profound amazement and great satisfaction of everyone in the last two years. The very attendance at this Conference on Psychiatry of people who are harassed with twice as many responsibilities and important duties as they had a year ago is a measure of the incredible responsibility and public-spiritedness developed by these essentially very individualistic physicians. They have been showing this, to my personal knowledge, for the past two years, whereas the morale of medicine in general has by no manner of means been so uniformly and unswervingly very high over that period. This is interesting, quite aside from their being psychiatrists, because here is one profession, a community within a much larger community, and in many ways very closely related, identical in many aspects of training. As I said, morale in regard to national objectives among psychiatrists is extraordinarily high, even though there is one region—and that not in the great middle country—where it is not yet perfect.

What of the morale of agricultural communities? I do not know "the agricultural community." I know only of communities in such and such counties where they grow so and so. Almost uniformly their morale is remarkably high. They are frightfully distressed at the present labor shortage not because their crops are going to waste and they are suffering monetary loss, but because they grew these crops to feed the Army and the United States and they hate to see crops rotting. That is what is distressing people in many agricultural communities around the country. That is impairing their morale. But in general their morale is excellent, because the government has seen that the agricultural communities should have organization of leadership. To the extent that this program has succeeded they have become most exceptional among American communities.

In industry, unhappily, morale is widely varied from one plant to another and the nearest we have come to organizing leadership is something about which a psychiatrist, I believe, is entitled to feel bored. When a factory seems to be doing badly somebody in Washington sends our a cheer leader who beats the drums and tells the workmen how utterly essential to winning the war their production in this particular factory may be, and so forth.

Finally, I wish to mention a group of communities in the United States in which morale is in general anything but satisfactory, where problems of morale are literally gravely pressing. I refer to most of the negro communities. The present state of our long neglected brown brethren is a source of very great distress to some of the thoughtful. Time permits no discussion of this complex field of problems. Perhaps I have given you a notion of how the psychiatrist is confronted by the problem of morale, and have shown you why he must always get to something reasonably concrete in terms of interpersonal relations in his recommendations for alleviating low, and protecting uncertain, morale.

Psychiatry and Propaganda

By FOSTER KENNEDY, M.D.

Professor of Neurology, Cornell University Medical College

THE MEANING OF PROPAGANDA • THINKING AND SUGGESTION • THE ACCEPTANCE
OF AN IDEA, IN CONSONANCE WITH AN ALREADY ESTABLISHED EMOTIONAL TREND •
THE PLAY BETWEEN ACCELERATORS AND DEPRESSORS • LOWERED POWER OF PER-
SONAL JUDGMENT • THE KNIFE EDGE OF INDECISION • THE FOUNDATION OF A
BELIEF IN THE EXISTENCE OF THE ULTIMATE GOOD • NATIONAL BEHAVIOR AND
PERSONAL CONDUCT • THE UNITY OF WILL AND HEART AND CLASS IN AMERICA •
THE SUGGESTION OF FEARS AND TERRORS • THE SMOKE SCREEN OF DEFEATISM •
COMPREHENSION OF THE ISSUES • THE RELIGIOUS IDEA OF PERSONALITY • THE
DEMOCRATIC DUTY OF EACH MAN • EDUCATION IN GEOGRAPHY • MAL-EDUCATION
IN HISTORY • THE ORIGIN OF THE MONROE DOCTRINE • WEAPONS OF THE MIND
• SCHOOL OF CITIZENSHIP AND SCHOOL OF WAR • THE BEGINNING OF THINKING
FOR ONESELF • THE WORLD OF YESTERDAY AND OF TODAY • THE WORLD NEEDS
POLICE • ONCE AGAIN LAW • THE VICTORY OF YOUTH • THE SPIRIT OF GOOD

WHEN DR. SULLIVAN described the young fellow who
lost the use of his trigger finger when about to go
over the top, I remembered another officer who, waiting to
take his battalion over the top, looked at his watch for the
zero hour and noticed that his knees were rubbing the skin
off each other from shivering. He looked down at them and
said, "You may shake now, but if you knew where I am going
to take you in one and two-fifths minutes, you'd shake a
damned sight more!"

When one thinks of propaganda, as one does every day
now, there comes to one's mind the quip of the civilian Roman
senator who told his military colleague across the floor of the
Senate that if he were given an ass saddled with two paniers
of gold, he would undertake to capture any city! And Germany has spent between three and four hundred millions every
year since 1935 for that idea.

The word "propaganda" is an odd one. I thought it might

341

be a Latin neuter. I thought it might be a gerund. I looked it up before coming here. It was not very enterprising of me that I never looked it up before. Fowler says it is a telescoped Latin brevity, shorthand for a phrase that first appeared in the Middle Ages as the title of an organization of the fifteenth century: "Congregatio de Propagandâ Fide,"—"The Association for the Propagation of the Faith." Words go through "ups and downs" in social life. My grandfather, if he wished to say that a woman was a lady and well-bred, would have said that she was very "genteel." If we were to say that anybody was very genteel now we would be saying practically the opposite of what my grandfather would have meant. "Genteel" has gone down the social scale. So has "propaganda." Propaganda has gone down with use, largely because we were exposed to what in many instances we found to be lies.

I was amused in 1937, when a taxi driver in Berlin, thinking I did not know the city, insisted on pointing out the various buildings: he showed me the Ministry of War, the Ministry of Navy, the Ministry of Foreign Affairs, and then he pointed out the Ministry of Propaganda. In 1937 I had never seen the outside of a Ministry of Propaganda and I was amused at the matter of fact way in which the taxi man had accepted the fact of its existence.

But, as I have said, there can be propaganda for *the faith;* that is what we must have. If we cannot raise the social status of the word "propaganda" we must use some other word. It is important to get *a word,* for, on the whole, men do not live so much by bread, as they live by catchwords. Catchwords are the stuff to remove the need of thinking. I think Dr. Sullivan said that depressed people did not like to think. I do not see why he said "depressed" people. Everybody tries to avoid thinking—just as much as possible. The process is painful. We do not mind living in daydreams, and wool-gathering, and chatter; but to think!—that is the hardest thing the human animal does, and he avoids it when he can. So we can be exposed to suggestion. We hear "suggestion" bandied about a great deal, without anybody quite understanding what it is.

I always describe suggestion as "the acceptance of an idea, already in consonance with previously established emotional trends." That is to say, it is like hitting a baseball the way it is going, instead of the way it is coming. And you remember what was said to Alice in *Through the Looking Glass,* that "Everything I say three times is true." The third time you hear something you begin to believe it, even if it be nonsense. Most of the newspapers have built their fortunes on this. (If you really dig through *Alice in Wonderland* you will get a great deal of wisdom.) We have always a quick, uncritical acceptance of an idea in consonance with an already established emotional trend. Should we hope and be afraid, we overreadily believe in our security and in our victory.

The Germans early in the war, in October, 1939, danced in the streets and everybody gave everybody else schnapps because of the false rumor of an armistice. They thought their nightmare war was over. If we hate, we believe almost any evil of those we hate. If we envy, we listen readily to malice. If we love, we can hear only good things of those we love. And if we are afraid and be lily-livered, we tremble before the radioed rumor, and the innuendoes and half-threats of the Artificer of Fraud.

Our standards of personal dependence on the sturdy virtue of our individual opinions have been weakened through the assault on imaginative reason. We have seen it going on in the world for forty years. You see in modern activities an effort everywhere to demote intellectual authority. For example, in psychology, we have overmuch beaten the drum of the subconscious to drown the still small voice of the intellect. The drum said "You don't really think what you think; you think what you think you don't think!" In painting, the discipline of drawing has been exchanged for meaningless, crazed abstractions. Much the same may be said about most modern music since 1911; it is either a cacophony of fire irons descending a nude staircase, or a sentimental, crooned aphrodisiac to impotent youth. And in literature, compare the style of our modern writers with the letters of Junius. Perhaps Winston

Churchill is like Lincoln. Lincoln had to speak in Stuart English, for he knew only four books: Blackstone, Bunyan, the Bible, and Shakespeare, all by heart, written in the grand manner. So he talked Stuart English, having learned no other. Perhaps Churchill's style is founded on the same books. The impertinent idiocies, for instance, of Gertrude Stein, James Joyce, e. e. cummings—folk like that are far less important than are the lack of judgment, the lack of independent personal opinion, the lack of reverence for the great tradition of language present in many half-educated and wholly uninstructed persons who take such "advertising" seriously. People have feared to admire or condemn on their own hook a play or a book until they have read the criticism, often foolish, of the critics. The smattered education to which we have all been exposed has lowered the sturdy, critical faculty we inherited. Words and facts, therefore, have held people in jeopardy and suspense, partly by dint of not being precise; we have lacked individual judgment with which to fight evil generalities.

All things in the physical, chemical, or natural world exist as a more or less unstable equilibrium between opposing forces. We ourselves maintain health and well-being in our bodies by reason of the balance between the accelerators and the brakes of the pressor and depressor nervous systems. Since Law runs absolute in the Universe, there is in the realm of morals and behavior the same opposition of positive and negative power. There *is* an ultimate Good and there *is* an ultimate Evil. We have been swimming in a solution of relativity in these matters, and because we weakened in our critical judgment regarding them, we became the prey and ready victim of the constant impact of evil counsel, and of lies, made to destroy us. Through lowered power of personal judgment we swayed for years on the knife edge of indecision. But indecision locks up energy; it stabs the heart; whereas decision clearly taken, brings calmness, strength, the quiet mind and a flow of power. It is so in every human experience; and since men make nations, it is so in national life, in the field of battle, and in the field of civil living.

If one be unaware of the stream of history, of the fall and rise of energy in nations, then one can be, by successive crises, shaken and made afraid. A man must have within himself a quiet place wherein he lives, however torn seemingly he may be by the passions of the world. That is his citadel which must be kept inviolate against assault. That quiet place must be founded upon a rock, and the rock must be a belief, a fervent and passionate belief, in the existence of the ultimate Good, and a willingness to put forth his strength against the ultimate Evil. Only by so doing, can he tap the flow of power needed to produce between one nation and another the same natural impulse for helping each other, the same natural acceptance of law and of legal procedure that obtains at present between people walking together in a city street. We must transfer to the national units of the world the same reign of law and helpfulness that now exists between individuals; as was said by Spinoza "There is nothing more serviceable to man,—than man." It is an evidence of weak growth that we could have put up with a standard of national behavior which we would not think of tolerating in personal conduct.

Now the decision of war has been made by those who lead and by those who follow. Energy for this high adventure has been poured into us. Again one must say, by decision, power has come. The lamp in the uplifted arm of our Statue of Liberty must be guarded by ourselves. Evil and wicked men in many vast and powerful countries are trying to snuff it out. If they should overcome our friends who think of life as we do, we could not survive to live our own way alone. So, we must believe good things of our leaders who plan our courses, think well of our friends who die in the same battle we are fighting. To die is much the same, after all, for a Chinese, a Russian, an Englishman, a Hollander, or an American. And greater love hath no man than this: to lay down his life for his friend. We have at last found in our country a unity of will and of heart and of class against which no ruse or trick or lie can avail at all. America is called to arms, a noble and most honorable occupation.

Priestley, speaking of his own country of Britain, said that the Nazis have done everything possible to paralyze opposition by "invading the emotions and the imagination of the more sensitive minds, suggesting a dark host of fears and terrors, creating a smoke screen of defeatism. But, fortunately, the British are not a very impressionable people. The ordinary folk are probably the hardest to rattle or to panic in the world. They are not very imaginative; a free and easy and complacent people." One may add they have the inestimable advantage, by social custom, of not being allowed to show fear, however much they be afraid.

The majority of Americans have detested Fascism and all it stands for; but apathy long stopped action, indecision stabbed the heart and locked up power. The adrenalin that would have girded us for the battle, in the absence of battle frittered the nervous system and made for us a world of jibbering shapes where the witches rode.

What seems to be the weakness of American political life which lowered resistance to the Fascist affront in our minds? First, there was a lack of intellectual comprehension of the issues at stake; second, large parts of our people lacked active interest in political affairs; third, corruption in many municipal offices made the name "politics" a mere term of abuse; fourth, mal-education in history, and almost no education in world geography. In speaking of the attitude, before Pearl Harbor, of many of our, what used to be called, "privileged fellow citizens," Buell in his *Isolated America* quoted a bit of slang of particular significance: "Don't stick your neck out." Those five little words were the core of defeatism, the signs and symptoms of which always are egotism, fear, anxiety, panic, lack of self-respect. If democracy continues to think in terms of a scramble for privilege, without reciprocal obligation, if our psychology persists in reducing man to his lowest common denominator and tries to explain his poetry by way of his perversions, and identifies self-indulgence with self-expression, then we have fled the deeply religious idea of personality, and the democratic duty of each man to train himself to betterment. Rugged sturdiness gets exchanged for indolence, a clean shave for a safety razor—even an electric razor. The American "pioneer spirit" gets swamped in insurance coupons payable "to the third and fourth generation of those who will love and call us blessed."

I said no "education in geography." I have stressed that carefully. In most of our states I find that whether you go to Sarah Lawrence or Radcliffe or Miss Chapin's, or to Groton or St. Paul's, or whether you go to the smallest public school in America, you are not asked to read a map or learn it by heart after the age of eleven and one-half. Can you deny it? As a teacher, I have always been interested in education. I contend that when 134 million people have never seen a map —unless they have passion for maps—since the age of eleven and one-half, they cannot possibly be expected to know a map at twenty-two! This sounds like scolding, but I assure you that this is a fundamental thing. It occurs in no other country. When I went up to my matriculation examination at the University of Dublin, there were two little items that I saw, of just two words each in the examination prospectus. The rest had more description attached to them—how much history, etc. But the book said "all arithmetic" and "all geography." That was in order to obtain admission to any university!

Of course, people who do not know the maps cannot but feel a sense of living, like Mohammed's coffin, swung between earth and heaven. Such a position is bound to give one a sense of great security against attack from either earth or sky. It is bound to enable us to swallow the absurdities that Lindbergh put before 25,000 cheering people when he said, "We have two oceans and nothing can get over them. We are protected by the seas." Well, as far as I know, every white and negro person in America came to America by water. Water has always been the highway of the nations. It becomes a barrier only when battling men and ships are put upon it to prevent its being a thoroughfare and to prevent an enemy stronger than ourselves from constraining our commerce in distant parts of the world. It is not necessary to come to America to stop American trade. A superior naval force in every waterway of the world, or even half a dozen waterways of the world, would stop American foreign trade, like a conjuring trick. With a combination of fleets in the Mediterranean, the Straits of Sumatra, Panama, and the English Channel, it might be done. So we must beware!

One of my juniors went into the army four or five months ago. He took the battalion he was attached to and talked to the men for a half-hour each evening on world affairs. I know he is a truthful man and he told me that he was shocked and amazed to find that nearly eighty percent of his battalion, when shown a map of the world, were unable to point to the land shape called Africa. That is to say, they knew America, but, I suppose, not many of its details. They did not know where Africa was and could not distinguish it from other land masses near it, or from Australia. How are we going to make men have "morale" and understand what the war is about, if we shove them off to Libya when they have not the remotest idea where it is or how any threat could possibly come out of Libya against the United States?

They have mal-education in history. I hope you will not mind my saying this. I am saying it as an American deeply concerned about it. Perhaps I have had the advantage of having lived rather more than half my life on this hemisphere and the other half in Europe: the advantage at least of seeing two sides. I am talking now of something that naturally makes the attitude of most of our people apathetic, a feeling that the war has nothing to do with us and then, "Well, I'm sure we'll get along O.K." The absence, for example in school histories, of one piece of information is important and intellectually misleading, and that is the origin of the Monroe Doctrine.

Now nearly everyone of our people brought up in the public schools, in fact any of the schools, is told that President Monroe in 1823, threatened with the overpowering of South America by the great powers of continental Europe, declared that no sovereignty could change in this hemisphere without war from us. And that is all there was to it; it sounds like a gallant, chauvinistic, David-like defiance against the rest of the world. Not until after the fall of France did I see the details of the origin of the Monroe Doctrine in print where any average American, who did not want to go to libraries or was not majoring in history, could find it. It was an article by Walter Lippmann and, of all places, in the magazine Life.

The truth is that the allies of Russia in 1822—the whole of central Europe, France and Spain and Portugal, I would say—called the Holy Alliance, got together to stop the liberation, the cutting away of the colonies of South America. They were going to take South America, a great virgin continent; this would have reduced the position of this country to a very difficult one. George Canning, British Secretary for Foreign Affairs, said, "We must call in the New World to redress the balance of the Old." He sent a messenger to Monroe to make the proposal for a de facto, not de jure, alliance between American and British sea power. British sea power was then utterly supreme, having been so since the recent destruction of the French and Spanish Fleets in the Napoleonic Wars. Monroe presented this suggestion to only one member of his cabinet, Secretary of the Navy Adams. He called in, very wisely, the two elder statesmen, Madison and Jefferson, and Jefferson's writings on the proposal are to be found in any good library. He summed it up by saying, "The only hope of survival of a young country like the United States is an alliance with the strongest friendly naval power, which is a major American power as well." Many people wrinkle their eyebrows when I ask them, "What is the second American western hemisphere power?" And most of them try to decide between Argentina, Canada or Brazil. Of course, it is Britain! It is that alliance which gave us one hundred years of peace, and only because of the rise of continental power in 1914 was the Monroe Doctrine challenged and America had to fight in 1917 to make good; she could not afford to lose control of the North Atlantic any more than she can afford to lose it today.

Together, we can do this thing, but we cannot do it without knowing each other's office, duties and responsibilities. We must know our facts. We must not conceal expression of the details of such great things on behalf of fabricating a strong nationalistic feeling. As a matter of fact, Nationalism was the canker of the nineteenth century, out of which came the great war—everybody feeling that he was better than the next fellow. It is only a diluted form of Hitler's "Herrenvolk," our feeling that we are better than everybody else. We shall have to lose much of our national-sovereignty feelings if we would make a better world. In England it has been said by H. L. Fisher that the idea of educating the British army, in world history, geography and current affairs is one of the greatest military inventions since gunpowder.

This war is being fought with weapons of the mind as well as weapons of the body. So, we speak of propaganda today. We know from the example of France the consequences of this warfare upon the mind of an army ill-equipped to meet it. It used to be said in 1937 that there were no more Frenchmen. Everybody there with $5000 a year or upwards was a Fascist and everybody below it was a Communist. We were getting rapidly into that phase in our hatred over the last presidential election. My wife heard a lady boast that she and her brother last fall had been invited to a dinner party at Long Island and when they went into the house and found that Marshall Field was one of the guests, they turned, said "Good-night" to the host and left. And she said with pride, "And so did everybody else." When class feeling, money feeling, runs as high as that, the country is in danger. Plato said that long ago.

Now our army spends many months in camp. The officers particularly suffer often from boredom. They have been parted from their former professions and their family life, and many become a culture medium for apathy, rumor-mongering and general lowering of tone. The British have had to meet the same threat over a much longer period. They have met it by turning each platoon in camp into a school of citizenship as well as a school of war. Bulletins are issued to officers for compulsory study—bulletins on current events, on history, on the geography of the world and the geography of this war.

This bulletin is used as a basis of a talk given by the officer. The officer then resigns temporarily his rank, and his position as a teacher, and acts simply as Speaker of the House. The platoon goes into parliamentary session and they question and answer each other. In this way officers and men learn together, they have a chance to express their views and show and share their knowledge. Possibilities in such a training system are immense. They are intrinsically democratic and lift contemplation of political and social problems out of the sphere of second-hand thought and party feeling. The men are taught the beginning of thinking for themselves. There could be no better bulwark, no better buttress against mental invasion by fools, or Nazi spokesmen than the truth which the men would learn of the world of yesterday and the world of to-day. There could be no surer path to a world, organized to live in peace, than one laid down as a solid foundation of knowledge in the minds of our soldiers, sailors and airmen, all of whom will return in victory and power to civil life. I hope that then none will be for the Party, and all will be for the State.

But this cannot be achieved by mere proclamation, however added to education. The world needs *police*. Does anyone imagine that if we took away our police force there would be less crime in our cities; that nobody would again steal Cadillac cars? Does the missionary's virtue alone stop the cannibal from eating him? Should we scrap our law courts, would there be any chance of justice for the simple and the humble man? No, we must make no mistake about the peace, if we would win it. The United Nations will once again bring into this world, Law. International Law at German behest, has been going downhill hard ever since 1866 and earlier. We will aim for it in human society, and shall with our strong hands make the Good come forth. The will to this purpose is written in the Atlantic Charter, to which the United Nations have all subscribed, and for which all must be integrated in the truth. We shall not fail again as we did in the last war. Selfishness, hatred and envy in the hearts of any group, instead of compassion for the world, shall not frustrate the wishes of our fighting men when they come home. The fighting man wants a better world to come out of his blood; this time he will not be denied.

Before I close I want permission to put to you two pieces of "propaganda." There appeared what I thought and what some of my colleagues thought, an unfortunate and unhappy statement from some of our profession, running the length of two columns in the *New York Times* of a week ago, which in vague and pseudoscientific language drew pictures of what would happen to men of eighteen and nineteen if they saw the face of war, all this in a way to strike terror into the parents of any such young men. I felt very much for the parents of those people; particularly since I knew from my experience of four years in France in every part of the field that the thing said was meretricious and untrue. Some of us made a short statement to reassure the public and reassure those parents, but before that was done I had been asked for my opinion, and this is what I wrote: "It is well known that the last ounce of physical reserve needed for speedy emergency is only to be found in very young manhood. Sports like bull-fighting cannot be played successfully after twenty-five, if the players would attain finest physical performance. Only the other day Joe Louis is reported as having said that he was too old for boxing. Such physical excellence in healthy men is found at eighteen. It is on the wane by twenty-three or twenty-four. And it is the last ounce that makes the difference between death and survival in physical combat." One could not help being impressed in the last war by the easy, humorous, carefree attitude of the very young soldier. They brooded never. Their elders brooded often. It was rare to find nervous breakdowns in men under twenty. I never saw it in such young persons. I did not even see a conversion hysteria in a young man.

After the retreat of the British Fifth Army on the 21st of March, something like 340,000 men, Britain's last reserves, were sent over the Channel in the course of five weeks. I was one of the officers to inspect them. They were seventeen years old, nearly all of them; some of them were eighteen, a gay, droll lot. Not one of that crowd, but another one, I remember, had a head wound; his field card with his history on it, said, "Private So-and-So, age 17, in France 3 years, wounded twice." I looked at it steadily and long and said, "What in the devil's name is this! This must be wrong." "No, it is not wrong. Quite right, sir, quite right," was the reply. I said, "You were in France when you were 14?" "Yes, sir. Was in the retreat from Mons as a drummer boy, sir." I said, "You have been wounded twice?" "Yes." "You've got a daisy there on the left side of your head." I said, "Look here, I am going to have you boarded out of the army. You are only a child." "I am not a child, sir. Got a wife and baby, sir." And he brought out of his bag a tintype of a nice young girl with a baby on her arm. Oh, no, those young men don't brood; they breed.

In England to-day, the doctors are finding that even the children who have been under heavy bombing recover much more speedily than do grownup people. The younger one is, the more one lives in the immediate present, and the less that immediate present persists in memory. The youngsters in the last war were terribly afraid that something might happen to end the war before they could see it. I am sure the same romantic enthusiasm exists today. I go further—if a man of eighteen does not feel it to be an extraordinary and lovely adventure to fight for his country in the Coral Sea and across the Mountains of the Moon, he must have been either badly brought up or badly endowed. There's something deeply wrong with him.

The second piece of "propaganda of the Faith" that I want to read is a letter that came to a physician of my acquaintance from the parents of a young man of twenty. This physician had been successful, happily, in ridding a seventeen-year old daughter of theirs of a grave malady. And this is the letter he received from the father:

"I want to send you a note of appreciation. I can hardly tell you there is no financial reward to compensate what you have done and are doing for my wife and me in your work for my daughter. Her advancement continues. She is beginning her studies with real interest, and her teacher after three days, having also taught Kay last fall, is greatly pleased over her progress. Since our last visit with you, we have received word that our eldest son, George, a lieutenant in the Marines, has been killed in action in the Solomon Islands. We have not yet received any notification from the government so that there is still a hope that the report may not be true. [It was true.] However, because of the origin of our information, we feel the chance is slight, although we are, of course, not in any way giving up hope. My wife is magnificent, and a constant inspiration to me; we have determined that if the boy has given his life to his country, he has done the most that can be done, and it is our job to display the same courage he has shown, and to rejoice in the feeling that after a life without fault as a son, he has now proven himself an equally fine soldier. You can appreciate how deeply grateful we are to you that our Kay is so well at such a time. Regards."

The wife sent a letter along with that:

"Pop [as she called her husband] and I think so alike that after his letter to you, it is not necessary for me to add anything, but I cannot help telling you myself what a great part you are playing in the thankfulness of our hearts now. Through our heritage and preparation it is the greatest feeling in the world to know that we are able *now* to keep our thoughts turned away from selfishness and straight toward the truth. Thank God for everything, and for His mercy to our daughter."

This is the spirit of Good which we must believe will utterly overcome whatever may be said or done by the spirit of Evil.

PART V

SYMPOSIUM I
THE PHILOSOPHY OF PSYCHIATRY

SYMPOSIUM II
PSYCHIATRY AND THE WAR

Symposium I
The Philosophy of Psychiatry

Introduction to Symposium I

By THEOPHILE RAPHAEL, M.D.

Professor of Clinical Psychiatry, University of Michigan; Psychiatrist,
University Health Service, Ann Arbor

THIS IS our final session and, it is to be hoped, our most significant one. I say this in full awareness of the many truly splendid contributions which have been given us thus far in this Conference, in many ways unique. I say this because, at this extremely important and crucial time for the world, when we must everyone of us contribute our very best, our most informed and intelligent best, we have now an opportunity, together, to sum up, to bring to a head, the rich and varied material presented at the previous sessions relating to our work. It is anticipated that this morning will yield a real critique and synthesis of the very full and rich experience of the last two days and thus render it of maximum value and significance.

How useful this summing-up process can be depends naturally, in final analysis, upon how purposefully, sincerely and thoughtfully we all of us approach it and work it through. In other words, now that we have had this Conference at this very special time, what can be crystallized from it, what essential meanings can be expressed from it? That is, how useful, how functional, can we make it, for ourselves as individuals and professional implements, and for others, for the world at large, in its present troubled state?

In this summing-up, in this enterprise of inter-thinking and search for values, we will as you know, be assisted by two very carefully selected and distinguished panels. What actually comes of it, however, depends upon what we all of us together do with it, how we all of us collaborate. Open discussion from the rest of us, therefore, has been planned and is just as important as the preliminary panel contributions themselves. It is hoped therefore that all will take the fullest advantage of this opportunity both in their thinking and in their expressions.

The working through of this morning divides itself into two phases—first, psychiatry in general, its philosophy, what it is, what it means, what it covers. We have heard so much about it, facts, implications, interrelations. Certainly it is obvious that properly conceived and thought through, it has much of value as an interest and science, and as an aid to mankind in its living. The second phase in our summing-up will deal with the very immediate and practical proposition of psychiatry and its implications and possibilities in the present war situation.

The first session will be led, as you have seen in your programs, by Dr. Adolf Meyer, who will introduce the individual members of his panel. Before calling on Dr. Meyer, I would like to express what I sense we all feel, namely, that because of its atmosphere and the way it has gone and the time, this meeting emerges as a very important moment, a very important occasion for psychiatry. If psychiatry has anything to contribute to society, to life, this certainly is the time to think out concretely what it is, and to put it to the fullest use.

Dr. Meyer needs no introduction. You all know who he is and what he stands for; so I will not introduce him formally. I will simply ask him to come forward to take over the discussion, the working-through of this first phase "The Philosophy of Psychiatry."

Symposium I
The Philosophy of Psychiatry

Presentation of the Subject of Symposium I

By ADOLF MEYER, M.D.

Psychiatrist-in-Chief, Emeritus, Henry Phipps Psychiatric Clinic, The Johns Hopkins Hospital; Henry Phipps Professor of Psychiatry and Director, Department of Psychiatry, The Johns Hopkins University

WE DO well to heed the responsibility that today's chairman has put upon us for this morning's session. The purpose of this Conference on Psychiatry is that of finding ourselves, of finding where our feet are, what we stand on, and where our head makes us *head*. This directional purpose has found introductory expression in "Philosophy and Meaning and Scope of Psychiatry." There followed presentations by a group of workers and speakers who took up special viewpoints and lines of practice—those of the schools of psychology, those of the physician and the internist, the surgeon, and the pediatrician. Geriatrics, too, the field which has become more and more important now through the fact that more people reach the upper age limits, came in for review. Following these presentations we heard psychiatry discussed in its relation to the training, experience and education of the individual; and finally, psychiatry and the war. There thus resulted in this manner a perspective; and it would be presumption on my part to want to do for you what you have no doubt done for yourselves, namely summarize that first session.

It is nevertheless important to state succinctly some upshots in which I want to emphasize as precisely as possible some of the implications of the original introduction and the perspective of the principles in speaking of the philosophy and the fundamental concepts. This I must do before I ask my cooperators in the panel to formulate their data and special points of view, preparatory to our opening the discussion from the floor in the remaining time for this orientation.

I welcomed the fact that the committee which arranged this program introduced the word "philosophy." It is unfortunate that so many have the habit of saying, "Of course I am not a philosopher," as if to absolve themselves of the responsibility of at least a temporary synthesis. None of us would claim to be *the* philosopher; but, when we speak of philosophy at all, we mean the application of the wisdom which has developed from the approach to the many subdivisions of that large field of thought and action for which any individual, as a conscientious worker and thinker, especially in a democracy, must make himself reasonably responsible, in order to know himself, and to make clear to others, where he stands.

There are sets of data to which sciences may want to limit themselves, keeping clear of any philosophy. However, there are also principles which deal with the *use*, the implications and the interrelations of data, and which must not be treated as "philosophy" in a haphazard way and with a derogatory slant. This is especially true when one actually deals with methods and principles of interdependences and questions of correlation not immediately resolved to an either-or of "mind or matter." It is not only the wealth and real charm of pluralism and the rich differentiations in actual life, but also the actual significance of the reality and objectivities of life, that call for a respect for *specificities*. Too often statistical science wants to eliminate qualitative features beyond the few primary distinctions so dear to Locke and the epistemologists, with dismissal of "secondary" sensations. In spite of the "conflicts" between the physical and the mental, and the physician's assignment to the "physical," we have become more properly objective in the consideration of what is "subjective" in man and his difficulties. More precisely we speak of them and treat them as person-facts or ergasia. As we have worked ourselves to clearness, and have found our common denominator in behavior or action, we have come to understand the die-hard character of the intransigence, or refusal of compromise, which does require effort to surmount without surrender, and have found rather a gain of human dignity. When we see the one-sidedness of the development of specific categories of science, especially at the point at which the non-living and the living, and the non-mental and the mental come into coexistence, we feel more and more the need of harmonious and positive consideration. We may as well learn to heed the importance of the fact of pluralism, and the necessity of considering specificities in operative formulation as well as relational principles and statements, which the statistical method must not turn into its narrowing goal without also respecting that for which we do not as yet have adequate statistics.

Our program calls explicitly and justly for the philosophy and scope of a field, the term for which, namely "psychiatry," might historically seem to imply a challenging contradiction, when we consider the burden of implications and suggestions carried by the "two components" of the expression "soul-physician." It would look as if to include the troubles and the capacities of the soul implies a presumption on the part of the physician, and a break of the pact between the guardians of mind and soul and the physician, whose very name would pledge him to focus on the physical preoccupations. Church and philosophy evidently meant to grant science and the physician professional status and license only as long as he left the mental and spiritual problems to the priest (that is, the "elder"), or to the philosopher (even Kant claimed that the insane and mental cases should be handed over to the philosopher). Law demands that the ordinary man be allowed to consider himself the best judge of what the physician should or should not consider his domain of competence, with our institution of the jury or the judge deciding on mental health versus insanity. Yet even if the physician wanted to heed the pact of "minding" the body and leaving alone the mind and soul, he still would have to cope with his own and the patient's sense, common and sharable, or questioned. As one realizes how loosely the "primitive" and the "less primitive" man resorted to animism in nature generally, and how in turn one indulged in speaking of animal "magnetism" to explain some "mental" events, one comes to understand the confusion about the nature of the pact. Quite apart from any pact, however, there has always been a tendency not only in the very early animism, which invented human-like forces and spirits and fairies for the moving of supposedly inert matter, but also throughout the periods in which the debate over mentalism was the "soul" of philosophy and religion, to let traditional philosophy keep alive the fundamental contrast between the purely physical and the purely mental. It was helped along by the contrasts of mechanistic and vital, and spontaneous activity as being actually due to mentality in the use of memory and thinking, emotion and choice and planning, and conscious and unconscious. This latter contrast is still obvious also in the divisions of the many standard psychologies, all of which are apt to keep up confusion. The doctrines of parallelism have aimed to keep mentality out of the domain of conservation of energy.

It would, however, go against all common sense to assume that the physician should or could surrender his recognition of the inseparable functioning of mind with body, even if only for matters of description and for means of understanding. This is quite apart from the fact that even the word "psyche" and the corresponding word "spirit" are literally derived from "breath," and the inseparable organismal condition of person-function for the continuity within specific life-durations.

It certainly is interesting that in the search for a term for the flight from mere earth to the inclusion of heaven, the common verbal and conceptual denominator in the development of the science of nature and the science of mind and ideals, was found in the unifying fact of *breath* as *psyche,* and the *wind* as *anima* and respiration for aspiration and inspiration. But we also have to realize that it was the primitive poetical tendency to personify the forces of nature and the motion of the things of the earth and the heavens in spirit-form (or breath-form) as *animism,* and that in the differentiation of the sciences, natural and social and formal, mind and soul appeared to be additive rather than integrational, not unlike the biblical "God formed man of the dust of the earth and breathed into his nostrils the breath of life and man became a living soul."

Evidently it is more in its primitive sense that the naive—and the erudite—use the prefix "psycho" in psychology and in psychiatry, as implying the "addition" of mind. But today our usual concern in man and the living is with the presence and use and implication of the mentality in which culture and science can find their conjoint home, and we see more and more of the inherence and the process and the results of integration and integrates, so strongly and distinctively in evidence whenever we use the "psycho" prefix. In our own conception of psycho-bio-logy, the prefix frankly accepts the prevailing of the specific *life-* and *working-function* as *person.* The primitive addition was on the side of sensation and feeling and the agency of will, present where there was life, and life of a special kind, the differentiation of symbol-process and its use in memory and anticipation, self-referring subject-function. Are these not also action?

Historically mankind started its organized thinking from a storywise conception that oriented itself first in mythology and in various forms of religion connected therewith. By religion I emphasized those ways of finding oneself bound and ob-*lig*-ated together, because that is what is meant by the *lig*-factor in the word religion, namely, that one *belongs together* and one enters into a responsibility for a whole—in conscience, hope, and charity, and fair deal, and reciprocity, and respect for a divine guiding principle of it all. That has to operate in keeping with fact, and with our democratic idea, in and between individuals. This is the nature of our operational philosophy.

What we call "psychological functioning" is the actual functioning of the real "individual," and the working and holding together in one world and one world force. This obligatory *vitally and mentally and memory and symbol integrated* function is what we have in mind when we speak of "psycho" this or that and the inherence principle.

For our scientific and practical purposes with the unit presenting mind, body and soul, the unit-word *individual* or *person* has assumed its status because there is no greater responsibility than that of recognizing that whatever happens in psycho-function refers to a natural reciprocity of such biological entities. This consists of entities with a specific genetic origin, and with a life-period in which they have to form or constitute themselves as infant, child and adolescent, as biographic person, in order to do one's best in the mature adult life; and to see that one can have an honorable age and leave a useful and meaningful kind of record with the young and one's contemporaries and survivors.

How does philosophy help us to actual order?

In philosophy, the science of the nature of things and our relation to them, we have learned to *distinguish between metaphysics*—that is to say, the study of essences and absolutes and beliefs—and the *science of the philosophy principle* itself as method and progression in differentiation and invention. *Philosophy* is that methodology and that science and that substance of knowledge and wisdom which deals with the *materials and the methods* of the individual sciences and their belonging and working together, blended into a way of life. There, of course, tradition immediately gets us into some problems, in the sense and practice of some of us left open (instead of cutting a "Gordian knot") and intent on a peaceful solution. Metaphysics and the metaparts of our preoccupations and contemplations deal with items and questions for which the objective sciences offer no final data, so long as they are allowed to keep aloof in their own glory of perfection, but for which we all have to adopt solutions either from dogma or from thinking them out for ourselves, since it is difficult to reach expressions of finality which everybody would accept. Finality evidently is not final; it has to face progress and new terms and new changes. While metaphysics claims to answer the question of the "to be," philosophy in its narrower sense aims at dependable *methods* of epistemology, logic, aesthetics and ethics, and the *operational procedure,* and stands true to those methods also in an active "philosophy" as *vision of life.*

What does philosophy do for us with regard to the sciences?

We work with our ways of *grouping sets of facts* which we speak of as *sciences,* with their own problems and answers and methods of proving their nature in nature and man's experiments. Some of them are spoken of as fundamental and all-pervading, formal and methodical, and some as the "natural sciences"; others figure as social or cultural or largely formal sciences, such as history and mathematics and logic and aesthetics and ethics, culminating in a self- and group-responsibility of all science and philosophy. Nature, of course, points specially to all that which "comes into existence by birth" (*natus, naturus*) and consists of a process of existence, that is actually a going on and change and movement. One likes to begin with physics and chemistry, and, where there is a process of individuation, one reaches that which in our experience holds together as biology, as the domain and the products of the living. Tradition speaks of the mentally and spiritually and humanly integrated reality of special "wholes" as something different from the natural sciences. Are we not seeing unity in the midst of it all? Within that frame of our type of integrates, we have come to speak naturally and seriously of the individual as I described him, as *person* and as groups.

Each of us has to figure as a sort of microcosmos of one's own, within which we operate as responsive and answerable or responsible entities, where the majority wants something final, fixed for the time at least in a personal "eternity" and the state of "belonging." We must recognize in contrast to a great deal of current science, that orderly entity-formation is a reality and actuality of momentous importance. This should be without overdrawing on the perpetuation of that which, with its self-referring feature of mentality, constitutes psychology, viewed either as the body of events, as purely "mental" facts and operation, or as what we may prefer to call behavior and action with mental content as solvent, as ergasiology, in order to keep the whole entity together in one term and concept pertaining to the unit and non-divisible individual. When I say *self-referring* and *self-appertaining*, I mean that which forms in our case the unit "man." When we speak of psychology (and psychiatry) and philosophy, we speak of man-science, the functioning of man as a responsible and answerable entity, with all the unity implied by "mind," by "soul," and by "life." Those are words which we cannot profitably subject to analysis by splitting, if we want to know more about their substance and meaning. We are inclined to accept them as the virtual units, not with something behind, but rather with specificity *inherent in,* those step-wise special fields that we then call "sciences," the cultural sciences and the so-called "natural" sciences—as sets of integrates.[1]

The order to which we belong is "mentally integrated." What does philosophy tell us about that?

To be as clear and concrete as possible, see Chart I, a tabulation of *grades or steps of nature and sets of integrates,* forming sciences, chapters of procedure and concepts forming natural units, from the least personal to the most personal, with relative discontinuities, but, in this essentially organismal scheme, not an all-out contrast such as the traditional one of mind and body. Evidently that which preoccupies us here is man and man-science, and not only pieces of man. We have to be prepared to have as our foundation those features of our-

[1] Evidently the vital and spiritual "breaks of continuity" between the physical and the mental had to be met and brought to a smooth understanding as to whether the presence of the mental was to be taken as a problem of addition *from the outside,* or rather the development *from an integrate,* and whether this process of integration among the sciences would appear as the continuum with imperceptible steps, or in the form of steps or levels of the type of jumps by mutations, in stages of species-making fixations; hence the grouping of the sciences to be studied for what they are and do and deal with, within definite categories of specific organization. "Integration" is the principle and "integrates" does not always mean that we know the process of the transition specifically.

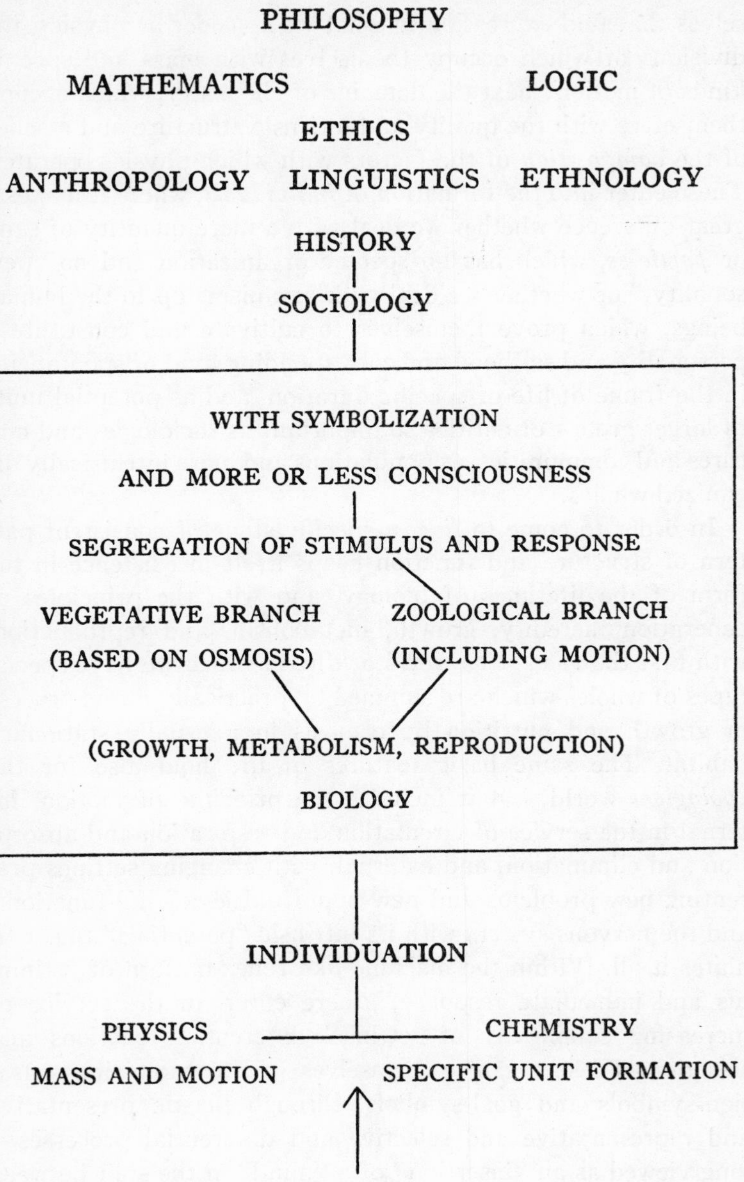

PHILOSOPHY

MATHEMATICS   LOGIC

ETHICS

ANTHROPOLOGY   LINGUISTICS   ETHNOLOGY

HISTORY
|
SOCIOLOGY
|

WITH SYMBOLIZATION

AND MORE OR LESS CONSCIOUSNESS
|
SEGREGATION OF STIMULUS AND RESPONSE

VEGETATIVE BRANCH   ZOOLOGICAL BRANCH

(BASED ON OSMOSIS)   (INCLUDING MOTION)

(GROWTH, METABOLISM, REPRODUCTION)

BIOLOGY

INDIVIDUATION

PHYSICS _____|_____ CHEMISTRY

MASS AND MOTION   SPECIFIC UNIT FORMATION
↑

CHART I

selves that find expression in what we consider as physics, the divisions of which occupy themselves with mass and specific kinds of motion; next the domains of chemistry, which occupy themselves with the quality and intrinsic structure and essence of the *composition* of the factors with which physics operates. These enter into the formation of *individuals,* where it makes a great difference whether we deal with a mere quantity of sand or *particles,* which has no specific organization and no "personality," or whether we deal with organisms up to the human beings, which prove themselves to cultivate and constitute a personality and selfhood and corresponding kind of spontaneity in the frame of life of specific duration, and as potential units of larger groups or entities so important as sociologies and cultures and communities, as populations and more intrinsically organized wholes.

In order to come to *live,* a specific stage of consistent pattern of structure and function keeps itself in existence in the form of the lifetimes of biology, and with the principles of generation, heredity, growth, metabolism, and reproduction, with first the *vegetative* world of life, in which we have special types of wholes which are summed up practically in the process of growth and nutrition by osmosis in a usually stationary habitat. The same basic features of life hold also for the *zoological* world, but it includes the principle of motion, internal in the service of circulation and respiration and absorption and elimination, and external, with changing settings presenting new problems and new opportunities of life-functions, and the nervous system with its intrinsic "potentials" that regulates it all. Within the machine-like reflex-pattern of "stimulus and immediate response," there enter, in the service of increasing complexity of settings, differential reactions and selection. These organize themselves with economizing sensation-symbols and goal-symbols, through plastic presentative and representative and selective and differential processes— long viewed as an "insertion" of a "mind" in the split between substance and function—but really a receptive and elaborative and effective *process* of symbolization and mentation, bringing together the symbols of present, past and future, and potentialities, as clearly organismal, space-time bound.

We have come to recognize as very definite and lawful static and mechanical physics with its dynamic-*kinetic* transformations, and chemistry dealing with the *intrinsic modes* of dynamic change; and in structured organisms the function of organs and the physiology of immediate basic reflexes; and finally, between stimulus and response, the mentally integrated system operating in the delayed response, as organized selfhood, and fullfledged overt behavior, with its amplified flux of implicit economizing symbolization—primary (speechless, pictorial and attitudinal) and secondary (in terms including language) and tertiary (in concept-formation)—in receptive, elaborative and effective processes and interrelations for plastic life in plastic settings and plastic demands. There thus develops that whole world which in us comes to further culmination, not only of the behavior which we share in general with all animals, but the specific feature of man, that huge organization of *language symbols,* so obviously as systems of *meaning-function,* so characteristic and specific for our individual and group "mentation," in which the picture of the whole ultimately gets unified into the common denominator of the activity of the person and group. Symbolization yields the more or less of a blending and linking together and feeling of more or less cohesion and differentiation in *consciousness* (born of the self-feeling and situation-feeling, differentiated by and for the complex needs of a complex life), which each of us has to learn to nurture and to guard. We are not "all there" all the time in a comprehensive fashion, and there enters the problem of the mentally integrated person as organism and performer, and the grouping of the performers, the family, the community, and all the potential super-units.

That the specific person-function in our individual and social nature is qualitatively so different from the not biologically organized physico-chemical processes must not overawe one. That indeed the subject-formation rests on a highly differentiated orderly organization is clearly brought home in the organization of the nervous system, with its sequence and background of sets of structure-functional integrates. The basic "segmental" set consists of the head and the headlights of vision, and smell, followed topographically (see Chart II) by the feeding and breathing and speech mechanisms in the neck and the trunk, in the viscera, and the pelvic organs, and the extremities. These are the organs in gradients of differentiation of the soma, unified and brought under a regime of the segmental nervous system that is laid down in the order of our body-structure as in the motor plate and receptor plate of the tube; and within the roof plate of the head segments of the nervous system, the dorso-median structures of the neural tube constituting the operators of relationships, cerebellar and mesencephalic, and especially within the forebrain (thalamus, striatum and cortex). We recognize that relationship through its function of discrimination, of association, of orientation, of affective life and of effective living, unified in a cortical top function and its integration of the special helps in intermediate structures of thalami, midbrain, cerebellum, etc., the whole suprasegmental system built upon and operating with and through the segments.

What philosophy actually brings home is the history-making process with which we operate. The reference to scientific organization must not distract us from returning to actual life in which we do not see the "inert" skeleton and structure, but the actual living and performance, in which we also blend in our descriptions the actual wealth of mental processes going on while we may be walking or using our hands, at the same time carrying on our verbalizations and those flashes of associations or digressions that remain the unexpressed part and wealth and continuity of actual living. We are dealing here with a wealth of reactivity such as remains unanalysed, for instance, one's including the whole picture of the room and the views through the window, with detail that is more or less passed by, unless it contains things that get into competition or conflict with leading trends of thought and action. It is obvious that the subject himself inherently makes *choices* from what is

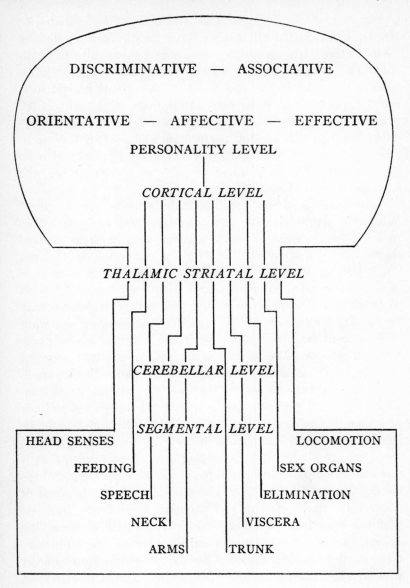

DISCRIMINATIVE — ASSOCIATIVE

ORIENTATIVE — AFFECTIVE — EFFECTIVE

PERSONALITY LEVEL

CORTICAL LEVEL

THALAMIC STRIATAL LEVEL

CEREBELLAR LEVEL

SEGMENTAL LEVEL

HEAD SENSES   LOCOMOTION

FEEDING   SEX ORGANS

SPEECH   ELIMINATION

NECK   VISCERA

ARMS   TRUNK

CHART II

pertinent or distracting, and what will be later remembered or not remembered. In all this we have to stipulate a selective (intel-lective) process which pertains just as much to theoretical work as to the ordinary way of getting along in the pluralistic universe. "Science" will make its classifications and sorting out according to impersonal correlations; and "actual life" according to personal and temporary *interests*. Actual psychobiological existence and performance submerges the mechanisms as merely incidental, and we obviously must also be able to sort our own pictures as parts of phases of life, the history in the making.

Consideration of use does not make science "unscientific." With this perspective we can consider ourselves justified to make a "declaration of independence" from a great deal of dogmatism which forced the "rigidly scientific" to cut out much that we do not want to have excluded from a free use of free science. Instead of having a completely prefixed system of order and conception of nature and reality, which we may borrow from a supposed basic "physical" science, we also want to be free to take from our experiences with the actual problems all that we have to include in science, but with more of *meaning,* and not necessarily only the tenets of orthodox tradition. We would then have certain *principles of logic or philosophy for general guidance* rather than fixed categories, and our new chapters of issues at hand and the inclusions would be shaped for *use* and according to use. We want to be able to focus on any kind of item according to its *importance*—that is our first principle. Within the psychobiological or ergasiological domain we deal not only with the detailed relationships of nerve cells, nerve centers and chemical ingredients, but also with the evaluations and inter-relationships of history-making events. In that sense we go beyond the average natural-history type of description, without, however, coming into conflict with it. The material obviously has to be a matter of *selection,* which then involves a second principle, that of *scrutiny,* for its better understanding, and, in the place of mere reasoning, a third principle, the *operative formulation.*

Provided that we use the safeguards and foundations of procedure and control required by the particular field of integration or integrates, we do not have to be afraid of surrendering the dogmatically narrowing orthodoxy of Lockian epistemology and of those who want to limit science to quantity and its mathematics, where we are sure that qualitative meanings become more important than mere quantities and forms.

You might call that a special philosophy—which it is—but it is one which gives the sciences the form required by the facts to be studied, instead of forcing innocent but valuable facts into arbitrary channels, copied from other fields and lost for use.

The admirable array of contributions in this present conference has brought before us a consistent sequence of chapters which give us striking sets of specific knowledge blending into the picture of the whole entity as unit. They contribute to the idea of the *whole* that also gives us the sense *inherent* in the working together of all the parts. During the largely mythologic-animistic period of man's culture, the *wholeness* was so accentuated and lifted out of and beyond the setting, as mind and soul, that the division into particular centers of clearness was either submerged or overdone; whereas now our wisdom, our philosophy, our critically scientific knowledge, call for a consistent unity with "chapters of emphasis." We cannot have a "psychology" that has not an anatomy and a physiology and a broader setting in it. There is an equal obligation that psychology also be considered in that big chapter of science which then forms the frame of *history,* with the biological function in its time and its subdivisions into a lifetime, and in lifewise interests and spatial and dynamic settings. This characteristic plan can be expressed to advantage and significantly with its equally characteristic specifications, in the so-called life-chart, which, in a rack of time-spaces, has limited notations within which the particular effects of memories and attitudes of history-making importance can be made to stand out as summary. There are, as I say, those of us who like to make "chapters by *emphasis*," and others who make chapters very much more sharp, as an *either* mental *or* physical process, and finally those who want to have no chapters, and no philosophy of relations and words, and leave man-science at loose ends in the traditions of mythology and traditional "religions" and mere storylike life histories on the one hand, and dry non-discriminating statistics on the other. This lends itself to a handing on of tradition if one is not critical; only I would say it is probably very difficult to demonstrate what kind of order one has without singling out emphases and chapters.

Our present chapters are those which have been exemplified in the various parts of the First Session of our Conference, and also in the divisions which have occurred in the contemplation of education, which is "history in the making, shaping itself under guidance." The question, then, is in what *form* we have our "natural" history, and how we deal naturally with our psychobiological and cultural organization. I had a hesitation in my presentation of the First Session to enter on all this detail before we had discussed the various concrete topics, and at present I have no right to go far into all the desirable detail. I simply would like to affirm what I consider the essence of modern philosophy, that it gives a frame of broad and yet specific principles for the material and the correlation of the sciences. It is that philosophy which I described to you as having been strongly assisted by those who came from the University of Michigan to the University of Chicago, and who belonged, of course, to the body of scientific and thinking and responsible men of the world at large. We had to meet materialism and idealism, absolutism and elementalism, monism and dualism, but also pluralism and various epistemological stipulations and restrictions to maintain and justify the dogmatic formulations. We knew that what we studied never exists completely detached, and we had to get our freedom of orderly choice according to perspective and work, critically and pragmatically and responsibly and truly religiously and philosophically, with a determined evaluation of man as agent and creative person and member of groups.

The principles used in handling the material present themselves in three very simple sets of considerations. As the *first requirement* in the selection of the data, I would stipulate that *anything which proves itself by orderly and characteristic specifications deserves to be made into serious chapters of investigation*—topical mental facts, emotional facts, just as well as chemical facts—a *frank pluralism* guided by evaluation; only we then want to have something of an order such as I tried to depict to you. In contrast to Locke's primary and secondary sensations, I should, indeed, consider myself free to select any item or topic of knowledge and dynamics worth discussion and consideration, the presence or absence and the operation or non-operation of which makes a difference.

The *second requirement* comes when we have found and determined the points that we want to stress; we have to see *in what specifications they occur*. We have to study the topics of concern as we find them. It is a serious mistake to work under the obsession that to be scientific the data must be turned into the "something else" and the "somewhere else" of some traditional scientific (science-making) category. Begin to recognize and study and work with the fact that you actually find and are concerned with, and do it to your best capacity. Have the courage of starting with the things which you are working on and for which you make yourself responsible, whether it be a complex item or topic or event, or a simple one. That depends on your judgment and what you are driving at. Science so far has had a habit of cutting things into stereotyped pieces, very often until the character of that which one started with was practically lost: "More and more about less and less." I seldom find in "chemistry" a complete formula for those things with which we are most concerned when we have a human being in function, when we have psychology or ergasiology in action. We do not want to begin by cutting or breaking things into pieces before we have determined what they are and do, uncut and unbroken. The first condition in any science and in any consideration is to take a view of what is at hand and, further, as the *prime issue, what it belongs to*.

I start from the point of view of the person who picks up any kind of find and tries to orient himself. He does not want to pick it hastily out of its setting. He wants to know what it is in itself and of what it is an immediate livable part. Out of consideration of what things belong to, what relations they have, we get some of the most important understandings that we really have to consider and get sense from. Only when we have that clear do we have a right to go into the most customary *specifications by analysis,* and even then not into particles and fragments which, Humpty Dumpty fashion, we would have difficulty to put together again. Humpty Dumpty offers a very interesting unit-concept. The symbol comes from the nursery, but the nursery very often is closer to an unprejudiced consideration of things than the preoccupations of complex erudition.

Hence I emphasize, (1) *"What* are you talking about?" Anything really worth-while, making a difference? (2) In what actual events and examples has it presented itself, quasi an experiment of nature? If not directly clear by itself, determine *what it may belong to or be part of.* Only when this is clear do we proceed to what it is made of. That is a matter of more or less technology, important, but unfortunately a technology which has outrun our interest in what things belong to, what they do, what we can expect of them, what we have to do with them, and what we can emphasize them for.

The *third and most important* requirement in our philosophy of science is what the modern trend of philosophy describes as the *operational formulation.* Instead of cutting things into pieces and standing before these as if they were the important and final fact, let us see what the component factors are, and how they operate, and what the total events are to which they belong. In this way all science becomes history, a development and study of events. What are the *factors* which enter into any one particular element of history, event, or topic of concern? How do those factors operate? What are the results, the ranges of results, and what are our means of modifiability?

That puts us to the task in which we have to acquire the skills and the obligations in life, so that we actually can make ourselves responsible. Here are facts—whether they are lines of thought, or habits, or matters of art, or obligations—as topics or as experiments of nature. We have to be clear as to what the factors are that enter into it all. This to me is a fundamental law and frame of psychiatry, and of the study of all science, but particularly that of life as person. Let us find out what is *worth* discussing, what it belongs to, what it is made up of, what enters into it and how it operates, with what range of natural events and with what opportunities for use to arrange and organize it so that it leads to a goal. It is not identification and definition that is the chief goal; it is *specification* and understanding and application in operational formulation of the setting and pertinence. I want from the start *action* as my frame; I want also the results in final performance, and then I have a complete picture, free of arbitrary and prejudicial classification.

This represents the philosophical as well as the scientific arrangement, and philosophy with all the desirable room for scientific organization and technique, provided that this actually adds something and is not merely an attempt at display of verbalization or an empty obsession of working for science for science's sake that breeds disdain of science for use.

It is now high time that I should ask my fellow-members in the panel to express themselves for your orientation, so that in a second hour, if there is time for discussion, you will know to whom to address yourselves, about whom and what to speak, from whom to expect an answer, and what to try to work towards as an upshot from the considerations that we have given in this whole Conference. I should like to ask Dr. Lewis to give a brief orientation of that for which he would like to make himself particularly responsible.

Symposium I

The Philosophy of Psychiatry

First Scheduled Discussion of Symposium I

By NOLAN D. C. LEWIS, M.D.

Professor of Psychiatry, College of Physicians and Surgeons, Columbia University; Director, New York State Psychiatric Institute and Hospital

IN THIS Conference, as in many others on psychiatry in recent years, the main focus of attention has been placed on the individual in action among other human beings. On Thursday, and also again to-day, Dr. Meyer stressed the point that the philosophy we are concerned with here is one of action rather than one of metaphysical speculations. Philosophy in most of its forms attempts to find a meaning in natural phenomena and the particular philosophy of psychiatry is concerned with the discovery and outlining of principles and unities common to every type of human activity. With it man tries to understand himself, his surroundings, and some of his disorders. Psychiatry has progressed far beyond the days when it was considered within the limiting framework of a minor specialty in the medical curriculum.

Philosophical systems develop in keeping with keenly felt needs and concentrate on problems requiring solution. They define the difficulties, work them over with their special methods, and usually come to some fairly satisfactory solution. Scientific thought is a derivative and an extension of philosophy

378

since it submits this solution to an experimental test and makes its final appraisal on the basis of the experimental findings. Science thus continues and completes the act of thought initiated in philosophical realms, and scientific methods are concerned with the understanding of the relationships among observations, laws, theories, and interpretation of data in the scientifically controlled procedure.

It is natural to assume that any expansion of the knowledge of natural processes will enrich psychiatry along with other branches of science. Psychiatry still needs a great deal of development along qualitative lines; and no psychiatrist needs to consider himself as "unscientific" when engaged in non-quantitative studies of his material. To do satisfactory research in psychiatry will require a more accurate formulation of human nature than psychiatrists or psychologists have yet produced. However, it is the psychiatrist who, by virtue of his training and experience with distorted minds, is best prepared to study the problems. He is accustomed to observing people from the viewpoint of the nature of their patterns of reaction, their life adjustments, and the significance of their ideas. Therefore, it is the duty of the psychiatrist to bring his specialty as soon as possible into the proper relationship and cooperation with other branches of medicine. But only the psychiatrist is capable of estimating the value of research in his own field, which obvious point is not always taken for granted.

Many different categories of problems in psychiatry and allied to psychiatry have been presented and discussed during this Conference, but there is one opportunity for valuable research which has not been emphasized. I refer to that great field represented by the institutions for the mentally deficient. The feebleminded and the constitutionally deficient are "experiments of nature." They are instances where definite limits have been placed on the individual by nature in a way which should encourage experimental work. Here there is a greater degree of fixity than is found in the more modifiable conditions known as "psychoses" and "neuroses." These constitutional deficiencies appear in many different types, degrees, and localizations of the abnormal process. There are anatomical developmental gaps in the central nervous system organization, nutritional deficiencies, physiological, endocrinological, biochemical, and psychological abnormalities which are awaiting investigation with instruments of precision and with experimental psychological methods under conditions a step beyond the level of animal experimentation, the results of which we are often reluctant to interpret in terms of human activity. In a relatively large percentage of institution cases, it is possible to obtain an autopsy which allows for an evaluation of the final chapters in the life story under investigation. There is a deplorable scarcity of pathologists as well as of other research workers in hospitals for the mentally deficient. Therefore, the bulk of this valuable material remains for future recognition and utilization.

While we cannot hope to accomplish as much therapeutically as with some other types of disorders, a thorough study of this material should serve to enlighten us as to both the physiological and psychological nature of the mechanisms of behavior. Apparently we have allowed the current attitude of defeatism toward therapy to blind us to the research opportunities.

In our work there are, in addition to the study of the individual as such, familial, social, communal, and national units to be considered both "biologically" and "socially." We should keep in mind that any science of life must deal with life's different aspects wherever and in whatever form it finds them, and regardless of whether they can be brought finally under the control of a laboratory experiment. It is only necessary for us to develop and maintain a sense of balance and to exercise a mixture of stability and plasticity in our thinking.

Symposium I
The Philosophy of Psychiatry

Second Scheduled Discussion of Symposium I

By SAMUEL T. ORTON, M.D.

*Professor of Neurology and Neuropathology, Columbia University, 1930-1936.
New York City*

I DO NOT feel that I am equipped to speak on the Philosophy of Psychiatry, particularly when included in a session under the leadership of Dr. Meyer who is so well prepared for such a task. However, I have been a close observer of the trends of thought which have influenced the development of psychiatry for about thirty-five years and actively at work in certain phases of its field during the same time. This period has been one of marked change in emphasis among psychiatrists and of marked expansion in their fields of interest and endeavor, and I hope that a brief review of my observations during that time may prove of interest.

While still a medical student I became interested in pathology, and on graduation I was fortunate enough to be accepted for a period of training under one of America's best teachers of general pathology, Dr. Frank B. Mallory, at the Boston City Hospital. At the end of that service an opportunity was offered to me in neuropathology, and I spent a short time adding a knowledge of the special techniques of this field and in becoming pretty thoroughly familiar with the problems of cerebral localization under the guidance of Dr. E. E. Southard at the Danvers State Hospital in Massachusetts. Those who had the opportunity of working under Dr. Southard will appreciate how much stimulus and enthusiasm he was able to inject into all of those who had the good fortune to serve with him.

Thus I started with unusually good preparation, and it was a period when neuropathology was thought to offer as much promise in the field of mental disease as its parent subject, general pathology, had held for the somatic diseases. Nissl's method for staining the extranuclear chromatin granules in nerve cells was comparatively new and Nissl and Alzheimer had described the histological changes in paresis and had given for that one mental disease a definite diagnostic criterion. This led to the hope that new methods of staining and finer histological detail would in time reveal structural alterations in other diseases. The older explanations of insanity as being due to magic, the influence of evil spirits, and over-exposure to moonlight had dropped out and the new science of neuropathology was considered the most promising field of exploration.

It was only shortly thereafter, however, that the swing away from the organic or structural causation toward that of functional disorders began to be apparent. There were two reasons for this change. First, the structural attack was not so productive as had been hoped, and it gradually became obvious that the brains of about eighty percent of our admissions to the state hospitals did not show organic changes pathognomonic for the corresponding clinical pictures; and second, new concepts of the importance of disorders of function began to bear fruit. On the first or negative side of the picture stood such work as that of Dunlap who, after several years of intensive study of the brains of cases of dementia praecox, reported that not only could he find no distinctive pathological picture in them but he could find no way in which they differed from the brains of nonpsychotic individuals. The second or positive side was supported by the studies of Freud and Jung and their pupils. Freud and Jung were at that time sufficiently in agreement to appear on the same platform, and the series of lectures which they gave at Clark University on the invitation of President G. Stanley Hall gave added impulse to the swing of the pendulum toward a functional explanation of many phenomena.

While recognizing the importance of the emphasis so placed on the enormous part played in our behavior by our instincts and emotions, I think it may be fairly said that the swing went to the extreme and gave us a whole generation of psychiatrists who had not even a nodding acquaintance with the structure of man's brain. The discussions at that time would, I think, bear me out in that. There was a great deal of talk about the possibility of lay analyists handling psychotic cases as well as borderline ones, and I even heard a very active and somewhat acrimonious discussion among one of the leading groups of the American Psychiatric Association as to whether we ought not to relegate all the organic psychoses to be studied exclusively by the neurologists, i.e., to group together with the spinal cord and midbrain diseases all that showed a lesion of the brain or cortex, and confine our own interests to the so-called functional groups. The continuation of the study of the brain, of its structures, its functions, and to some extent of its changes and alterations, was turned over during that period very largely, except for a few of us who maintained our old interests, to the physiologists, to the brain surgeons and even to the psychologists.

Another movement which began at about that period was the development of the psychopathic hospital. It had been recognized for some time past that the state institutions, while fulfilling the custodial need very well for the most part, were not the place for the best possible treatment for acute psychotic cases and particularly for borderline cases. Also, there was need for institutions which would segregate the more interesting material for research so that it would not be lost in the maze of large ward groups and used for the expansion of the teaching facilities. These three needs—that of a hospital for treatment, of selection of cases for research, and of material for teaching—led to the establishment of the genuine psychopathic hospital. Many institutions which were merely receiving hospitals subsequently borrowed that title but were not covering the whole field. The first of the genuine psychopathic hospitals was established here in Ann Arbor under Dr. Albert M. Barrett. Your city and your University may rightly claim to be the pioneers in that regard. The second followed relatively shortly after, with the development of the Phipps Clinic under Dr. Meyer in Baltimore. The third was that of Dr. Southard in Boston, and it was my good fortune to organize and direct the fourth unit, in Iowa City.

Another movement of about the same time was the tendency toward extension of psychiatric work through mental hygiene societies and mental hygiene clinics. In Iowa we made an experiment in this direction at quite an early date. Our original experiment was carried out by a group of volunteers from the Psychopathic Hospital staff who offered to go to any community in that state which wanted us and to study cases referred by the doctors, by the courts, by the county social agencies and, finally, by the schools. We felt we could offer service to these various agencies since our unit was made up of a psychiatrist, a psychologist and a trained psychiatric social worker. The yield was very good and we were able to extend it, through a liberal grant from the Rockefeller Foundation, to an enlarged two-year experimental period with the Mobile Mental Hygiene Clinic, as we called it, moving from city to city through the state and studying intensively the cases that were referred to us, on the ground, rather than having them sent to the Hospital in Iowa City.

There was also a growing tendency toward extension of psychiatric interest into the period of childhood, which Dr. White so aptly spoke of as the "golden period of mental hygiene." I think also it was a golden period for research of various types. The interest in children's work has spread very widely and, as you have heard from papers on this program, is still actively enlarging. Still more recent is the broadening interest in the application of psychiatry to sociology, both to the understanding of how social factors affect the psychotic disturbance in a given individual and also the influence that psychotic ideas and psychopathic personalities, particularly when they occur in natural leaders of men, may have on society at large.

When I began work at Danvers, Dr. Southard introduced me to a recent book and suggested that a study of the brain of an extreme case of chronic internal hydrocephalus along the same line might be interesting. It was Campbell's *Histological Localization of Cerebral Function,* and it was, I believe, the first complete map of the human brain based on the histological differences between various areas. This book was followed shortly afterward by much more extensive works by German writers, one of which has since become the popular guide to which to refer in identifying given cortical regions. Campbell's work was much simpler but at the end of the description of each cortex type he reviewed the evidence concerning its function. This forms a much more serviceable chart for correlation of clinical findings. His successors have carried the separation of areas showing minor differences in cellular and fibrous architectonics beyond our ability to subdivide functions with security.

I have carried Campbell's map and its interpretations in mind ever since and have applied it extensively in interpretations. I cannot emphasize too strongly my belief that the enormous organ which evolution has developed in man's head has a much wider part to play in his behavior than that of a generator of emotions, and that a thorough knowledge of the functions represented in each of the various large areas which show a markedly different histologic structure is of enormous value in the study of many clinical syndromes. Moreover, I believe not only that emotional variations may modify the efficiency of the various brain functions, but also that differences in physiological activity of specific areas may generate emotional deviations as well, and that thus observed concurrent emotional disturbances may often be an effect rather than a cause of disordered functions. One of the best illustrations of this relationship is to be seen in a critical study of the earliest stages of stuttering—a disorder which frequently makes its first appearance in childhood. When stuttering is studied in an adult who has labored under this handicap all of his life, many neurotic traits are seen which are not obvious in childhood and may quite logically be explained as the results of experience—for example the withdrawal from social contacts and the avoidance of other situations which require fluent speech. Thus fear of the telephone which is a frequent finding in adult stutterers may be a result of past difficulties with that instrument rather than a phobia which causes the stuttering, as it is so often interpreted. Stuttering children, early in the course of their trouble, do not avoid social contacts nor do they fear the telephone, and they do not as a group show any consistent apprehensiveness which might be considered a constitutional factor sufficient to explain the later development of phobias. Indeed many of these children are of a distinctly social, garrulous and venturesome make-up both before and immediately after the onset of their difficulty. They often exhibit reactions to frustration, when their attempts to speak are blocked, but this would seem to be an entirely logical behavior reaction. Stuttering may, of course, occur in a true neurotic individual, as would be expected in any group selected by including those showing one given type of disorder, but our observations in children have led me to believe that a marked injustice is often done when the presence of stuttering is accepted as prima facie evidence of the existence of a neurosis.

In the course of an extended program of research covering a period of about seventeen years, I have also become convinced that certain developmental disorders in childhood may rest not on structural alterations of a given area of the brain but on a failure to acquire the normal physiological pattern of action of that area. This rests partly on our studies of the reading disability—strephosymbolia—and the very close parallel which exists between its symptoms and those seen in acquired alexia in the adult and partly on the extension of these studies to the problems of developmental aphasia and developmental apraxia. This last syndrome is still a research problem and our most thorough piece of work on it has not as yet been published.

The reasons for accepting a physiological hypothesis concerning the developmental delays of childhood are too varied and too complex to go into in detail within the time allotted here but suffice it to say that they seem to harmonize with modern neurological opinion and to take cognizance of both the intrinsic or hereditary factors and the play of extrinsic or environmental factors and finally to meet the therapeutic test of response to proper retraining methods. While the determining factor seems best explainable on the basis of a faulty physiology we must, of course, grant the emotional factors a prominent place in the picture. I believe that the interplay between these two must always be taken into account. We can no more isolate one from the other than we can discard either the warp or the woof of a piece of cloth. With either gone, it is no longer cloth.

Finally, in closing, since our studies point to a failure to acquire the normal adult pattern of unilateral cerebral dominance as the source of the developmental language disorders and of developmental apraxia and since the pattern of control from one side of the brain is also disturbed in injuries to critical areas of the dominant hemisphere, we are hopeful that the somewhat better understanding of the principle of unilateral dominance gained in our studies of the special disabilities of childhood and the methods of retraining derived therefrom which have been so effective, may prove helpful in the rehabilitation of cases with war injuries of the brain. We are convinced, as outlined above, that the classifying of all stutterers as neurotics is an error and the assumption that non-readers are mentally defective can be readily shown to be untenable. We feel sure that some of our observations on right-brained (left-handed) children and on those with mixed or confused dominance could profitably be used for better understanding the troubles which lead, in the Army, to the awkward squad or to the failures of a strongly left-eyed soldier in the rifle pits, and that such understanding would in turn be serviceable in the proper assignment for service of these men who do not conform to the more common pattern.

Symposium I
The Philosophy of Psychiatry

Third Scheduled Discussion of Symposium I

By WALTER FREEMAN, M.D.

Professor of Neurology, George Washington University

I WOULD INTRODUCE my remarks with the quotation from Alexander Pope, "The proper study of mankind is man." During the past few years we have been engaged in the intensive study of a particular type of man, a man whose frontal lobes have been partially inactivated. Since the frontal lobes represent such an important part of man in his relation with his fellows, it seems worth while to present facets of his personality and to discuss the frontal lobes in relation to the ego, the future and psychosis.

James W. Watts and I have performed prefrontal lobotomy on about 140 mentally disordered individuals during the past six years and have observed them in detail over the ensuing period. Most of them are now steady, industrious, undistinguished citizens; some are cheerful drones; some have slipped back into the world of fear from which the surgeon's knife temporarily rescued them; and three have succumbed in the first groping attempts of the surgeon to make their lives more worth living.

What are the behavioral characteristics of a patient who has undergone prefrontal lobotomy? He is friendly, cheerful, agreeable, relaxed and interested in what goes on around him. He enters readily into conversations, stating his opinions positively rather than diplomatically. With strangers he is dignified, but with the members of his immediate family he occasionally indulges his high spirits by unrestrained speech and sometimes salty jest, with a spice of profanity. He is always ready for the next meal and never complains of indigestion. He sleeps soundly and without dreams, wakes refreshed, and attends to his needs and his business with equal unconcern over the horrors of war or the empty shelves of the corner grocery. Sometimes he is genially indolent, answering in petulant fashion when his family tries to rouse him to greater efforts. At other times, he is a dynamo of industry, and seems oblivious to sensations of fatigue. He is a procrastinator. His intelligence is intact, but his distractibility may be so great as to stamp him as a scatterbrain. He likes to spend money when he has any, but gets along just as well when he has none. He is interested in people and his conduct is grave and respectful if they are not too intimate with him. He delights in the simple pleasures of family life and in spectacles of all sorts, movie programs, radio entertainment, life and movement on the streets. He is able to worry, but more about externals than about himself. He is the complete extrovert.

What has happened to the previously psychotic individual as the result of prefrontal lobotomy? This operation, in essence, cuts across the fiber connection in the frontal lobe that unites the thalamus with the frontal pole. It is fairly well agreed that the thalamus represents the central mechanism for emotional experience. What then may be said of the functions of the frontal lobes?

For a few weeks after operation, one of our patients was a very restless, noisy fellow who pulled the screens from the windows and tore the telephone and light cords from the walls. On this particular day he rang the fire alarm of the hospital. When the excitement subsided he was duly repentant and agreeable. He was asked about the occurrence: "Now that I've done it" he said "I realize that it wasn't the thing to do, but beforehand I couldn't say whether or not it would be all right."

It would seem from this observation, the quality of fore-sight is one of those that is mediated by the frontal lobes. We have erected the hypothesis that the cerebral hemisphere may be considered as being divided into two portions by the rolandic fissure. The parts posterior to this fissure are those concerned with the reception of impulses through the various channels of perception, and their elaboration into engrams. Memory and intelligence, everything concerned with the past, are presided over by the cortex behind the fissure. The parts anterior to the fissure of Rolando would seem to be concerned in the projection of the individual as a whole into the future, enabling him to visualize beforehand what the effect of an act will be before he has commenced it.

This quality of foresight is permanently altered in those whose frontal lobes have of necessity been sacrificed for the removal of tumors or other mass lesions. No patient with bifrontal lobectomy has been reported as able to work for gain. However, in the case of prefrontal lobotomy, the cortical zones are not sacrificed, and even histologic preparations show no change in the architecture of the frontal cortex. It is the thalamus, and particularly its nucleus medialis dorsalis that has undergone atrophy. Consequently, in cases of prefrontal lobotomy, it is the emotional component in relation to foresight that has been reduced. Our patients know beforehand that their laziness and tactlessness may be offensive, but they do not have the urge to conform to the high standards that they formerly set for themselves. As one man said of his wife: "She's so full of don't-give-a-damness."

Another property of major importance among the functions of the frontal lobes is consciousness of the self. The patient who has undergone prefrontal lobotomy under local anesthesia is at first disoriented completely, may even deny that he has been operated upon, although he may remember the shaving of the scalp, the drilling of the holes in his skull, and frag-ments of the conversation that he carried on during the opera-tion. Some of this profound disturbance of ego relationships must, of course, be attributed to the diaschisis following interruption of any considerable number of axones, but in the succeeding days, this lack of consciousness of the self is revealed in a variety of ways. In many respects the patients are childish in their instant replies to questions and in their lack of embarrassment at being laughed at or reprimanded for their undignified behavior. They are no longer sensitive and their feelings cannot be hurt. This unconcern applies equally readily to the "self" as a collection of organs. Hypochondriacal complaints are arrested abruptly by operation, and fear of contamination or disease is abolished.

Brickner has stressed synthesis as the outstanding intellectual function of the frontal lobes. We also would emphasize the function of the frontal lobes in the selection and elaboration of all the factors to be considered in the solution of a problem, upon the contemplative aspects of behavior, and especially upon mental concentration, the following of a single line of argument through all its ramifications, envisaging everything of importance and excluding the irrelevant. Ambition and singleness of purpose are important results of frontal lobe activity. And yet here again the personal aspect weighs heavily in all such activity. I recall demonstrating on the lecture platform a very intelligent draftsman who had made a brilliant recovery from a very long-standing and disabling obsessive compulsive neurosis. He described in detail the various characteristics of a machine that he had invented for grinding elliptical bearings. Obviously this invention required concentration, singleness of purpose, ambition, visualization and foresight for its successful completion. The patient went on to describe, in my presence and before a medical gathering, how the use of non-heat-producing foods and his devotion to spiritualism had been responsible for his recovery. Other patients have engaged successfully in various occupations such as legal work, radio operation, clerical work of all kinds, telephone operation and the like, making a pronounced success in the practical and impersonal aspects of their jobs, while still manifesting slightly erratic behavior in interpersonal relationships. "The fellows tap their foreheads and call me nuts, but

I don't mind that. I just go ahead and do my work." This from a previously shy, sensitive, preoccupied schizophrenic.

What is the importance of these observations in the field of psychiatry? What have foresight, self-consciousness and concentration to do with mental disorders? Stated succinctly, there may be too much of a good thing.

Foresight is surely of value to the normal individual. But some individuals become mentally sick from trying to see too far ahead into the mazes of life in this world and the next. Where the road is clear, there is little emotion, but where it is dark and where answers are equivocal, the emotional charge becomes overly heavy and ideas of personal failure and incompetence creep in. The bridge-crossers and the molehill builders are suffering from too much foresight with the corresponding emotional building up. The practical question, "What shall I do next?" becomes converted, shortened but unanswerable, "What shall I do?"

Consciousness of the self is an undeniable blessing, representing man's highest endowment. But let self-consciousness become elaborated until the individual begins to hear his name mentioned, to see total strangers follow him, to see people in conversation look at him covertly and to hear the horns of automobiles signalling to one another about him, and this self-consciousness cannot but have a grave effect upon his ability to meet his fellows on a plane of equality.

Consciousness of the self as a collection of organs prevents abuse of their capacity, but a patient with "nervous indigestion" is all too apt to blame the food or the cook or his stomach. Almost anybody suffering from indigestion, becoming aware of improper functioning of such an important part of the body as his stomach, seeks for a cause, and this seeking for a cause and foreseeing the probable consequences is an important function of the prefrontal regions. Concentration and synthesis are now in order. The individual summons his past experiences with regard to bellyaches, his knowledge of appendicitis gained from the press, the experiences of his friends and the reports of men in high places who have died of cancer of the stomach. He projects himself into the future, visualizing the doctor's examination, the hospital, the operation, the lingering death in agonizing pain and the children left fatherless while the widow demonstrates her lack of rudimentary financial sense.

Thus again, consciousness of the self, projection into the future, and contemplation *as regards the self,* may erect upon the base of simple hypertonicity of smooth muscle some of the most ghastly consequences. Anterograde algimnesia is the painful contemplation of events that will never happen.

To sum up, it is well for the individual to have a little fear, a little anxiety, a fairly high ambition, a bit of the perfectionist spirit, an abundance of foresight and an awareness of himself both as regards his internal functioning and as regards his functioning as a social unit. It is well for him to be able to select a group of ideas and to elaborate them into an hypothesis that governs his conduct, excluding from consideration the non-essential and the irrelevant. He should build a few castles in the air, and people his world of fantasy with good and bad genii. But all the good can be turned to bad by excessive elaboration, and especially when indecision brings about rumination, inaction and pure fantasy, and further retreat from reality with feelings of guilt and inferiority. The emotional charge in such instances probably serves further toward fixation of the complexes to the exclusion of normal outward interests. If fixation of ideas becomes the criterion of a psychosis, then anything that prevents or relieves such fixation can be of benefit.

To the normal individual the frontal lobes are indispensable; to the sick individual they may be destructive. Without the frontal lobes there could be no functional psychoses.

TABLE 1

STATUS OF PATIENTS FOLLOWING PREFRONTAL LOBOTOMY.

September, 1936-October, 1942

Disease	No.	Regularly Employed	Studying or Partially Employed	Housekeeping	At Home	Institution	Dead
Involutional Depressions	62	6	4	27	11	6	8
Obsessive Tension States	30	12	4	5	7	—	2
Schizophrenias	31	4	7	4	11	4	1
Psychoneuroses	8	4	—	2	—	2	—
Undifferentiated (Schizoid)	5	1	1	1	1	1	—
Totals	136	27	16	39	30	13	11

TABLE 2

RESULTS OF PREFRONTAL LOBOTOMY.

September, 1936-October, 1942

Disease	No.	Results			Deaths	
		Good	Fair	Poor	Operative	Subsequent
Involutional Depressions	62	48	10	3	1	7
Obsessive Tension States	30	22	4	2	2	—
Schizophrenias	31	21	5	5	—	1
Psychoneuroses	8	6	1	1	—	—
Undifferentiated (Schizoid)	5	1	3	1	—	—
Totals	136	98	23	12	3	8

Symposium I
The Philosophy of Psychiatry

Fourth Scheduled Discussion of Symposium I

By LAWSON G. LOWREY, M.D.

Editor, American Journal of Orthopsychiatry; Director, Brooklyn Child Guidance Centre; Psychiatrist, Brooklyn Hebrew Orphan Asylum and New York Travellers Aid Society

THIS large group of psychiatrists has not been concerned with symptom patterns or polite squabbling over terminology, but has been really discussing what psychiatry can contribute to the problems of everyday living.

It was my misfortune to be absent the first day and I shall therefore concentrate my remarks into a summation of what I gained through yesterday's program. My remarks are still further focused by Dr. Meyer's comment that I represent the field of orthopsychiatry. It should be borne in mind that orthopsychiatry is largely concerned with prevention of a particular type, i.e., therapeutic prevention. Working largely with children, the orthopsychiatrist is inevitably deeply concerned with the family drama in all of its permutations and substitutions. Accordingly, the concentration, in yesterday's program, on the problems of family life and what happens to the individual as he grows up in the family and then widens his social group living in school and college, was to me most important. It was especially heartening to see the extent of recognition of the importance of family experiences in determining personality trends, behavior reactions and social adaptation.

I can not, of course, agree with some of the viewpoints expressed yesterday because they are contrary to experience and observed facts. But a true and most important emphasis was given to the point that in any extra-family care of children we must approximate as closely as possible the best conditions of normal family life. Apparently we shall presently have to embark upon extensive programs of out-of-home care of children, the war situation and demands for production being what they are. And in terms of the future of these children, and therefore of this country, we must keep clearly to the fore at all times in such programs the need for a real, valid, emotionally healthy substitute for family life.

I should like to support, and perhaps explain to some extent, the emphasis on this point by citing data derived from two different studies. A mental hygiene unit, of which I was director, spent two years working directly in kindergartens, i.e., we were in the rooms observing, testing, examining, during every school day for two years. We made extensive and intensive studies of one hundred children, followed for two years. The teachers invariably said the aggressive, impudent, demanding youngsters were "spoiled," had obviously always had everything they wanted and were given their own way at home. What we learned in studying the family life of these children was that, *without exception, these were rejected children;* either obviously and openly rejected, or suffering from a less overt rejection, often masked as over-solicitude. There were among the one hundred children some who really were the family pets, loved, respected, indulged. In the classroom, again without exception, these children were poised, secure, well-behaved, and regarded by the teachers as their dependable leaders. May I leave you to draw your own conclusions?

The second set of data is derived from studying children reared in infants homes. These homes conform to the description Dr. Gesell gave yesterday, so far as physical equipment and care are concerned. But it is highly significant that if children are placed in these homes prior to twelve to fifteen months of age and are removed for placement in foster or own homes at three to three and a half years of age, they all present the same type of solitary, hostile, destructive, aggressive, demanding behavior. This behavior does not correlate with any other factors, such as intelligence, heredity, physical disorders, etc. In a more recent study of this group it is found that, when discharged from care at the age of sixteen to eighteen years, they still present this same kind of asocial, isolated behavior pattern.

These observations, and others of a similar sort, seem to me of the greatest importance with reference to the responsibilities of psychiatrists in advising regarding the care of large numbers of children. The factor of human relationship and its quality is transcendant in such arrangements for young children, far more so than for older children. It seems to me conclusively shown from all sides that the early stimuli to emotional response play a major role in determining the later type of personality and possibilities of adjustment to the wide range of variable situations all must encounter.

Long ago I made a distinction betweeen the psychiatric and the mental hygiene or orthopsychiatric approaches. The former is highly individual, while the latter is concerned not only with the whole individual and how he functions, but with the totality of situations in which he must live and have his being. This Conference program has been, to me, mental hygiene on a large scale. The philosophy I see in what I have heard has been one of penetration of many areas in which psychiatric viewpoints are extremely valuable if they are correctly presented. To do the last is not always easy, and should engage our best attention.

Symposium I
The Philosophy of Psychiatry

Discussions from the Assembly

LEO KANNER, M.D.

Baltimore

THIS CONFERENCE, which Dr. Raphael has rightly called unique, has impressed me profoundly. The majority of the presentations has indicated a gratifying fulfillment to myself and, I am sure, to other psychiatrists of my generation. It has brought to focus three concepts which, among many other things, I have been fortunate to learn from Dr. Meyer and have tried for many years to make my own. These are the concepts of meliorism, pluralism and relativism.

When most of us started on our psychiatric careers, psychiatrists and those lay people who were interested in psychiatry were more or less divided into two groups: those who viewed psychiatry with pessimistic gloom, and those who indulged in day dreaming, wishful thinking and enthusiasm which mostly spent itself in verbal profusion. The intercourse between those two groups sounded very much like a monologue between Cassandra and Pollyanna. I think these two ladies have been conspicuously absent from this meeting.

Pluralism denotes many things. It denotes the realization of a plurality of people and the ways in which people react. It indicates a plurality of factors which enters into the performances and feelings of people. It also indicates a plurality of the means of studying man, a plurality which keeps one, I think happily, from indulging in what Dr. Meyer has referred to as "exclusive salvationism." Pluralism further indicates a plurality of avenues through which man can be studied and

reached and helped. We have heard quite a bit of this plurality during the meeting—the avenues of the home and family life, of education for the younger person, on through industry and the armed forces, in urban as well as rural areas,
through the physician both in general practice and in the spe-
cialties, through sociology and criminology. More than anything else the concept of relativism has been emphasized, both
directly and by indirection. It became quite clear that man's
performance is no longer studied and viewed as detached from
everything else, but definitely in relation to the performing
person. The performing person, in turn, is not studied in a
vacuum but definitely related to his life situation. The life situation, in turn, has been viewed and studied and treated in
the larger constellation in which it occurs, economic, political,
cultural, international. The present has been viewed in its
relation to the past and to the future. There is very definitely
a respect for connections and pertinences, which takes us
away from the idea of absoluteness.

One of the greatest minds in Germany and one of the most
brilliant writers of our time, after being forced to leave Germany and come to this country, was at first distressed by, and
published a paper in which he deplored, the lack of absoluteness in American thinking. He could think only of looseness
as the alternative. I am sure that he has learned meanwhile
that what seemed looseness to him is much more a respect for
both relativism and pluralism, and denotes breadth and width,
and, I think, much more depth than our culture is usually
given credit for.

I might say one more word. Another thing that has come
out is this: it may seem to the person who thinks in absolute
terms or in terms of exclusive salvationism that such a formulation is not scientific in the sense of having a set of prepared
tools, verbal and otherwise, in a rigid form. I think this Conference has shown more than anything else that just these concepts make for a true scientific spirit, and it has been evident
that psychiatry has been viewed as a science dunked in the
milk of human kindness.

TEMPLE BURLING, M.D.

Providence

AMONG MANY reasons why I found this Conference valuable to me is that it has given me an opportunity to make a diagnosis for myself of the present status of psychiatry.

This Conference has demonstrated over and over again that we have at length learned how to talk about personality without getting tangled up in the old body-mind antithesis. But it has demonstrated equally clearly that we have not yet learned to talk about society without falling into the analogous group-individual quandary. It appears to me that learning to do that is the next important forward step in the philosophy of psychiatry.

FRITZ REDL, Ph.D.

Detroit

I WOULD LIKE to draw your attention to an additional field in psychiatry for which we need more material than we now have.

In working in camps with children and adolescents, I am constantly struck with the high degree of *unpredictability of group behavior.* This is evident even in those cases in which the most elaborate psychiatric case histories were available on the youngsters in question. This means, then, that the reaction within a group is not *only* a function of a person's case history, though we know that it is partly that. It also means that a number of factors come in about which as yet we know little, in spite of the fact that group psychologists, on the one hand, and sociologists and social anthropologists, on the other, have given us some general studies on group structure. The exact place where group psychological influences and the individual case history of a person get together to produce his in-group behavior is still rather unknown.

I seriously think we shall not get very far in the help we have to offer to people in the *armed forces,* in *youth move-*

ments and in *civilian group life,* without a more thorough consideration of the *psychology of group phenomena.* We have, yesterday, heard about the suggestion that wars are nowadays fought by "ideas" as well as arms. However, I should like to add to this "by ideas imbedded into a group psychological power-system." For it is only then that "ideas" assume their dynamic forcefulness. We need much more concrete knowledge on exactly that problem of group-imbeddedness of an idea than we now have.

In short, I would like to challenge this assembly very strongly to add to the research which has been done in the field, a much more elaborate and widespread as well as thorough research in the direction of group psychology. In fact it is a *psychiatrically founded group psychology* of which there is very little yet and which is badly needed if the knowledge gained from individual psychiatry is to be fruitfully applied on the group phenomenon of war and army life.

C. MACFIE CAMPBELL, M.D.

Boston

I HAVE BEEN wondering what those who are responsible for the Conference feel they have got out of it. We have learned a great deal with regard to many aspects of human nature, the somatic, the personal and the social. What are we going to do about it? What can we do? When we go back home, do we just resume our tasks and have pleasant memories of Ann Arbor and the Conference? What authority do we have? There is a vast amount of knowledge available in this room. Is it going to be utilized? How can it be applied? What principles referred to can be translated into productive activity?

We have learned that in regard to chemical research there are some important practical steps to be taken. It has been emphasized that a great deal of help can be given to an innumerable number of individuals groping about with frustrations and difficulties in life, having nobody with whom to talk over their difficulties, and perhaps finding in the medical profession an inadequate sensitivity to these issues.

One can think over the concrete results of a conference like this in regard to some practical topics. Of the practical topics, I think those dealing with childhood stand out in my mind most clearly. Perhaps from the point of view of social organization and its values the problems connected with courtship and marriage may be of equal importance. The needs of the child and the lack of help available to the average parent are things which we might very well think about. How can we organize the community so that people will get a little more help? Will the average mother in America get more insight into her own needs and those of her children as a result of this Conference? Will the conclusions formulated here be made available to the community in general?

Well, perhaps they will be through a process of filtering down. There are many teachers here. Through their students and their colleagues and their association with the ancillary disciplines such as social work, education and psychology, etc., that knowledge may slowly filter down. Is there any way in which that process could be made a little more rapid and perhaps a little more systematic?

As to the industrial field and the needs of the individual worker, more knowledge and clear formulations are much to be desired.

I think it might be possible to draw up a list of the needs of several types of individuals in a community, the housewife, the mother, the skilled factory worker, the unskilled laborer, the friendless roomer, the ambitious executive, the emancipated adolescent, etc. With their respective needs, what resources does the community offer? It may not be impossible to provide satisfactory resources and there may be enough good will in the community to make them available to those most in need of them. The physician and teacher see repeatedly in individual cases the transformation of human lives by very practical procedures. They may not see how they can extend these procedures to the community in general. Enough insight and conviction have been slowly acquired to make vaccination acceptable to the community, but in regard to the preventive measures of mental hygiene the community still requires adequate demonstration and education. Specific topics can be dealt with efficiently by individual communities, specially interested in and competent to deal with these topics. A local demonstration may be necessary preliminary to state-wide or nation-wide organization.

The resources of the individual community may not be so very meagre after all. The psychiatrist may irritate or stimulate his colleagues in the local medical society so that the medical society may feel its conscience awakened as to the absence of clinical facilities. The medical group may win the support of the whole social service group, of district nursing organizations, of teachers, of the clergy, of industrialists, of all those interested in the cultural level of the community. Thus it may be possible to organize the resources that are available in the light of principles which have been clearly formulated for some time and which have been focused so very well in this Conference.

RICHARD L. JENKINS, M.D.

Ann Arbor

I WAS STRUCK yesterday by the comment that Colonel Porter made with respect to the difficulties of adjustment which members of our profession often have in the armed services. There is an old admonition: "Physician, heal thyself." We psychiatrists have not always been too good at that. In such a situation we ought to have, however, the strength and courage of our convictions to apply the thinking of our profession to the problem which exists.

In addition to the problem of adjustment which exists in any new position, there is the problem of adjustment to a highly rigid, disciplined life which leaves essentially no escape from responsibility except through illness. There is further the problem of adjustment to an altered life objective. Most of us have as our life objective the practice of the healing art. Here, as we have had stated, the shift is to the objective of promoting the efficiency of a machine for killing men. This is a rather gross reorientation. Even though intellectually a man may accept it, one does not suddenly sweep aside the emotional loyalties which have developed from twenty-four centuries of professional tradition. The psychiatrist in the armed forces is faced with a problem of divided loyalties—loyalties to his patients, loyalties to his service.

What have we from a mental hygiene point of view to help him make this adjustment, or what have we from a mental hygiene point of view to help the adjustment of the selectee trained in the values of democracy, taught to regard human life as sacred, and suddenly pushed into the profession of killing?

I should like to follow up the point brought up by Dr. Burling and Dr. Redl, and perhaps some bridging between this discussion and the next session is not inappropriate, since that is the objective of this Conference. Psychiatry has been the science of abnormal people. Many people are seeking to make it a science of interpersonal relations. I am in sympathy with this. But in the Army the problems of interpersonal relations are the responsibility of the line officer. The responsibility of the psychiatrist begins when the man is deemed unfit for interpersonal relations. The psychiatrist will get the conduct problem when the sergeant, having exhausted his resources, concludes that "the man must be nuts." Now probably we can never expect that in a fighting organization we can achieve the degree of flexibility which would recognize that in order to cure the private it might be necessary to give psychotherapy to the sergeant. But is there no middle ground, accepting the objective before us of winning the war? The child is easily forgiven for trespassing in forbidden areas from ignorance —and if I stir up some sacred cows, I hope that as a child psychiatrist some tolerance may be extended to me.

In mechanized warfare morale and the will to fight inevitably depend in no small measure upon the sense of confidence which a group of teammates have in each other, on the personalities which easily work together. Colonel Reinartz cited the German bomber where the crew is in close proximity to each other for the purpose of preserving morale. Now men are not and never can be made to be interchangeable, regardless of any program of military machine-processing. Some teams will function smoothly and will function better than the men who make them up; other teams will function badly and worse than the men who make them up, and may be lost as a result of that. That is a point of tremendous importance for military efficiency. To what extent is it recognized? Many years ago when I had my very limited military training, an infantry company was *divided* into squads. What was to a considerable extent the fighting unit was grouped together on the basis of stature. Why? Because it looked well on the parade ground. Real team play, if it develops under such circumstances, is a little bit accidental and spurious. In Germany I understand they group men now to have those in the same unit of the same blood group. I wonder what the possibility is of a company *composed* of squads. Certainly I would expect that an aviation unit *composed* of flying crews would be superior to the same aviation unit *divided* into flying crews. I suspect that the traditional line officer may be troubled by this thinking in the fear that consulting in any direct way the preferences or attitudes or personalities of the men may break down morale and remove the premium for doing one's duty as ordered under any circumstances, regardless of personalities.

There is the effort to develop an interchangeability of fighting men, but any conclusion that men can be absolutely interchangeable in team positions is unrealistic. I wonder if anyone would suggest that human beings are interchangeable in marriage relationships or in foster home placements? I suspect that under the pressure of military necessity the degree of personality interrelationship between teammates in a fighting unit is at least as high as between school-age children and their foster parents. There are techniques which have been developed and experimented with (as Dr. Redl can elaborate) in children's camps, in institutions, in settlement houses, for finding the resonances and dissonances of personalities with each other. I wonder whether this is something which receives full consideration at present? I have no doubt that in cases where there are unmistakable dissonances in a fighting unit, they are likely to be corrected by regrouping, but I wonder if this area of mental hygiene has been utilized to its full possibilities in our war effort.

GEORGE H. STEVENSON, M.D.
London, Ontario

As, I think, the only Canadian of those invited able to attend, I should like to thank the Committee which has arranged for the privilege of my participating in the program. This generous courtesy in an international way is only one of the many kindnesses that your people have so often shown to us Canadians.

In the philosophy of psychiatry there is just one aspect which perhaps has not been touched on particularly, although the Program Committee included it as a subject for discussion; namely, psychiatry in national and international affairs, which was handled so ably by Dr. Appel. But he limited his remarks to the war period. We are talking a great deal about post-war planning, and I would suggest that preventive psychiatry can play an important part. There are people living in Germany and people in Russia and people in France, people in the United States. That in itself presents the problem of of interpersonal relations on an international scale. This is one of the most important research problems facing psychiatry and the other social sciences. The international psychopathology which has led to the present war and past wars is also a field for serious research on the part of members of this association and of psychiatrists in general.

May I state in closing that the American Psychiatric Asso-

ciation has recently appointed a committee on international
relationships under the chairmanship of Dr. Glenn Meyer of
California. I think the only member of that committee present is Dr. Kubie.

FRANZ ALEXANDER, M.D.

Chicago

I SHOULD LIKE to express very briefly my impressions about
this Conference. I was very much impressed, as was Dr.
Kanner, by the lack of absolutism and by the multiplicity of
approach exhibited. The fact that we came here with our pet
ideas and approaches and then were able to listen to each
other and learn from each other is a sign that psychiatry is
coming of age and giving up a certain amount of dogmatism
and exclusiveness.

I believe Dr. Campbell is right that we should fight more;
it would be a sign of more juvenile or even more infantile
vigor. On the other hand we are settling down and becoming
wiser, which may be deplorable, but it also has its advantages.
We are less vigorous but more wise, I think.

There is one cleavage which I should like to see disappear
and that is the one between behavioristic psychiatry and motivation psychiatry. I shall try to explain what I mean very
briefly.

I listened with the greatest interest to Professor Gesell's
presentation of how the institutionalized child behaves and
how, under his or her influence, the newcomer begins also to
assume this catatonic-like behavior, weaving back and forth.
The young child coming in from outside, so to speak, succumbs to the social atmosphere, succumbs to some kind of
mental infection or contagion, and behaves also like the institutionalized children, namely, in a more primitive, less differentiated way. The behaviorist psychiatrist explains this interesting phenomenon by what he calls social contagion, imitation,
or identification. The motivation psychiatrist asks, why does
the child, the newcomer, behave that way, why does he get

affected? There is a very important factor which I do not think was sufficiently brought out in this meeting, namely, that the newcomer child behaves like the institution child, imitates him, because something in his own nature responds to this type of behavior. There is a certain amount of magic attraction to this weaving back and forth, which is mobilized also in the catatonic who regresses to that phase. In other words, we can say that one cannot propagandize, one cannot inculcate, into people, something which is not in them. What propaganda does is only to appeal to certain potentialities which are preformed in human nature. There is no simple imitation. You do not imitate something if this something does not emotionally appeal to you—at least this imitation will not stick, will not sink in—if there is not something in you which responds to the external influence.

It seems that human nature has tremendous possibilities. It can become a totalitarian Nazi and it can live peacefully in constructive work like people in democracies. The same person may be transplanted from one atmosphere to the other and will change his attitude from one type to another, as Dr. Gesell's children do. They come in as fresh, let us say, progressive, democratic children and then they become conformed and they begin to behave in a termite-like fashion. Here we deal with something which requires a knowledge of human motivation, the potentialities of human nature, which cannot be guessed simply by describing people's external behavior as the behaviorists do, but can only be reconstructed in speaking with people, taking advantage of verbal communication which differentiates psychology and psychiatry from all other disciplines; that is to say, we can talk with the object of our study, with our fellow man, who can tell us something about the motivations and their internal processes which make them behave as they do.

MARIAN J. FITZ-SIMONS, Ph.D.

Detroit

MAY I SPEAK for the people in related fields who I know are very appreciative of being invited to attend this Conference, and extend our thanks to McGregor Fund and the University of Michigan for including us.

I have gained courage from listening to Dr. Campbell and Dr. Alexander to bring up some controversial issues which apply in the field of education. I believe that Dr. Alexander's point of studying the motivation of activity applies to the main point in which I disagree with Dr. Hohman, who talked about the education of young children. With regard to the child he spoke of, who was brought into the nursery school and taught to smile, it seems to me that before you decide to teach a child to smile, you must find out why he doesn't smile naturally and what the factor is in the home background which has brought that child to the nursery school in that condition. Also, when you impose drill before you have developed interest in children, you are running the danger of developing negative attitudes not only toward the thing which you are teaching but also to the person who is doing the teaching, to the entire subject, and perhaps to anyone in authority who attempts to impose his ideas on that child, throughout the rest of his life. The best example of this sort of thing I believe we all know is found in the teaching of music. How many children have been taught to go through the practicing and have been drilled in music who, as they grow older, never touch the piano? Of course, there are many other illustrations.

Dr. Burling's discussion of school problems was obviously based on keen first-hand experience in school work. If psychiatrists are to help school people, they need much of that first-hand experience. I believe that no teacher ever caused any child's personality problems; that the origin of the maladjustments which we see in school lies in the home and is always well set before the children reach school. A teacher may aggravate a child's problem and bring it into the open or she may, if clever, be able to alleviate some of his difficulties. Teachers cannot carry the burden of preventive mental hygiene alone. The problem of teaching a group is quite different from helping a child to make a fundamental readjustment, and trained therapists are needed in addition to the regular training of the school teachers. If you have tried to work with difficult school children and with school teachers, you realize that the things you want the teacher to do for that child in a group are often contrary to her methods, which she must use because her responsibility is to the group first and to the deviate second. What she can do for the difficult, maladjusted child has to be fitted into her first major responsibility, which is that of the development of the group, all the children in the group.

As Dr. Kanner pointed out in his discussion of pediatrics, the pediatrician is in the most strategic spot because he reaches the children who are not developing satisfactorily before they come to any school, even the nursery school. The pediatrician also needs to have much training from the psychiatrist in order to learn how to teach the parents, because that in itself is something which we have been learning in the child guidance clinics is very difficult to achieve. The problems of the parents need to be understood before a successful attempt can be made to influence them to change their methods of handling the child.

I would agree with Dr. Burling that it is distressing to see on a school visit the loss of color as one progresses from kindergarten through high school, but I disagree with him on the fact that a greater knowledge of subject matter rather than method would improve high school teaching. In my experience the interest in subject matter on the part of the teacher increases as one goes up through the grades with a corresponding lack of interest or knowledge of personality development. And that is one reason for the loss of color, I believe, as one progresses through the school. A greater knowledge of the application of mental hygiene to the methods used in high school would very radically change the high school teaching and would, I believe, bring life into it.

JOHN W. APPEL, M.D.

Philadelphia

I HAVE A point which I hesitate to make, but feel should be considered.

From the papers presented in this Conference, one might conclude that we psychiatrists are ready to turn from the problems of the individual patient to the problems of society as a whole. I am not sure that society is ready for us to turn in this direction. I believe that among large segments of society psychiatrists are regarded with suspicion and mistrust. In the last ten months I have had over fifty interviews with various non-psychiatric members of society in Washington, Philadelphia, Boston and New York City—advertising men, newspaper men, government officials—and I have heard the following beliefs and criticisms regarding psychiatrists.

A. Psychiatrists have closed systems of thought. The Rankian school is at odds with the Freudian. The analysts fight the non-analysts. All psychiatrists disagree among themselves.

B. Psychiatrists live in their own worlds of mental disease and know little about the outside world.

C. Psychiatrists deal with crazy people. They don't know much about normal people.

D. Psychiatrists deal with individuals. That doesn't necessarily indicate that they have knowledge of groups.

E. Psychiatrists are clinicians and not scientists. Their opinions are based on clinical impressions rather than scientific evidence.

F. Psychiatrists have not worked well as members of groups themselves.

G. Many psychiatrists have proven inadequate in their personal relationships.

These are the opinions, criticisms, or perhaps I should say "sentiments" which I have heard. I think any psychiatrist planning to shift from the problems of individual patients to the problems of society as a whole must regard this matter as important.

NORMAN MAIER, M.D.

Ann Arbor

I SHALL TRY to make my point as briefly as possible. In a meeting of this sort, one hears much about needs and about frustrations. In other words, it is the problem of the explanation of motivated behavior as against behavior instigated by frustration. Similarly, when one reads about normal psychology, one hears one set of concepts and when one reads about abnormal psychology, one runs into an altogether different set of concepts. Nevertheless, we speak of abnormal behavior as being a deviation from normal behavior. To me the concepts describing these two classes of behavior seem to be quite different. I wonder whether this distinction which we make between normal and abnormal, and between frustrated and motivated behavior may not really represent a sharp distinction in mechanisms.

There are many types of behavior mechanisms in the organism and it is conceivable that different types of mechanisms take over and dominate under different situations. We have had the difficulty of trying to explain or bring together normal and abnormal behavior. Maybe we should not try to bring them together. Maybe that has been one source of the difficulty.

In our laboratory we have been doing some experiments to try to see whether we can distinguish between behavior instigated by frustration and behavior instigated by goals (i.e., motivated behavior). The procedure is to match the behavior produced under the two conditions. After we have obtained similar samples of behavior based upon frustration and upon motivation, certain symptoms turn out to be very different. This shows up particularly when we try to alter the two forms of behavior. In other words, a response based upon motivation and a similar response based upon frustration show very different symptoms when one tries to break them up. Thus our attempts to see whether we could distinguish between frustration and motivation have led us to the belief that they are fundamentally different mechanisms.

If we accept the possibility that these two mechanisms may be altogether different, what is that going to do to our thinking? We are going to analyze separately the types of behavior which are released or instigated by frustration and, of course, we will run into such symptoms as aggregation and stereotypy or fixation. In contrast we will find that motivated behavior is characterized by good problem-solving behavior. In other words, the so-called rational behavior is characterized by situations that are goal-motivated.

If we carried our distinction further, we would probably find that social groups may be organized on different bases: one type organized around frustration, the other organized around goals. The behavior of the two types of groups would be very different, and you would expect it to be different if you accepted the assumption that you were dealing with different mechanisms. The same kind of propaganda which would influence the behavior of one type of group would not influence the behavior of the other type of group because each is based on a different psychological principle.

It also follows from our analysis that certain distinctions which we have been making between the conscious and the unconscious might really be a distinction between motivated behavior and frustration-instigated behavior.

NORMAN CAMERON, M.D.

Madison

IN ONE respect I must disagree decidedly with Dr. Burling when he implies that we no longer have to contend with the mind-body problem. I wish that were the case. But we cannot settle our difficulties simply by agreeing that none exists. I think, for one thing, we all stand in too much awe of the philosophers; and although in psychopathology we have actually been indulging in the most florid theorizing for the past fifty years, we are most reluctant now to re-examine the hypotheses we have evolved. The mediaevals said, "Physician beware of metaphysic!" Already we in psychiatry are far too late to profit from this warning. Even so, if we mean by meta-physics a critical investigation into the fundamentals of our materials and our theories, I can see no reason for our being afraid to tackle the job.

I was much heartened by Dr. Alexander's emphasis on the fact that there are different legitimate ways of going at things in psychopathology. In my own report I emphasize the concept of varying degrees in the accessibility of human behavior, as a substitute for the hypothetical split into a conscious and an unconscious. There is a very fundamental and practical difference between the attitude that we are working with human beings in varying phases of accessibility, and the one that we are working with a lot of psychic "forces" or "energies." It is no mere quibble over words. As physicians we deal with a single biological organism. We can study it at the behavioristic level which, while adequate for some purposes, is obviously incidental and superficial for others. We can go further and investigate emotional, situational and motivational aspects which, however, can also be adequately formulated in terms of conduct; and we can go right on into personal attitudes, trends, wishes and phantasies, without once having to jump from a physical into a psychic world.[1] All these are the reactions of biological organisms, including day-dreaming and night-dreaming, talking and thinking, the unacknowledged as well as the acknowledged, the expressible and the inexpressible.

The psychoanalytic techniques have contributed greatly to the advance of psychiatry, even though some of their theoretical assumptions have stood in their own way. As they appear to me, psychoanalytical techniques are no magical devices for transmuting unconscious gold into conscious brass, but rather highly developed instruments for rendering accessible to the patient and the therapist things which had remained inaccessible to other methods. I look upon hypnosis, out of which Freud developed his later techniques, also as an instrument

[1] Otto, M. C. et al. William James, the man and the thinker. Madison, University of Wisconsin Press, 1942.

which renders accessible certain human reactions—attitudes, responses, wishes, or whatever you want to call them—which are inaccessible to more direct approaches. In either instance we are no more introducing a new kind of reality than we are when we turn to the stethoscope or ophthalmoscope to bring out what has been eluding the naked ear or eye. It is exactly the same reacting biological organism, now being studied more minutely and by more refined methods.

I should like to make this point, while I still have the opportunity, that one of the greatest fallacies in our present psychiatric methods is the one of trying always to make emotionally determined conduct square with verbal logic. Very often this can be achieved only by changing emotion into something else; and as soon as we do that we are deceiving ourselves. We are studying words and not emotional events. Dr. Meyer has said that he hoped we would have the courage to study things as we actually find them. To investigate the emotional I believe we have got to study it the way it occurs and not try to change it into verbal logic, whether according to Aristotle or according to Hartmann and Schopenhauer.

The most glaring examples of the sort of thing I mean can be found even in the current literature, as in the papers of Glover and of Melanie Klein, where the phantasies ascribed to six months old babies by the theorists are speculated upon without hesitation, and in terms of a sophisticated adult verbal logic! This is very thin stuff. In the last century, philosophers and psychologists used to do that with animals, too, and it led them nowhere; we call these romantics *anthropomorphs*. Dr. Kubie tells me that psychoanalysts who dream about babies' phantasies this way in public are known as *adultomorphs*. The phantasies which we really can elicit from ourselves and our patients are, to my way of thinking, not only the biological activities of biological organisms, but are themselves derived also from the social field. Even the most personal of phantasies go back ultimately to social activity and not merely to individualistic rumination.

Finally, I should like to say a word about *psychosomatic*

medicine. From the standpoint of our further advance this seems to me an extremely unfortunate term. It leads our colleagues and our students to expect some new and magical revelation about mind and body; it encourages them to go on thinking in a nineteenth century framework. Why can't we speak instead of physiological psychiatry, that is, the physiology and biochemistry of abnormal behavior? We already have physiological chemistry and physiological psychology. The term psychosomatics only saddles us with an archaic prejudice. It is nothing in the world but a translation of mind-body; and to me "mind-body medicine" sounds like erudite nonsense. After all, the men working on the physiological aspects of psychiatry, Drs. Gildea, Whitehorn, Ziegler, Katzenelbogen, Ewen Cameron, Freeman, Malamud and many others, have something worth while to say about the potentialities and limitations of this approach. Why should we commit it to the confusing proposition that part of each of us lives in a psychic and the other part in a physical world of reality?

Returning then to what I started out with, we are not disposing of this mind-body dualism by saying that it does not exist, while at the same time we go right on formulating our research problems, our pathology and our therapy in its terms. Translating it into Greek only makes it more remote and unintelligible, however attractive and deceptively scientific it may sound. On Thursday Dr. Hartmann spoke of the contributions Gestalt psychology has made to our field. One of these is the experimental finding that tasks and problems left in an unsettled and unfinished state are apt to be best remembered and better worked on later. Therefore, I think that if we can leave the Conference with such problems as this one still open and in a controversial state, it is much more likely that when we finally disband and go to our homes we will keep them alive, and something will come of them.

ADOLF MEYER, M.D.

Baltimore

I HOPE THE words can be few; the thoughts in the minds of the individual members of this group are many. To try to bring them together in my own imagination would be my own business and limited to my limited capacities.

There is one thing I would like to mention. In the first place, let us take these discussions as they were offered. Let us think of the necessity of making our choices. We cannot think of all the things at any one time. We are individuals dependent on the choice of the occasion. Let us make ourselves *responsible* for the courage of *choices*. Select what is important to work with and to discuss (now and here?) and eliminate the things which are merely distracting. That does not mean an arbitrary exclusiveness, but the courage and necessity of the judgment of the individual.

The last remark I want to make is in connection with something that one of my Scotch friends wrote to me about early in the war conflict. He spoke of the demands that had been made on him from all sides to give talks to the public for guidance in crises and impending danger, and all that sort of thing. He was struck by one thing that I would like to have remembered. In the many questions which came to him, there was one general feature—they all always referred to helping somebody else, and never asked about the questioners themselves, as if they never could be perturbed. There we are apt to be hesitant. We are talking about *the child* as if it were the only real toy or victim on which we could expend ourselves. *It is our own responsibility, the responsibility of the adult, the responsibility of all of us, from the youngest to the oldest, that we have to emphasize.* Instead of having the human being torn to pieces, into little special advantages and special disadvantages, we have got to recognize that, after all, we have to see that we pay attention to the *formation of complete personalities and groups,* which we then treat as our units for discussion as worthwhile concrete material, i.e., person with more or less responsibility implying a certain ethical estimation.

I never speak of "mind" as our subject in general discussions. I like to speak of persons and groups. Invariably we are occupied with the two sets, so that what Dr. Burling emphasized as the social nature of his material is one of the fundamental features, actual or potential, of "mental" material. We do speak of the person as the *agent* of *contacts*. It is not *merely* interpersonal relations with which we are occupied. We are also occupied with that which has got to work in and for the individual who has to do the choosing in his interpersonal material, and has to choose the telling active objectives. The person is an object with subject capacity. And that is the essence and concern of the objects of psychiatry as far as I can see it at the present time. We try to make of man an objective body of data, with the investigation including also the sharable subjectivity nature.

It has, I think, been a matter of *genius* that has led to the courage *of making up this program* which may have seemed so difficult and so bewildering on first reading. As far as I can see, it leads to something which is bound to have individual reactions, such things as Dr. Campbell has specified to us. I hope we will go home, not to enter a shell but to work with "ourselves as physicians," and get through with some of that timidity, especially of the disgustingly narrowing fear and cause for fear which physicians have about the speech, conduct and assertions of their professional etiquette. Let's be colleagues ourselves, individuals encouraging each other toward free and yet common goals, and frank and free discussion and sharing, leadership and followership, and confidence that action requires a sound sense of determination and courage of action with plenty of room for modesty and tact, but not as an excuse for indifference.

Symposium II
Psychiatry and the War

Introduction to Symposium II

By THEOPHILE RAPHAEL, M.D.
Ann Arbor

WE NOW pass to the second topic in this final summarizing session, Psychiatry and the War. This, it need hardly be stated, constitutes a consideration of truly vital moment, since in such important measure it refers to what psychiatry can do here and now. The tremendous importance of the "here and now," at this critical time in world affairs, certainly is obvious. It is unusually fortunate that so many psychiatrists who are in the military service can meet with us here today to give us the benefit of their views and experience and in return, receive the thoughts of those engaged in other areas, so that we may all approach the question and work it through as it really is, in terms of one large common front, one large common job calling for the utmost and clearest collaborative effort of all.

Leading the panel on this topic "Psychiatry and the War" is Colonel Roy D. Halloran. He is known to all of you as an outstanding worker in the Massachusetts field and recently and very deservedly appointed to the Office of the Surgeon General, to direct and develop the neuropsychiatric work of the Army. Colonel Halloran will speak first and then will introduce those of his panel who are present, after which there will be a period for general discussion.

Symposium II
Psychiatry and the War

Presentation of the Subject of Symposium II

By COLONEL ROY D. HALLORAN, M.C., U. S. Army

Chief, Neuropsychiatry Branch, Office of the Surgeon General, U. S. Army, Washington, D. C.

IT IS a distinct privilege and a signal honor to be invited to participate in these deliberations of national scope and importance among such an outstanding group. I am happy to bring to you the warm greetings of the Surgeon General of the Army and to express his regrets that he is unable to be here in person.

I have been asked to take part in summing up the high lights of this Conference. I feel that it would be more profitable and perhaps better judgment to present first some thoughts which have been in the minds of our recently organized division, Colonel Farrell and myself, and then proceed to a generalized discussion stimulated by my associates on the panel. Your committee has assigned to me a topic of such latitude that I am tempted to generalize upon the intangible factors of human behavior which are so inevitably associated with the etiological background and precipitation of the titanic struggle in which we are now engaged. However, I fully realize that while a dissertation of such magnitude might well be interesting and provocative of much discussion, it would inevitably prove lengthy, reflect personal bias and mirror the mutual experiences and opinions of large numbers.

421

I believe that at this time we are faced with practical problems which demand and have been given definite consideration and action. I shall present to you, first, a general picture of the special needs of the country for neuropsychiatric assistance in a war of this type, and then, as a representative of the Army, indicate some special observation, plans and procedures which have been initiated and developed by the Army toward the building of a fighting force mentally fit for the vast job ahead. May I assure you at the beginning that the Army welcomes this opportunity to keep the country informed of its vital interest and efforts to maintain the necessary mental health of the forces in so far as military plans will permit.

Certainly there never has been an era—and I think I am safe in saying this—in American history, or for that matter perhaps, in the history of the world, when neuropsychiatry and its allied field of psychology have been called upon to play such an important and complex role. For the past twenty-five years the democratic nations have developed a comfortable and progressive individualism that has contributed momentous advances in the art of living. We are now faced with a real and ominous threat to our freedom of thought and action and must be made to realize, if we do not already, that we can retain it only by a unified fight to the finish. Never have we been called upon for such a colossal, coordinated effort in which every man, woman and child must join hands if we are to keep what we have or any part of it. Since the entire globe is now aflame with a conflicting mass of ideologies and emotions, it is no small wonder that those who have been quietly working in homes, offices, hospitals and laboratories with the many behavior problems of individuals and small groups should now be called upon to apply their talents to the much larger and more critical field of mass motivation. Without doubt this emergency presents not only a challenge but the greatest opportunity in history for those specializing in the field of mental medicine to make a magnificent contribution to the war effort and to the type of humanity which will exist in the years to follow. We as a nation have accepted somewhat complacently the old adage, "In union there is strength." In fact, we have symbolized it in song, story and sport. And now we are again called upon, especially in our field, to demonstrate its practical value.

Throughout our entire economic structure the value and efficiency of cooperative organization has been clearly demonstrated. The armed forces from early times have furnished ample proofs. It would appear that in the wide field of behavior in modern warfare affecting both civilian and soldier alike the uniform no longer symbolizes the only element of risk. Since the danger is commonly shared there can be only an artificial distinction between the needs of civilian and military preparation. Again, the health and spirit of the armed forces reflect the same factors that we find in the civilian population, modified only by preparatory selection and training. It seems essential, therefore, that with neuropsychiatric problems closely related in the civilian and military field there should and must be a closely coordinated effort between the specialists operating in both spheres.

It is not my purpose or province to discuss at length the civilian effort—I think that has been very ably done during the course of this Conference—but rather to discuss it as a part of the total picture related to the military effort. I am aware that there are many helpful investigations and splendid efforts being made to study and bolster the mental health of the communities against the incidence of actual warfare. I have been recently told of the fine plan in one large city to instruct the district nurse in the principles of mental hygiene, since she reaches so many families. The older community neuropsychiatrist, with so many of the younger specialists in the service, must respond to the added burden of wider practice. Undoubtedly he will deal with special exigencies of domestic separation and economic hardships due to enlistment and the war demands. He will have to spend long hours in hospital work due to staff shortages and will assume added responsibilities in teaching. He will give thought to the special preparation of medical students by emphasizing instruction in military neuropsychiatry.

As a matter of fact, the whole orientation of medicine will have to deal with this very important phase of behavior as related to the military effort. If we are to follow through in our total warfare, it seems logical that we must inculcate those principles of preparation from the first year of medical teaching. The medical schools have contributed many of their experienced teachers to the armed forces and must continue to do so. Mental hygiene clinics will take on the additional function of defense advice and thereby contribute greatly to civilian morale. The general medical problems of the community must be shared by specialist and general practitioner alike due to the shortage of physicians. This will provide an excellent opportunity, perhaps the best opportunity we have ever had, for a better understanding of the individual as a whole and a closer relationship between all branches of medicine. Experienced specialists from medical schools who are practicing in the community and in hospitals have felt and should feel a patriotic obligation to offer their services on induction boards, especially since these are most critical points both for the Army and the individual, requiring infinite skill under trying conditions. It is obvious that there will be fewer physicians available and mistakes may be costly.

The neuropsychiatrist must prepare not only to handle civilian casualties due to enemy action but he must also play as important role in an organized effort to rehabilitate those who have been rejected from military service and the war casualties returned to civilian life. I have neither the time nor the wisdom to indicate the various organized channels through which this may be done, but there have been some excellent suggestions during the course of this Conference. Carefully planned programs should be directed toward the maximum utilization of those returned to civilian life or rejected from the armed forces for their use in industry and defense activities. It should be demonstrated to the individuals who cannot actually serve in the armed forces that they, too, can contribute greatly to the war effort, thus conserving the nation's manpower to its maximum degree.

There are many specific problems which are inevitably the result of war and need not be exhaustively discussed. For example, while it has been shown in Great Britain that the incidence of neuroses under the stress of total warfare has not met expectations; on the other hand, juvenile delinquency has shown a marked increase and will present a challenge to the combined efforts of the neurophychiatrist and community agencies. The question of morale is too large and too important to be only casually entertained. It can well be considered an integral factor in mental hygiene. It is recognized that where community morale is high, psychiatric casualties are low. Again, armed forces drawn from communities with a high degree of morale are better prepared for the hardships of warfare. The neuropsychiatrist by his very experience and training is well qualified to assume leadership in a program designed to stimulate the vigorous mental attitude required for victory. This will to win is as essential as the equipment.

I like to think of the military and the civilian groups as joint members of a large football team. I wonder if the men going into a game expect the opposing side to defeat them? What goes on in the locker rooms? Is there an emphasis on defense or is there an emphasis on offense? We must be prepared for defense, but it seems to me that we have to catch that offensive spirit which emanates from the coach and an organized trained group such as a football team. It has the will to win. We all know that nothing succeeds like success, and if we are oriented on the side of success, if we adopt the philosophy of success and are still prepared for defense, it seems to me that we will have gone a long way toward adopting that aggressive spirit we all need; that will to win which is so essential in both the civilian and military effort.

Now let us consider the practical application of neuropsychiatry in military service and more especially in the Army, with which we are more intimately concerned.

Methods of warfare have constantly changed, especially since World War I. Armies are not merely composed of physically able fighters but consist of highly mobile, specially trained technical groups which are closely integrated. The mental agility of the individual is now fully as important as his physique. Furthermore, the theatre of operations may now cover not only the so-called front but homes, farms and factories many miles distant.

Psychiatrists have long recognized that the average American must make a relatively rapid adjustment to military life. He is uprooted from a community tolerant to his shortcomings and transplanted into a necessarily rigid and routine environment, where his individuality and personal liberty must be largely submerged. The hope for a peaceful existence must be exchanged for the will and ability to fight.

The neuropsychiatrist should recognize that he too must make not only a personal but also a professional readjustment when he enters the military service. He leaves behind him at considerable sacrifice a position of individual authority and expression to become another cog in a vast machine. Many of the attributes regarded as essential to succeed in civilian life must be subordinated. The neuropsychiatrist, because of the known needs for his services and the nature of his practice, expects to follow the same channels of professional activities in the Army and his adaptation is therefore correspondingly more difficult. He soon finds himself engaged in a neuropsychiatric practice peculiar to military life where cause and effect manifest a close interplay. There is frequently a fairly rapid development of abnormal mental reactions which may respond with surprising readiness to relatively simple therapeutic procedures.

He is imbued with the necessity of weeding out as soon as possible those who are mentally unfit to adapt themselves to military regime. He must operate through a well established and lengthy line of regulations, which have been established to protect the rights of the individual as well as of the Army. While a certain amount of temporary therapy is applied, as it should be, the main objective is to direct the more serious mental disorders back to community care. This must be a primary consideration if the Army is to use its fighting strength effectively. I quote from Army Regulations: "The mission of the medical corps is the conservation of manpower and the preservation of the military forces"(AR 40-5). Its hospital facilities must be utilized to speedily restore soldiers to health and fighting efficiency and cannot be burdened with cases requiring prolonged care.

In addition to the essential detection and elimination of the mentally unsound, there are other and wider fields in which the neuropsychiatrist should have much to offer. Here, as in the civilian field, the question of morale is a very critical one. Again, no other person is better qualified by training, experience and understanding of mental mechanisms to render a valuable service. All physicians worthy of the name must interest themselves in prevention. What more important and timely aspect of neuropsychiatry is placed in the hands of the specialist? It is well known that the maintenance of morale and discipline is a prophylactic against psychiatric disability.

All too often one hears complaints from psychiatrists in the Army that they are in field units and "not doing psychiatry." There are two types of Army hospital units in general. There is the numbered hospital unit which trains and prepares for service in the combat area, and there is the named hospital which is a fixed hospital on a military post to care for and dispose of casualties in this country. Those in numbered hospital units should understand that they will not have patients under their care until the hospital functions at the point of intended action. They are essentially in a training, toughening period. Psychiatrists have to be tough just like the men on combat duty. Some do not catch that idea at first, but I assure you it is a very important one. In the meantime, they have much to learn in the art of soldiering. They must become medical officers first, and neuropsychiatrists secondarily. They must develop themselves physically and become an integral part of their organization. Neuropsychiatrists attached to combat units have an unprecedented opportunity to practice the specialty at its best and in its widest scope. During the training period they will observe at first hand under simulated tactical conditions the reactions of men who are potential patients. Thus the psychiatrist will be better prepared to institute appropriate therapeutic measures at a most critical time. These medical officers have an unexcelled opportunity within their grasp not only to contribute in fullest measure to the military effort but also to collect valuable data from many sources which will be priceless and will further enrich psychiatric understanding and literature. Just as psychiatry received a tremendous impetus from the last war, so the present conflict can also make a momentous contribution, provided neuropsychiatrists seize the opportunity within their reach.

The training period of a unit is extremely critical. Many personality difficulties first appear at this time, due to the change in environment, separation from friends and loved ones, anxiety over family responsibilities, strangeness of camp life, change of diet habits, discipline and loss of personal liberty. Gillespie has indicated that the most common cause of breakdown in the English forces is the breaking up and dislocation of families. While to some these factors are beneficial, to others they may be detrimental, and may appear during the most critical period of combat when individual failure might spell disaster for the organization. Here the old maxim "A chain is no stronger than its weakest link" is amply illustrated. I do not think that there is any supportive argument in the fact that one of the heroes of the last war was below par intellectually. We cannot build a fighting force on such elusive expectations. If we have one who performs in this manner, we must regard him as fortuitous.

Every advantage should be taken of training opportunities, no matter how irksome or monotonous. The eventual efficiency and safety of the unit and its individuals depend upon the proficiency acquired through training. Hard work and diligent application are excellent preventive measures. If the officer or enlisted man successfully completes his training, his chances of serving efficiently the military cause will be greatly enhanced. He will thus fortify himself against the rigors of modern warfare in which noise and lack of food, fatigue, fear of death and fear of being wounded or captured are expected hazards. The English have found that many of the neuropsychiatric casualties can be traced to a lack of adequate training. The neuropsychiatrist must be able to interpret these factors to his fellow officers, and through them, to the unit.

When there are complaints by the neuropsychiatrist in the Army of poor cooperation and failure to accept his recommendations, he should be certain that the fault is not his. He may not have inspired confidence or adequately sold himself and his ideas. It has been said, and rather aptly, that a good medical officer in combat is worth two hundred rifles.

In considering the organization necessary to provide properly for expected neuropsychiatric casualties, it has been broadly intimated that the experience of World War I should have taught valuable lessons, although it is understood that we are now faced with a radically different type of warfare. A general outline of the organized neuropsychiatric procedures thus far developed in the Army may furnish some evidence that learning, although sometimes insidious, may consist in adjustments of such nature that generalized deductions are likely to be misleading. For a considerable period the Surgeon General has been actively interested in developing an organization to make appropriate use of experience and its adaptation to the present problems on a large scale.

In line with this policy there has been established a separate Branch of Neuropsychiatry in the Surgeon General's Office where there is a close relationship with other branches of medicine. An understanding of the psychological factors in the incidence of physical disease and the reverse has been an accepted viewpoint in the Army and coincides with modern concepts in the community. This factor has prepared the way for the necessary and helpful coordination which exists between the neuropsychiatric and other medical sections in Army hospitals. Out-patient consultations of considerable volume and benefit on medical wards and through the posts have already developed. The alert neuropsychiatrist through his experience and widening association has done much to encourage this commendable relationship.

Neuropsychiatric screening has been developed at induction centers to a far wider degree than during the last war, and neuropsychiatric service at this point is considered of paramount importance, however tedious and demanding. In spite of the relatively large and necessarily rapid mobilization, evidence already indicates that a greater percentage of potential neuropsychiatric misfits have been prevented from entering the armed forces than during a comparable period in the last war.

It is inevitable that under the most exacting examination possible some will be missed. An attempt must be made to weed these out during the training period. Accordingly, steps have been authorized already to place well qualified neuropsychiatrists on the staff of replacement training centers. The soldier after induction goes to a reception center and spends anywhere from a few hours to a few days becoming oriented, getting his uniform and going through certain forms of introduction, and then proceeds to the replacement training center. Here for the first time the problems incident to the new life in the Army begin to appear. The function of the psychiatrist at the replacement training center will be concerned with adjusting normal individuals and detecting and eliminating the mentally unstable who are or may become a distinct liability to military training, discipline and morale during the early weeks of training.

There are a large number of trained neuropsychiatrists giving excellent service in their specialty at various hospital units throughout the country and with the forces overseas. In order to coordinate neuropsychiatric service properly a plan has been placed in operation to provide eminent consultants in their specialty with the headquarters of service commands and with the large overseas forces. The experience of military authorities in these areas has convinced them of the need for such assistance.

For newly commissioned neuropsychiatric medical officers an effort has been made to provide a period of instruction and indoctrination at one of the large established Army general hospitals where they will see psychiatry at work, the neuropsychiatric casualties as they are seen during the training period, and also casualties actually returned from the combat areas. Assurance may be given that those with proper qualifications will be located where their training and experience can best be utilized, taking into consideration the requirements of the military service. There is a need and a definite place for the broadly trained neurologist and psychiatrist who feels the urge to offer unselfishly his professional experience, foregoing his personal ambitions during this critical period.

In summarizing this part of the presentation, it has been pointed out that both the civilian and the military neuropsychiatrist, by a readjustment of concepts and full participation in the greatest organized effort in our history, can make an outstanding contribution to the successful conclusion of the present military effort and to the neuropsychiatry of the future.

I know that there are many aspects in this wide field under consideration which have been so splendidly covered during this Conference. There are many questions which have come to your minds. Since this is a total effort and may be one of the last opportunities for all of us who are so vitally interested in this field to express ourselves and to unleash questions which perhaps some of us cannot answer, it has been arranged that Dr. Lawrence Kubie as associate leader and Doctors Frederick Parsons and Edwin Zabriskie will cover some of the wider problems suggested by the Conference.

Symposium II
Psychiatry and the War

First Scheduled Discussion
of Symposium II

By LAWRENCE S. KUBIE, M.D.

*Associate Neurologist, College of Physicians and Surgeons, Columbia University;
Associate Psychiatrist, Mt. Sinai Hospital, New York City*

WE HAVE heard a record of such high achievement and of such high goals, that criticism will sound carping, and any commentary critical. Nevertheless, comments to be constructive must not merely repeat the picture of what has been accomplished. They must take as their starting point the lessons of the last twenty-five years and apply these lessons to the future. They must not say, "Look how well we have done," but "Let us see if we can do still better."

In approaching this question we must first acknowledge that as a nation we are paying a high price for our very virtues. An individualistic psychology is an inevitable product of a long period of peaceful democracy. The organized action which is forced upon us by total war has almost no purpose or value in a peaceful culture. But the individualism which thrives in peacetime and which has its great cultural values, also has the serious effect of making us feel less close to one another. Aggressive impulses which have no external targets turn against our neighbors, against the people in the next apartment, against business or professional colleagues. A slow, insidious alienation of man from man takes place. This is one of the most important psychological tolls of peace; and it is this which has made it hard to reorient ourselves to war. It is this centrifugal force which has produced the tendency to scoff at patriotism, at sacrifice for common ideals, and at democracy itself, which we have all observed during the recent years of short-sighted cynicism.

We have seen this happen in our own country, and we should examine it in ourselves. One serious consequence has been a socially destructive attitude towards the one group in the country which continued to represent the idea of group solidarity, namely our military forces. The habitual attitude of condescension towards the military, which is characteristic in a peaceful democracy, is a very serious phenomenon. As we look forward to the future, it seems to me that we as psychiatrists can make one of our most important contributions to the problem of preserving the virtues of individualism (on which depend so much of our culture, art and science), without losing that sense of unity of one man with his neighbor, in the absence of which there can be no such thing as idealism, generosity, the willingness to sacrifice, or even elementary safety.

If we cannot solve that problem, then what Henry Adams called the "Degradation of the Democratic Dogma" becomes unavoidable; and whenever the tidal wave of total war breaks over us we will always suddenly be forced to draw into the armed forces and into industry men and women who are psychologically wholly unprepared for united effort. This is our major problem in social psychiatry: to learn how to keep these United States from becoming in long periods of peace a conglomeration of disunited states of mind and heart. It is heartening to find that all of us are aware of the urgency of this problem. On this point there is no divergence of purpose here today.

On the other hand, there are natural differences of opinion as to the techniques by which we can best meet the problems of the present emergency; and there may be a legitimate difference of opinion as to how satisfied we ought to be with the present status. On this issue we should be carefully and meticulously self-critical—not with any implication that the job could easily have been done better and that therefore somebody is at fault, but in a spirit of healthy dissatisfaction with anything less than the best. Considering the state of mind in the country as a whole, it is amazing that the reorientation towards war has gone as well as it has. It would be wholly unwarranted to say that things are in a bad way. But this should not deter us from facing the fact that they can be and must be even better—better in terms not only of the present situation but even more of the future which lies ahead of us. Ultimately, this will entail important cultural reorientations, and a realignment of all of medicine towards psychiatry.

This is something which many have been thinking about for a long time. At Johns Hopkins, Dr. Meyer has stood for this trend for many years. In the junior branch of the armed services, the Air Corps, it is taking place already, in that every flight surgeon is pressed to be at the same time a psychiatrist. It is taking place in many of our general hospitals, where psychiatry is slowly infiltrating into every ward. That such a revolutionary change as this has to occur slowly must be borne in mind when any suggestion is made which aims at a possible improvement of the present system.

In this spirit, then, let us consider the whole selective process in terms of how it might conceivably be done better. The essential job of a small army is to expand; and the essential job of a small medical organization in a small army is to expand. This basic fact is the source of a whole group of curious and paradoxical problems. The sudden occurrence of war immediately creates a series of bottlenecks. The induction station is a bottleneck, the narrow end of a funnel through which manpower streams most swiftly. Yet it is just here that ever since January, 1942, we have been trying to evaluate that manpower. At that time, medical screening was taken out of the hands of the Selective Service Boards and placed at the induction stations. This moved it from a relatively broad area in the stream into the narrow channel where the flow is fastest. The reason advanced was that the process of selection is of such importance to the armed forces that it cannot be delegated to anyone who is not directly under military supervision. This point is valid; but the concentration of the process of selection at the induction station is not an adequate solution. It may work during peace when men are inducted a few at a time. But it creates an impossible bottleneck during periods of rapid expansion. Instead, there is need of something which does not exist at present, namely a selective agency whose job is selection, and selection only. It should be led by men who have had years of service in all phases of the armed forces. It should be composed also of psychologists, of men experienced in sampling methods, of statisticians, of experienced social service administrators, of penologists, of internists, surgeons and psychiatrists. Such an agency would be part of the Army and Navy; and its function year in and year out through peace and war should be the study of the techniques of selection and their administration. Selection is a specialty in its own right, wholly different from the treatment of disease. Because he is a good doctor, a man is not necessarily competent to estimate rapidly either physiological or psychological fitness for combat. To perform this task, special methods must be devised and tested, and a special personnel must be trained in their use.

What would such a selective agency have to do? In the first place, it would have to develop group screening devices. The feasibility of such tests has been demonstrated by the classification tests which are being used by the psychologists in the Adjutant General's Office. Similar screening methods for the induction process have not been developed by the Medical Corps, because the primary preoccupation of the medical services is always the *treatment* of illness and casualties; and consequently neither in the Army nor in the Navy have physicians been allocated exclusively to the problems of selection. No one has been devoting five, ten, fifteen, twenty years to the study of the process of screening manpower by the millions. We have relied instead on the inadequate procedures of peacetime recruiting, expanded by additional personnel.

Furthermore, the Selective Agency would have to validate the tests it devises. No test is worth the paper it is written on until it has been tried in the field. That is to say, every test must itself be validated by correlating the scores made with the actual performance of the tested men under military conditions. This can be done slowly over a period of years; or it can be done rapidly by subjecting to the same tests sample groups of men who have already done outstandingly well in the field and of men who have done badly. In the process of working out such tests it is important to bring to bear every technical facility which we have. Here, therefore, is an opportunity to heal the old breach between psychology and psychiatry.

Instruments other than special screening tests are also needed. The most exacting test of good medicine is the quality of a medical history. We are more likely to recognize the potential peptic ulcer on the basis of the history rather than the examination. This is equally true for the so-called "effort syndrome." We cannot practice good medicine and we cannot do good medical selection for the armed services if we cannot take a medical history. Yet no one can take a medical history at an induction station. Useful compact medical histories could be gathered, however, if appropriate forms were evolved, and if the work were done where the stream moves relatively slowly, i.e., before the men reach the induction stations. The development of appropriate methods of history gathering would thus become another problem for the Selection Agency.

In yet another respect the concentration of the selection process at the induction station creates a bottleneck, namely with respect to medical personnel. When the armed forces must expand rapidly, the physicians of the medical corps are needed with the troops. They cannot simultaneously serve at induction centers. Furthermore, the newly inducted physician needs special military training too, which he does not get at the induction station.

Clearly, therefore, it is necessary to train and organize a special personnel for selection, consisting of those who for any reason are not eligible for active service with the armed forces. They should nonetheless be organized as a definite and recognized branch of the service. This requires that work must be so planned as to make it possible for them to perform necessary civilian functions at the same time. A man in New York, for instance, who is practicing, visiting at a hospital and teaching, cannot also go to Governors Island eight hours a day as is required at present. But if their hours were wisely allocated, all civilian doctors, psychologists and social workers should and could become part of this service, as a definite part of the mobilization of total manpower. *They would be trained and supervised by the selective agency of the armed services, thus fulfilling the valid argument of the Army and Navy that the armed services must pick their own fighting men.*

The selective agency would also have to attack the problem of collecting social histories economically, efficiently and quickly. It would have to devise quick methods of gathering together the information available in social service files, in police files and in mental hospitals, and all other relevant important information.

Finally, it would organize mobile units to function in those parts of the country where there are not enough doctors, social workers, psychiatrists or psychologists to do the work. Mobile units of this kind are imperative if the selective process is to be carried on equally well everywhere throughout the country.

Without such an agency how well are we doing? Every day informal reports reach us from physicians in the services, from internists and surgeons as well as psychiatrists. Their impressions are that in station and base hospitals the general medical wards are half-filled with neuropsychiatric problems which are not listed in official statistics. One man who has had several years of training both in general medicine and psychiatry said that according to personal records which he kept over a period of several weeks, between thirty-five and fifty-two percent of the patients on the general wards were neuropsychiatric. We must not underestimate the importance of this. It means that we have not screened out as many camp casualties as we could if we had an adequate organization and adequate methods.

The distribution of medical manpower would be a less difficult problem if the job of screening were adequately done, because we would then need fewer physicians in the armed services. It is, after all, a bit ridiculous to take a man into the Army only to have him break down in camp, and then to have to take care of him in the Army, using up the time of Army physicians, nurses, and medical corps personnel, when he could have remained healthy in the civilian community in the first place.

Evidently, then, it is essential that we should re-examine with a fresh mind the whole set-up of the selective process, beginning with the fact that it is impossible in a time of emergency to select men by the millions with the recruiting methods of times of peace, merely by multiplying the number of physicians who do the selecting. The job needs different methods, a different organization, and a specially trained personnel; and for this entire task we need a separate branch of the armed services.

Thus far we have spoken only of the selection process. Much could also be said of psychiatry within the armed services themselves. Here, however, we are on happier grounds, and I will say little about it. Primarily I would like to emphasize what Dr. Bartemeier has already said in discussing the use of psychiatrists in the care of the civilian population. As he pointed out, the vast majority of our psychiatrists know only hospital psychiatry. Yet in the armed services that aspect of psychiatric training is most useful which deals with the neuroses, neurotic and psychopathic behavior disorders, perversions, criminalistic trends and psychosomatic disorders. With these one has little contact in mental hospitals. Therefore, it is for this type of work that the Army psychiatrist needs special indoctrination, not in the phenomenology of the psychoses with which the hospital-trained psychiatrist is already thoroughly familiar.

Secondly, just as we need mobile selection units, so we need many *mobile psychotherapeutic units*. Even if we eliminate a large percentage of the existing errors in the screening process and thus reduce training camp breakdowns to a minimum, there will always be the traumatic war neurosis to deal with. If this is to be dealt with adequately, it must be treated promptly. This is very important from the point of view of the community, because the traumatic war neurosis is an acute emergency, like an acute appendix or a severed artery, and prompt treatment can make the difference between recovery and a life of chronic illness. It is this fact which necessitates the organization of mobile psychotherapeutic units.

In summary, then, we would urge a basic reorganization of the whole framework of selection, with a centralizing of authority and responsibility in a Selective Agency of the armed services themselves. And within the services, we would urge first the adequate training of the inducted psychiatrist in the problems of extra-hospital psychiatry, and secondly the formation of mobile psychotherapeutic units.

COLONEL ROY D. HALLORAN
Washington, D. C.

I want to bring out a point which was not emphasized in the general presentation; that is, the liaison between the psychologist on the post and the neuropsychiatric service in general and station hospitals. The psychologist is used as part of the team, where available, to assist the psychiatrist and will be similarly utilized in these replacement training center units. I want to emphasize also the fact that there is a rapid mobilization going on and it should not be inferred that the neuropsychiatric services have reached their maximum effort. We are really only on the threshold but there is sufficient evidence of progress. There are psychiatrists at practically all the larger stations and general hospitals throughout the country. There is available the machinery for good neuropsychiatric work, and from my own observation thus far, excellent work is being done in view of facilities available.

Symposium II
Psychiatry and the War

Second Scheduled Discussion of Symposium II

By FREDERICK W. PARSONS, M.D.

Member, Temporary Commission on State Hospital Problems, New York City

I EXPECT THAT the principal function of a discussant is to refer occasionally to the papers under discussion. Yesterday afternoon we had a series of six excellent papers on the Army, the Navy, the Air Force and International Affairs.

Colonel Porter gave you a realistic survey of the Army's needs. He touched on the exigencies of psychiatry in the military situation, something which we civilian psychiatrists are prone to forget. Captain Harrison spoke forcibly of the place which psychiatry has in the Navy, and Colonel Reinartz, who with his psychiatric associates, flies with men whom they suspect are too sick to fly, brings our medical specialty into a spot we rarely occupy. These men know the realities.

Finally Dr. Kolb, close to Dr. Parran, the Surgeon General of the Public Health Service, visualized post-war psychiatric problems. Dr. Kolb's realistic survey justifies our hopes of the continued federal interest in our specialty.

So much for the uniformed services. That would have been a full measure but it was pressed down and running over by papers by Dr. Bartemeier of Detroit and Dr. Appel of Philadelphia, on the place of our special medical interest in civilian defense and national and international affairs, respectively.

I feel that it is quite impossible for a discussant to discuss intelligently the very excellent material which has been presented. I look upon the papers somewhat as the elements of a glorious cake which will some day be mixed together and evolved as a delicious morsel. You do not expect me to present you with this confection. I shall perhaps assist in the stirring only; the expert chef who will finally put this cake before you will be the operation of your own minds. The things which you have heard consciously, the things which have unconsciously penetrated into your minds, will by that mysterious machine evolve into something comprehensive and worthwhile. You will do the evolving, not I. It will not be presented to you this morning. It will not come this afternoon, but with the meditation and with the operation of your own minds, nourishment and stimulation will be yours.

I tend to be overwhelmed by the opportunity which psychiatry has in the present emergency. All kinds of people tell us what we can do, what we should do and what we must do. It seems to me they forget one important factor, that is, the psychiatrists will have to be spread very thinly. They can be augmented, but they can never be increased so that all desirable tasks can be accomplished. I take comfort from remembering that heading the psychiatric forces in the Army is a person who has had state service. Anybody who has been in public life and operated a public hospital has come to the conclusion that you have to do your best with the materials at hand. So I get comfort from Colonel Halloran's appointment, because I think the psychiatric forces will be wisely led and efficiently utilized. Those who point the way have worthwhile goals. We need them. We need them just as the ship captain needs the beacons, but it does not necessarily follow that a good captain steers for the light. If he does, he either runs his ship aground or has a collision with the lightship.

The important things have been mentioned by the authors to whom I referred earlier. I think we will conclude that armed services do well when they provide as best they can for these essentials:

1. Keeping out of the armed forces those constitutionally unsuited to military life.
2. Speedy detection of those who escape the Induction Board screening.
3. Prompt detection of those who break during intensified training and during combat.
4. Elimination of those not fit for any military service.

An alert mind can name other psychiatric objectives. It is proper to think of them. Listing them and speaking of them guide us on our way. They, however, are not the "first things." Many can be tackled by the civilians but they are not for the armed services until the Army, the Navy and their flying arms have solved the essentials.

I should like to assure the representatives of the uniformed services that organized psychiatry stands behind them. We are proud of our professional brothers and are ready to help in any way possible.

Symposium II
Psychiatry and the War

Third Scheduled Discussion of Symposium II

By EDWIN G. ZABRISKIE, M.D.

Attending Neurologist, Manhattan Eye, Ear and Throat Hospital;
Attending Physician, Neurological Institute, New York City

I CANNOT HELP but yield to the temptation to contrast the technique of psychiatric screening used in building up an army today with what we did in the last war. Just to touch on that briefly, in the last war it was a mad rush to get everybody overseas if we could. There was little chance to do any training at all, and one felt forced to adopt the attitude of whether or not the individual examined, either as officer or enlisted man, was stable enough to warrant his transportation overseas. A six weeks or possibly two months training period was all he got then.

I must say that our results on practically that basis showed up pretty well. For instance, our record of admissions to the mental wards of the large base hospitals in the A.E.F. corresponded very closely to the yearly admission rate of the civilian population, which seemed an astounding thing, we thought, in view of the careful screening. As a matter of fact, the best results seemed to appear in the rather limited number of alcoholics and drug addicts who came into conflict with authority. We did not have any screening of psychiatrists at that time. And if you will keep my secret, I will say that I know of at least three psychiatric casualties which we had up

443

at the front. One insisted on being sent back as an influenza. The second insisted that he had been gassed at a time just before the Germans began to send over gas. He pointed with pride to the verdigris on his brass buttons and said, "There is the evidence." I do not know whether you would call the third psychiatrist a casualty or not, but he was darn near murdered when they caught him in bed with a hot water bottle on his way up to the front. The advantage of our set-up is very clearly illustrated in those three cases. They were not sent back too far. They were sorted in the advanced neurological hospitals, and were retained for other jobs which they did very well.

I wonder—and it is pure speculation on my part—how essentially different conditions are in the present war from the past war. To be sure, the mobilization is different; the mechanized implements are entirely different; but when I hear about the so-called mysterious tank black-out, I wonder whether that is really so different from the artilleryman who was subject to constant fire, constantly handling shells in an atmosphere of the gasses formed by the explosions of those shells, and who often broke down, fainted, passed out, and was sent back as a gas casualty. My own real combat experience was around the Marne. Our advanced posts in trenches and nests were subject to the same conditions as in the Solomons (perhaps not quite psychologically the same, because we were not on an island; we always had a good area back of us to which we could retire), but as far as the constant noise and the constant bombing and the privations went, with the exception of the time element, from the reports in the papers, conditions differ very little from what is going on in Guadalcanal now.

I am apt to indulge in speculation where I should not, I suppose, but I asked our psychiatric friend Harrison the other day whether there was any difference in the type of neurological or neuropsychiatric response of the men in the Navy in the different types of ships, torpedo boat or destroyer as contrasted with a battleship, submarine or subchaser. Much to my surprise he said there was not. It has always seemed to me that life on a torpedo boat or destroyer was very similar to the life in the trenches, with just the same hardships, just the same privation, just the same lack of food. The only difference was, in the trenches you were apt to be bombed.

One thing more and then I shall not burden you further. I have heard Colonel Halloran talk of the replacement centers, and the chance to screen out and utilize as well as classify the material which comes up in those centers. I do not see how, in this era of total war, we can afford to let the least possible unit or individual go who can do something. We had a very amazing instance of that in the last war, where the Germans threw all their important and dominating personnel up into the front lines and left their service of supplies to a very weak outfit, and as a result it broke down. I was very much cheered to hear that such careful screening is going on now, and we have more time to do it.

Symposium II
Psychiatry and the War

Discussions from the Assembly

LOWELL S. SELLING, M.D.

Detroit

I AM SURE we all realize that there are many aspects of military psychology which cannot be touched upon in a meeting such as this. Many of us who have the historical background Dr. Kennedy emphasized in his talk remember that Von Moltke won his decisive battle at Sedan because he was able to find out what the French plans were ahead of time by reading the newspapers. So we must have military secrecy to some degree, even in a meeting such as this. I think what is lacking here, unfortunately, is non-secret information about practical uses of psychiatrists in other spheres than examining psychotics. Their use as teachers of personnel specialists in the armed forces can be compared with the use of psychiatrists who are able to exert their influence upon a very large number of people in the child guidance clinics where they act as consultants or directors of the activities of others. Just so could they handle problems in the armed forces in the field of morale. In this field the Russians had "political commissars" for many years. They were only recently removed, but not because they were a nuisance or because they interfered with military matters, but because they had such training and experience that they offered a vast reserve force for officer replacement. These men, though not psychiatrists, were doing psychiatric work on the troops. Their equivalents now in our own army could very well be trained and directed by psychiatrists who are too few to do the work themselves. The German

Central Psychological Station was doing just this sort of thing at the outbreak of the war.

It seems to me that a few psychiatrists could exert immense influence upon men who are going into some unit to do personnel work, not to do classification permanently, but rather to correct emotional difficulties. They could be supervised in the same way that social workers are supervised in a child guidance clinic, and those supervised can actually be assigned to service with troops in the field.

Another possibility is the use of psychiatrists to guide non-medical experts who have to do technical classification, for the psychiatrist is skilled in the study of attitudes and can transmit his knowledge of this particular field, thinly, it is true, but competently, to a large number of workers who deal with the selection of men for special jobs. An example of this comes from the traffic clinic in which psychologists under the guidance of psychiatrists have graduated from the brass instruments to find that most of the difficulties lie in the attitudes, interests and emotional reactions of the problem driver, for a man may be physically very deficient—blind in one eye, lacking a leg, or even a little feebleminded—and yet, with a good attitude he would be a safer driver than a man who is physically intact but has a bad attitude.

The use of psychiatrists as consultants can be extended, I think, even to the problem of selecting leaders. I recall that last spring, in a publication of the Army Recruiting Service, there was a picture of a board to check officer material coming from civilian life into the Officers' Candidate School. On that board was a physician but he was not known to me as a psychiatrist. There are undoubtedly too few psychiatrists to supply the need for examining men for selection of officers from the lower ranks. Perhaps there are not even enough to take care of field officers. Perhaps we do not know enough about attributes which make for good officer material to help very much. After all, Napoleon's best officers were all ego-centric, problem individuals to some extent, and were also somewhat antisocial. Many of them, including Napoleon himself, were psychopathological and Napoleon's marshals, while good subordinates, could never take command. On the other hand, we have had such bizarre personalities as Thomas Jonathan (Stonewall) Jackson who was a poor subordinate but was extremely able in separate command. Jackson's personality was certainly as bizarre as those of Napoleon and his marshals. His subordinates often called him a "crazy man."

It is such problems as these that psychiatrists are able to solve if there are enough of them to do the job, and there are many other phases of military psychology which would be of interest to us. I am sorry that they could not be touched upon in this meeting.

I wish that Major Hans von Hentig who is now at the University of Colorado could have been here because he wrote that magnificent book, a unique work, on the psychological strategy of the Great War and from his writing much of the psychological strategy of the German Army has stemmed.

LOUIS A. SCHWARTZ, M.D.

Detroit

I SHOULD LIKE to make one point which can be told quickly and simply. I think out of these sessions we ought to employ the best thinking of psychology and psychiatry as a distinctive agency in developing techniques for the indoctrination of the ideals of democracy to all groups of the American people, starting with children, as a dynamic and vitalizing force throughout all groups. We have taken democracy for granted. This is a war of ideologies. Can we learn the psychological import of the emperor-worship of the Japanese and the notion of racial supremacy of the Nazis for the purposes of learning the technique of indoctrination of democracy? Democracy has as its basic psychological formulation that which may be described as rugged individualism through which we may have lost the broader relatedness of the individual to his social responsibilities. A psychological technique of this kind will then help automatically in the development of civilian morale, prevent delinquency by the better utilization of the energies of children, help men in knowing what they are fighting for, and thereby help them to become better fighters and aid in the complex problems of the relationships between capital and labor.

MARION E. KENWORTHY, M.D.

New York City

I WOULD LIKE to add just one small constructive suggestion. Yesterday there was mention of the use of psychiatric social workers in the armed forces. In my experience, having trained psychiatric social workers for many years, I find at the present moment that although there are seventy men psychiatric workers, only five are being made use of in the Army —I mean as psychiatric social workers. The others are doing infantry jobs. This group of five is being used in that small unit, the reclassification center, now called the mental hygiene unit, at Fort Monmouth.

Another aspect of this which is tremendously important is that there are many other schools of social work over the country which have turned out men highly prepared for being an assistant to a psychiatrist in this particular job of meeting the emotional problems, not the severe psychiatric problems, but the emotional problems of those individuals who may be returned to service. This is the group effort which is being made at Fort Monmouth, and I hope that, out of the deliberations of this body and out of the fine kind of leadership which Colonel Halloran will give us, this may be possible at all of the reclassification groups over the country.

FREDERICK H. ALLEN, M.D.

Philadelphia

I WOULD JUST like to add one word in support of that very important note which Dr. Kenworthy has just brought before us. I have been quite thrilled with not only the opportunity but also the service which some of these men working in that Monmouth Clinic have been able to achieve. One of the men working in that unit happens to have spent a year in my clinic in Philadelphia, and he has brought to me some of the types of things that he has been able to work with right within the structure of the Army. It is not a matter of picking out those already upset but of really working with individuals simply and quickly in order to prevent them from becoming upset, and of helping them to retain their effectiveness as units in the service. It seems to me that this opens up a very important new service and new area which should be extensively utilized, particularly with a desire to utilize those people in the service of the type Dr. Kenworthy mentioned. They can, I am sure, give psychiatry a very much more effective application right within the Army itself.

LESLIE B. HOHMAN, M.D.

Baltimore

I HAVE BEEN working now for two years solely on screening processes in the induction centers and in the draft board, and have developed techniques for rapid examination. I do not know whether they are good or bad. All I can do is to go to camps from time to time and check on the patients who are already in camp hospitals and find out whether my routine examination would have excluded them. To date I find it has. I would like to suggest that we could test very simply whether we are having effective screening methods or not by taking two contrasted groups, one that has been through careful screening boards such as the board in Boston or perhaps the board in Baltimore, and contrast that with groups selected where there have been very few psychiatrists, or none at all, to find out whether we are really doing a good job or not. That would aid us in our techniques and methods of examination.

WALTER J. FREEMAN, M.D.

Washington, D. C.

THROUGHOUT THIS Conference I have gained the impression of an attitude, a spirit, one might say, pervading it. That attitude is compounded of doubt, anticipation, pessimism, emphasis on the difficulties, the recognition of why men fail; and not so much of why they succeed. Paradoxically, those speakers who have emphasized all these difficulties and all these dangers to mental health still admit that mental health improves during wartime. And the figures all back them up. Why not *study* those figures, the whys and wherefores? I think the reasons for improvement in mental health in wartime are pretty evident.

Sometime ago I suggested a few.[1] (1) The difficulty of choice is removed. It is no longer a question of what book we will read or what suit we will wear or what we will have for dinner. When the emergency comes, indecision is banished. We run for the shelter. (2) Banding together for the common good; organization, unification, discipline, leadership and followership. (3) Hate, that burning, purifying hate which burns away the mists of petty fears and causes us to band together with strangers and even erstwhile enemies for the common good. Now without fear there can be no hate. *We have not been scared.* (4) Trust in God. Fortunate is the person who can say to himself, "God's will be done." That is the unassailable, the unshakable answer to catastrophe. (5) Finally, there is the opportunity of putting aside anticipation and contemplation and getting into action. It is in action that we can thrive.

Throughout this Conference I think there has been too much emphasis upon the thought processes, too much intellectualization, one might almost say emasculation, of the emotions, by the study and contemplation of our experiences.

---

[1] Freeman, W. J. Wartime neuroses, Hygeia, *20*:492, 1942.

COLONEL ROY D. HALLORAN

Washington, D. C.

I THINK THAT the keynote sounded by those who have discussed this rather important section is the necessity for coordination, the necessity for unity, not only in neuropsychiatric circles but in the whole processes of living together. Here we are faced with the Army, an organized group; and over here, civilian life, a group only partly organized, or organized for defense but with a great deal of loose thinking and cross purposes. This Conference and those speakers who have discussed it, have emphasized the need for a planned coordination between military and civilian activities. Perhaps we should first keep our own houses clean by good example in our own special field.

I should also like to give some assurance that the proper mental hygiene instruction is being made available to officers and men. This is a developing situation and will be greatly augmented by the development of the replacement training center clinics similar to the excellent one mentioned at Monmouth. As a matter of fact, although the one at Monmouth is the best known, there are other clinics of similar character which have already been developed.

As to the question raised by Doctor Hohman with regard to the screening groups, it is well recognized that, to check adequately the criteria for screening, one must have a sufficient number of casualties checked against the induction area. That, may I assure you, is a mammoth task. It is one which can be done but whose consummation may be too late to help the local boards, because of the intricate processes needed to carry it out. At this time we can gain some generalized impressions only. If in certain areas the rejection rate is higher than in others, it may well be that the criteria used by that group is more satisfactory or even too critical. That could be brought out roughly by a check of the rejection rates against the actual casualties coming from each area. There are many complex factors, and we hope that some means may be devised to secure that check.

I am very happy to get Dr. Freeman's rather forceful emphasis on mental improvement during wartime. I have no figures. He probably knows more than I do about that. I would like to emphasize the fact that there are constructive features and that the whole tone should be one of aggression rather than passivism. If in our discussions we think only of destructive factors, we are apt to overlook something important at this time, stimulation of the whole tone of the community and consequently the armed forces drawn from the community.

In concluding our presentation here I want to express my very sincere appreciation for the privilege of being invited to take part in this outstanding Conference in such an appropriate atmosphere for critical soul searching.

Conclusion of Conference

By THEOPHILE RAPHAEL, M.D.

Ann Arbor

WITH THIS panel discussion, the Conference comes to a close. I think it has been most worth while and successful. This is not only by reason of content, but also because of the original intention and the planning of the sessions; the place and setting; the gracious atmosphere of hospitality and friendliness; and the spirit of comradeship in working together within the frame of a momentous crisis in which we are all involved, and in which we all have a definite responsibility and task to perform. While, to be sure, everything has not been covered, while all questions have not been answered or completely answered—they cannot be, that is not the way of life—much nevertheless has been accomplished. Much good material has been presented and there has been great stimulus of thinking and insight. There is much we have gained to take away with us, for our greater development and that of the work we have to do. We have been aided to a definite step forward at a juncture when every step is so important.

And so, I beg leave to express what is undoubtedly in the minds of all of us, that is, our very deep and heartfelt appreciation of the opportunity thus to have come together at this very special time, and to convey this feeling to McGregor Fund and the University of Michigan whose interest and vision have made this Conference possible. Also, reciprocally, on behalf of McGregor Fund and the University, I wish to convey a like appreciation and thanks to those who have been willing and able to come and participate. Frankly, I feel quite moved. It has been truly a most valuable, stirring, and in many ways rather wonderful experience and *not* just another meeting! And now, formally, on behalf of the Committee I declare this Conference on Psychiatry closed. May there be another! And, in our breaking up, to us all, Godspeed!

Halloran

Colonel Roy Dennis Halloran, chief of the neuropsychiatric branch of the Army Medical Department, died suddenly November 10th, 1943. Thus was completed the work of a second leader in this Conference on Psychiatry (see footnote page 94), the representative of the Surgeon General of the Army, and an important contributor to the psychiatry of this war. His remarks on pages 421-431 and page 452 in this record attain even greater significance on this account. (Editor)

Index

THIS BOOK

PSYCHIATRY AND THE WAR

Edited by FRANK J. SLADEN, M.D.

was set, printed and bound by Kingsport Press, Inc., Kingsport, Tennessee. The type face is Linotype Old Style No. 7, set 11 point on 13 point. The type page is 24 x 42 picas. The text paper is 50-lb. White Eggshell. The binding is Bancroft Linen Finish, Color 3, Smooth. The jacket is Tan Laid Antique Linweave Text.

With THOMAS BOOKS careful attention is given to all details of manufacturing and design. It is the publisher's desire to present books that are satisfactory as to their physical qualities and artistic possibilities and appropriate for their particular use. THOMAS BOOKS will be true to those laws of quality that assure a good name and good will.